The World Bank Glossary

Glosario del Banco Mundial

English-Spanish
Spanish-English

Inglés-Español
Español-Inglés

The World Bank
Washington, D.C., U.S.A.

Copyright ©1996

The International Bank for Reconstruction
and Development/The World Bank

Banco Internacional de Reconstrucción
y Fomento/Banco Mundial

1818 H Street, N.W.
Washington, D.C. 20433, U.S.A.

First printing April 1996
Primera impresión: avríl de 1996

Manufactured in the United States of America
Hecho en los Estados Unidos de América

Library of Congress Cataloging-in-Publication Data

The World Bank glossary : English-Spanish, Spanish-English = Glosario
   del Banco Mundial : inglés-español, español-inglés.
        p.   cm.
     ISBN 0-8213-3595-2
      1. Economics—Dictionaries. 2. English language—Dictionaries—
   Spanish. 3. Economics—Dictionaries—Spanish. 4. Spanish
   language—Dictionaries—English. 5. Finance—Dictionaries.
   6. Finance—Dictionaries—Spanish. 7. World Bank—Language—
   Glossaries, etc.   I. World Bank.
   HB61.W615   1996
   330'.03—dc20
                                          96-10217
                                              CIP

Table of contents/*Indice de materias*

World Bank Glossary

Foreword

This edition of the World Bank Glossary has been revised and expanded by the Terminology Unit of the Bank's Translation, Interpretation and Conference Services Division, in close collaboration with the English and Spanish Translation Sections.

The Glossary is intended to assist the Bank's translators and interpreters, other Bank staff using Spanish in their work, and free-lance translators and interpreters employed by the Bank. For this reason, the Glossary contains not only financial and economic terminology and terms relating to the Bank's procedures and practices, but also terms that frequently occur in Bank documents, and others for which the Bank has a preferred equivalent. Although many of the terms, relating to such fields as agriculture, education, environment, housing, law, technology and transportation, could be found in other sources, they have been assembled here for ease of reference.

Comments and suggestions from users will be most welcome and should be addressed to:

Terminology Unit
Translation, Interpretation and Conference Services Division
World Bank
1818 H Street, N.W.
Washington, DC 20433
USA

Glosario del Banco Mundial

Prefacio

Esta edición del Glosario del Banco Mundial ha sido revisada y ampliada por la Unidad de Terminología de la División de Servicios de Traducción, Interpretación y Conferencias del Banco, en estrecha colaboración con las Secciones de Traducciones al Español y al Inglés.

El Glosario tiene por objeto servir de ayuda a los traductores e intérpretes del Banco, a otros funcionarios que utilizan el idioma español en su trabajo, y a los traductores e intérpretes independientes que el Banco contrata. Por esta razón, el Glosario contiene no sólo términos financieros y económicos y expresiones relacionadas con los procedimientos y prácticas del Banco, sino también algunos vocablos que suelen emplearse en sus documentos, así como otros para los cuales se prefiere una determinada traducción. Aunque muchos términos --propios de esferas como agricultura, educación, medio ambiente, vivienda, derecho, tecnología y transportes-- pueden encontrarse en otras fuentes, se han incluido aquí para facilitar la consulta.

Se agradece a los usuarios que envíen sus comentarios y sugerencias a:

Terminology Unit
Translation, Interpretation and Conference Services Division
World Bank
1818 H Street, N.W.
Washington, D.C. 20433
EE.UU.

English-Spanish Glossary

Glosario inglés-español

- A -

"A" loan
préstamo "A"
Standard World Bank loan.

abatement technologies
técnicas de reducción de la contaminación
Technologies designed to reduce (but not eliminate) the amount of pollutants released into the environment, e.g. from a factory.

above quota
por encima de la cuota

above the line (item)
(partida) ordinaria
A customary balance-sheet or revenue-or-expense position in a **financial statement** as compared to a **below the line item**.

absolute poor
personas, grupos que viven en la pobreza absoluta
Those with an average annual per capita income of less than that needed to pay for a minimum consumption basket, based on the food necesary for a recommended calorie intake, and for nonfood needs, consistent with the spending patterns of the poor. This rate will vary from country to country.

absorptive capacity
capacidad de absorción

abstract (of a publication)
extracto

academic research
investigación académica

accelerate a loan
exigir el reembolso anticipado de un préstamo; exigir el reembolso de un préstamo antes de su vencimiento

accelerated depreciation
depreciación acelerada, decreciente
Depreciation at a higher than usual rate in the early years of an asset's life and a lower than usual rate in the later years of its life.

accelerated recall [MOV]
reintegro acelerado

accelerated recovery
recuperación acelerada
Recovery of currency used in lending operations subject to **maintenance of value**. Recovery is accelerated at the request of the member, provided that such recovery does not result in a material reduction of the sum of repurchases.

acceleration of maturity (of a loan) [IBRD]
aceleración, adelanto del vencimiento
Declaration by a lender that the outstanding principal is due and payable immediately, together with the interest due, following non-compliance with loan covenants.

acceptance, accepting house [UK]
casa de aceptaciones
Merchant bank in the U.K. specializing in accepting **bills of exchange**.

acceptance; bank acceptance; banker's acceptance
aceptación bancaria
A **bill of exchange** which has been accepted by a banker.

acceptance rate (by beneficiaries of a project)
tasa de aceptación

accession
accesión; adhesión; introducción [agricultura]

accommodation type
tipo de alojamiento

accountability
responsabilidad; rendición de cuentas

accounting see also accrual (basis) accounting; business accounting; cost accounting; current cost (value) accounting; double entry accounting; full cost accounting; general price level accounting; inflation accounting; job order accounting; management accounting; managerial accounting; single-entry accounting; social accounting matrix; standard cost accounting; stock accounting

accounting entries; entries
asientos (contables)
The record of a transaction in a book of accounts.

accounting period
período contable; ejercicio contable

accounting practices
prácticas contables

accounting price
precio de cuenta
A price used for accounting purposes (i.e. not a market price). Often used synonymously with shadow price.

accounting procedure
método, procedimiento contable, de contabilidad

accounting rate of interest - ARI
tipo de interés contable - TIC
Discount rate used to convert future values of benefits and costs into equivalent **present values**.

accounting ratio
relación de cuenta
Ratio of **accounting price** to market price of a good.

accounting unit
unidad contable
A business enterprise or other economic unit for which a system of accounts is maintained.

accounts payable
cuentas por pagar
Amounts due and payable to third parties for goods and/or services purchased for which payments have not been made.

accounts receivable; receivables
cuentas por cobrar
Amounts due from others within one year of report date for goods and/or services sold in the normal course of business, but for which payment(s) have not been received.

accrual see nonaccrual status; overaccruals

accrual (basis) accounting
**contabilidad en valores devengados;
contabilidad según registro de derechos
adquiridos u obligaciones contraídas**
A form of accounting wherein all transactions are recognized and recorded at the time income is earned or expenditures are incurred, irrespective of whether or not cash is paid or received.

accrual rate
tasa de acumulación
The rate at which interest is accrued. In pensions, the rate at which benefits accrue.

accruals
acumulaciones [acreencias; obligaciones]
Revenues and expenditures recognized as earned or incurred and recorded in the **financial statement** of the periods to which they relate.

accrued depreciation; accumulated depreciation
depreciación acumulada
The total depreciation suffered by an asset or asset group, based on customary or fairly determined rates or estimates of useful life.

accrued income
ingresos devengados, acumulados
Income earned but neither received nor past due.

accrued interest - AI
intereses devengados, acumulados
Interest earned but not yet due and payable.

accrued liabilities
pasivo acumulado
An amount of interest, wages or other expenses recognized or incurred but not paid.

accrued loan commissions
comisiones devengadas, acumuladas sobre préstamos
Loan commissions earned but not paid.

accumulated depreciation **see** accrued depreciation

accumulated profit [accounting]
utilidades acumuladas

achievement **see** educational achievements

achievement tests [education]
pruebas de aprovechamiento, de progreso escolar, de rendimiento; exámenes
Test for measuring learner's present ability in a particular subject or skill (as opposed to his potential ability).

acid deposition
depósitos ácidos

acid rain
lluvia ácida

acid-test ratio; liquid ratio; quick ratio
relación activo disponible-pasivo corriente
The standard IBRD definition is the ratio of cash plus marketable securities plus **accounts receivable** plus other amounts readily convertible into cash to **current liabilities**. Other definitions include ratio of **current assets** less **inventories** to **current liabilities**, ratio of **quick assets** to **current liabilities**, ratio of cash plus near-cash assets to **current liabilities**, and ratio of cash plus **accounts receivable** plus the market value of selected investments to **current liabilities**.

ACP countries [Lomé Convention]
países ACP (Africa, el Caribe y el Pacífico)
European Union country classification, consisting of countries that have established a cooperation scheme (the Lomé Convention) with the European Union. Consists primarily of the former colonies of the European Union members.

acquired immune-deficiency syndrome - AIDS
síndrome de inmunodeficiencia adquirida - SIDA

act of state
acto de gobierno
Legal theory according to which the courts of one country should abstain from passing judgment about the legality of a sovereign act.

action plan **see** mitigation plan

active borrower
prestatario activo
Country that still receives World Bank loans.

active loan
préstamo activo
A loan on which disbursement is still being made.

activity brief [EDI]
resumen de actividades previstas; sinopsis de actividades (no relacionadas con proyectos específicos)

actual costs
costos efectivos, reales
Amounts determined on the basis of costs incurred as opposed to forecasted costs.

actual figures
cifras efectivas

actuarial lump sum
monto global actuarial

ad valorem (customs) duty
derecho (aduanero) ad valórem
A tax or duty levied as a given proportion of the value of a commodity or service. It grows with inflation.

adaptive research
investigación con fines de adaptación
Research which adapts to local conditions.

additionality
adicionalidad
Used to refer to the provision of extra loan flows to developing countries.

additional facility [ICSID]
mecanismo complementario

Additional Facility Rules [ICSID]
Reglamento del Mecanismo Complementario

adjective law; procedural law
derecho procesal, adjetivo, de forma

adjustable peg [foreign exchange]
vínculo ajustable

adjustment
ajuste; reajuste
[see also agricultural sector adjustment loan; exchange adjustment; export adjustment loan; financial adjustment; industrial and trade policy adjustment; industrial and trade policy adjustment loan; price adjustment clause; sector adjustment loan; self-adjustment; Structural Adjustment Facility within the Special Disbursement Account; structural adjustment lending; translation adjustment]

adjustment aid
asistencia para fines de ajuste

admeasurement contract see unit price contract

administered arbitration system [ICSID]
sistema de arbitraje administrado por una institución

administered price
precio administrado, controlado, impuesto
The price per unit of commodity where the amount to be paid or received is directly established or substantially influenced by a controlling agent. Such a price is ordinarily the result of planned control. Includes **ceiling prices, support prices** and fixed rates (government) and base prices, computed prices and millnet or netback prices (industry).

administrative machinery
sistema, mecanismo administrativo

advance account
cuenta de anticipos

advance contracting
contratación anticipada
In World Bank loans, procedure whereby the borrower enters into a contract before the signing of the relevant loan agreement.

advance contribution scheme (for IDA-10)
plan de acceso anticipado a las aportaciones (correspondientes a la décima reposición de los recursos de la AIF)

advance deposit
depósito previo, anticipado

advance deposit requirements (on imports)
requisito de depósito previo, anticipado (a la importación)

advance payment
pago anticipado

advance payment bond
fianza, garantía por pago anticipado
A bank bond guaranteeing the **advance payment** made by the employer to the **contractor** in case of bankruptcy or other cause.

advance payment security
garantía por pago anticipado
A bank security guaranteeing the **advance payment** made by the employer to the **contractor** in case of bankruptcy or other cause.

advance procurement action
licitación anticipada
Initiating and processing the procurement, up to the point where bids have been received and evaluated and an award decided upon. It stops short of entering into a contract, to avoid committing the borrower before the Bank funding for the operation is assured.

advance repayment
reembolso anticipado

advanced export payments
pagos anticipados de exportaciones, por concepto de exportaciones

advanced farmer
agricultor innovador

advanced studies
estudios avanzados, superiores, de perfeccionamiento

advanced training
formación avanzada, especializada; especialización

adverse selection [MIGA]
antiselección de riesgo

advocate [ICSID]
abogado

aeromagnetic survey; airmag survey
estudio aeromagnético; levantamiento aeromagnético

affiliate
institución afiliada; afiliada

affiliate bank
banco afiliado

affordability
accesibilidad financiera; capacidad de pago; capacidad de acceso a ...

affordability ratio **see** housing expenses/income ratio

afforestation
forestación; repoblación forestal; plantación de árboles

age-standardized death rate
tasa de mortalidad normalizada según la edad
Death rate corrected so as to allow for the effects of the differences in age structure of a population.

agency line; credit line on a agency basis [IFC]
línea de crédito a través de un agente

agency (line) subprojects
subproyectos gestionados a través de agentes

agency securities, obligations [U.S.]
títulos de organismos federales; emisiones de organismos federales

agent **see also** billing agent; buying agent; extension agent; field agent; fiscal agent; procurement agent

agent [bank syndicate]
agente

agent [ICSID]
apoderado

agent bank
banco corresponsal; banco agente
1. Bank acting for a foreign bank.
2. Bank handling administration of loan in a syndicated credit.

agglomeration economies
economías de concentración
Economies of scale resulting from urban concentration. Cf. **localization economies, urbanization economies.**

aggregate
agregado; monto global; suma total

aggregate demand
demanda agregada, global

aggregate measure of support - AMS
medida global de la ayuda - MGA
A way of measuring domestic agricultural support, proposed by the European Union, whereby all government support provided to a specific farm product is measured.

aggregate model
modelo agregado, global
A mathematical model which models a combined sample instead of several units in a group, e.g. it takes representative factors for a farm instead of modeling a number of farms and the interactions between them.

aggregative planning
planificación global, agregativa

aging schedule [accounts receivable]
estado, informe de cuentas por cobrar según fecha de vencimiento
Classification of **accounts receivable** according to whether they are current or past due. If past due they are classified into categories based upon the period when they became due.

agreed budget plan; contract plan
plan presupuestario
A selective statement of the major tasks and performance indicators - including dates and anticipated costs - to be used in tracking and evaluating quarterly progress during the budget year. A cornerstone of the Bank's budget policy. Both terms are used, though agreed budget plan is the official one.

agreement to reimburse **see** irrevocable agreement to reimburse; qualified agreement to reimburse

agribusiness; agroindustries; agro-based industry;
agroprocessing industries
agroindustrias

agricultural credit intermediary
intermediario de crédito agrícola

agricultural extension
extensión agrícola

agricultural extension officer - AEO
agente de extensión agrícola; extensionista

agricultural production and export (apex) bank
**banco, caja de crédito para la producción y las
exportaciones agropecuarias**

agricultural production and export (apex)
cooperative
**cooperativa de producción y exportaciones
agropecuarias**

agricultural sector adjustment loan - ASAL [World
Bank]
préstamo para ajuste del sector agrícola

agriculturist
agrónomo; técnico agrícola

agro-based industry
agroindustrias

agro-economist
agroeconomista

agroforestry
agrosilvicultura

agroindustries
agroindustrias

agroprocessing
elaboración de productos agropecuarios

agroprocessing industries
**industrias de elaboración de productos
agrícolas; agroindustrias**

agrosupport industry
industria de apoyo a la agricultura

aid dependency
dependencia de la ayuda exterior
Refers to the poorest countries that need foreign
aid merely to maintain their present low quality of
life.

air dried ton
tonelada en seco, secada al aire
A ton of an agricultural product which has been
dried in the air and will therefore weigh less than
the same quantity not dried in the air.

airmag survey; aeromagnetic survey
**estudio aeromagnético; levantamiento
aeromagnético**

airshed
zona atmosférica
An area with similar air mix and affected by the
same air pollution sources, thereby having similar
air quality.

algae, algal bloom
proliferación de algas
Proliferation of algae due to excessive release of
nitrogen and phosphorus (e.g. from fertilizer
runoff or detergents).

all risk insurance
seguro contra todo riesgo

alley cropping; strip cropping
cultivo en franjas
Growing two or more crops in alternating strips or
blocks on the same piece of land at the same time.

allocated costs
costos imputados

allocation of loan proceeds
**asignación de los fondos del préstamo;
distribución del importe, de los fondos del
préstamo**

allocation of net income
asignación de los ingresos netos

allocation of profits; appropriation of profits
**asignación de las utilidades; distribución de las
utilidades**

allocation of resources
asignación de los recursos; distribución de los recursos

allotment [budget]
asignación presupuestaria; crédito presupuestario

allowance for contingencies; reserve for contingencies; contingency allowance
reserva para imprevistos, para contingencias

allowance for depreciation **see** reserve for depreciation

alternative [projects]
variante; opción [proyectos]; alternativa

alternative bid [procurement]
oferta alternativa

alternative energy
energía sustitutiva

amendment, amending agreement
convenio modificatorio

amendments to the Articles of Agreement
enmiendas al Convenio Constitutivo

American short staple cotton; Arabian cotton; herbaceous cotton; Levant cotton
algodón herbáceo

amortization schedule
plan de amortización

andropogon
Andropogon gayanus
Grass used for erosion control.

animal husbandry
ganadería; cría de ganado, de animales; zootecnia

animal unit - AU
unidad de ganado
Measurement based upon the amount of feed eaten and manure produced by an average mature horse or cow or the equivalent. The equivalent is taken to be two heifers over one year, four calves under one year, seven ewes or bucks, two and a half

brood sows or boars, five hogs raised to 200 pounds each or 100 hens.

annotated agenda
temario anotado, comentado

announcement effect
efecto de anuncio
The change in market price or other economic condition that occurs upon the mere knowledge of something later that will cause the change. For example, if a developer plans to buy land for a shopping center, land prices will rise when his intentions are known.

Annual Meeting [ICSID]
Reunión Anual

Annual Meetings (of the Boards of Governors) of the World Bank and the International Monetary Fund
Reuniones Anuales (de las Juntas de Gobernadores) del Banco Mundial y del Fondo Monetario Internacional

annualization
cómputo sobre una base anual; anualización

annuity bond
bono perpetuo, de renta vitalicia
Bond on which interest is paid indefinitely and which has no maturity date.

annuity system [debt service]
sistema de pagos iguales de principal e intereses

annuity-type repayment terms
condiciones de reembolso con pagos iguales de principal e intereses

anthracite; hard coal
antracita; carbón antracitoso

anticipatory rate setting - ARS
fijación anticipada del interés
Similar to **deferred rate setting** but which allows purchaser to lock in the underlying Treasury yield at one or more points in time *preceding* the date of the issue.

antidumping duty
derecho antidumping

apex bank, cooperative see agricultural production and export bank, cooperative

apex bank, institution
banco, institución principal
Institution receiving money from the World Bank under an apex loan which it, in turn, onlends to other borrowers.

apex loan
préstamo en pirámide, en cascada
Loan whereby IBRD lends money to an apex development financial unit which onlends it to participating financial institutions which, in turn, onlend it to industrial companies.

apex report
informe presupuestario trimestral
Quarterly report issued on the previous quarter's budget. They show the extent to which agreed budget plans are being implemented and highlight areas where corrective action or resource redeployment would be appropriate.

application fee [MIGA]
comisión de solicitud
Fee charged for every definitive application for a guarantee filed with MIGA.

application for membership
solicitud de ingreso

application for withdrawal (from loan account or credit account)
solicitud de retiro de fondos (de la cuenta del préstamo o crédito)

application of funds
empleo, uso, utilización de (los) fondos

applied research
investigación aplicada

appraisal (technical and economic)
evaluación inicial (técnica y económica); evaluación previa; evaluación ex ante

appraisal fee [IFC]
comisión inicial (por evaluación)
Fee levied under various IFC facilities (APDF, MLF), payable by borrower at time of signing relevant loan agreement.

appraisal mission
misión de evaluación inicial, previa, ex ante

appraisal team [IFC]
equipo de evaluación
The investment officer, engineer and economist for a project.

appreciation (in value)
valorización

approach paper
documento expositivo sobre...; síntesis sectorial
Issues paper.

appropriate technology - AT
tecnología apropiada
The application of a technology appropriate for the factor endowment that exists. As developing countries usually have a large labor force and relatively little spare investment capital, labor-intensive industries are appropriate for them.

appropriation [budget]
autorización presupuestaria; crédito presupuestario; asignación presupuestaria

appropriation law [US]
ley del presupuesto
US statute that generally provides authorization for federal agencies to incur obligations and to make payments out of the Treasury for specified purposes.

appropriation of profits; allocation of profits
asignación de las utilidades; distribución de las utilidades

aqua privy
letrina de pozo anegado
Consists essentially of a squatting plate situated immediately above a small septic tank that discharges its effluent to an adjacent soakaway.

Arabian cotton; American short staple cotton; Levant cotton; herbaceous cotton
algodón herbáceo

Arabian crude see light Arabian crude

arbitrage see covered interest arbitrage; tax arbitrage

arbitrage pricing theory - APT
teoría de los precios en operaciones de arbitraje
An economic theory that determines prices of assets and the associated risk premia for each kind of pervasive risk assets face, on the assumption that the expected return of an arbitrage portfolio is zero.

Arbitral Tribunal [ICSID; MIGA]
Tribunal de Arbitraje

arbitration clause
cláusula de arbitraje, compromisoria
Clause in contract requiring some or all disputes between the parties to be settled by arbitration, usually final, rather than litigation.

Arbitration Rules [ICSID]
Reglas de Arbitraje
[see Rules of Procedure for Arbitration Proceedings]

arbitrator [ICSID]
árbitro

area development
desarrollo subregional

area of operational emphasis - AOE
campo de atención especial de las operaciones
Sectors which the Bank wishes to give specific focus to. They include poverty reduction and food security; debt, financial intermediation, and adjustment; human-resource development; private-sector development and public-sector management; and environment and natural-resource management.

area specific project
proyecto en un sector específico

arm's length contract
contrato entre iguales, entre compañías independientes
Contract negotiated on an equal basis between two parties, excluding favoritism or irregularity.

arm's length negotiation
negociación en pie de igualdad, entre iguales

arm's length price
precio de mercado, de plena competencia
Price between corporations under fully competitive conditions (the opposite of transfer price).

arm's length principle
principio del trato entre iguales, entre compañías independientes

articles of incorporation
escritura de constitución

ash farming; burn-beating; burning
artiga; roza; roce
Cutting and burning rough fallow on land to prepare for tillage.

assessed income
renta presunta; ingreso imponible

assessment for tax; tax assessment
avalúo, tasación para fines impositivos; estimación de la base impositiva

asset and liability management
administración de activos y pasivos
[see also **liability management**]

asset price inflation
inflación de los precios de los activos
Steep increase in equity and property prices.

asset quality ratios
coeficientes de calidad de los activos
Ratios that measure the quality of assets of a lending institution. They include ratio of undisbursed loans to disbursements, reserves to disbursed loans and loans to rescheduling countries to total loans outstanding.

asset stripping
liquidación de activos
When a company takes over another company and sells off for profit the valuable assets of the company taken over, usually because these assets have been undervalued by the stock market.

assets
activo(s); bienes
Physical objects or rights which have economic value.
[**see also** capital assets; contingent asset; current assets; domestic asset formation; domestic assets; earning assets; fixed assets; foreign assets; intangible assets; liquid assets; nonperforming assets; performing assets; real assets; saleable assets; self-liquidating assets; sight assets; sundry assets; tangible assets; temporary assets]

assignee
cesionario

assignment agreement
acuerdo de cesión

assignor
cedente

associated cost
costo asociado
The value of goods and services over and above those goods and services included in the project costs incurred to make the immediate products or services of the project available for sale. Used in US Government practice for computing the **benefit-cost ratio** at market prices.

associated crops, cropping
cultivo(s) asociado(s)
Growing two or more different crops on the same piece of land.

associated gas
gas asociado
Gas deposit capping an oil deposit.

at the margin
en el margen
The last point of production or consumption.

attachment [legal]
embargo preventivo
Act or process of seizing property by virtue of a writ or other legal order to satisfy a judgment to be entered in action subsequent to the attachment.

Attitude Survey [IBRD]
encuesta de actitudes

attrition rate
tasa de desgaste, de eliminación, de atrición

audit **see also** energy audit; internal audit; pass-through audit; project audit; project performance audit, memorandum, report; tax audit

audit, to
verificar, comprobar cuentas; auditar

audit [energy]
estudio de recursos energéticos [de un país]; examen del uso de la energía

audit [finance]
auditoría; verificación de cuentas; comprobación de cuentas
Inspection of accounting or other records in order to provide a basis for third-party evaluation or appraisal.

audit [projects]
evaluación de los resultados

audit; management audit [management]
evaluación administrativa
A review and appraisal of any or all parts of management activity.

audit mission; evaluation mission
misión de evaluación *ex post*

audit report **see** project performance audit report

audited statement of accounts
estado de cuentas verificado, auditado

auditor
auditor
[**see also** management auditor]

authenticated specimen of signature
espécimen de firma autenticado; facsímil de firma autenticado

authority [IDA] **see** commitment authority

authority [legal]
autorización; facultad

authorized bank
banco autorizado

authorized capital stock [MIGA]
capital autorizado
For MIGA, it equals one billion Special Drawing Rights.

authorized officer
funcionario autorizado

authorized positions [personnel]
cargos autorizados

authorized share capital
capital accionario autorizado

autoconsumption of food
producción de alimentos para consumo propio

automatic resetting mechanism [IFC]
mecanismo de reajuste automático (del tipo, de la tasa de interés)
In an IFC fixed rate loan, an option under which the interest rate would be reset every five years, based on current interest rates. As a result, the initial loan rate would be around 1% less than the normal fixed term rate.

availability [transportation]
disponibilidades (de equipo)

availability fee [IFC]
comisión de disponibilidad
Fee set by IFC, initially at 0.25%, which would guarantee a borrower that the rate set for a loan on signing would remain in force when the loan became effective.

average earning assets - AEA
rendimiento medio neto, rentabilidad media neta de los activos productivos
Average interest return on earning assets less average rate of borrowing costs.

average effective tax rate - AETR
tasa impositiva efectiva media
Ratio of total revenues collected through the company's income tax to the company's economic profit.

average incremental cost - AIC
costo incremental medio
[**see also** long-run average incremental cost]

average loan life - ALL
vigencia media de los préstamos
A composite indicator of how long a loan remains outstanding. For a specific loan it is calculated by dividing the cumulative debt disbursed and outstanding over the total time the loan is outstanding by the principal amount (net of cancellations).

avoidable cost
costo evitable
Marginal cost that a corporation can avoid by adopting one solution rather than another.

avoidance **see** tax avoidance

avoided cost
economía(s); reducción de costos

award [contracts]
adjudicación

award [ICSID]
laudo

awarding committee [contracts]
comité de adjudicación

- B -

"B" loan
préstamo "B"
Loan made by the World Bank involving cofinancing.

back value
ganancia neta
Value of oil or gas taking the price paid downstream for the product less the transportation and other costs incurred between the **wellhead** and the downstream place of sale.

background [education]
antecedentes (profesionales); formación

background noise
ruido de fondo

background paper
documento de antecedentes, de información básica

backhaul traffic
tráfico de regreso
Goods carried on a return journey.

backstopping
apoyo; servicios, mecanismos de apoyo
Provision of technical support.

back-to-back credit
crédito con garantía de otro crédito

back-to-office report - BTO
informe sobre misión realizada

backup (underwriting) facility
mecanismo de suscripción de reserva

backup (underwriting) facility fee
comisión de garantía de compra

backward-forward integration, linkage
integración, vinculación vertical
The "push" (i.e. the extent of demand which a development project generates for the output of all the production sectors of the economy) and "pull" (i.e. the extent of demand generated for the output of a project by an overall expansion of the production sectors of the economy).

backward integration, linkage
integración, vinculación regresiva
The extent of demand which a development project generates for the output of all the production sectors of the economy, i.e. the push exercised on the economy by a development project or group of them.

bad debt
deuda incobrable; deuda de pago dudoso

badly performing loan
préstamo poco rentable, de escaso rendimiento
Loan with poor prospects for future gains and a low **rate of return**.

bag filter; baghouse filter
filtro de tela
Fabric filter used in industrial operations to recover valuable matter as well as to control atmospheric pollution at the source.

bail out, to
sacar de apuros

bailout loan
préstamo, crédito de emergencia
Loan made to borrower whose ability to service outstanding indebtedness has become doubtful.

balance, to (an account)
cuadrar (una cuenta)

balance carried forward
saldo traspasado

balance of payments see current balance of payments

balance of payments position
situación, posición de balanza de pagos

balance-of-system costs
costos de instalación y suministros
Cost of auxiliary hardware and installation of electrical systems.

balance of trade see trade balance

balance sheet see consolidated balance sheet

balances [cash]
saldos en efectivo; fondos en efectivo

balances held on a covered basis
saldos retenidos para cubrir operaciones a término, a plazo

balancing equipment
material complementario
Extra equipment (usually small-size) needed to complete a project.

balancing item, entry
partida compensatoria; contrapartida
An entry having the effect of balancing an account.

balancing subsidy
subvención equilibradora
A subsidy given by the central government to help balance the budget of a local authority.

balloon loan
préstamo "balloon"; préstamo amortizable en su mayor parte al vencimiento
A loan repayment scheme, under which the last repayment is larger than the previous repayments. In some cases, the term is used to refer to a scheme, under which the whole loan is repaid at maturity.

balloon payment
pago final, global

ballpark figure
cifra aproximada; dato aproximado

bank acceptance, bill; banker's acceptance
aceptación bancaria
A bill of exchange which has been accepted by a banker.

bank examiner
inspector, superintendente de bancos

bank exposure
monto de los préstamos bancarios vigentes; monto de los préstamos desembolsados y pendientes; riesgo de los bancos
The total of all investments made by a bank.

"Bank first" principle
principio de utilización de los fondos del Banco en primera instancia
Principle according to which the resources of the Bank are drawn down first. Used, for example, in reference to allocation of IBRD funds to IDA where the funds made available by the Bank are used before other funds.

"Bank last" principle
principio de utilización de los fondos del Banco en última instancia
Principle whereby the funds of the Bank are used last. Used, for example, in reference to allocation of IBRD funds to IDA where these funds are drawn down only after all other sources of funds have been used.

bank money
dinero bancario
Money on deposit at a bank.

bank of issue; issuing bank
banco emisor, de emisión

Bank performance see performance

bank rate [UK]
tipo, tasa oficial de descuento

banker's acceptance; bank acceptance, bill
aceptación bancaria
A bill of exchange which has been accepted by a banker.

banker's markup; banker's spread; gross margin; gross earnings margin [banks]
margen (bancario) bruto
A bill of exchange which has been accepted by a banker.

bankable assurances
seguridades aceptables para los bancos

bankable project
proyecto financiable (por el Banco)

bar chart
gráfico, diagrama de barras

barefoot doctor
médico "descalzo"

barrels of oil equivalent - boe
barriles de equivalente en petróleo - bep
The energy equivalent to a barrel of crude oil, i.e. 5.8 million btus.

barrels per day of oil equivalent - bdoe
barriles diarios de equivalente en petróleo - bdep

barriers see tariff barriers

barter terms of trade
relación de intercambio de trueque
The relationship between the prices of exports and prices of imports in terms of the value of goods. Net barter terms of trade (also known as commodity terms of trade) is the quotient between an index of export prices and an index of import prices. Gross barter terms of trade is the quantity of imports divided by the quantity of exports. When weighted by the volume of exports the net barter terms of trade are called **income terms of trade**.

bartered exports
exportaciones en régimen de trueque

basal dressing; bottom dressing
abono, estercoladura de base

base; road base [highways]
capa de base; base
The part of the road structure below the base course and above the sub-base.

base convention see establishment convention

base costs; baseline costs
costos básicos; costos iniciales [proyectos]

base course [highways]
capa intermedia
The part of a road structure below the wearing course and above the road base.

base (lending) program [IBRD]
programa (de financiamiento) básico
The lending program of projects that will definitely be ready for the fiscal year in question.

base load [electricity]
carga de base, fundamental
The minimum load over a given period of time.

base load station [electricity]
central de carga de base, fundamental
A power station where generation is held constant.

base year
año base

baseline costs; base costs
costos básicos; costos iniciales [proyectos]

baseline data
datos básicos

baseline survey
encuesta básica; estudio básico
A preliminary survey.

basic account [balance of payments]
cuenta básica

basic education
educación básica

basic health care
atención básica de salud

basic research
investigación básica

basic skills
capacidades básicas; competencia básica; conocimientos básicos

basic subjects see core subjects

basin irrigation; level border irrigation
riego por compartimientos
Irrigation by division of the field into small units so that each has a nearly level surface. Levees are constructed around the areas forming the basins, within which the irrigation water can be controlled.

basis point
centésimo de punto porcentual (0,01%)
0.01 percent of yield (e.g. of a security).

basket extractor, exit mechanism [GATT]
mecanismo de salida de cesta
GATT mechanism that triggers new quotas in the textile field semiautomatically within existing restraint agreements.

basket unit
unidad de la cesta de monedas; unidad monetaria compuesta

basket unit of account
unidad de cuenta basada en una cesta de monedas
A **unit of account** linked to a basket of currencies.

bear market
mercado bajista
A prolonged period of falling prices.

bearer bond
bono al portador

"before-and-after" test
prueba de "antes y después"
An analysis of a country or region before and after the completion of a project.

beggar-my-neighbor policy
política de empobrecer al vecino
Protectionism, usually with the intention of improving domestic employment but without concern that any such gain in employment in one nation must cause an opposite change in employment in the trading partner.

behest project
proyecto emprendido a instancias gubernamentales

bellwether (of economic trends)
indicador primario de las tendencias económicas

below the line (item)
(partida) extraordinaria
An out-of-the-ordinary revenue or expense item or a nonrecurrent item requiring a separate entry in a balance sheet. Compares to **above the line item**.

benchmark crude; marker crude [oil]
crudo de referencia

Saudi Arabian (gravity API 34 degrees) light crude oil employed as the standard on which OPEC price changes have been based.

benchmark jobs
empleos de referencia

benchmark portfolio
cartera modelo
An assessment of the most efficient passive portfolio strategy the Bank could adopt for each major currency if it decided to abandon its active trading strategy while keeping an average portfolio duration of 12 months.

benchmark price; marker price [oil]
precio de referencia
The reference price used by OPEC for oil price changes, based on the price of Saudi Arabian light crude oil.

benchmark provisioning rate
porcentaje estándar para el establecimiento de reservas para pérdidas
The standard percentage of outstanding principal balance of non-accrual loans set aside for provisioning.

benchmark spread
margen estándar
Standard spread in IFC loans which is added to six-month **LIBOR** to determine the IFC loan rate. It is based on risk level and is closely aligned with the market, where available, for the risk and maturity in question and will, in general, reflect risk factors related to the particular investment and any special characteristics of the loan.

beneficial interest
beneficio contractual; (derecho de) usufructo
Profit, benefit or advantage resulting from a contract for the ownership of an estate as distinct from the legal ownership or control.

beneficial owner
usufructuario
... ave title to property but ... which are the normal ... property. Cf. **record**

beneficiary assessment
evaluación con la participación de los beneficiarios

beneficiation [minerals]
beneficio
Improvement of the grade of ore by milling, flotation, sintering, gravity concentration or other processes.

benefit-cost ratio [US]; cost-benefit ratio [UK]
relación costos-beneficios
[see also entrepreneurial benefit-cost ratio; private benefit-cost ratio; social benefit-cost ratio]

benefit stream
serie de beneficios
A succession of benefits over several years.

benefit taxes [IBRD]
impuestos por beneficios
A recovery of costs and benefits in a project, considered necessary beyond those through efficiency pricing, if any, or existing general taxes.

benefits [social security]
prestaciones

berth see multipurpose berth

berthing capacity
capacidad de atraque

berth throughput
capacidad de despacho de buques
The handling of ships in a port.

best available technology - BAT; best practicable means - BPM
tecnología óptima disponible
In the US, in environmental control, used to refer to environmental control standards which are at least as stringent as the uniform national technology standards but taking into account cost-effectiveness. In other countries, e.g. UK, New Zealand, Norway, the requirements may be more or less stringent than national standards and are legislated for individually by group of facilities or hazards (e.g. large combustion plants). BAT is the US term, BPM the UK term.

"best effort" project [IBRD]
proyecto en que se hará todo lo posible para lograr la participación de la mujer
A regular Bank project where "best efforts" are used to involve women.

"best efforts" sale
venta sin compromiso de garantía de emisión
A new issue which is not underwritten and not purchased as a whole from the issuer, but is sold by securities dealers on a "sell what can be sold" basis. Used in the U.S. securities and syndicated Eurocredit markets.

best practicable means - BPM see best available technology - BAT

best practice
práctica óptima

betterment levy, tax
impuesto de valorización; impuesto sobre la plusvalía
A tax on betterment (i.e. an expenditure to extend the useful life of an existing fixed asset).

beverage crop
producto agrícola para elaboración de bebidas

bias [economy; statistics]
tendencia; inclinación; sesgo; predisposición

bid see also alternative bid; examination of bids; invitation to bid; lowest evaluated bid; model bid documents; takeover bid; unsuccessful bid

bid bond, garantee, security
garantía, fianza de la oferta
Financial or other security supplied by a **bidder** when the bid is submitted which guarantees that he will not withdraw his bid during the period of bid validity specified on the **bid form**, will execute the contract form, if required, and will supply **performance security**. If he fails to do any of these the security is forfeit. The security is refundable if the bid is unsuccessful.

bid documents see model bid documents

bid form
modelo de oferta
A document submitted by the **bidder** for a contract which offers to supply and deliver the goods and/or services which are the subject of the bid, in accordance with the **conditions of contract** and specifications. In the document the **bidder** undertakes to commence delivery within a specified amount of days and obtain a **performance security**.

bid guarantee **see** bid bond

bid opening
apertura de ofertas
Examination of all bids submitted for a contract. The Bank requires this to be done in public, i.e. in the presence of those **bidders** or their representatives who choose to attend.

bid package
conjunto de bienes (obras, servicios, elementos) a licitar
Usually refers to bids where there is more than one item involved.

bid price [contract]
precio de oferta
The price that a **bidder** specifies in the **bid form** for the delivery of goods or completion of the works.

bid security **see** bid bond

bid submission; delivery of bids
presentación de ofertas
The act of a **bidder** handing over his bid to the purchaser.

bidder (highest/lowest)
licitante (que somete la oferta más alta, más baja)
[**see also** highest bidder; lowest bidder; postqualification of bidders; prequalification of bidders; qualified bidder; second lowest bidder; successful bidder]

bidding **see** competitive bidding; competitive bidding in accordance with local procedures; component bidding; international competitive bidding; limited international bidding

bidding conditions
bases de licitación; pliego de condiciones de la licitación

bidding documents; tender documents
documentos de licitación
The collection of documents which specify the bidding procedures, the technical specification of the goods/works required and contract terms. They include the **Invitation for Bids, Instruction to Bidders, General Conditions of Contract, Special Conditions of Contract, Schedule of Requirements (or Bill of Quantities), Technical Specifications, Bid Form, Price Schedules, Bid Security Form, Contract Form** and **Performance Security Form**.

bill of exchange
letra de cambio

bill of lading
conocimiento de embarque
A contract for the delivery of goods to a buyer. It also represents the title to the goods and a receipt that the carrier has received the goods.
[**see also** through bill of lading]

bill of quantities
estimación cuantitativa
The specification of the quantity of materials to be used.
[**see also** priced bill of quantities]

bill of quantities contract
contrato basado en una estimación cuantitativa
A type of **unit price contract**, with a **detailed bill of quantities** calculated on the basis of the plans of the consultant **engineer** or architect. The **unit prices** are given and the totals worked out. As the contract is carried out, the quantities actually used are measured by a quantity surveyor and the **contractor** is paid on the basis of these amounts.

billing agent
organismo agente de cobranza

binding; bindings
consolidaciones arancelarias
In GATT, the fixing or freezing of certain trading advantages for a three year period.

biochemical oxygen demand - BOD
demanda bioquímica de oxígeno - DBO
A measure of the amount of pollution by organic substances in water. It is expressed as the number of milligrams of oxygen required by the micro-organisms to oxidize the organics in a liter of water.

biochemical oxygen demand over five days - BOD5; five day biochemical oxygen demand
demanda bioquímica de oxígeno en cinco días - DBO5
The standard **biochemical oxygen demand** test whereby a sample of the liquid is incubated at 20 degrees C for five days.

biodiversity
diversidad biológica; biodiversidad

biogas plant
central (productora) de biogás

biomass energy
energía de biomasa; energía a partir de biomasa

biomass (power) plant, station
central (generadora) de energía a partir de biomasa; central de biomasa

biosphere reserve
reserva de biosfera
An idea created by the UNESCO Man and the Biosphere Programme, which aimed to establish protected core areas with one or two surrounding buffer zones, with the core areas devoted to sustainable development and habitat restoration.

birth control
control de la natalidad

birth spacing
espaciamiento de los nacimientos
The deliberate effort of couples to postpone a birth. Also used as a synonym for birth timing.

bisque clause
cláusula de modificación parcial
Clause in loan agreement that entitles a borrower to postpone payments of interest and principal for limited periods of time in balance of payments difficulties.

black economy **see** parallel economy

black market
mercado negro, clandestino

black money
dinero negro
Money in the economy obtained through illegal means, such as money from the drug trade.

blanket effect
efecto generalizado

blanket purchase order - BPO
orden de compra general
A purchase of low value goods and services from a single vendor.

blanket release
liberación incondicional, irrestricta
Release by Bank member of its **18% currency** for indefinite lending or relending.

blend country
país que puede obtener financiamiento combinado (del BIRF y la AIF)
Country eligible to receive financing from both IBRD and IDA.

blend financing; mixed financing
financiamiento combinado (del BIRF y la AIF)

blending (of flows)
combinación de financiamiento

blind trust
fideicomiso cuya composición es desconocida por el beneficiario; fideicomiso "ciego"
An arrangement whereby a person places some or all financial affairs in trust, beyond his personal control. Used by public officials to avoid conflict of interest charges. Currently used by the President of the World Bank and the President of the United States.

block release **see** day release

block tariff
tarifa por bloques
A tariff in which the charge is based on a series of different kilowatt-hour rates applying to successive kilowatt-hour blocks of given size, supplied during a specified period.

block trading
negociación de bloques de acciones

block train
tren bloque
A permanently made-up train.

blue chip; blue chip security
acción de primera clase; valor de primera clase

blue projects
proyectos azules
Projects covering coastal and marine resources. Cf. **brown projects, green projects.**

blue stained cotton see gray cotton

blueprint planning
planificación detallada

Board seminar
reunión informal (del Directorio)

Board of Directors [IFC, MIGA]
Junta de Directores

Board of (Executive) Directors; Executive Board [IBRD, IDA]
Directorio Ejecutivo

Board of Governors
Junta de Gobernadores [Banco, AIF, CFI]

Boards of the Bank and the Fund
Directorios del Banco y del Fondo

body corporate; corporate body, institution
persona jurídica

boilerplate
cláusula tipo, modelo, estándar
Standard legal language used in legal documents.

bond see annuity bond; bearer bond; bid bond; convertible bond; corporate bond; coupon bond; deep discount bond; development bond; discount bond; exit bond; floating rate bond; government bond; indexed bond; noncallable; original issue discount bond; outstanding bonds; performance bond; perpetual bond; publicly issued; registered bond; serial bond; straight bond; Treasury bond; warrant bond; zero coupon bond

bonded area; free trade zone - FTZ
zona franca

bonded contractor
contratista con fianza, afianzado
Contractor who has taken out a surety bond to cover any claims against him.

bonded goods
mercancías en depósito, en almacén de aduanas
Taxable goods held in a government-licensed warehouse pending payment of customs duties and other taxes due.

bonded industrial estate
zona industrial en régimen de franquicia aduanera

bonded warehouse
depósito, almacén de aduanas
A government-licensed warehouse that holds taxable goods pending payment of customs duties and other taxes due.

bondholder
tenedor de bonos

bonding [customs]
depósito en almacén de aduanas

bonding company
compañía de fianzas
Company which issues **performance bonds, payment bonds** and other kinds of bonds.

bonus
prima; bonificación

bonus clause
cláusula de bonificación
Clause in a contract which provides for a bonus to be paid to **contractors** or suppliers for completion of works or delivery of goods ahead of schedule, when this is beneficial to the contracting agency.

bonus issue
dividendo en acciones

bonus share
acción recibida como dividendo
A share given as a bonus to purchasers of shares.

book value
valor contable, en libros
The net amount at which an asset appears on the books of account.

boomtown effect **see** induced development effect

booster pump
bomba de refuerzo
Pump installed in front of another pump to ensure satisfactory suction conditions for the main pump or to deliver water from a deep well to a second pump, which develops the final delivery head.

booster (pumping) station
estación (de bombeo) de refuerzo, de rebombeo
A pumping station in a water distribution system that is used to increase the pressure in the mains on the discharge side of the pumps.

border bias
sesgo (por defecto) de margen, de borde
In crop evaluations, under-representation of the crops at the edge of the plot, because of difficulty of placing the square used for these estimates.

border check irrigation; border ditch irrigation; border irrigation; border strip irrigation; gravity check irrigation; ribbon check irrigation; strip check irrigation; strip irrigation
riego por tablares, por eras; riego por gravedad con retenes
Flood irrigation in which land is divided into border strips and water is delivered into each strip from a head or field ditch at its upper end.

border currency (unit)
(unidad de) moneda fronteriza
In a project, values measured in foreign exchange but denominated in the local currency.

border ditch irrigation **see** border check irrigation

border industry
industria fronteriza

border irrigation **see** border check irrigation

border point price **see** cost, insurance and freight port of entry/border point price

border price
precio en (la) frontera
Price of a **tradable** good at a country's border or port of entry.

border strip irrigation **see** border check irrigation

border taxes
impuestos fronterizos
Taxes levied at national frontiers.

borrower ownership
adopción (por el prestatario) de un programa como propio; autoría; identificación
In adjustment programs, when the borrower adopts the Bank program as its own. Criteria for this include launching of economic reforms preceded or accompanied by productive policy dialogue and operationally-oriented economic and sector work by the Bank, a timely program tailored to country-specific circumstances and supported by adequate external financing and the borrower endeavoring to build a strong consensus for the program at key points in the administration.

borrowing capacity
capacidad de endeudamiento

borrowing cost
costo de los empréstitos

borrowing from the public
oferta pública; emisión ofrecida al público

borrowing pool [IBRD]
conjunto de empréstitos
Pool of IBRD **funded debt** used to determine on a semi-annual basis the IBRD **lending rate**.

borrowing rate **see** depositor rate of interest

bottleneck
estrangulamiento; *a veces*: **congestión**

bottleneck analysis
análisis de la capacidad limitante
Type of analysis concentrating on bottlenecks in system, e.g. delivery systems, transportation systems.

bottom dressing; basal dressing
abono, estercoladura de base

bottom line
conclusión; resultado final

bottom out (of a recession)
pasar, superar el punto más bajo

bottom up (approach) [projects]
de abajo arriba
Planning which is decentralized and which takes place at the development project level.

bracket creep, progression [taxation]
paso gradual a tasas impositivas más altas
The situation in which incomes rise due to inflation and that rise puts taxpayers in higher income tax brackets so that a larger percentage of their income is automatically paid to the government.

bracketing
restricción a la admisibilidad de licitantes
Restriction indicating which **bidders** may submit a bid, e.g. by stating that only certain **bid prices** may apply. The Bank does not allow this procedure in international bidding.

Brady bond
bono Brady
Bond created when existing developing country debt is concerted into new debt. The new bond has a smaller face value or a lower nominal interest rate than the original bond but may be enhanced through, for example, collateralization of principal and/or part of the interest payments.

brain drain
fuga de cerebros, éxodo de intelectuales

branch ministry
ministerio responsable de una sola industria
A ministry responsible for just one industry.

brand name drug
específico; especialidad (farmacéutica)

brand name product
producto de marca registrada

... oslavia Precedents
... establecido por Brasil y Yugoslavia
... RD share allocations to restore a ... shareholding in IBRD parallel to its ... . Named after the first two countries to ... .

... ontract
... iento de contrato; violación de

breach of contract risk [MIGA]
riesgo de incumplimiento de contrato
Repudiation or breach of a specified commitment by the host government to the **guarantee holder** in cases where (1) the **guarantee holder** does not have recourse to a competent, independent judicial or arbitral forum to determine the claims of repudiation or breach, or (ii) a decision by such a forum is not rendered within a reasonable period of time, as defined in the contract of guarantee, or (iii) a final decision cannot be enforced.

bread grains
cereales panificables

breadwinner
sostén de la familia

breakbulk
carga fraccionada
Cargo packed in separate packages or individual pieces of cargo, loaded, stowed and unloaded individually, as distinct from bulk cargo.

break clause; escape clause; jeopardy clause
cláusula de salvaguardia, de elusión, de escape
A clause in a Eurocurrency agreement specifying that, if certain events curtail the lender's activity or the operation of the Euromarkets, other designated actions will come into effect.

breakdown
desglose; distribución

breakeven analysis
análisis de punto muerto, de equilibrio
An analysis of expense and revenue factors, often expressed graphically, aimed at determining at what cost and price points a product, product line or company break even.

breakeven (dollar) depreciation
(tasa de) depreciación de equilibrio
Depreciation rate of the dollar such that the Bank's **headroom** is at breakeven point.

breakeven point
punto muerto, de equilibrio
The level of product sales at which financial revenues equal total costs of production. At higher volumes of production and sales financial profits are generated. Point where two strategies are equivalent.

breed [livestock]
raza

breeder [agriculture]
genetista [especies vegetales]; criador; reproductor [ganadería]

breeder seed
semilla de primera reproducción, del mejorador

breeding **see** plant breeding

breeding material
material genético, de mejora [especies vegetales]

breeding station [commercial breeding]
puesto de monta, de cubrición, de reproducción

breeding stock
(animales) reproductores; sementales

breeding unit
centro de genética ganadera

bridge, bridging loan
préstamo transitorio, de transición, "puente"

bridging arrangement, credit
disposiciones transitorias; financiamiento transitorio

bridging facility
mecanismo de financiamiento transitorio; servicio de financiamiento transitorio

brief [project]
datos básicos de un proyecto

broad money
dinero en sentido amplio
Equivalent to M3, i.e. M2 plus the average of the beginning- and end-of-month deposits of non-bank thrift institutions.

broadcasting (seed, fertilizer)
siembra a voleo; aplicación de fertilizantes a voleo

broken cross rates
tipos cruzados dispares
In foreign exchange, disparity among three or more rates, e.g. if DM 1 = 30 cents and FF 1.5 while FF 1 = 22 cents a Deutschmark will bring 30 cents if converted directly but 33 if converted first into francs and then into dollars.

broker
corredor (de cambio, de bolsa); agente (de cambio y bolsa)

brokerage
corretaje

brown coal
carbón bituminoso; lignito
A low-grade coal which commonly retains the structures of the original wood. It is high in moisture, low in heat value and checks badly upon drying.

brown projects
proyectos marrones, pardos
Projects covering the immediate and most critical environmental problems facing cities; they include three main areas--energy use and efficiency, urban and industrial pollution control, and urban environmental management. Cf. **green projects, blue projects.**

Bruno ratio
relación de Bruno
The **present worth** of the domestic currency cost of realizing a foreign exchange saving divided by the **present worth** of the net foreign exchange saving. A project is accepted if it is less than the official exchange rate in financial analysis or less than the **shadow exchange rate** in economic analysis.
[**see also** modified Bruno ratio]

bubble concept
criterio de contaminación total permisible
The concept whereby the total pollution level for an area must be set collectively but the market can allocate that total among competing uses by exchange of emission permits.

bubble-up effect
efecto de capilaridad, ascendente
The opposite of the **trickle-down effect**. The benefits of a project, change in economic policy benefiting the lowest paid and gradually rising up the scale.

bucket latrine
letrina de cubo
A latrine where the sullage falls into a bucket which can be removed for disposal of the sullage.

budget **see also** capital budget; cash budget; current budget; exchange budget; investment budget; midyear review; operating budget; partial budget; performance budget; program budget; special budget; unit activity (crop) budget; whole farm budget

budget amendment [U.S.]
enmienda presupuestaria presidencial

budget appropriation
autorización presupuestaria [EE.UU.]; crédito presupuestario; asignación presupuestaria

budget authority
facultad presupuestaria

budget closure
cierre del presupuesto
Lapsing of authority to incur approved budgetary expenses. In the Bank, this is at the end of the fiscal year for the regular and reimbursable budgets and after three years for capital budgets.

budget cuts
reducciones presupuestarias

budget deficit; budgetary gap
déficit presupuestario

budget estimates
proyecto de presupuesto; estimaciones presupuestarias

budget neutral
que no afecta al presupuesto
Outputs having no influence on the budget.

Budget Planning Framework [IBRD]
parámetros de planificación presupuestaria

budget process
proceso presupuestario

budget surplus
superávit presupuestario

budgetary aid
ayuda presupuestaria, para el presupuesto

budgetary gap; budget deficit
déficit presupuestario

budgeting **see** full budgeting; planning, programming, budgeting system; zero base budgeting

buffer fund
fondo de regulación, de estabilización
Fund set up to regulate **buffer stocks**.

buffer stock scheme
plan de existencias reguladoras

buffer stocks
existencias reguladoras
Stocks of a commodity held in an attempt to even out price fluctuations in primary commodities. The operators use the stock to mitigate fluctuations in prices by selling from the commodity stock when prices are high and by buying the commodity when prices are low.

build-own operate - BOO
construcción-propiedad-operación
Type of construction contract whereby a private firm finances some or all of the initial investment and is remunerated directly from revenues earned by the project from selling output to a public utility. The project is kept by the private firm and not transferred back to the government.

build-operate-transfer; build-operate-turnover - BOT
construcción-operación-transferencia - COT
Type of construction contract whereby a private firm finances some or all of the initial investment and is remunerated directly from revenues earned by the project from selling output to a public utility. Ownership is eventually transferred to the state or to private domestic investors.

build-own-operate-transfer - BOOT
construcción-propiedad-operación-transferencia - CPOT
Type of construction contract whereby a private firm finances some or all of the initial investment and is remunerated directly from revenues earned by the project from selling output to a public utility. Ownership is initially held by the firm but eventually transferred to the state or to private domestic investors.

built-in evaluation [projects]
evaluación incorporada en los proyectos

built-in stabilizers
elementos estabilizadores, automáticos, internos, intrínsecos
Relationships which reduce the amplitude of cyclical fluctuation in the economy without any direct action by government, firms or individuals, e.g. a progressive tax which reduces the spending power of consumers in amounts which change faster than incomes, resulting in contractionary tendencies during expansionary periods and vice versa.

built-in tendency
tendencia intrínseca

bulk, in
a granel

bulk procurement
compra, adquisición en grandes cantidades, en grueso

bull market
mercado alcista
A rising market.

bullet issue
emisión, empréstito reembolsable de una sola vez a su vencimiento

bump integrator [highways]
integrador de irregularidades
Type of machine for measuring uneven road surfaces.

bunching
acumulación; congestión
[see also debt bunching

bunching of maturities
acumulación de vencimientos

bund
dique; terraplén
[see also contour bund]

bunker [coal]
carbonera

bunker; bunker oil
combustible para calderas, barcos
A heavy residual fuel oil used by ships, industry and for large-scale heating installations.

bunkering
aprovisionamiento de combustible [barcos]
To fill a ship's bunker with coal or oil.

buoyancy [economics]
capacidad de reacción; dinamismo
[see also tax buoyancy]

buoyant demand
demanda intensa

buoyant market
mercado activo

burden sharing
**participación en el financiamiento de los costos,
gastos [beneficiarios]; participación en la carga;
distribución de la carga [donantes]**

burn beating **see** ash farming

burning [agriculture] **see** ash farming

bush fallow
barbecho en maleza
Poor quality land covered with scrubby vegetation.

business accounting
contabilidad de empresa, comercial

business community
**medios, esferas, círculos empresariales,
comerciales**

business cycle; trade cycle
ciclo económico; coyuntura

business cycle policy
política coyuntural

business expenses
gastos de explotación, de operación

business line
actividad comercial; ramo

business plan
plan de actividades (empresariales)

business (profit) tax; corporate income tax [US];
corporation tax [UK]
impuesto sobre las utilidades

buy-back agreement; take-out agreement
acuerdo de recompra

buyer credit; buyers' credit
crédito de compradores

buyer's market
**mercado de compradores; mercado favorable a
los compradores**

buying agent [commodities]
agente comprador; agente de compras

buying rate of exchange
tipo de cambio comprador
The rate at which foreign exchange banks and
brokers agree to buy foreign currency.

bylaws
reglamento; a veces: estatutos

- C -

calendar quarter
trimestre del año civil

call for capital; call of capital
requerimiento de capital
Request for paying in of **callable** capital.

call in a loan, to
exigir el reembolso de un préstamo

call loan
préstamo a la vista
A loan on a demand basis (i.e. which either the borrower or lender may terminate at will).

call money; day to day money; demand money; money at call
dinero exigible; dinero a la vista
Money deposited in an interest-bearing account, that can be called by the depositor on a day's notice. Often applied to money lent by banks to stock exchange **brokers**, which may be called at any time.

call of capital **see** call for capital

call option
opción de compra
Option to purchase designated **securities** at a predetermined price within a specified time limit.

call order contract
contrato de servicios ocasionales
Contract whereby an entreprise engages staff on a short-term basis but does not know when it needs them so reserves the right to call them when needed.

callable (capital, subscription)
exigible
That part of capital which is not yet paid up and on which payments can be called for.

called up (share) capital; paid in (share) capital
capital pagado

calling in of a currency
retiro de una moneda de la circulación; desmonetización

calorie intake
ingestión de calorías

calving rate
tasa de parición
The number of calves born alive in any year expressed as a percentage of the number of females let to the bull in the previous year.

cancellation
condonación (de una deuda); anulación; cancelación
Voiding a debt by annulling or paying it.

cancelled debt
deuda anulada

cap
tope; *a veces*: **contrato, préstamo con interés tope**
A **floating rate note** with an upper limit on the interest rate to be paid.

capability [urban development]
capacidad

capacity **see** rated capacity

capital **see also** commercial capital; domestic capital formation; equilibrating capital flow; equity capital; floating capital; foreign capital; frozen capital; General Capital Increase; gross fixed capital formation; incremental capital-output ratio; loan capital; marginal efficiency of capital; noncash working capital; official capital; overhead capital; paid-in (share) capital; paid-up capital; public (capital) expenditure; quasi-equity; recycling (of capital); return of capital; return on capital; return to capital; risk capital; seed capital; Selective Capital Increase; share capital; social overhead capital; uncalled capital; unimpaired capital; venture capital; volatile capital; working capital

capital account
cuenta de capital
In balance of payments, it measures the short- and long-term financial movements which may be associated with the purchase of physical assets, stocks and shares, or with the placing of money on a short-term basis.

capital adequacy
suficiencia de(l) capital

capital assets; fixed assets; permanent assets; fixed capital [accounting]
activos fijos; capital fijo
All **tangible assets** (movable and immovable) held by an entity and used in its normal operations for the production of goods or services. These assets have a normal life longer than one year and are not normally acquired for resale.

capital base
base de capital
Total capital of an organization, i.e. capital plus reserves.

capital budget
presupuesto de capital
A budget which is limited to showing planned expenditures and sources of funds for purchases of **capital goods**. In the Bank, one of three budgets, it is for funds used to incur costs that result in capital assets being created in the balance sheet. Includes computing and office technology equipment, buildings, building renovation, furniture and other equipment costing more than $50,000.

capital consumption allowance
reserva para depreciación
An entry in the national income accounts which reflects the depreciation of equipment and machinery within a given period of time. Usually based on tax reports of depreciation.

capital cost
costo de inversión

capital deepening
aumento del capital con respecto al trabajo
Action which increases the relative value of capital in relation to labor (see **capital widening**).

capital deepening investment
inversión orientada a aumentar la eficiencia de la producción y reducir los costos
Investment aimed at increasing production efficiency and lowering costs.

capital-deficit oil exporter
exportador de petróleo con déficit de capital

capital efficiency
productividad del capital; rentabilidad del capital

capital endowment
dotación de capital

capital equipment; capital goods
bienes de capital, de equipo
Production goods, i.e. instruments of production such as buildings, machinery, equipment, etc. rather than items for immediate consumption.

capital expenditure; capital outlay
gasto(s) de capital; inversión en capital fijo

capital flight; flight of capital
fuga de capitales

capital flow; capital movement
movimiento, flujo de capital

capital formation
formación de capital

capital gain
ganancia de capital; plusvalía

capital gains tax
impuesto sobre la plusvalía; impuesto sobre ganancias de capital

capital gearing ratio **see** gearing ratio

capital goods; capital equipment
bienes de capital, de equipo
Production goods, i.e. instruments of production such as buildings, machinery, equipment, etc. rather than items for immediate consumption.

capital grants
transferencias de capital (no reembolsables)

capital impairment
reducción del capital
The estimated loss in an investment.

capital inadequacy
insuficiencia de(l) capital

capital inflow
entrada, afluencia de capital

capital infrastructure
infraestructura (económica); capital social básico

capital intensity
intensidad de capital

capital-intensive
con gran intensidad de capital; con uso intensivo de capital; con alto coeficiente de capital

capital investment
inversión (de capital)

capital-labor ratio
relación capital-trabajo
The ratio at which labor and capital are combined within the production process. Generally labor and capital are measured as flows per unit of time.

capital loss
pérdida de capital

capital market
mercado de capital(es)
The market for buying and selling long-term loanable funds, in the form of bonds, mortgages and the like. Unlike the **money market**, where short-term funds are traded, the capital market tends to center on well-organized institutions such as the stock exchange. However, there is no clearcut distinction between the two other than that capital market loans are generally used by businesses, financial institutions and governments to buy capital goods whereas money-market loans generally fill a temporary need for **working capital**.

capital movement; capital flow
movimiento, flujo de capital

capital outlay; capital expenditure
gasto(s) de capital; inversión en capital fijo

capital-output ratio
relación capital-producto
The ratio of the amount of capital to the amount of output produced by that capital.

capital position
posición de capital
The amount of capital held.

capital recovery factor - CRF
factor de recuperación del capital
The annual payment that will repay a loan of 1 currency unit in x years with compound interest on the unpaid balance. Also called the "partial payment factor." The reciprocal of the **present worth of an annuity factor**. Generally obtained from a set of compounding and discounting tables. This factor permits calculating the equal installments necessary to repay (amortize) a loan over a given period at a stated interest rate. The total payment is a varying combination of both interest and repayment (amortization) of principal.

capital-service ratio
coeficiente, relación capital-servicio
Contractual service payments on long-term debt plus remitted profits on direct investment divided by exports of goods and services.

capital stock
capital social, accionario; capital nacional [para un país]

capital structure
estructura de capital

capital subscription [IBRD]
suscripción al capital, de acciones del capital

capital supply
oferta de capital

capital-surplus country
país con superávit de capital; país superavitario

capital transfer
transferencia de capital

capital widening
ampliación del capital; aumento del capital
Investment that increases the absolute value of capital (*see* **capital deepening**).

capital works
instalaciones físicas

capitalized expenses
gastos capitalizados; costos capitalizados
An item of cost usually charged to profit and loss but, because related to a period of construction, added to a capital-asset account.

capitation approach [health financing]
sistema de capitación

capitation tax; poll tax; head tax
(impuesto de) capitación

capture (e.g. of public services)
captación
The use of a significant amount, e.g. of public services or resources by relatively narrow special interests.

capture fishery; harvest fishery
pesca
Fishing for wild fish, normally from a boat, as opposed to aquaculture, where the fish are bred in a controlled environment.

carbon fixation, sequestration
fijación de carbono
Conversion, through photosynthesis, of atmospheric carbon dioxide into organic form in plants.

carbon sink
zona de absorción de carbono
Natural structure, such as a forest, that absorbs carbon dioxide and other carbon-based emissions.

carbon tax
impuesto a las emisiones de carbono; recargo o multa para reducir las emisiones de carbono
A tax levied on products that emit **greenhouse gases**.

career development
planificación del avance profesional

carried interest [petroleum industry]
participación pasiva
A fractional interest in oil and gas property, usually a lease, the holder of which has no personal obligation for operating costs, which are to be paid by the owner or owners of the remaining fraction, who reimburse themselves, therefore, out of production receipts.

carrying capacity (of the Earth)
capacidad de absorción
The ability of Earth to absorb emissions and waste.

carrying capacity [pastures]
capacidad de carga; capacidad de sustento; capacidad ganadera
The amount of feed available from a pasture area, generally stated in **animal units**.

carrying capacity [transportation]
capacidad de acarreo

carrying cost (of capital); charge of capital
costo de inactividad del capital
The interest on debit balances.

carrying costs, charges [goods]
costo de mantenimiento en existencia
The cost of carrying commodities held in a warehouse, such as charges for storage, insurance, haulage and loss of interest on the investment.

carrying gain
diferencia positiva
The positive difference between the return on a portfolio and its average cost.

carrying loss
diferencia negativa
The negative difference between the return on a portfolio and its average cost.

carryover loan
préstamo a corto plazo para salvar una dificultad temporal

carryovers
créditos, saldos que se traspasan; créditos, saldos traspasados
Funds unused during a financial year which are transferred to the budget for the following financial year.

cascade tax
impuesto en cascada
A tax levied at several stages of the manufacturing process.

case study
estudio de un caso práctico, de casos prácticos

cash advance
anticipo de caja

cash balance; cash holdings; cash in hand; cash on hand
saldo de, en caja
Cash in immediate possession represented by coin, paper money and negotiable checks and other paper commonly accepted for immediate credit by a bank in a deposit of cash.

cash-based budget planning
planificación presupuestaria en valores de caja, en efectivo
Budget planning based on actual cash outlays for the budget, rather than for a fixed amount of items, with allowances for cost increases.

cash (basis) accounting
contabilidad según registro de caja; contabilidad en valores de caja
A form of accounting wherein transactions are recorded only as cash is paid or received. Related **financial statements** are usually restricted to a summary of receipts and payments.

cash basis, on a
según registro de caja

cash budget
presupuesto de caja
An estimate of cash receipts and disbursements for a future period, cash requirements at various points within the period, and cash on hand at the end of the period.

cash buybacks
recompras en efectivo

cash crop
cultivo comercial
A crop sold directly on the market as compared to one which is fed to animals or otherwise used but not sold.

cash deficit
déficit de caja

cash economy
economía monetaria

cash expenditures
gastos en efectivo

cash flow
flujo de fondos; corriente de fondos; liquidez; flujos de caja
A narrow definition for **funds flow**, restricted to cash or cash equivalents. Sometimes used synonymously with **funds flow**.

cash flow system of taxation
sistema impositivo con deducción de gastos efectuados en el mismo año
System of taxation whereby all expenditures are deducted from the income base in the same year as they are incurred.

cash forecast
previsiones de caja

cash generation; internal cash generation; internally generated funds
recursos propios; recursos provenientes de las operaciones

cash grant
donación en efectivo

cash holdings **see** cash balance

cash income
ingresos monetarios, en efectivo

cash inflows
afluencia de fondos; entradas de fondos

cash in hand **see** cash balance

cash input [accounting]
aportación, aporte en efectivo
The cash component of an investment, as compared to the capital, labor, etc. component

cash input [agricultural projects]
insumo de fondos en efectivo
An **input** into a project used to produce an output in the form of cash.

cash management
gestión de caja
Control and use of liquid assets.

cash market **see** spot market

cash on hand **see** cash balance

cash payment
pago al contado; pago en efectivo

cash position
situación de efectivo, de liquidez

cash projections
proyección del flujo de fondos

casual labor
trabajadores ocasionales; mano de obra ocasional

catalytic converter
convertidor catalítico
A device installed in motor vehicle exhaust systems that reduces the emissions of hydrocarbons and carbon monoxide.

catalytic role
función catalizadora
The way a project encourages other potential cofinancers to join in the project.

catch basin; catchment area
cuenca de captación; zona de captación [riego]; zona de captación, de influencia [educación, etc.]

catch crop
cultivo intercalado, intermedio
A quick-growing crop, planted and harvested between two regular crops in consecutive seasons or between two patches of regular crops in the same season.

catchment area; catch basin
cuenca de captación; zona de captación [riego]; zona de captación, de influencia [educación, etc.]

categorical grant; targeted grant
donación para fines específicos, para un fin específico
Grant given by central government for specific purposes.

Category I countries [IBRD]
países de la Categoría I
Industrial member countries.

Category II countries [IBRD]
países de la Categoría II
Developing member countries.

cattle on the hoof
ganado en pie
Live cattle.

cattle unit
unidad ganadera
Unit for measuring number of animals - cattle = 1, sheep = 1, goat = 0.05, fowl = 0.01, pig = 0.2-0.4. [**see also** tropical cattle unit]

caucus (of countries at Annual Meetings)
grupo

ceiling price
precio tope, máximo
The maximum price which may be charged, regardless of what price would be reached through the natural forces of supply and demand.

center pivot sprinkle irrigation
riego por aspersión con pivote central
Type of irrigation which consists of a central pivot linked to a water supply and a long arm extending from this central pivot which sprays water on crops, often with subsidiary arms extending from the major one.

centrally-managed costs
costos, gastos centralizados
Costs which are the responsibility, for budgetary purposes, of the institution as a whole, as opposed to those that are the responsibility of individual units (see unit-managed costs).

centrally planned economy (country)
economía de planificación centralizada; país con economía de planificación centralizada

central rate [exchange rates]
tipo de cambio central

central vicepresidencies [IBRD]
vicepresidencias centrales
Vicepresidencies in IBRD responsible for the central research and operations support functions.

certificate of deposit
certificado de depósito
Certificate of an interest-bearing time deposit with a bank.

certificate of payment
recibo; comprobante de pago

certified seed
semilla certificada
The progeny of **breeder**, select, **foundation** or **registered seed** so handled as to maintain satisfactory genetic purity and identity.

ceylon cotton; tree cotton; Siam cotton; China cotton
algodón arbóreo

chain index
índice en cadena
An index number derived by relating the value at any given period to the value in the previous period rather than to a fixed base.

chair, constituency of an Executive Director [World Bank]
país(es) representado(s) por un Director Ejecutivo; *a veces:* **jurisdicción**

chair representing ... [World Bank Executive Directors]
representante de ...

changes clause [US]
cláusula de modificación unilateral
A clause in a contract giving a contracting officer the right to make unilateral changes to a contract, provided that the changes are within the general scope of the contract.

changes in working capital statement **see** statement of changes in financial position

channel [trade]
conducto, cauce, vía de comercialización

channel, river
cauce, lecho, canal de un río

charge; lien [legal]
cargo; gravamen; embargo preventivo

chargeback
cargo al usuario

charge number [currency pool]
base de cálculo de la tasa de interés
An intermediate variable used to calculate **currency pool** interest, it is determined by revaluing each day's current dollar-equivalent balance to the present using the product of the duality **revaluation factors** between that day and the present, with the sum of these daily revalued balances representing the charge number.

charge of capital; carrying cost (of capital)
costo de inactividad del capital
The interest on debit balances.

charges [utilities]
tarifas; cargos

chart **see** bar chart; chart of accounts; construction progress chart; flip chart; flow chart; performance chart; process chart; progress chart; scatter chart

charter (of a company)
escritura de constitución; escritura social

charter party - c/p
contrato de fletamento
A contract between shipowner and charterer for the carriage of goods or hire of vessel for a period of time.

chart of accounts
plan de cuentas
A systematically arranged list of accounts applicable to a specific concern giving account names and numbers, if any.

cherry picking
selección de lo mejor

chief economist
economista principal (Oficina Regional)

child mortality
mortalidad en la niñez [uno a cuatro años de edad]
[see also infant mortality]

China cotton; Ceylon cotton; Siam cotton; tree cotton
algodón arbóreo

chlorofluorocarbon - CFC
clorofluorocarbono - CFC

churn factor
oficinas en alquiler temporal
Leased space to handle demand surge and space modifications.

cistern flush latrine
letrina de cisterna y sifón
Latrine where the water for flushing comes from a cistern.

civil commotion
conmoción civil
Events which have all the characteristics of a **riot** but which are more widespread and of longer duration, without, however, attaining the status of civil war, revolution, rebellion or insurrection. Covered by MIGA under the **war and civil disturbance** category. Cf. **riot**.

civil service
administración pública; cuerpo de funcionarios públicos

civil works; public works
obras civiles

claim
reclamación; demanda; exigencia; derecho; afirmación; etc.; acreencia [banca]; (título de) crédito [finanzas]
[see also financial claim; financial claims of government]

claim [mining]
denuncio; concesión

claim (on resources)
utilización de recursos

claused bill of lading; dirty bill of lading
conocimiento de embarque con reservas, objeciones
A **bill of lading** that has been endorsed by the shipowner as the goods described in the bill do not conform to what is offered for shipment, e.g. package missing, goods damaged, etc.

clawback provision
cláusula de suscripción preferente
Clause in an underwriting agreement for a security that restricts the issue to a certain group, e.g. domestic buyers, till demand from that group is satisfied.

clean bill of lading
conocimiento de embarque sin reservas, objeciones
A **bill of lading** which has no superimposed clause(s) expressly declaring a defective condition of the packaging or goods.

clean coal
carbón limpio, libre de impurezas
Coal produced by a cleaning process.

clean fuel
combustible no contaminante
Fuel that causes little or no pollution

clean-up (environmental)
(tarea de) reparación de los daños ambientales; remediar los daños sufridos por el medio ambiente; limpieza (del medio ambiente)

clearance
autorización; compensación [cheques]; despacho aduanero; aprobación; espacio libre; luz [entre cuerpos]; despeje [transporte]
[see also slum clearance; tax clearance]

clearing [agriculture]
desmonte; desbroce

clearing house
cámara de compensación [bancos]; centro de intercambio de información
An organization set up by financial institutions agreeing to initiate and receive among themselves **electronic funds transfers** authorized by their customers.

client country
país solicitante; país que recurre a los servicios del Banco

clinker
clínquer; clínker [fabricación de cemento]

closed-end investment company, fund [US]; investment trust [UK]
sociedad de inversión con número de acciones fijo
Investment company with a fixed number of shares outstanding. The shares represent an interest in the fund's portfolio. New shares may not be issued.

closely-held corporation
empresa con pocos accionistas
A corporation whose stock is held by a small group, usually with an agreement that if a member of the group desires to sell any part of the ownership, it must first be offered to the other members of the group.

close of business - c.o.b.
cierre de las actividades

closing date
fecha de cierre

closing stock [livestock]
número de animales al final del período contable
Number of animals held at the end of an accounting period.

closure of the proceeding [ICSID]
conclusión de los procedimientos

club deal
operación concertada por, con un club bancario, consorcio
Loan whereby, instead of one bank being designated **lead bank** and others comanagers or **underwriters**, the various functions these carry

out are divided among a limited group of members, in order to save fees.

club loan
préstamo concedido por un club bancario, por un consorcio
Loan whereby, instead of one bank being designated **lead bank** and others comanagers or **underwriters**, the various functions these carry out are divided among the members, in order to save fees.

cluster analysis
análisis por conglomerados, grupos
A statistical procedure for arranging a number of objects in homogeneous subgroups based on their mutual similarities and hierarchical relationships.

cluster audit
evaluación *ex post* combinada
OED audit of several operations together in one audit in order to analyze critical issues in a wider sector or country context.

cluster sampling
muestreo por conglomerados, grupos
When the basic sampling unit in the population is to be found in groups or clusters (e.g. human beings in households) the sampling is sometimes carried out by selecting a sample of clusters and observing all the members of each selected cluster.

coal-based fuel
combustible derivado del carbón

coal field
yacimiento de carbón

coal fired power station
central eléctrica de carbón, que utiliza carbón como combustible

coal gasification
gasificación del carbón

coal liquefaction
licuefacción del carbón

coarse grain(s)
cereales secundarios
Cereal grains used to feed livestock.

coastal shipping
cabotaje

coastal state
estado ribereño, costero

coastal strip country
país de franja litoral estrecha
Country consisting of a small strip of land with an outlet to the sea. Examples include Gambia and Togo.

codetermination; comanagement; management participation system
cogestión; coadministración; sistema de participación en la gestión, administración
System which gives employees the right to be represented in the decisions of a corporation.

co-exposure [insurance]
riesgo conjunto

cofinanc(i)er
cofinanciador

cofinancing
cofinanciamiento

coinsurance
coaseguro(s)
Insurance where a number of insurers share the risk or where insured and insurer share the risk. [**see also** qualitative coinsurance; quantitative coinsurance]

coke oven gas
gas de horno de coque

coke oven plant
coquería

coking coal
carbón coquificable
Coal which can be converted into useful coke that must be strong enough to withstand handling.

colead manager
(banco) codirector [emisiones de bonos]
Lender ranking next to lead manager in a Euroloan.

collateral
garantía

collateral financing
financiamiento con garantía

collect call; transfer charge call; reverse charge call
llamada de cobro revertido

collection of data
recopilación de datos

collection of taxes
recaudación de impuestos

collective self-reliance
autosuficiencia colectiva; confianza de la colectividad en sí misma
Term used to describe the economic independence of the developing countries from the industrial countries and economic cooperation among the developing countries. Embodied in the Arusha Programme for Collective Self-Reliance, 1979.

collegial management
administración colegiada
Management system based on the manager being supported by an advisory committee (consisting of senior staff) which helps him in his decision-making.

collusive oligopoly
oligopolio colusorio
Oligopoly where participants act as a cartel.

collusive tendering
licitación colusoria

coloan
préstamo cofinanciado
A cofinanced loan.

comanagement; codetermination; management participation system
cogestión; coadministración; sistema de participación en la gestión, administración
System which gives employees the right to be represented in the decisions of a corporation.

combined cycle [energy]
ciclo combinado
Designation of a power plant that uses two technologies to generate electricity. Usually applied to gas-turbine and steam-turbine combinations.

combined heat and power - CHP
producción combinada de calor y electricidad

command-and-control instrument, regulation
mecanismos oficiales de control
Government issued regulations, bans or other control mechanism.

command area [irrigation]
zona bajo riego controlado
An area which could be profitably irrigated or has effectively been irrigated.

command economy; controlled economy; directed economy
economía dirigida
An economy in which a significant amount of end results is due to the deliberate decision of government bodies rather than to consumer choice plus forces of supply and demand.

commercial bank
banco comercial, privado

commercial bills; commercial paper
efectos comerciales; papel comercial; papeles de comercio
Promissory notes normally having a maximum maturity of 270 days sold by companies or institutions to raise cash for purposes of **working capital**. A major borrowing instrument for first-class borrowers in the U.S. and Canada.

commercial capital
capital comercial, en condiciones de mercado

commercial conditions
condiciones de mercado

commercial debt
deuda con los bancos comerciales, privados

commercial deposit [mining]
yacimiento rentable

commercial energy
energía comercial

commercial, commercialized GDP
PIB comercial
The gross domestic product of commercial activities, i.e. excluding invisibles, services, etc.

commercial lending
préstamos, financiamiento en condiciones comerciales
Lending not always at market rate but under normal market conditions (e.g. as regards maturity, reimbursement) (*see* **market-related lending**).

commercial paper **see** commercial bills

commercial production
producción a escala comercial

commission, to
encargar; encomendar; poner en servicio

commissioned company
empresa comisionista; compañía comisionista [emisiones de bonos]
Agent in Japan which acts for the IBRD (or other non-Japanese financial institutions) in the issue of bonds on the Japanese market.

commitment authority; authority [IDA]
facultad para contraer compromisos
The authority that IDA has to make credit commitments based on the amount of resources it has received or had committed from donors.

commitment charge, fee
comisión por compromiso, por inmovilización de fondos
A fee paid by a borrower to a lender in the period between approval of a loan and disbursement of the loan. Intended to reimburse the lender for the cost associated with meeting a disbursement request on demand. Usually stated as a percentage of the loan amount approved and much less than the interest rate charged for the loan commencing with disbursement.

commitment deflator
deflactor de los compromisos
A **deflator** which translates Bank commitments into constant dollars.

commodity
producto básico, primario; bienes
[see also core commodities; international commodity agreements; international commodity organizations; non-food agricultural commodity; primary commodity; self-targeting (commodity)]

commodity agreement
acuerdo, convenio sobre un producto básico, primario

commodity assistance
asistencia en especie

commodity loan
préstamo en especie

commodity producing countries, sectors
países, sectores de producción primaria

commodity trade
comercio de productos básicos, primarios

common share; common stock; ordinary share; equity
acción ordinaria
Units of ownership in a public corporation.

communication hub
centro de comunicación

community facilities; social infrastructure
instalaciones comunitarias; infraestructura social

community health services
servicios comunitarios de salud

community health worker - CHW
trabajador de salud de la comunidad; agente de salud comunitaria

commuter
viajero frecuente o cotidiano (por razones de trabajo, de negocios)

companion crops
cultivos simbióticos
A crop sown with another crop on the same land, often to increase returns from the first crop, e.g. by attracting predators of pests of the primary crop.

comparatio [staff compensation]
comparatio (la)
A statistical measure which shows the relationship of average salaries of a given population to the midpoint(s) of the applicable salary range(s).

comparative advantage
ventaja comparativa

compensation
indemnización; remuneración; compensación

compensatory damages
indemnización compensatoria
Damages to compensate an injured party for his actual loss and/or injury and no more, as opposed to nominal damages and punitive damages.

competent court or other authority (to enforce awards) [ICSID]
tribunales competentes o cualquier otra autoridad (para ejecutar laudos)

competing claims (on resources)
competencia por la obtención de recursos

competitive bidding
licitación pública

competitive bidding in accordance with local procedures; local competitive bidding - LCB
licitación pública según procedimientos nacionales, anunciada localmente; licitación pública nacional
Competitive bidding advertised locally and in accordance with local procedures. Used where foreign competition is unlikely to be attracted.

competitive market
mercado de competencia, competitivo

complementarity
complementación; aspectos complementarios
The provision of funds from extra sources. Used to refer to cofinancing arrangements.

complementary financing
financiamiento complementario
Form of cofinancing whereby the lead agency (e.g. the Bank) in addition to making its own loan for an investment project or program, could participate in a commercial bank loan for the same project or program with the sales of participations being pre-arranged (i.e. before the financing is executed).

complement control
control de la dotación de personal
Management imposed constraints on the number of staff at certain grades.

completely knocked down - CKD
completamente desmontado
Components of a piece of machinery that have not been assembled.

completion certificate (of a project)
certificado de terminación

completion coefficient
coeficiente de semanas-personal hasta la aprobación del proyecto
Staffweeks per project from identification to approval, excluding dropped projects.

completion economic rate of return
tasa de rentabilidad económica a la terminación
The **rate of return** on completion of a project.

component (of a project)
elemento; componente

component bidding
oferta parcial
Bidding for part of a contract instead of a whole contract.

composite currency unit
unidad monetaria compuesta
Currency units denominated in a basket of currencies. The two main ones are the Special Drawing Right (SDR) and the **European Currency Unit** (ECU).

composite mission
misión multidisciplinaria

composite peg [foreign exchange]
vínculo compuesto; vínculo a una combinación de monedas

composting
producción de abonos a partir de desechos

compound [West Africa]
recinto (ocupado por una familia extensa)

compound fertilizer; mixed fertilizer
fertilizante compuesto
A formula or mixture of fertilizer compounds such as nitrogen, phosphorus and potassium, in definite proportions.

compound interest
interés compuesto

compound rate of growth
tasa compuesta de crecimiento

compounding factor
factor de interés compuesto
What an initial amount of 1 becomes when growing at compound interest.

comprehensive auditing
evaluación, auditoría general, integral, a fondo
Auditing going beyond financial auditing into evaluation and examination of other non-financial aspects of projects.

comprehensive insurance
seguro contra todo riesgo

comprehensive planning
planificación global, integral

comprehensive school
escuela diversificada, polivalente
In the United States, a secondary school that includes both general education courses and specialized fields of study in its program and thus offers academic, commercial, trade and technical subjects. In the United Kingdom, a non-selective secondary school providing all types of education for all or most of the children in a district.

comptroler
contralor
An accountant in charge whose technical skills and professional interests are confined to a single organization or organizational group and who has been given that title by the management of the organization(s).

compulsory saving
ahorro forzoso

computable general equilibrium (CGE) model
modelo computadorizado de equilibrio general
A mathematical model developed by the World Bank to model national economies. Used in providing projections and aiding policy analysis as it is able to analyze the effect on a country of project results, macroeconomic factors, etc.

computer **see** mainframe computer

computer aided design - CAD
diseño con ayuda de computadoras

computer aided manufacture - CAM
fabricación con ayuda de computadoras

computer language
lenguaje de programación de computadoras

computer virus
virus informático

computerized
computerizado; informatizado

concealed unemployment; covert, disguised, hidden unemployment
desempleo encubierto, oculto, disfrazado

concentration ratio
coeficiente de concentración
Percentage of total sales or output accounted for by largest firms in a country.

conceptual design
diseño conceptual

concertina reduction
reducción de las tasas máximas de cada tramo arancelario, del arancel
Method of reducing a tariff structure by reducing the top rate at each step of the transition to the next highest level, leaving the lowest rates unchanged.

concessional; concessionary
concesionario; en condiciones concesionarias, muy favorables

concessional, concessionary aid
asistencia, ayuda en condiciones concesionarias, muy favorables

concessional, concessionary element
factor, elemento concesionario, de donación

concessional flow
flujo, corriente (de fondos) en condiciones concesionarias

concessional terms
condiciones concesionarias, muy favorables

concessionary; concessional
concesionario; en condiciones concesionarias, muy favorables

Conciliation Rules [ICSID]
Reglas de Conciliación
[see Rules of Procedure for Conciliation Proceedings]

concurrent indicator
indicador contemporáneo
A statistic which has no value for predicting purposes because it changes at the same time as the economy in general, e.g. many types of sales will peak out and bottom out simultaneously with overall economic conditions.

conditionality
condicionalidad
Conditions attached to financing, often used to refer to IMF financing, e.g. upper credit tranche limits.

conditions of effectiveness
condiciones de entrada en vigor

condominial sewerage system
sistema de alcantarillado "en condominio"
Shallow, small-diameter sewers laid at flat gradients run through backyards, receiving flows from short lengths of house connections before making a single, "block" connection to the public sewer.

confirmed letter of credit
carta de crédito confirmada
Form of **irrevocable letter of credit** whereby the correspondent bank of the issuing bank gives an undertaking to the beneficiary that payment will be made, provided that the beneficiary complies with the terms of the credit. May be used as **performance security**.

conformed copy
ejemplar autenticado; copia autenticada
Copy of a legal document which is certified as authentic.

connection [electricity]
conexión de servicio

consent (to jurisdiction) [ICSID]
consentimiento (a la jurisdicción)

consequential damages
daños indirectos
Damages resulting from a breach which could have been reasonably foreseen.

conservation **see** energy conservation

consideration, for a; valuable consideration, for
a título oneroso

consideration [legal, economic]
contraprestación; compensación; honorario; pago
Something given, done or foreborne in return for the promise or act of another party.

consolidate maturities, to
consolidar los vencimientos

consolidated balance sheet
balance (general) consolidado

A balance sheet in which the assets and liabilities of a controlling company are combined with the corresponding items of the organizations it owns or controls in such a manner as to disclose the financial position of the related companies as though they were a single financial unit.

consolidated income statement
estado consolidado de ingresos y gastos
A statement combining the **income statements** of two or more associated enterprises as a single economic unit.

consolidation, land
concentración parcelaria

consolidation (of companies)
fusión (mediante fundación de una nueva empresa)

consortium (for a country)
consorcio (de coordinación de la ayuda a un país)

conspicuous consumption
consumo suntuario, de ostentación

constant dollar budgeting
presupuestación en dólares constantes
Budgeting where expenses are adjusted for changes in the purchasing power of the dollar, caused by price changes. Cf. **current dollar budgeting**.

constant elasticity of substitution - CES
elasticidad constante de sustitución
Elasticity of substitution which is linearly homogeneous.

constant energy intensity
intensidad constante de utilización de energía

constant prices
precios constantes

constituency, chair of an Executive Director
países representado(s) por un Director Ejecutivo; *a veces*: **jurisdicción**

constituent(s) of an Executive Director
país(es) representado(s) por un Director Ejecutivo; *a veces*: **jurisdicción**

constituent subdivision or agency (of a Contracting
State) [ICSID]
**subdivisión política u organismo público (de un
Estado Contratante)**

constructed value
valor calculado

construction allowance
asignación por construcción
Allowance paid to those subject to involuntary
resettlement under a Bank project for income
foregone while the resettlers build their houses.

construction progress chart
gráfico de ejecución de las obras

construction sector
sector, industria de la construcción

consulting firm
firma consultora, de consultores

consumables
bienes fungibles, de consumo

consumer [telecommunications]
usuario; abonado

consumer credit
crédito a los consumidores

consumer demand
demanda de los consumidores

consumer durables
bienes de consumo duraderos

consumer goods
bienes de consumo

consumer price
precio al consumidor

consumer price index - CPI
índice de precios al consumidor

consumer subsidy
**subsidio a los consumidores; subvención a los
consumidores**

consumer subsidy equivalent - CSE
equivalente de subsidio al consumo
Measures the implicit aggregate tax on consumers
generated by agricultural policy.

consumer surplus
excedente del consumidor

consumption bundle
consumo
What is consumed by an individual, population.

consumption conversion factor - CCF
factor de conversión basado en el consumo
In evaluating project benefits, a factor used to
adjust welfare change in **border prices**, based on
the expenditures of the average consumer, when
benefits accrue to consumers.

consumption economy
economía de consumo

contact farmer [agricultural extension]
agricultor de enlace
A farmer that has been selected in an **agricultural
extension** scheme who will assist in spreading new
practices to most farmers in the area quickly.

containerization
uso de contenedores; contenedorización

contingencies
imprevistos

contingencies, physical
asignación para exceso de cantidades físicas

contingencies, price
asignación para alzas de precios

contingency allowance; reserve for contingencies;
allowance for contingencies
reserva para imprevistos, contingencias

contingency mechanism [IMF/World Bank]
mecanismo de emergencia
A joint scheme between the Bank and Fund to
assist troubled economies initially applied to
Mexico.

contingency plan
plan para situaciones imprevistas

contingent asset
activo contingente
An asset the existence, value or ownership of which depends upon the occurrence or nonoccurrence of a specified event or upon the performance or nonperformance of a specified act.

contingent commitment [IFC]
compromiso contingente [CFI]

contingent interest
interés condicional, contingente

contingent liability
pasivo contingente
An obligation which is conditional upon the finalization of certain transactions or may arise in consequence of a future event now considered possible but not probable.

contingent obligation
obligación contingente
Type of IBRD **"B" loan** whereby the loan is initially financed entirely by the commercial lender with IBRD having a contingent commitment to finance at a given date (i.e. at the end of the duration considered "normal" by the commercial markets for the specific borrower) the remaining balance of principal (if any), if the commercial lenders choose not to finance this amount.

contingent reserve
reserva para imprevistos
Retained earnings appropriated in anticipation of possible future losses or expenses.

continuation rate [contraception]
tasa de continuidad de utilización
The rate of continuation of use of contraceptives after a certain lapse of time.

continuing education; lifelong education; recurrent education
educación permanente

continuous cropping
cultivo constante, continuo

Continuously Offered Longer-Term Securities - COLTS
valores a más largo plazo de oferta continua - COLTS
Program of securities issued by the World Bank, starting in 1986. Buyers can obtain maturities from 3 to over 30 years as they choose. The program is indefinite (hence continuously offered) and of a longer term than the Bank's previous discount note system. It extends the range of paper available in the medium-term note market (initially medium-term meant 2-4 years but now covers up to 30 years or more).

contour bund
dique en curva de nivel; terraplén en curva de nivel

contour farming
cultivo en curvas de nivel

contraceptive prevalence rate - CPR
tasa de uso de anticonceptivos

contract see arm's-length contract; breach of contract; breach of contract risk; call order contract; cost-plus fixed fee contract; cost-plus percentage fee contract; fixed cost contract; fixed term contract; lump sum contract; man-month contract; open-ended contract; percentage (fee) contract; performance contract; product in hand contract; production-sharing contract; program contract; risk contract; schedule contract; schedule of rates contract; "slice and package" contract; subcontract; take-and-pay contract; take-or-pay agreement, contract; time-based contract; turnkey contract; unit price contract

contract documents
documentos contractuales

contract out, to
dar en contrato; contratar

contract performance
cumplimiento de contrato

contract plan see agreed budget plan

contract price
monto del contrato; precio contractual

Contracting State [ICSID, MIGA]
Estado Contratante

contractionary policy
política de contracción

contractor **see** bonded contractor; prime, principal, main contractor; subcontractor

contractual savings institutions
instituciones de ahorro contractual
Institutions dealing with contractual savings, i.e. savings that have to be made such as pensions.

contribution value [MIGA]
valor de contribución
The initial value of the resources contributed by the **guarantee holder** to the investment project.

contributory school; feeder school; preparatory school
escuela preparatoria
School where students go on to a specific higher-level school, for which it is the feeder.

control
lucha contra [enfermedades, desastres, etc.]; control; ordenación; etc.

controlled economy **see** command economy

controlled flooding
anegamiento controlado

controlled plot; control plot
parcela testigo, de control

controlling interest
participación mayoritaria
Ownership of a corporation in excess of fifty percent. Can also be used for ownership of less than fifty percent if the remainder of the stock is distributed among many owners.

conurbation
conurbación

conventional energy
energía de fuentes convencionales

conventional terms
condiciones corrientes, comerciales, de mercado

Convention on the Settlement of Investment Disputes between States and Nationals of other States [ICSID]
Convenio sobre Arreglo de Diferencias Relativas a Inversiones entre Estados y Nacionales de Otros Estados

convergent indicator
indicador coincidente

conversion at par
conversión a la par

conversion forest
bosque destinado a convertirse en...
Forest assigned for conversion to agriculture or other nonforest use.

convertible adjustable stock
acción ajustable y convertible

convertible bond
bono convertible
A bond that, at the option of the holder, may be exchanged for another asset, generally a fixed number of shares of common stock.

convertible debenture loan investment [IFC]
préstamo representado por obligaciones convertibles [CFI]

convertible release (of 18% currency) [IBRD]
liberación con autorización de convertibilidad
Release by Bank member of its **18% currency** for lending or relending, with permission granted to the Bank to exchange the **18% currency** for the currency of any other member.

cooperative program
programa de cooperación

core **see** drill core; dwelling core

core commodities [IBRD]
principales productos básicos, primarios
This term is used by the Bank to describe the ten major world commodities as defined by UNCTAD; UNCTAD, itself, does not use this term.

core curriculum
currículo, plan de estudios común
A curriculum design in which one subject or group of subjects becomes a center or core to which all the other subjects are subordinated.

core departments **see** core ministries

core fund [GEF]
recursos básicos
The basic funding for the Global Environment Facility.

core hours; core (working) hours
horario (de trabajo) básico

core housing; nuclear housing
unidad mínima de vivienda; vivienda mínima
A basic structure, often just the shell, built for low-income families. Additional facilities are provided by the family themselves, often in self-help groups.

core inflation
inflación básica
The basic level of inflation over a period of time (e.g. a decade) as opposed to temporary fluctuations in the rate.

core ministries, departments
ministerios de hacienda y de planificación
The key ministries, i.e. planning and finance.

core process [IBRD]
actividad básica
Includes country, economic and sector work; country programs; the project cycle and project evaluation.

core project
proyecto básico
A project based on certain key activities as designated by the Government.

core staffing
dotación mínima de personal

core subjects; basic subjects [education]
materias básicas
A subject that is considered so essential that everyone must have instruction in it.

core working hours **see** core hours

corporate body, institution; body corporate
persona jurídica

corporate bond
bono de una empresa privada, de una compañía, de una sociedad anónima

corporate finance
gestión financiera de las sociedades

corporate income tax [US]; business (profit) tax; corporation tax [UK]
impuesto sobre las utilidades

corporate management
gestión, dirección de la institución, empresa

corporate restructuring
reestructuración empresarial, de empresas

corporate sector
sector empresarial
The business sector.

corporate stocks
acciones

corporate structure
estructura social

corporate tax
impuesto a las sociedades; impuesto a las empresas

corporation tax [UK]; business (profit) tax; corporate income tax [US]
impuesto sobre las utilidades

corporatization
transformación (conversión) de empresas (públicas) en sociedades comerciales, entidades previstas en la ley de sociedades
Conversion of an economy from state-owned enterprises to joint stock companies.

correction **see** monetary correction

correspondent bank
banco corresponsal

corrugation irrigation
riego por corrugación; riego por surcos pequeños y próximos
An irrigation method whereby water flows down the slope in small furrows, called corrugations or rills. Used for irrigating uncultivated close growing crops such as small grains or pasture on steep slopes.

cost accounting
contabilidad de costos
A specialized field of accounting which deals with the ascertainment, classification, recording, allocation and summarization of the various elements of cost of production, operation and maintenance (including overheads) of an entity, using accounting and costing principles and methods and techniques.

cost and fee contract **see** cost-plus (fixed fee) contract

cost-benefit analysis
análisis de costos-beneficios

cost-benefit ratio [UK]; benefit-cost ratio [US]
relación costos-beneficios

cost center
centro de costos
An organizational unit for which accounts are maintained containing direct costs for which the head of the center is accountable.

cost-effective
eficaz en función de los costos; eficiente y de costo mínimo; eficiente y de costo más bajo

cost-effectiveness
eficacia en función de los costos

cost estimate
estimación de costos; presupuesto

cost, insurance and freight - CIF
costo, seguro y flete - c.i.f.
Applies to goods where the seller must pay the costs and freight necessary to take the goods to the named destination and procures any insurance required.

cost, insurance and freight (CIF) port of entry/border point price
precio c.i.f./puerto de entrada

cost-of-living differential factor
coeficiente de ajuste por diferencias del costo de vida

cost overrun
costos superiores a los previstos; sobrecostos

cost-plus contract
contrato al costo más honorarios, más porcentaje
A contract in which the parties agree that the **contractor** will submit bills for payment based on costs actually incurred plus either a fixed fee or a percentage of those costs.

cost-plus (fixed fee) contract - CPFF; cost and fee contract
contrato al costo más honorarios (fijos)
A contract in which the parties agree that the **contractor** will submit bills for payment based on costs actually incurred plus a fixed fee.

cost-plus percentage (fee) contract; cost-plus percentage of cost contract - CPPC
contrato al costo más un porcentaje (honorarios)
A contract in which the parties agree that the **contractor** will submit bills for payment based on costs actually incurred plus a percentage of those costs.

cost-plus pricing system
sistema de determinación de precios en función del costo más honorarios

cost price
precio de costo

cost pricing
determinación del precio de costo; fijación de precios en función del costo

cost-push inflation
inflación provocada por el alza de los costos
A type of inflation caused largely by wage-price spiral, that consists of upward pressure on the cost of production caused by wage increases, followed by price increase, then further wage increases and so on.

cost recovery
recuperación de costos

cost reimbursable contract
contrato con reembolso de costos
Contract which provides for payment of allowable incurred costs, to the extent provided for in the contract. Cf. **cost-plus fixed fee contract, cost-plus percentage fee contract**.

cost sharing
participación en los costos; distribución de los costos

cost-sharing fee [APDF]
comisión de participación en los costos
Set of fees charged by the Africa Project Development Facility to project promoters in order to have them share in APDF's costs in preparing the project.

cost underrun
costos inferiores a los previstos; infracostos

costing
determinación de costos

cottage industry
industria familiar, casera, artesanal

Council of Governors [MIGA]
Consejo de Gobernadores

counsel [ICSID]
consejero

counterfactual
hipótesis; caso hipotético
An economic what if? Used to imagine what might have happened to an economy if some condition was different from actual reality, e.g. if inflation were only x%, then...

countermemorial [ICSID]
contramemorial
In proceedings before ICSID, a response to the memorial submitted by the requesting party which outlines the basis for the case.

counterpart agency
organismo de contrapartida

counterpart funds
fondos de contrapartida
Local currency payments by the ultimate beneficiaries of a Bank loan or IDA credit that accumulate in the hands of the government or an intermediary, in advance of payments due to the Bank or the Association, as the case may be.

counterpart staff
personal, funcionarios de contrapartida

countertrade
comercio compensatorio
The reciprocal and contingent exchange of goods and services specified by contract, with each flow of deliveries being valued and settled in monetary units.

countervailing duty
derecho compensatorio
An import duty established specifically to restore the competitive position of businesses that are put at a disadvantage by a tax which raises their costs.

countries in nonaccrual status
países excluidos del régimen de contabilidad en valores devengados

country assistance management - CAM
administración de la ayuda a los países

country economic and sector work - CESW
estudios económicos y sectoriales de países

country exposure [IBRD]
compromisos por países; préstamos (a un país) desembolsados y pendientes
The extent to which a financial institution has lent money to one country.

country loan [IBRD]
préstamo para programas de un país, de países

country study
estudio sobre un país, países

country WID action plan
plan de acción nacional relacionado con la función de la mujer en el proceso de desarrollo
Plan, at country level, intended to provide an operational framework, based on sectoral analysis, for targeting and designing Bank assistance in a manner that will effectively reach women and improve both their contribution to economic development and the benefits they derive from it.

country-wide project
proyecto de ámbito nacional

coupon bond
bono con cupón

coupon equivalent yield
rendimiento equivalente a un interés nominal
The yield obtained from the difference between the purchase price and the **face value** of a short-term noninterest-bearing instrument, expressed as a percentage, determined by the difference divided by the purchase price.

coupon rate (of a bond)
interés nominal; tasa de emisión
Interest to be paid regularly on the **face value** of a bond or other long-term debt instrument.

course **see** base course

course interchange [education]
curso de elementos intercambiables
In education, a course with interchangeable features.

covenants [loan agreements]
estipulaciones

cover **see** plant cover

coverage
cobertura; campo de aplicación; alcance

cover crop; nurse crop
cultivo protector, de cobertura
A **companion crop** grown to protect some other crop sown with it, as small grain is sometimes seeded with clover.

covered interest arbitrage
arbitraje de intereses con cobertura
Investing dollars in an instrument denominated in a foreign currency and hedging the resulting foreign exchange risk by selling the proceeds of the investment forward for dollars.

covering memorandum
memorando de transmisión

covert, concealed, disguised, hidden unemployment
desempleo encubierto, oculto, disfrazado

crawl [noun]
deslizamiento (de un tipo de cambio dentro de una banda)

crawling peg [rate of exchange]
vínculo móvil; paridad móvil; ajuste gradual del tipo de cambio
A form of international exchange in which monetary authorities make frequent small changes in the rate at which the nation's monetary unit officially trades with others. In some cases the change is triggered when certain conditions are met.

creative financing
financiamiento innovador, imaginativo; formas novedosas de financiamiento
Financing using unconventional means, e.g. special **swaps**, etc.

credit **see also** back-to-back credit; financial credit

credit account [IDA]
cuenta del crédito
Account opened by IDA on its books in the name of a borrower to which the amount of a credit is credited.

credit arrangements
acuerdos de crédito

credit balance **see** unspent credit balance

credit ceiling; credit limit
límite, tope de crédito

credit crunch
restricción pronunciada del crédito

credit facilities
sistemas, mecanismos, servicios de crédito, crediticios

credit-in-kind
crédito en especie

credit limit; credit ceiling
límite, tope de crédito

credit line [IFC]
línea de crédito
Credit line (also known as **equity line** or **agency line**) set up by IFC in favor of an intermediary which would draw on the line to make loan and equity investments for IFC's account.

credit line on an agency basis; agency line [IFC]
línea de crédito a través de un agente

credit multiplier
multiplicador del crédito
The ratio of change in the volume of lending by a group of deposit-taking financial intermediaries (especially banks) to the change in reserve assets which initiated the change. More commonly, it denotes the ratio of change in bank deposit liabilities caused by the increased extension of credit, to the initiating change in **reserve assets**.

credit rating
clasificación del crédito, de créditos, crediticia

credit spread trades
transacciones conforme a márgenes de riesgo y rendimiento
Investment in higher risk paper on the one hand (in the case of the Bank this includes **agency securities, Eurobonds** and off-the-run securities) and current government securities on the other. The yield spread between the two is monitored. When the higher risk paper is trading at a higher than normal yield spread, the higher risk security is bought and the lower risk security sold; when the spread narrows, the trade is reversed.

credit squeeze; credit tightening
restricción del crédito

credit standing
reputación en materia de crédito; crédito
The current **creditworthiness** of a borrower.

credit tightening; credit squeeze
restricción del crédito

creditworthiness; financial standing
capacidad crediticia; solvencia
The likelihood of a borrower to pay back a debt, based on past credit performance.

creep see grade creep

creeping inflation
inflación progresiva

critical consumption level - CCL
nivel crítico de consumo - NCC
Poverty line at which additional consumption changes are equally valuable to investment.

critical path method - CPM
método del camino crítico
Type of planning method which shows the interrelationship in sequence of all the activities involved in undertaking a project. The network of activities highlights those operations or activities which are critical for the successful completion of the project within the scheduled time scale.

cronyism
favoritismo; preferencia por los amigos; amiguismo

cropping intensity
intensidad de cultivo

cropping pattern
sistema de cultivo

crop-cut method
método de los cuadrados de rendimiento
Method for estimating agricultural production, consisting of taking a few small subsamples in the form of small squares, selected by using a grid, and extrapolating from these results.

crop production
producción agrícola, de cultivos

crops
cultivos; cosechas; productos agrícolas

crop tree
árbol de cultivo, aprovechable

crop year
campaña; año agrícola

cross-border; transterritorial
transnacional; transterritorial; transfronterizo;
a veces: **internacional**

cross-bred progeny [livestock]
animales de cruza
The results of crossing two different breeds or varieties.

cross-classification
doble clasificación; clasificación cruzada

cross-conditionality clause
cláusula de condicionalidad recíproca
A clause in a World Bank/IMF loan agreement that makes action affecting one organization apply to both organizations.

cross-country studies
estudios comparados entre países

cross-default clause
cláusula recíproca en caso de incumplimiento
A clause in a loan agreement specifying that default on any other loans to the borrower shall be regarded as default on this one.

cross-effectiveness clause
cláusula recíproca de entrada en vigor
A clause in a loan agreement that states that the agreement only comes into effect when the cofinance loan comes into effect.

cross elasticity
elasticidad cruzada
A measure of the influence of a price of one good on the demand for another.

crossover discount rate; equalizing discount rate
tasa de actualización de equilibrio
The **discount rate** that equalizes the net **present value** of two streams of benefits and/or costs.

cross-placements
colocaciones cruzadas

cross price elasticity
elasticidad-precio cruzada
Same as **cross elasticity**.

cross rate
tipo cruzado; tasa cruzada
The exchange rate between currencies A and C which is derived from the rate between A and B and the rate between B and C.
[see also broken cross rates]

cross-reference clause
cláusula de referencia
A clause in a Bank loan document referring to a loan by a commercial bank.

cross-sectional analysis
análisis transversal
An analysis on the basis of a cross section, i.e. the same things at the same time as opposed to a time series, i.e. the same things at a different time.

cross-sectional data [econometry]
datos transversales
A set of data involving observations taken at one point in time.

cross section(al) survey
encuesta (de sección) transversal
Survey which provides a snapshot of an entire population or of a sample population.

cross section sample
muestra representativa

cross subsidization
subvención cruzada; subsidio cruzado

crosswalk document
documento, matriz de referencia cruzada, comparación
Document that provides cross references between, for example, two budgets which use different systems of classification. The most common form consists of a matrix which helps the reader to determine where an item in the multiyear planning budget may be found in the annual budget.

crowding in
atracción; invasión
Occurs where government bonds are sufficiently good money substitutes so that bond issues reduce demand for money balances, leading to an expansionary impact via their effect on portfolio composition.

crowding out
desplazamiento
Any displacement of private economic activity by public economic activity.

crude birth rate - CBR
tasa bruta de natalidad
Birth rate for an entire population.

crude death rate
tasa bruta de mortalidad
Death rate for an entire population.

culled cow
vaca de desecho
A cow that has been eliminated from the herd because of disease, low quality, etc.

culture fishery
piscicultura
Fish breeding in a controlled environment.

cumulative charge number [currency pool]
base de cálculo de la tasa de interés de los desembolsos acumulados; base de cálculo acumulada
The **charge number** for cumulative disbursements.

cumulative letter of credit
carta de crédito acumulativo; crédito acumulativo
Form of **revolving letter of credit** where amounts from unused or incompletely used portions may be carried forward and used in a subsequent period.

cumulative write offs
anulaciones, cancelaciones acumuladas en libros
The total amounts written off since operations began.

curb market **see** over-the-counter market

currency **see also** border currency; calling in of a currency; composite currency unit; domestic currency; 18% currency; 18% currency out on loan; eligible currency; Eurocurrency market; European Currency Unit; foreign currency; gold-pegged currency; hard currency; intervention currency; local currency; major currency

currency-hedged transaction
transacción cubierta contra riesgos cambiarios
A transaction where assets/liabilities are matched by currency.

currency liabilities
pasivos monetarios
In national accounts, the liabilities of a country denominated in another currency.

currency mix
combinación de monedas

currency option bond **see** multiple currency option bond

currency pool
fondo común de monedas
A system set up by the World Bank to equalize among all borrowers at any time the risks inherent in fluctuations in the exchange rates of the currencies disbursed and repayable on all Bank loans included in the system. Equalization is achieved by pooling all currencies disbursed and outstanding on participating loans and by expressing the outstanding principal amount of each such loan as a share of the pool. As a result, loan-service obligations on each participating loan are related to all amounts in various currencies disbursed and outstanding on all loans in the system.

currency-specific costs
costos relativos a monedas específicas

currency swap
swap, intercambio de monedas
System whereby an institution with funds in one currency converts them into another and enters into a forward exchange contract to recover the currency borrowed.

currency transfer risk [MIGA]
riesgo de transferencia de moneda
One of the **covered risks**. Defined as "any introduction attributable to the host government of restrictions on the transfer outside the **host country** of its currency into a **freely usable currency** or another currency acceptable to the holder of the guarantee, including a failure of the host government to act within a reasonable period of time on an application by such holder for such transfer."

currency translation
traducción de monedas
Recording in accounts of assets (or liabilities) in one currency when they are actually in another. No actual exchange of funds takes place. The World Bank and IFC, for example, translate all their assets and liabilities into U.S. dollar amounts, regardless of the actual currency in which they are denominated.

currency unit
unidad monetaria

current account deficit
déficit en cuenta corriente

current account pattern
configuración de las cuentas corrientes

current amount **see** current insured amount

current assets
activo corriente; activo disponible y realizable a corto plazo
Unrestricted cash or other asset held for conversion within a relatively short period into cash or other readily convertible asset or currently useful goods or services.

current balance of payments
balanza en cuenta corriente

current blend [IFC]
índice combinado de desempeño de la cartera
A rate used by IFC to assist in determining the performance of its loan portfolio, it is based on actual and projected **debt-to-equity ratios**.

current budget
presupuesto ordinario, corriente
The projection of income and expense at anticipated levels of activity rather than in terms of ideal goals.

current cost [accounting] **see** current (entry) value

current cost (value) accounting; current value accounting; value based accounting
contabilidad según el costo (valor) de reposición
Accounting approach designed to reflect changes in the value of assets or goods themselves for changes in specific prices by the use of several methods. The methods commonly used are specific price index, **replacement cost**, current entry prices, current exit prices, reproduction cost and discounted **present values**. Current cost deals with the effects of changes in prices of resources used by the enterprise and is concerned with values to the business rather than costs.

current dollar budgeting
presupuestación en dólares corrientes
Budgeting where expenses are not adjusted for changes in the purchasing power of the dollar but represent actual prices. Cf. **constant dollar budgeting**.

current (entry) value; replacement value; current cost [accounting]
valor de reposición
The amount of cash (or its equivalent) that would have to be paid if the same asset - either an identical asset or an asset with equivalent productive capacity - were acquired currently, computed by applying to **historical cost** one or more index numbers (= adjusted **historical cost**) or by substituting for historical prices prevailing prices of equivalent goods and services.

current equity investment **see** net book value

current exit value; exit value; net realizable value [UK] [accounting]
valor de realización
The estimated selling price in the ordinary course of business less costs of completion and less costs necessarily to be incurred in order to make the sale. It is often used to determine a measurement of an asset value in terms of the amount of cash or its equivalent expected to be derived from the sale of the asset, net of costs required to be incurred as a result of the sale.

current insured amount; current amount [MIGA]
cantidad asegurada corriente; cantidad corriente
The amount of the **guarantee**. Some countries use this amount as the basis for compensation.

current international payments
pagos internacionales corrientes

current liabilities
pasivo corriente; pasivo exigible a corto plazo
Liabilities that are to be paid out of **current assets**
or transferred to income, usually within one year
or less.

current maturities
vencimientos a menos de un año
That portion of debt falling due for repayment in
the accounting year following the date of the
balance sheet (i.e. within twelve months of the
balance sheet date).

current prices
precios corrientes

current ratio; working capital ratio
**relación corriente [América Latina]; coeficiente
de solvencia [España]**
Ratio of **current assets** to **current liabilities**. It is
the main **liquidity ratio**.

current revenues
ingresos corrientes; ingresos fiscales corrientes

current terms, in
en términos, cifras corrientes

current value
valor actualizado (principal)

current value **see** current (entry) value

current value accounting **see** current cost (value)
accounting

current yield
rendimiento corriente

curriculum
plan de estudios; currículo
[see also core curriculum]

custom retrofitting
modificación de productos fabricados en serie

customs duty bill
letra aduanera garantizada
Special type of credit in France granted by the
state to corporations to allow them to pay indirect
taxes or customs duty, with a guarantee provided
by a bank or other financial institution. These
bills allow the corporation to defer payment of

value-added tax or customs duties. The state
draws up a bill for the amount in question which
the corporation agrees to pay on maturity.

customs valuation (practices)
(prácticas de) avalúo aduanero, de aduana

cutoff date [debt]
fecha límite

cutoff point (for Bank or IDA financing)
**límite (para la concesión de financiamiento de
la AIF o del Banco)**
Point at which a country is no longer eligible for
Bank or IDA financing.

cutoff rate (of return) [projects]
**tasa de rentabilidad aceptable, de desistimiento;
tasa límite de rentabilidad aceptable**
The rate of interest (commonly the **opportunity
cost** of capital or the **accounting rate of interest**,
Little-Mirrlees method, or the **consumption rate
of interest**, UNIDO method) below which capital
investment projects should be rejected. It is often
taken to be the **opportunity cost** of capital. The
cutoff rate would be the minimum acceptable
internal rate of return for a project or the
discount rate used to calculate the **net present
worth,** the net benefit-investment ratio or the
benefit-cost ratio.

cut-over forest
bosque de segundo crecimiento, bosque talado
Secondary forest that has already been logged but
regrown.

- D -

dam see diversion dam; earthfill dam; storage dam

data collection
recopilación de datos

dated information
información desactualizada

day release; block release
licencia de tiempo completo
The system by which a trainee is authorized to be absent from work, usually for one or two complete days a week, with or without pay, in order to attend part-time courses of related instruction and general education constituting part of his training program.

day-to-day money see call money

days receivable
días de atraso en el pago de las cuentas por cobrar
The average number of days overdue of **accounts receivable**. It is used as an indicator of the efficiency of the commercial operations of a corporation, as it reflects its ability with regard to collection of bills. The Bank target is around 60 days.

dead storage (capacity)
capacidad no utilizable

deadweight (losses)
(pérdidas de) peso muerto
Loss of consumer surplus incurred by buyers and not captured by producers, which is consequent upon an initially competitive industry becoming monopolistic and therefore, ceteris paribus, charging a higher price and selling a lower level of output.

deadweight tonnage - DWT
toneladas de peso muerto
The weight in long tons that a vessel can carry when fully laden.

deadwood equities [IFC]
capital improductivo, "lastre"
Investments that either have a loss reserve, a write-off, paid less than half of the portfolio's average dividend rate the past two years, are presently valued at less than 1.2 times cost, or whose prospects for future price appreciation are estimated to be poor.

dealer see securities dealer

dean (of the Board of Directors)
decano

debenture (bond)
bono sin garantía específica; debenture [EE.UU]; bono con garantía de activos [Reino Unido]
1. U.S.: Unsecured bond.
2. U.K.: Loan secured against specific or general assets of a company.
[see also convertible debenture loan investment]

debt bunching
acumulación de vencimientos

debt burden ratio
relación intereses de la deuda - exportaciones
Interest on debt as a percentage of exports.

debt cancellation
anulación, condonación de una deuda

debt carrying capacity
capacidad de endeudamiento
Conversion of debt into equity (see debt-equity swap).

debt conversion
conversión de la deuda

debt-creating
que genera deudas

debt distressed country
país agobiado por la deuda

debt due
deuda vencida

debt enhancements
mejora de las condiciones de la deuda

debt-equity conversion; debt-equity swap
capitalización de la deuda; conversión de la deuda en capital

debt-equity conversion fund [IFC]
fondo de conversión de la deuda en capital; fondo de capitalización de la deuda

debt-equity ratio; debt-to-equity ratio; debt-to-capital ratio
relación deuda-capital; coeficiente de endeudamiento
Mainly used to describe the ratio of total liabilities to **shareholders' equity (net worth)**. It can also be used to describe the ratio of long-term debt to equity, net long-term debt to equity, total or long-term debt to tangible equity (= equity plus revenue plus capital reserves). All these definitions are used in the World Bank and IFC, so care should be taken in translation to ensure the correct term is used. Other definitions are used outside the World Bank.

debt-equity swap; debt equity conversion
capitalización de la deuda; conversión de la deuda en capital

debt financing
financiación mediante endeudamiento

debt forgiveness
condonación de deudas, de la deuda

debt-for-health swaps
conversión de deuda en programas de salud
Exchanges of developing country debt for assistance for health programs.

debt funding
financiamiento de la deuda

debt outstanding and disbursed - DOD
deuda desembolsada y pendiente

debt overhang
deuda pendiente
1. The total outstanding debt.
2. The total debt that cannot be readily covered by expected growth.

debt ratio
relación de endeudamiento
Ratio of total liabilities to total assets.

debt relief
alivio de la carga de la deuda

debt rephasing; rescheduling of debt; rephasing of a debt; debt rescheduling
reprogramación (del servicio) de la deuda

debt representation letter
carta de declaración de la deuda externa
A letter from a member to the Bank outlining the country's external debt.

debt rescheduling; rescheduling of debt; debt rephasing; rephasing of a debt
reprogramación (del servicio) de la deuda

Debt Restructuring Facility - DRF
servicio de reestructuración de la deuda

debt retirement
rescate de la deuda
Paying off a debt.

debt sales
descuento de instrumentos de deuda

debt service coverage
cobertura de servicio de la deuda
Ratio of net income after taxes plus interest on long-term debt plus depreciation to debt service.

debt-service ratio
coeficiente del servicio de la deuda
External public debt-service ratio (i.e. interest and principal payments) as a percentage of export earnings from goods, **nonfactor services**, and **workers' remittances**.

debt service requirements
obligaciones relacionadas con el servicio de la deuda

debt service schedule
calendario del servicio de la deuda

debt servicing capacity
capacidad para atender el servicio de la deuda

debt strategy
estrategia ante (de) la deuda

debt-to-capital ratio **see** debt-equity ratio

debt-to-equity ratio **see** debt-equity ratio

debt workout program [World Bank]
programa de reestructuración de la deuda

Debtor Reporting System [World Bank]
Sistema de notificación de la deuda al Banco Mundial

decapitalize
descapitalizar

decision-maker
persona responsable de adoptar decisiones

decision-making body
órgano decisorio, de decisión

decision-making power
facultad decisoria, de decisión

declining balance method; reducing charge method
sistema (de amortización, de depreciación) de saldo decreciente
In depreciation where the annual charge for depreciation is the amount obtained (a) by applying a fixed percentage to the diminishing balance of the asset account, that is the balance after deducting preceding depreciation provisions; or (b) by applying a diminishing rate to the original cost of the asset.

deductible [insurance]
franquicia

deduction **see** tax deduction

deed of trust
escritura de constitución de deuda; escritura de fideicomiso

deep discount bond, note
bono de descuento intensivo
Bond with relatively low-**coupon rate** of interest, offered with a **discount** in excess of what can normally be treated as capital gain by the investor.

deep market
mercado muy activo
A very active market.

deep sea fishing
pesca de altura

deep water port
puerto de aguas profundas

deepening **see** capital deepening; capital deepening investment; financial deepening

deepening of the industrial structure
modernización de la estructura industrial

default [ICSID]
rebeldía (únicamente en el sentido del Art. 45[2] del Convenio)

default on obligations
incumplimiento de obligaciones

defensive expenditures
gastos preventivos
National accounts concept for expenditure to protect the environment and to combat those undesirable aspects of economic activity that lead to environmental decay, resource degradation and depletion and pollution.

deferrable participating loan
préstamo participatorio con obligación contingente de pago de intereses
A loan used by IFC whereby the interest paid is linked to the profits of the company.

deferred charges, expenses
cargos diferidos; gastos diferidos
Expenditures carried forward as an asset until they become relevant (such as an advance rent payment of insurance premium).

deferred depreciation
depreciación diferida

deferred rate and currency setting
fijación diferida de la tasa de interés y la moneda

deferred rate setting - DRS
fijación diferida del interés
Method of locking in a spread over a Treasury benchmark while distributing the rate fixing over several months. Treasury securities are purchased, with the pricing benchmark being the issue at the time the borrowing was launched and the securities are sold when the borrower wants to fix the Treasury yield component of the borrowing cost. The issue spread is locked in at time of issue and the Treasury yield component of the cost is stripped out. Any decrease in interest rates after the issue date would mean the **Treasury notes** could be sold at a profit which would reduce the borrowing cost of the issue to a level reflecting the original issue spread and the Treasury yield at the time the **Treasury notes** were sold. Conversely, any increase in interest rates would mean a loss on the sale of the Treasury securities and an increase in the borrowing cost to a level reflecting the higher Treasury yield.
[**see also** anticipatory rate setting]

deferred recovery
recuperación diferida
Recovery of currency used in lending operations subject to maintenance of value. Recovery is deferred for any currency outstanding on loan since June 30, 1987.

deficiency **see** vitamin deficiency

deficit country
país deficitario

deficit financing
financiación con, mediante déficit presupuestario

definitive application for guarantee
solicitud definitiva de garantía
An application for a MIGA guarantee, to be made once investment plans are established. It provides the detailed information with which MIGA will determine investor, investment and project eligibility; the details of the investment to be insured and the types of guarantees desired; the economic and developmental effects of the project on the **host country** and the basis for confirming the economic viability of **project enterprise**. **See** notice of registration, preliminary application for guarantee.

deflate, to
deflactar

deflation
deflación

deflationary gap
brecha deflacionaria

deflator
deflactor
An implicit or explicit price index used to distinguish between those changes in the money value of **gross national product** which result from a change in prices and those which result from a change in physical output.
[*see also* **commitment deflator; GNP price deflator; implicit deflator; implicit gross domestic product deflator**]

deforestation
deforestación

degree of concessionality
medida en que la asistencia es concesionaria, muy favorable

degressive scale
escala decreciente

dehusking; husking
descascarar; deshojar

delegation of authority
delegación de atribuciones, facultades

delink, to [foreign exchange]
desvincular

delinking [foreign exchange]
desvinculación (de divisas)

delinquent taxes
impuestos en mora

delivered at frontier - DAF
entregado en frontera
Applies to goods that the seller must deliver to the frontier of the country named in the sales contract.

delivered duty paid - DDP
entregado con derechos pagados
Applies to goods that the seller must deliver to the buyers' premises.

delivered energy
energía entregada

delivery (of a contract)
formalización; perfeccionamiento

delivery of bids **see** bid submission

delivery system; supply system
sistema de prestación, de suministro (de un servicio); sistema, red de distribución, de reparto

demand deposit
depósito a la vista
Deposits payable within thirty days.

demand management
gestión, regulación de la demanda
Influence over the wants of buyers, usually consumers, e.g. advertising.

demand money **see** call money

demand note
pagaré a la vista

demand-pull factors
factores de atracción (del lugar de destino) relacionados con la demanda
Factors that attract migrants into another country.

demand-pull inflation
inflación producida por la (presión de la) demanda
A rise in prices brought about by consumers and investors with rising incomes as they compete for a relatively limited supply of valuable goods.

demand shift
desplazamiento de la demanda

dematerialization of manufactures
aumento del componente de servicios en los productos manufacturados
The phenomenon whereby the service content of manufactured goods is increasing.

demerit goods
bienes de escaso interés social
A **merit good** in which the merit is negative, e.g. alcohol consumption.

demonstration activity
operación, actividad de demostración

demonstration effect
efecto de demostración

demonstration plot
parcela de demostración

demonstration school; laboratory school; model school; practice school
escuela de aplicación; escuela experimental
A school attached to a teacher-training establishment in order to allow students to observe experienced teachers at work and to undertake teaching practice themselves.

demurrage
sobrestadía
The money payable to the owner for the delay for which the owner is not responsible in loading and/or discharging after the **laytime** has expired.

dendrothermal power plant
central eléctrica dendrotérmica

denominated in (dollars, etc.)
expresado; denominado

departmental forces **see** force account

departmentalization [education]
departamentalización, división de la enseñanza

dependency allowance
asignación por cargas familiares, por persona a cargo

dependency ratio
relación de dependencia (por edades)
Proportion of children and old people in a population in comparison with everyone else.

dependent
persona a cargo; carga familiar

depletion allowance, reserve
asignación por agotamiento; reserva por agotamiento
An allowance for exhaustion of a natural resource.

deposit see geothermal deposit

deposit liabilities
obligaciones en, por concepto de depósitos

depositor rate of interest; borrowing rate [banks]
tipo, tasa de interés sobre los depósitos; tipo, tasa pasivo(a)
The rate of interest paid by banks on deposits.

depository bank
banco depositario
A bank that is designated and authorized to accept deposits of funds belonging to the federal government or other government bodies, or funds from other banks which the latter are required by law to maintain as reserve against deposits.

depreciation see accelerated depreciation; accumulated depreciation; allowance for depreciation; deferred depreciation; straight-line depreciation

depreciation allowance see reserve for depreciation

depreciation on a straight line; straight line depreciation
amortización (depreciación) lineal, constante, de cuotas fijas

depressed industry
industria en decadencia, en crisis

Deputy [Dev. Comm.; IDA]
suplente

Deputy Secretary General [ICSID]
Secretario General Adjunto

deregulate
desreglamentar; desregular; liberalizar

derivative instruments
instrumentos derivados
A contract whose value changes as prices move in a related or underlying commodity or financial instrument. The term covers standard **futures** and

options, as well as over-the-counter **swaps**, options and similar instruments.

design
diseño; idea; creación; proyecto; plano; modelo; concepto; formulación; etc.
[see also conceptual design; detailed design; engineering design; preliminary design; project design]

design capacity
capacidad nominal, de diseño

design engineering
ingeniería de diseño

design speed
velocidad de diseño, nominal
The highest continuous safe vehicular **speed** as governed by the design features of a highway.

design standards
normas de diseño

designated forest
bosque reservado
Forest legally set aside for preservation or production.

Designating Authority (of Panel Members) [ICSID]
autoridad que efectúa la designación

designer
proyectista; diseñador

desk officer
funcionario encargado de un país

desk study
estudio documental, de referencia

desktop publishing
edición, publicación mediante microcomputadora

despatch money; dispatch money
prima, bonificación por descarga rápida
The money payable by the owner if the ship completes loading or discharging before the **laytime** has expired.

destination taxes
impuestos según mercado final

detailed design, engineering
**diseño detallado; estudios técnicos detallados;
planos técnicos detallados**

deterrent
factor, elemento de disuasión, disuasivo

developing island country
país insular en desarrollo

development
**desarrollo; fomento; aprovechamiento;
evolución; preparación; elaboración;
bonificación; urbanización; explotación;
mejoramiento; auge; progreso; adelanto;
acontecimiento; invención; creación; avance;
nueva circunstancia; nueva situación; etc.**
[see also area development; engineering
development; Evaluation Capability Development
Program; land development; letter of development
policy; management development; manpower
development; site development; skills
development; staff development; whole farm
development; World Development Indicators]

development area
zona en desarrollo

development bank
banco de desarrollo, de fomento

development bond
bono de desarrollo

development credit agreement [IDA]
convenio de crédito de fomento

development drilling
perforación de explotación
Drilling in a known producing field as opposed to
exploratory drilling.

development finance company - DFC
institución financiera de desarrollo

development finance institution - DFI
institución financiera de desarrollo

development period (of a project, of a company)
fase, etapa inicial

development planner
planificador del desarrollo

development planning
planificación del desarrollo

deworm
desparasitar

diagnostically related groups - DRG
grupos homogéneos de diagnóstico
Groups of related ailments for which identical fee
schedules can be prepared.

diesel fuel; diesel oil
(combustible) diesel; gasóleo

diesel (fired) power plant
planta eléctrica diesel; central eléctrica diesel

dietary energy supply - DES
suministro de energía alimentaria - SEA
Kilocalories per capita per day of food
consumption. A standard measure of food intake.

dilution see stock dilution

diminishing returns
rendimientos decrecientes
[see also law of diminishing returns]

dip [stockbreeding]
baño

dipping tank
tanque de inmersión

direct contracting [procurement]
contratación directa
Award of a contract without using competition.

direct costing
**cálculo de costos directos; determinación de
costos directos**
The process of assigning costs as they are incurred
to products and services.

direct labour see force account

directed credit
crédito dirigido

directed economy **see** command economy

direction of lending
distribución del financiamiento (entre los países)

directly unproductive profit seeking (DUP) activities
actividades con fines de lucro directamente improductivas

direct overhead budget
presupuesto de gastos generales directos
In the World Bank, a budget for those overhead expenses controlled by the manager. Include office equipment, direct communications, equipment depreciation, field office costs, supplies and materials.

direct shopping [procurement]
compra directa
Procurement based on direct comparison of price quotations. No **bidding documents** are used.

direct work **see** force account

dirty bill of lading **see** claused bill of lading

disadvantaged group
grupo desfavorecido

disbursement deflator
deflactor de los desembolsos
Coefficient used to convert disbursement amounts into constant dollars.

disbursement letter
aviso, notificación de desembolso

disbursement officer
oficial de desembolsos

disclaimer
declinación de responsabilidad

disclosure of information
libre acceso a la información

discontinuance [ICSID]
desistimiento (únicamente en el sentido del Art. 45 del Convenio)

discount
descuento
[see also exchange discount]

discount, to [finance]
descontar; actualizar

discount bond
bono descontado
Bond selling at a price less than its par value.

discount factor
factor de descuento, actualización
How much 1 at a future date is worth today.

discount note
pagaré descontado
Note (i.e. short- or medium-term bond) issued at a **discount** from its **face value**. On maturity, the investor receives the full **face value**. The **discount** from par, thus, corresponds to the return on the investment.

discount rate [central bank]
tasa, tipo de redescuento
Rate at which a central bank (Federal Reserve System in the U.S.) (re)discounts certain bills for financial institutions.

discount rate [project appraisal; securities]
tasa de actualización
Annualized rate of **discount** applied to debt **securities** issued below par (e.g. U.S. **Treasury bills**).
[see also shadow discount rate; social rate of discount]

discount window [central bank]
redescuento

discounted cash flow (DCF) method
método de actualización de los flujos de fondos
A type of analysis based on discounting cash flows to the present by a given **discount rate**. It allows an analyst to take into account the fact that a dollar of benefit received a year from today is not as valuable as a dollar of cost incurred today, for example, because if the cost had not been incurred, the dollar could have been invested, and in a year's time at an interest rate of, say, 10%, the capital would have grown to $1.10. Because projects vary widely in the pattern of their costs and benefits over time, DCF is necessary to place them on a common **present value** basis for comparison.

discretionary expense budget
presupuesto de gastos discrecionales
In the World Bank, a budget for those expenses directly controlled by the manager. Include salaries, temporary staff costs, overtime, operational travel, representation, hospitality, consultants, contractual services, internal computing and language services.

discretionary income
ingreso discrecional
Income available after payment of necessaries such as housing, taxation, etc.

discretionary liquidity
liquidez discrecional
The amount of liquidity held by the Bank above the minimum prescribed.

discretionary spending
gasto discrecional

discussion paper
documento de trabajo

disease see pest and disease control; vectorborne disease; water-based disease; waterborne disease; water-washed disease

diseconomies
deseconomías
Occurs when, as a firm grows larger, management becomes less efficient, raw material costs rise because local supplies are exhausted or for similar reasons.

disestablish, to
suprimir

disguised unemployment; concealed, covert, hidden unemployment
desempleo oculto, encubierto, disfrazado

dishoarding
desatesoramiento
Returning an item to either the real flow or the money flow so that it can be circulated, consumed or otherwise used in its intended function.

disincentive
desincentivo

disinflation
desinflación

disinflationary
desinflacionario

disintermediation
desintermediación
1 Shift of funds away from financial intermediaries (**commercial banks**, etc.) into **Treasury bills** and other securities.
2. Shift by large corporations away from banks to a **parallel market**, involving other large corporations.

disinvestment
desinversión

dislocated worker
trabajador desplazado

dispatch money see despatch money

disposable income
ingreso disponible

disposal see waste disposal

dispose (of) for value, to
enajenar a título oneroso

disqualification [ICSID]
recusación

dissaver
ahorrador negativo

dissaving
desahorro; ahorro negativo

distance learning, teaching
enseñanza a distancia; educación a distancia
Teaching by remote media such as radio or television.

distress borrowing
endeudamiento forzoso
Borrowing in a situation of extreme need when there is no other alternative.

distressed loan
préstamo (que se halla) en dificultades
Loan on which repayment of interest and principal has been severely delayed or completely suspended.

distress price
precio de necesidad

distress sale, selling
venta de bienes embargados, secuestrados; venta a cualquier precio, de urgencia

distributional weight
ponderación distributiva

disutility
desutilidad

ditch rider; waterman
canalero
Person responsible for supervising an irrigation area.

diversion dam
presa, represa de derivación
A barrier across a stream built to turn all or some of the water into a diversion.

divestiture; divestment
privatización; venta (de una empresa); cesión; traspaso de intereses
Disposition of an asset or investment by outright sale, employee purchase, liquidation, etc.

divestment **see** divestiture

dividend **see** stock dividend

dockage; wharfage; wharfage charges
muellaje

documentary credit
crédito documental
An arrangement where a bank, on behalf of a customer, makes payment to a third party or authorizes such a payment to be made.

documentary evidence
pruebas documentales

dollar budgeting
presupuesto basado en los costos efectivos
Budget planning based on actual cash outlays for the budget, rather than for a fixed amount of items, with allowances for cost increases

dollar gap
escasez de dólares
When the inflow of dollars into the US is high, causing a shortage of dollars on the international market.

dollarization
dolarización

domestic asset formation; domestic capital formation
formación interna de capital
Gross fixed capital formation plus increase in stocks.

domestic content
contenido de origen nacional

domestic currency
moneda nacional

domestic economy
economía interna, nacional

Dollar-cost averaging
promedio del cost en dólares

... sobre ... nacionales

domestic preference; preference margin; ... preference

... resas nacionales; ... nacionales ... ods and services of ... ocedure.

domestic resource cost - DRC
costo en recursos internos
Cost of resources used in products that are not imported.

domestic savings
ahorro interno

domestic value added
valor agregado, añadido en el país
The value added to a product by local or domestic activities.

donor country
país donante

dose-response relationships
relación dosis-efecto
The direct relationship between a specific amount of environmental pollution and its environmental impact. This is the easiest way to cost the effects of pollution but is not always feasible.

double cropping; sequential cropping
cultivos dobles; cultivos sucesivos
Planting one crop after harvesting another.

double-day phenomenon
fenómeno de la doble tarea (de la mujer)
Phenomenon of women being wage-earners and responsible for children and household tasks.

double digit inflation; two digit inflation
(tasa de) inflación de dos dígitos, de 10% ó más

double entry accounting
contabilidad por partida doble
An accounting system in which every transaction results in corresponding debit and credit entries in the system. All credits equal all debits at all times.

double factorial terms of trade
relación de intercambio de dos factores
Terms of trade where changes in productivity in both trading partner countries are taken into account in order to estimate the division of the real gains from trade. They therefore vary proportionately with the net **barter terms of trade** and with productivity in the export sector but inversely with productivity embodied in imports.

double shift teaching system
enseñanza en doble jornada, de doble turno
System where, normally because of overcrowding, one group of pupils is taught in the morning, the other in the afternoon.

double taxation
doble tributación, imposición
A term widely used to describe double taxation of corporate earnings, once through corporate income tax and again through taxation of corporate dividends paid out of after-tax earnings. Also used to describe taxation paid on income first in one country and then another.

double-weighted borrowing cost [IBRD]
costo de los empréstitos con doble ponderación
When calculating borrowings, the IBRD takes the amount of the loan, multiplies it by the interest rate, and obtains a total for the interest. All the loans and all the interest totals are added. The first sum is then divided by the second to obtain the weighted average interest. This is the single-weighted borrowing cost. Recently, the IBRD has obtained the interest total by multiplying the amount of the loan by the interest and the number of years to maturity, to take into account the fact that it has loans of varying maturities. The weighted averaged interest obtained from this calculation is called the double-weighted borrowing cost.

doubtful debt
deuda dudosa, de cobro dudoso

down payment (on the budget deficit)
reducción inicial

down time
tiempo de inactividad

downgrade, to (a loan)
rebajar de categoría

downloading
transferencia desde el sistema principal

downsize, to
reducir de tamaño

downstream effect, benefit
efecto (o beneficio, etc.) mediato

downstream innovations
innovaciones inducidas por el usuario

downstream plant, facilities
planta de elaboración secundaria [petróleo]; instalaciones de elaboración, transporte y distribución

downswing
fase descendente, de contracción; movimiento descendente

downturn (economic)
iniciación de la fase descendente; cambio desfavorable de la coyuntura

downward trend
tendencia descendente

drainage system **see** storm water drainage system

draw, to (funds)
girar, retirar, utilizar fondos

drawback [customs]
reintegro
An amount of money which is collected as a customs duty on imported goods and then refunded when the goods are reshipped as exports.

drawdown
disminución; reducción; giro; utilización

drawdown of equity
utilización del capital

dressing **see** basal dressing; surface dressing; top dressing; window dressing

dressing section, hall [slaughtering]
sección de evisceración
Area where excess fat and bone is removed from a meat carcass.

dribble irrigation **see** drip irrigation

drift fishing
pesca de deriva

drill core
testigo

drilling
perforación

drilling rig, platform **see** oil (drilling) rig

drip irrigation; dribble irrigation; trickle irrigation
riego por goteo
The application of water to the soil through small orifices in plastic pipelines.

droppage [IFC]
abandono; renuncia
When a borrower from IFC decides to cancel a loan before signature.

drop out [education]
desertar; deserción; desertor escolar

dropout rate [education]
tasa de deserción

drought stress
tensión debida a la sequía
Stress on a plant due to lack of water.

drug **see** brand name drug; generic drug

dry farming; dryland farming
cultivo de secano
A system of producing crops in arid and semiarid regions without the use of irrigation. Frequently alternate years of fallow and cropping are practiced.

dryland farming **see** dry farming

dryland(s) management
ordenación de tierras áridas
The management of arid and semi-arid areas.

dry process [cement manufacture]
elaboración, fabricación por vía seca
Method of manufacturing cement whereby no water is used in the process. Cf. **wet process**

dual executive director
director ejecutivo con doble función (en el BIRF y el FMI)
Executive director of both the World Bank and the International Monetary Fund.

dual-purpose cattle
ganado de doble finalidad
Cattle used both for beef and milk.

dummy variable
variable ficticia, artificial, simulada
A constructed variable used as a means of including factors that are not naturally quantifiable in an econometric model. It may assume two and only two values (usually 1 and 0) used to represent the presence of a factor and its opposite or absence.

dumping
dumping

dung cake
torta de estiércol

durable goods; durables
bienes duraderos
Any consumer good which has a significant life and which is not therefore immediately consumed.

dust collector **see** precipitator

dust separator **see** precipitator

dutiable
sujeto al cobro, al pago de derechos

duty-free
libre, exento de derechos

duty station
lugar de destino

dwelling core
núcleo habitacional; vivienda mínima
The basic shell of a building often constructed to allow family or self-help groups to have basic housing and add additional features themselves.

dynamic life index [commodities]
índice de vida dinámica
Index in years of a commodity, assuming a specified growth in rate of production.

- E -

early intensive adjustment lending (EIAL) country
país que recibió financiamiento para fines de ajuste antes de 1986
Country that received two structural adjustment loans or three adjustment operations, with the first taking place before 1986.

early (maturing) [crops]
de maduración temprana, precoz

early retirement scheme
plan de jubilación anticipada

early warning system
sistema de alerta anticipada

earmark, to (funds)
consignar, destinar (fondos) para un fin determinado

earmarked account
cuenta reservada, especial

earmarked tax
impuesto para fines específicos

earned income
ingreso(s) proveniente(s) del trabajo; *a veces:* **ingreso(s) salarial(es)**

earned surplus
utilidades no distribuidas

earning assets
activos productivos
Loans and investments.

earning power
rentabilidad; capacidad de obtención de ingresos

earnings
ingreso(s); ganancia(s); utilidad(es); remuneración

earthfill dam
presa, represa de terraplén
Dam constructed of excavated earth material.

earth resources satellite
satélite de exploración de los recursos terrestres; satélite para el estudio de los recursos terrestres
One of a series of satellites designed primarily to measure the natural resources of the earth.

earth road
camino de tierra
Unsurfaced road made entirely out of earth.

ease, monetary
relajación monetaria; flexibilidad monetaria
Policy of reducing restrictions on the availability of money, e.g. by easing credit restrictions.

easy money
dinero barato, abundante
A condition in which a combination of relatively low interest rates and great credit availability exists.

economic and sector work - ESW
estudios económicos y sectoriales

economic hardship
dificultades económicas
A reason for delaying Bank or IFC repayments.

economic indicator
indicador económico

economic internal rate of return **see** economic rate of return

economic life
duración, vida útil

economic man
homo economicus

economic management
gestión económica, de la economía

economic performance
comportamiento, desempeño de la economía; resultados económicos

economic policy note [EDI]
nota sobre política económica

economic price; efficiency price
precio económico; precio de eficiencia
Price reflecting relative value to be assigned to
inputs and outputs if the economy is to produce
the maximum value of physical output efficiency.

economic rate of return - ERR; economic internal
rate of return - EIRR
**tasa de rendimiento económico, de rentabilidad
económica**
An **internal rate of return** based on economic
prices.

economic recovery loan - ERL [World Bank]
préstamo para recuperación económica

economic rent
renta económica
The return for the use of a factor of production in
excess of the minimum required to provide the
service of the factor. The surplus remaining to a
project beneficiary after he receives the rewards
necessary to attract physical **inputs**, labor,
entrepreneurship and the willingness to bear risk.

economic soundness [MIGA]
solvencia económica
One of the criteria used in assessing a project
before a guarantee is provided.

economics of regress
**economía del retroceso; aspectos económicos del
retroceso**
The economics of negative growth. The opposite
of economics of progress.

economies of scale
economías de escala

economies of scope
economías de diversificación
Cost advantage of producing different products in
a single firm.

edge bias
sesgo (por exceso) de margen, de borde
In crop evaluations, inclusion of a plant on the
edge of the square delineating the area to be
measured, rather than excluding it, leading to an
upward bias.

edit (texts for publication)
editar

edited by
compilado por

editor
**editor (de un texto); compilador (de una
colección de textos); coordinador, encargado de
una edición; redactor jefe**

educational achievements
resultados escolares; rendimiento escolar

educational background
antecedentes académicos; formación

educational material
material didáctico

effective **see** cost effective

effective cut-off **see** operational cut-off

effective date
fecha de entrada en vigor

effective exchange rate
tipo de cambio efectivo
The domestic market price of a good divided by its
border price. In effect, the exchange rate actually
paid for a given good. Serves as an estimate of the
shadow exchange rate for that good.
[**see also** real effective exchange rate]

effective interest rate
tipo, tasa de interés efectivo(a)
The true rate of interest paid on an installment
loan.

effective protection coefficient - EPC
coeficiente de protección efectiva
A measure of protection through import duties,
etc. as related to domestic value added as opposed
to total value of output. Commonly measured as
the excess value added. It measures the protection
given to the production process per se, not just to
the product. Often useful as a partial, quick
indicator of economic acceptability.

effectiveness **see** conditions of effectiveness; cost
effectiveness

effectiveness of an agreement
entrada en vigor de un convenio

effects method [project appraisal]
método de los efectos
A method of project evaluation originated by
Charles Prou and Marc Chervel, widely used in
French-speaking African countries, which involves
valuing the product and its tradeable **inputs** at
shadow prices. A comparison is made between the
situation with the project and without the project.

efficiency cost of taxation; excess burden of
taxation
**costo de eficiencia de (los impuestos) la
tributación; carga excesiva de la tributación**
The difference between the resources that the
government gains and the sacrifice that is made by
taxpayers.

efficiency price see economic price

efficiency price; efficient price; long-run marginal
cost - LRMC [electricity]
costo marginal a largo plazo
The cost of meeting an increase in consumption,
sustained indefinitely into the future, when needed
capacity adjustments are possible.

efficiency unit
unidad de eficiencia

efficiency wage
salario de eficiencia
Wages measured in cost per unit output rather
than in actual wages received or paid.

efficient price; efficiency price; long-run marginal
cost - LRMC [electricity]
costo marginal a largo plazo

effluent charges
cargos por efluentes; descarga de efluentes
Payment for direct releases into the environment.

effluent sewerage; solids-free sewerage; small-bore
sewerage
**sistema de alcantarillado (alcantarillado) para
efluentes líquidos**
A hybrid between a septic tank and a conventional
sewerage system. Its distinctive feature is a solid
interceptor tank located between the house sewer
and the street sewer. The interceptor tank retains

the solids, thereby allowing smaller sewers to be
laid at flatter gradients and with fewer manholes.

18% currency [IBRD maintenance of value]
**monto(s) del 18% (pagado(s) por un miembro
en su moneda)**
The capital paid in to the Bank by a member
country in its own currency. Members have to pay
in 20% of their initial shares, of which 2% is in
gold and 18% in the national currency. This is the
18% currency. Though subsequent capital
increases have required a lower national currency
payment, this amount is still called 18% currency.

18% currency out on loan [IBRD maintenance of
value]
montos del 18% en préstamo

Egyptian cotton; kidney cotton; Sea Island cotton;
West Indian cotton
**algodón de las Islas Occidentales; algodón de
Barbados; algodón egipcio**

elasticity of demand
elasticidad de la demanda
The percentage change induced in one factor of
demand divided by a given percentage change in
the factor that caused the change. For example, if
the price of a commodity is raised, purchasers tend
to reduce their buying rate.

elasticity of substitution
elasticidad de sustitución
A measure of the ease with which one **input** can
be substituted for another when responding to a
change in the ratio of the prices of the s. For
instance, given a production function, suppose that
the ratio of the return to capital to wages declined
1%, making labor relatively more expensive than
capital. If the ratio of the amount of capital **input**
to labor **input** used increases more than 1%, the
elasticity of substitution is elastic, which implies
that it is relatively easy to substitute capital for
labor.
[see also constant elasticity of substitution]

elastic money
dinero elásticoinput
The situation occurring in a monetary system in
which the volume of currency in circulation can be
varied to meet different needs.

electronic funds transfer - EFT
transferencia electrónica de fondos

eligibility; eligibility conditions
habilitación; requisitos, condiciones que deben cumplirse

eligibility ceiling **see** formal eligibility threshold

eligibility to bid
elegibilidad para participar en una licitación

eligibility threshold **see** formal eligibility threshold

eligible [procurement]
elegible

eligible currency
moneda admisible

eligible expenses
gastos admisibles, aceptables, financiables

eligible host country [MIGA]
país receptor elegible
A member who is listed as a developing member country in Schedule A to the Convention.

eligible investment [MIGA]
inversión admisible
Investment accepted for coverage under the Convention. Includes equity interests, including medium- or long-term loans made or guaranteed by holders of equity in the enterprise concerned, and such forms of direct investment as may be determined by the Board.

eligible paper
efectos, valores negociables
Paper than can be freely traded on the market.

eligible risk
riesgo admisible

eligible source country
país de origen calificado

embodiment hypothesis
hipótesis del progreso técnico incorporado
Economic theory which states that investments in new capital equipment embody technical change.

emergency reconstruction loan - ERL
préstamo para reconstrucción de emergencia

emergency recovery loan - ERL
préstamo de emergencia para recuperación

emerging markets [securities]
mercados emergentes, incipientes

eminent domain
dominio eminente; derecho de expropiación
The power to take private property for public use by the state, municipalities and private persons or corporations authorized to exercise functions of a public nature.

emissions trading
intercambio de derechos de emisión, contaminación
Pollution dischargers who release less pollution than the officially approved limit may sell or trade the difference between its discharges and the authorized limits to another firm which can then increase its amount of discharge.

empower
dar participación; dotar de los medios; responsabilizar; dar poder de decisión

empowerment
habilitación; promoción de la autonomía; potenciación
Giving political power to disadvantaged groups, e.g. women, children.

enabling environment
entorno, ambiente, clima propicio, favorable; condiciones propicias, favorables

enabling legislation
ley(es) que autoriza(n); autorización legislativa

encashment [IDA]
conversión en efectivo
The conversion of notes and other securities paid in by member countries to IDA into cash.

enclave project
proyecto enclave
Project designed and supervised by foreign consultants, executed by foreign contractors and suppliers and managed with the help of expatriates.

end-of-mission document
informe de fin de misión

end of pipe pollution control
control de la contaminación en la descarga
Control of pollution where it is discharged rather than in the production cycle.

end use (of a commodity)
uso final

end use (energy) efficiency
eficiencia del uso final de la energía

end use tax
impuesto según uso final

energy **see also** alternative energy; biomass energy; commercial energy; constant energy intensity; conventional energy; net energy ratio

energy affiliate
organismo de energía afiliado al Banco; organismo afiliado de energía
Proposed organization, subsidiary of the World Bank, dealing with lending for energy. Never actually set up.

energy assessment
evaluación de recursos energéticos

energy audit
estudio de recursos energéticos [de un país]; examen del uso de la energía; balance de energía
A survey of energy usage in a system or organization and an examination of how energy may be used more economically.

energy cascading
utilización escalonada de energía
The utilization of energy, otherwise wasted, in the performance of work matched to the characteristics of the energy, e.g. the use of waste heat from an industrial process for a variety of purposes in sequence, performing work at a lower temperature at each stage. The sequence may include air heating, steam raising and water heating.

energy conservation
conservación, ahorro de energía

energy cropping
cultivos para fines energéticos
The growth of plants to be used for energy needs (i.e. wood, oil-bearing plants).

energy-efficient
eficaz en el uso de la energía

energy-intensive
de uso intensivo de energía

energy lending
financiamiento para energía

engender
considerar (una cuestión) desde el punto de vista de los roles del hombre y la mujer
Considering issues from the point of view of gender, relations between the sexes.

engineered road
camino trazado técnicamente
A planned **earth road**.

engineering **see also** design; design engineering; detailed design, engineering; environmental engineering; financial engineering; heavy (engineering) industry; preliminary design, engineering

engineering consultant
ingeniero consultor

engineering design
diseño técnico

engineering development
desarrollo técnico

engineering industry
industria técnica, mecánica, metalmecánica

engineering, preliminary
diseño técnico preliminar

engineering-related technical assistance; hard technical assistance
asistencia técnica relacionada con los componentes físicos; asistencia técnica relacionada con las inversiones en activos físicos
Technical assistance geared towards engineering projects as opposed to **institution-related technical assistance**.

engineering studies
estudios técnicos, de ingeniería

enhance new debt, to
mejorar las condiciones de la nueva deuda

enhanced recovery [oil]
recuperación mejorada
Increased recovery from a reservoir achieved by artificial means or by the application of energy extrinsic to the reservoir.

enrollment ratio
tasa de matrícula; coeficiente de matrícula
Ratio of pupils enrolled to total school age population.
[see also gross (primary) enrollment ratio]

enrollments
matrícula; número de alumnos matriculados

entrepôt trade
comercio de reexportación
The re-export trade of a country.

entrepreneur
empresario

entrepreneurial benefit-cost ratio - EBC
relación costos-beneficios empresariales, de las empresas

entrepreneurship
capacidad, espíritu empresarial

entries see accounting entries

entry level
nivel de ingreso

environment satellite accounts
cuentas subsidiarias del medio ambiente
Subsidiary national account for the environmental sector.

environmental action plan - EAP
plan de protección ambiental

environmental (advisory) panel
grupo de evaluación ambiental
An advisory panel of independent, internationally-recognized, environmental specialists, formed to advise on projects involving large dams. Normally required for Bank large dam projects.

environmental assessment - EA
evaluación ambiental
An intensive examination that is required for lending operation that have diverse and significant environmental impacts.

environmental audit
auditoría ambiental
Detailed study of the environmental problems of an area or industrial plant.

environmental degradation
deterioro, degradación ambiental
Deterioration in the environment. Includes pathogens in the environment, indoor air pollution, substandard housing and extensive industrialization.

environmental engineering
ingeniería ambiental, del medio ambiente; ingeniería ecológica

environmental enhancement
mejoramiento ambiental
Improvement to the environment. Used by the Bank to refer to improvement to the environment as an indirect effect of a project.

environmental goods and services
bienes y servicios ecológicos, para la protección ambiental
Goods and services provided for environmental protection purposes.

environmental health, sanitation
higiene ambiental; saneamiento ambiental

environmental hotspot
zona de singular riqueza ecológica
Area on the Earth where there is a considerable and often unique species diversity.

environmental impact assessment - EIA
evaluación del impacto ambiental; evaluación de los efectos ambientales
Evaluation of the effect of a project on the environment.

environmental management plan see mitigation plan

environmental reconnaissance
examen (ambiental) sobre el terreno
Bank mandated study, carried out by independent, recognized experts during project identification, to ensure that potential environmental effects are identified, ascertain the scope of further environmental studies and action needed, assess the availability of the borrower to undertake them and advise on the need for an environmental panel.

environmental review
estudio de los efectos ambientales
The whole process by which the Bank monitors the environmental effects of projects. It may involve fullscale environmental assessment or only limited analysis. It starts with screening at identification and continues through evaluation after the last disbursement.

environmental screening
estudio (ambiental) preliminar

environmental services
beneficios ecológicos
Functions performed naturally by forests, such as maintenance of waterflow patterns, protection of soil, support of economically important living resources and regulation of climate.

environmental stress
tensión, estrés ambiental; perturbaciones del medio ambiente

environmental sustainability
sostenibilidad ambiental

environmentalist
ecologistas; expertos en medio ambiente

environmentally adjusted domestic product - EDP
producto interno ajustado conforme a consideraciones ambientales - PIA

environmentally adjusted economic accounts - EEA
cuentas económicas ajustadas conforme a consideraciones ambientales

environmentally adjusted income - EAI
ingreso ajustado conforme a consideraciones ambientales

environmentally adjusted national income - ENI
ingreso nacional ajustado conforme a consideraciones ambientales - INA

epidemic disease [livestock]
epizootia

equalization fund
fondo de igualación, de equiparación
Funds made available by a national government to subnational or local governments to reduce the degree of inequality in the levels of revenue raised by the local governments.

equalizing discount rate **see** cross-over discount rate

equalizing rate of return
tasa de rentabilidad de equilibrio
The **rate of return** that equalizes the **present value** of two streams of costs. Used to compare two or more different project alternatives.

equilibrating capital flow
corriente de capital equilibradora

equilibrium climate change
cambio climático de equilibrio
The change which would occur once all the lags in the climate system have worked through the system, which may take decades or centuries. Cf. **transient climate change**.

equilibrium exchange rate
tipo de cambio de equilibrio
The exchange rate when offer and demand are equally balanced.

equilibrium income
ingreso(s) de equilibrio

equilibrium model **see** computable general equilibrium model

equilibrium real exchange rate
tipo de cambio real de equilibrio
The price of **tradables** relative to **non-tradables** that, for given long-term equilibrium (or sustainable) values of other relevant variables such as trade taxes, international prices, capital and aid flows and technology, leads to the simultaneous attainment of internal and external equilibrium and is compatible with long-term economic growth.

equipment
equipo(s); material (de transporte)

equipment grant
donación en, para equipos

equity
capital (social, accionario); patrimonio (neto); acciones; equidad
[see also capital; deadwood equities; debt-equity conversion fund; debt-equity conversion, swap; quasi-equity; real estate equity; stockholders' equity]

equity; common share [stock exchange]
acción ordinaria

equity capital; capital stock (of a corporation)
capital social, accionario
The **issued share capital** which is neither limited nor preferred in its participation in the distribution of its profits nor in the ultimate distribution of its assets. **Equity capital** is sometimes used as a synonym for **stockholders' equity**.

equity feature [IFC]
opción a participar en el capital social; préstamo convertible en acciones de capital [CFI]
IFC loan which has a feature enabling it to be converted into an equity participation.

equity financing, investment
inversión, participación en (el) capital social
Investment that confers whole or partial ownership in an enterprise and entitles the investor to share in the profits from its operation.

equity fund
fondo de inversión en acciones
Money market fund investing in equity stocks.

equity grant
donación en capital

equity-like instrument
instrumento financiero con características patrimoniales
A loan structured in such a way that it can be converted into equity. An example is an income note that acts as equity, i.e. it bears interest only if the project generates interest. This means it has the form of equity (cf. stocks where income is generated only if the company pays a dividend). An example of the use of this type of instrument is in high-risk countries where an equity investment would be lost at once but an equity-like instrument, if dollar-denominated, would guarantee the capital and ensure income if the project produced income.

equity line [IFC]
línea de capital accionario
Credit line (also known as **agency line**) established in favor of an intermediary which would draw on the line to make loan and equity investments for IFC's account.

equity loan
préstamo en forma de participación en el capital
Loan in the form of equity participation.

equity ownership
participación en el capital social
An interest in a property.

equity portfolio fund
fondo de inversiones de cartera

equity ratio
relación capital-activo
Ratio of assets to **net worth**.

equity security
certificado de participación
A certificate that designates a proportional ownership in a corporation. Includes rights, **warrants** and long call options.

equity subscription [IFC]
suscripción de capital social, de capital accionario
The purchase of shares in IFC by member countries.

equity-type loan; sponsored loan
crédito de accionistas, de participación
Loan made by equity holders of the borrower.

equity underwriting
compromiso de suscripción de acciones
Underwriting (i.e. finding buyers for a **security issue**) a share issue. This technique has been used by IFC, e.g. for the Korea Fund, a diversified **closed-end investment company** investing in Korean **securities**, that plans to offer its shares in the U.S. and other markets with IFC as one of the **colead managers**.

escalation **see** price adjustment clause; tariff escalation

escalation clause [prices]
cláusula de reajuste (de los precios)
Clause in a contract which allows for prices to increase as certain specified items, e.g. labor costs, increase.
[**see also** price adjustment clause]

escalator clause [wages]
cláusula de escala móvil
Clauses in labor agreements providing for automatic wage increases based on movements in a specific price index.

escape clause; break clause; jeopardy clause
cláusula de salvaguardia, de elusión, de escape
A clause in a Eurocurrency agreement specifying that, if certain events curtail the lender's activity or the operation of the Euromarkets, other designated actions will come into effect.

escrow
depósito en garantía, en custodia
A writing, deed, money, stock or other property delivered by the grantor, promisor or obligor into the hands of a third person, to be held by the latter until the happening of a contingency or performance of a condition and then by him delivered to the grantee, promisee or obligee.

escrow account
depósito en custodia
Account to set aside a sum of money for a specific purpose, e.g. loan repayment.

estimates of quantities **see** preliminary estimates of quantities

establishment convention; base convention
convenio básico
Basic agreement used in financing a major project.

Eurobonds
eurobonos

Eurocurrency market
mercado de eurodivisas

Euroissues
euroemisiones

European Currency Unit - ECU
unidad monetaria europea - ECU
A standard unit of account of European Community member countries.

European flotations
emisiones (de obligaciones) en Europa

Eurosterling
euroesterlina

evacuation road
camino de salida

evaluated portfolio [IFC]
valor estimado de la cartera
That part of the **disbursed portfolio** in companies which have a sufficient operating history for a reasonable review of their creditworthiness or profit potential.

evaluation [projects]
evaluación *ex post*

Evaluation Capability Development Program - ECDP [IBRD]
Programa de Desarrollo de la Capacidad de Evaluación Ex Post

evaluation mission; audit mission
misión de evaluación *ex post*

evidence [ICSID]
prueba; medio de prueba

examination (of witnesses or experts) [ICSID]
interrogatorio; examen

examination of bids
análisis de las ofertas

examiner **see** bank examiner

ex ante evaluation
evaluación previa, ex ante

ex ante financing gap
brecha financiera ex ante
Used by the IMF to denote a gap between the funds they need and the funds they have available at the start of a program of financing.

excellence center [education]
centro de excelencia
Training and research institutions for the training of highly qualified personnel and for undertaking research in scientific disciplines.

excepted period
período exceptuado
Period that does not count as **laytime** even if loading or discharging is carried out.

excepted risks
riesgos no cubiertos
Risks excluded from insurance under a contract. These often include war, revolution and similar acts of violence, as well as explosions, damage caused by radioactivity or aircraft and similar damage.

excess burden of taxation **see** efficiency cost of taxation

excess capacity
excedente de capacidad; capacidad excedentaria

exchange **see** foreign currency, exchange

exchange adjustment
ajuste cambiario

exchange allocation
asignación de divisas

exchange arbitrage
arbitraje de cambios

exchange budget
presupuesto de divisas

exchange control regulations
disposiciones de control de cambios

exchange cost
costo en divisas

exchange discount
descuento cambiario; pérdida cambiaria

exchange equalization account
cuenta de igualación de tipos de cambio
An account to stabilize the exchange value of the domestic currency by preventing excessive depreciation or appreciation. Used primarily in the United Kingdom.

exchange market **see** foreign exchange market

exchange premium
prima, ganancia cambiaria

exchange rate differential
diferencia(s) de tipos de cambio

exchange rate overvaluation
sobrevaloración de las monedas

exchange rate policy
política cambiaria

exchange risk
riesgo cambiario

exchange stabilization fund
fondo de estabilización cambiaria
A fund set up to stabilize the value of the domestic currency. Used primarily in the US.

exchange system
régimen, sistema cambiario

excise tax
impuesto al consumo

exclusive economic zone - EEZ
zona de soberanía económica
The area beyond and adjacent to the territorial sea over which the coastal state has sovereign rights for the purpose of exploring, exploiting, conserving and managing the natural resources of the bed, subsoil and superjacent waters and with regard to other activities for the economic exploitation and exploration of the zone as well as jurisdiction with regard to marine scientific research and the preservation of the marine environment. It should not exceed 200 miles.

execute an agreement, to
celebrar, firmar un convenio, un acuerdo

executing agency [UNDP]
organismo de ejecución
Organization that implements a project on behalf of another.

Executive Board; Board of (Executive) Directors [IBRD; IDA]
Directorio Ejecutivo

Executive Director
Director Ejecutivo

executive summary
resumen

ex factory price; price ex factory; factory gate price
precio en fábrica
The manufacturing cost excluding cost of distribution.

exhaustion of local administrative or juridical remedies [ICSID]
(exigir) el agotamiento previo de las vías administrativas o judiciales (de un Estado)

existence value
valor intrínseco; valor de existencia
Value of keeping something (e.g. a species of plant or animal) even when no benefit is expected to be derived from keeping it, now or in the future.

exit barrier
obstáculo a la salida del mercado
Legal mechanism that prevents from leaving a market (e.g. liquidating or merging a firm), often designed to protect workers from unemployment or to conserve scarce capital resources.

exit bond
bono de exclusión
Instruments issued by a debtor country to a creditor bank in place of a bank credit, that allows the creditor bank to be exempted from future requests for **new money** and restructuring. Used by Argentina and the Philippines (with its Philippines Investment Notes - PIN).

exit mechanism
mecanismo de opciones
Procedures to allow users of a service to use alternative services. In public sector management, these include deregulation, contracting out of services to multiple private providers and competition between the public and private sectors. The basic concept was developed by Albert Hirschman in *Exit, Voice and Loyalty* and adapted by Samuel Paul to the issue of accountability.

exit value **see** current exit value

ex-officio [ICSID]
ex officio

expansionary policy
política expansionista

expatriate
expatriado

expectation [mathematics] **see** expected value

expected value
valor esperado
The mean value of single observations drawn from a finite or infinite universe in repeated samplings.

expendable equipment
material fungible

expenditure-switching
reorientación del gasto
One of the policy alternatives necessary to remove an international trade imbalance. Examples are devaluation and import restrictions which are intended to encourage domestic output and also foreign expenditure on domestic output.

expense, to; to write down
castigar; rebajar el valor en libros; amortizar parcialmente

expert appraisal
tasación, avalúo pericial; peritaje

expertise
conocimientos especializados; pericia; expertos

explanatory variable; predictor; predicated,
independent variable; fixed variate; regressor
[statistics]
variable independiente, predictiva

(explicitly) collusive oligopoly
oligopolio colusorio explícito; cártel
An oligopoly where participants act as a cartel.

export adjustment loan - EAL
**préstamo para ajuste del sector exportador, de
exportación**
Loan made by the World Bank to assist a country
to adjust its export sector.

export credit
crédito de exportación, a la exportación

export development fund - EDF
fondo para el fomento de las exportaciones
A self-sustaining revolving fund set up to
recapture the foreign exchange advanced within a
specific period, typically 120-360 days, for use
again by eligible beneficiaries. It provides
mechanisms to give access to exporters to foreign
exchange for the purchase of intermediate **inputs**.
The Bank has made loans for these funds as part
of its Program of Special Assistance.

export earnings, proceeds
ingresos de exportación

export-enclave economy
**economía dependiente de la exportación de un
solo producto**
Economy which is geared towards the export of
one commodity only (e.g. oil).

export-oriented
orientado hacia la exportación

export parity price
precio paritario de exportación
The estimated price at the farm gate or project
boundary derived by adjusting the cif or fob price
by all the relevant charges between the farm gate
and the project boundary and the point where the
cif or fob price is quoted.

export processing zone - EPZ
zona franca industrial
An industrial area forming an enclave in the
customs area of a country (generally near a port or
airport).

export rehabilitation project - ERP [IBRD]
**proyecto de rehabilitación del sector
exportador, de exportación**
Project geared towards improving the export
performance of a country.

export shortfall
**insuficiencia de las exportaciones; insuficiencia
de los ingresos de exportación**

export subsidy
subvención, subsidio a las exportaciones

exports of goods and services - XGS
exportaciones de bienes y servicios

ex post cofinancing
cofinanciamiento *ex post*
Cofinancing after the initial loan has been made,
e.g. by selling part of the loan.

ex post evaluation
evaluación *ex post*, a posteriori
The process whereby the Bank, and in some
instances, an agency of the government, shortly
after completion of project implementation and
disbursements of the proceeds of the loan, review
comprehensively the extent to which the objectives
and expectations of the project, on the basis of
which the Bank loan was approved, have been or
show promise of being achieved.

ex post real interest rate
tipo de interés real *ex post*
The actual real interest rate.

exposure
**riesgo; préstamos pendientes; participación en
una inversión; compromisos netos**
Amount of investment made, with the additional
idea of risk. These translations are proposed. The
translation will often depend on the context.
[**see also** bank exposure; co-exposure; country
exposure]

exposure diversification
diversificación de los riesgos

ex quay (duties on buyers' account)
en el muelle (derechos por cuenta del comprador)
Applies to goods that the seller makes available to the buyer on the quay at the destination named in the sales contract. The seller bears the full cost and risk involved in bringing the goods to this destination, except for the liability for clearing the goods for import, which is the responsibility of the buyer.

extended family
familia extensa

extended payment plan
venta a plazos

extender [gasoline]
aditivo (que aumenta la cantidad)

extension [agriculture]
extensión; divulgación

extension [building]
ampliación

extension agent, worker
agente de extensión, de divulgación agrícola; extensionista
Low-level staff providing assistance and advice to farmers.
[see also field-level extension worker]

extension officer
oficial de extensión, de divulgación agrícola
A higher-level staff member providing assistance and advice to farmers.
[see also agricultural extension officer]

external current account deficit
déficit de la balanza en cuenta corriente

external debt outstanding
deuda externa pendiente

external debt reporting system
sistema de notificación de la deuda externa

external payment position
situación de pagos externos

external review mission
misión de examen externo

external viability
viabilidad de la balanza de pagos

externalities [projects]
efectos externos; externalidades [proyectos]
Costs and benefits of development projects which do not get captured by the market mechanism, e.g. revulsion caused by bad taste advertising, garbage dumped on the outskirts of a city and poor performance of sanitary services.

extra long staple cotton
algodón de fibra extra larga
Cotton with fibers of 1 3/8 inches long or more.

extraordinary budget; special budget
presupuesto extraordinario

- F -

face value
valor nominal

facility
mecanismo; servicio; instalación; medios

fact sheet
datos básicos

factor cost, at - f.c.
al costo de los factores

factor income
ingresos de los factores
Income derived directly from the current production of goods and services. There are normally four main categories: rent; wages and salaries; interest and profits.

factor income payments
pagos en concepto de ingresos de los factores

factor price
precio de los factores
The price of a factor of production (e.g. land, labor and capital).

factoring
factoraje
The purchase of trade debts, usually without recourse.

factory farming
agricultura industrial

factory gate price **see** ex factory price

facultative reinsurance
reaseguro facultativo
Reinsurance of a specific risk. Cf. **treaty reinsurance**.

fair market value
valor justo, equitativo de mercado

fair price shop
puesto de venta de productos subvencionados

fallacy of composition
falacia de composición
A wrong conclusion reached by taking a known fact about individuals and projecting it to apply to the entire population.

family planning
planificación familiar, de la familia

farm
explotación agrícola; granja; finca

farm budget
presupuesto de la explotación agrícola

farm forestry
agrosilvicultura
Forestry carried out on private farmlands.

farm gate price
precio a nivel de la explotación agrícola

farm income
ingreso(s) agrícola(s)

farmer-pull innovations
innovaciones inducidas por el agricultor

farming system
sistema de explotación agrícola

farming systems research - FSR
investigación sobre sistemas de producción agrícola

farming techniques
métodos, técnicas de cultivo

farming unit
unidad agrícola, de explotación agrícola

fast disbursing (loan); quick disbursing (loan)
(préstamo) de rápido desembolso

fast-track procedures
negociaciones por vía expedita
Procedures designed to facilitate negotiation of complex trade agreements. They give the president authority to conclude such agreements and submit them to Congress for approval or disapproval without amendment. Used by the Bush administration in the 1990-1991 Uruguay Round negotiations.

feasibility study
estudio de factibilidad, de viabilidad

fecundity
fertilidad

fee see availability fee; backup facility fee; commitment charge, fee; cost plus fixed fee contract; cost plus percentage fee contract; front-end fee; guarantee commission, fee; harbor fees; loan origination fee; management fee; percentage (fee) contract; service and support fee; stumpage fee; tuition fees; zero fee policy

fee-based service [IFC]
servicio a cambio del pago de honorarios
Services provided by IFC for which IFC charges a fee. Includes such services as technical assistance, advice on privatization, corporate strategies, financial risk management, project structuring, setting up capital markets, etc.

fee for lodging requests [ICSID]
cargo por presentación de solicitudes

fee-for-services basis
sistema de honorarios por servicios

feed balance; feed estimate
balance forrajero

feed conversion ratio
índice de aprovechamiento del forraje
Ratio which makes it possible to evaluate feed efficiency. Obtained from the amount of product obtained per kilo of feed given to the animal (i.e. daily average profit/feed).

feed estimate; feed balance
balance forrajero

feed grains
cereales forrajeros

feed unit
unidad forrajera
One pound of corn or its equivalent in feed value in other feeds which is fed to cattle under normal farm conditions.

feedback (of information)
retroacción; información obtenida; retroinformación

feedback loop
circuito de información

feeder road
camino de acceso, secundario, vecinal

feeder school; contributory school; preparatory school
escuela preparatoria
School where students go on to a specific higher-level school, for which it is the feeder.

feedlot
corral de engorde

feedstock
materiales básicos; materias básicas
Substance (e.g. gas) used as raw material for its chemical properties in creating an end product.

fellow [EDI]
ex participante

fertility rate
tasa de fecundidad
Births per thousand, usually related to individuals of same sex, age, marital status, etc.

fiber crop
planta textil

field see coal field

field agent
agente en el terreno

field assignment, mission
misión en el terreno, de observación en el terreno

field crop
cultivo; cultivo extensivo

field-level extension worker
agente de extensión a nivel de poblado

field mission, assignment
misión en el terreno, de observación en el terreno

field office
oficina exterior, fuera de la sede

field seeds
semillas, simientes de campo
The seed of **field crops**, as contrasted with vegetable and flower seeds.

field staff
personal de las oficinas exteriores, fuera de la sede; personal en el terreno

field trip
viaje de observación, estudio, etc.

field unit [agricultural extension]
unidad de extensión (agrícola)

field work
trabajo en el terreno

field worker
funcionario destacado en el terreno

Fifth Dimension Program
programa de "quinta dimensión"
World Bank program whereby the Bank provides additional IDA allocations to IDA-only countries that have outstanding IBRD debt, are current on their debt service to the Bank and have an IDA-support adjustment program.

filing of claims [MIGA]
presentación de reclamaciones
Submitting appropriate documentation to support a claim for a covered loss.

fill ratio [staff]
coeficiente de ocupación de cargos, puestos
Percentage of positions in an organization that are filled.

final design
planos definitivos

final design quantities
cantidades para los planos definitivos

final energy; secondary energy
energía final, secundaria

finance lease; financial, full pay out lease
contrato de arrendamiento con opción de compra; leasing; arrendamiento financiero
A lease involving payment over an obligatory period of specified sums sufficient in total to amortize the capital outlay of the lessor and give some profit. In other words, the lessee pays the full value of the asset.

finance plan
plan financiero

financial adjustment
ajuste, reajuste financiero

financial claim
título de crédito; acreencia; activo financiero

financial claims of government
uso de recursos por el gobierno

financial contingency
imprevistos financieros

financial credit
crédito financiero

financial deepening
intensificación financiera
Acquisition of financial assets at a faster rate than nonfinancial assets.

financial distress
dificultades financieras graves

financial engineering
técnicas financieras; ingeniería financiera [México]
Application of innovative techniques in major national and corporate **workouts**.

financial expenses coverage ratio
coeficiente de cobertura del gasto financiero
Net income plus non-cash charges plus interest payments divided by interest payments plus current portion of long-term debt.

financial flows
flujos financieros; corrientes financieras

financial futures
futuros financieros

financial intermediary loan - FIL
préstamo a un intermediario financiero
World Bank loan to a financial intermediary, such as a central bank.

financial internal rate of return **see** financial rate of return

financial intrinsics
situación financiera
An alternative word for financial position.

financial lease **see** finance lease

financial leverage **see** leverage

financial package
serie, conjunto de medidas financieras; paquete financiero

financial paper
efectos, valores financieros
Commercial paper issued by financial institutions.

financial performance, results
actuación financiera; resultado(s) financiero(s)

financial plan
plan financiero

financial rate of return; internal rate of financial return; financial internal rate of return - FIRR
tasa de rendimiento financiero, de rentabilidad financiera
The **internal rate of return** based on financial or market prices.

financial ratios
relaciones financieras

financial replicability
posibilidad de repetición financiera
Full recovery of the financial costs of the project entity.

financial repression
represión financiera
Distortion in the financial system, with negative interest rates, subsidy interest rates to some privileged borrowers, selective credit allocation, and excessive bureaucratic control over the financial system.

financial restraint, stringency
austeridad, moderación financiera

financial spread
margen financiero
Income from loans and investments minus cost of borrowing.

financial standing **see** creditworthiness

financial statement
estado financiero
A balance sheet, **income statement**, funds statement or any supporting statement or other presentation of financial data derived from accounting records.

financial year; fiscal year
ejercicio (económico)

financialization
financialización
The holding of assets (e.g. savings) in financial form (e.g. bills, bonds, cash) as opposed to in the form of fixed assets (e.g. gold, real property).

financing gap
déficit de financiamento

financing package
financiamiento; *a veces*: **plan de financiamiento**

financing plan
plan de financiamiento

fineness (of a precious metal)
ley (de un metal precioso)

fine tuning (of the economy)
afinamiento (de la economía)

firm bid rule
norma de oferta firme
Principle that a bid is irrevocable for a reasonable time after bid opening.

first in, first out - FIFO
salida en el orden de adquisición, fabricación, etc.
[see also last in, first out]

first-loss deductible [insurance]
franquicia correspondiente a la primera pérdida

first ranking security
garantía de primer grado

first refusal right; preemptive right
derecho prioritario, preferencial, de preferencia, de prelación
Right to have the first opportunity to purchase real estate when such becomes available, or right to meet any other offer.

first year rule - FYR [project analysis]
regla del primer año
A method of determining when to start a project. Two time streams of costs and benefits (using one-year intervals of discounting) are subtracted. The project should be delayed by one year if the net **present value** of this figure is negative.

fiscal agent
agente financiero
A bank appointed by the borrower as its agent for a new issue of **securities** when no trustee has been appointed. Its functions include those of a principal **paying agent** and a number of clerical functions but none of the fiduciary responsibilities of a trustee.

fiscal balance
equilibrio fiscal, del presupuesto
A balance between the receipts and expenditures of a government (not just taxes).

fiscal drag
lastre fiscal; rémora fiscal; freno fiscal

1. Reduction in real income due to the increase in income from inflation, resulting in income earners being placed in higher tax brackets.
2. Action by public financial authorities with regard to economic activity.

fiscal gap
déficit fiscal

fiscal policy
política fiscal

fiscal revenue
ingresos fiscales, tributarios

fiscal transparency
transparencia fiscal
Refers to the situation whereby certain partners and associates in certain companies are deemed to be the same as the company for taxation purposes. Used in France.

fiscal year; financial year
ejercicio (económico)

fishing by lamplight; lamplight fishing
pesca con luz artificial, al encandilado

five day biochemical oxygen demand **see** biochemical oxygen demand over five days - BOD5

fixed assets **see** capital assets

fixed capital **see** capital assets

fixed cost contract; fixed price contract
contrato a precio fijo

fixed costs
costos, gastos fijos

fixed investment
inversión en capital fijo

fixed price contract; fixed cost contract
contrato a precio fijo

fixed-rate financing
financiamiento con tipo de interés fijo

fixed rate matched funding loan
préstamo de contrapartida con tasa fija
One of two types of fixed rate loans made by the Bank to IFC, involving amounts in various currencies from which currency-specific tranches are established to fund new fixed rate IFC loans on a back-to-back basis.

fixed term appointment
nombramiento de plazo fijo

fixed term contract
contrato de plazo fijo

fixed term staff
personal contratado a plazo fijo

fixed variate; predictor
variable independiente, predictiva

fixing see price fixing

flag of convenience; open registry flag
bandera de conveniencia, de favor

flagship product
producto, publicación estrella
Used to describe key publications, summarizing Bank policy in a major area, e.g. poverty, adjustment, health in Africa.

flagship project
proyecto puntero, de punta
Project used to promote development in a key area, e.g. environment, **women in development**.

flat budget
presupuesto igual, sin cambio, sin aumento
Budget which shows no increase over previous budget period.

flat rate
tasa, tarifa uniforme, a tanto alzado

flattening out
aplanamiento de una curva; nivelación

fleet [transportation]
flota; parque

flexibility quotient
cociente de flexibilidad
Number of redeployable staff resources as a percentage of the total workforce.

flexitime; flextime
horario flexible

flight capital
capital fugado

flight of capital; capital flight
fuga de capitales

flip chart
rotafolio

float [banking]
efectos en cobro, cobranza
Checks, drafts, etc., in the process of collection.

float a loan, to
obtener un empréstito; lanzar una emisión de bonos

floating capital
capital circulante, flotante
That portion of the capital of an enterprise not invested in fixed or other capital assets but in **current** and working **assets**.

floating cash reserve
reserva flotante en efectivo; encaje circulante, flotante

floating rate
tipo de cambio flotante

floating rate bond
bono con interés variable, flotante
Bond on which the coupon is established periodically and calculated with reference to short-term interest rates.

floating rate note
pagaré con interés variable, flotante
Note issued from five to fifteen years with a fixed **spread**, usually over the six month **London Interbank Offered Rate (LIBOR)**, normally with provision for a minimum interest rate. Primarily used by banks to raise dollars for their **Euromarket** operations.

floating rice
arroz flotante

flock management; herd management
manejo de rebaños

flood control irrigation
riego por anegación controlada

flooded rice
arroz acuático

flood irrigation; spate irrigation
riego por inundación
A method of irrigation in which water is made to cover the surface of the land to a considerable depth and remains for a considerable period, after which so much of it as has not soaked in is drawn off, leaving the land ready for the growing of crops.

flooding see controlled flooding

floodplain
llanura inundada, de inundación; terreno aluvial, de aluvión

floodplain agriculture, cultivation
agricultura, cultivo en tierras de aluvión

flood recession crop
cultivo de decrecida
Crop planted on land which has recently been flooded.

floodway; high-flow diversion
canal de derivación
Natural or man-made bypass channels or conduits that redirect flood waters around or away from urban centers or area of high population density.

floor price
precio mínimo
Usually established by the government, the smallest price that a seller is allowed to charge.

floor rate of exchange
tipo de cambio mínimo
The minimum rate of exchange.

floor return
rendimiento mínimo
The amount of annual investment income projected at the beginning of the fiscal year for the Bank.

flotation [bonds]
emisión

flotation costs [bonds]
gastos de emisión

flow see capital flow; capital inflow; cash flow; cash inflows; concessional flow; discounted cash flow; equilibrating capital flow; financial flows; funds flows; inflow of capital; nonconcessional flows; official flows; other official flows; student flow

flow chart; process chart
gráfico de circulación; diagrama de movimiento, de flujo, de producción, de secuencia, de procedimiento
A graph or chart that illustrates the movement of money, credit, goods or some other economic element through various stages. In computer terminology it is a diagram of the processing of a problem in a computer by means of symbols and lines to show either the logic and sequence of specific program operations or a system of processing to achieve certain objectives.

flow meter; flowmeter
caudalímetro
A meter that indicates the rate of flow of water.

flow of funds see funds flow

fluidized bed combustion
combustión en lecho fluidizado
A method of burning particulate fuel such as coal in which the amount of air required for combustion far exceeds that found in conventional burners. The fuel particles are continually fed into a bed of mineral ash in the proportions of 1 part fuel to 200 parts ash, while a flow of air passes up through the bed, causing it to act like a turbulent fluid.

focus group
reuniones de grupos de representantes de los interesados; grupo muestra elegido

focusing effect
efecto de concentración
In crop estimations, the effect of selecting one specific part of a field over another. In most cases, the tendency is to select the center part of the field, where crop density is likely to be higher, thereby leading to an upward bias in the estimates.

follow-up
seguimiento; complemento; etc.

follow-up financing
financiamiento complementario

follow-up project
proyecto complementario

food crop
cultivo alimentario

food demand program
programa de demanda de alimentos

food-for-work programme
programa de alimentos por trabajo
A programme set up under the World Food Programme where food is provided as part-payment to men and women engaged in community improvement programmes.

food grains
cereales, granos alimentarios

food import dependency ratio
coeficiente de dependencia de la importación de alimentos
The ratio of food imports to the food available for internal distribution, i.e. the sum of food production, plus food imports, minus food exports.

food intake
ingesta, ingestión de alimentos; alimentos ingeridos

food plant
planta alimentaria

Food Price Index [IBRD]
Indice de precios de los alimentos

food processing industry
industria de elaboración de alimentos

food production
producción alimentaria, de alimentos

food security
seguridad alimentaria
The availability of adequate food supplies for a target population.

foodstuffs
productos alimentarios

footloose industry
industria no localizada, sin vinculación permanente
Industry not bound to particular location by specific locational requirements and thus can effectively locate anywhere.

forage tree
árbol forrajero
A tree whose leaves are used for forage.

forage unit
unidad forrajera
Unit of measurement of the energy **input** of feedstuffs based on the net energy value of 1kg of barley.

force account, by/on [US]; direct labour [UK]; direct work; departmental forces
por administración
Used to describe a situation whereby the owner of a project uses his own labor force to undertake the project, rather than hiring **contractors**.

forced investment
inversión forzosa
A requirement placed on a **commercial bank** (usually in a developing country) that it make specific investments (e.g. x % of its portfolio must be agricultural investments), sometimes at a specific rate.

forced sale value **see** liquidation value

forced savings
ahorro forzoso

foreclosure
ejecución (de una hipoteca); juicio hipotecario

foregone output **see** forgone output

foreign assets
activos en el exterior; activos sobre el exterior

foreign borrowing
empréstitos en el exterior

foreign capital (official, private)
capital extranjero, externo (oficial, privado)

foreign currency, exchange
divisas; moneda extranjera

foreign currency issue
emisión en divisas

foreign exchange auction
subasta de divisas
Auction of foreign currency, as used in some developing countries, whereby the price obtained for the foreign currency at the auction is the rate of exchange applied till the next auction.

foreign exchange component
elemento, componente en divisas

foreign exchange cost
costo en divisas

foreign exchange coverage fund
fondo de cobertura del riesgo cambiario

foreign exchange market
mercado de divisas, de cambios

foreign exchange position
situación en materia de reservas de divisas

foreign exchange reserves
reservas de divisas

foreign exchange resources
recursos en divisas

foreign exchange risk
riesgo cambiario

foreign-owned
de propiedad extranjera

foreign price
precio en el exterior

foreign tax credit
crédito por pago de impuestos en el extranjero

foreign trade
comercio exterior

forest canopy
cubierta, dosel forestal

forest fallow
barbecho forestal
All complexes of woody vegetation derived from the clearing of natural forest for shifting agriculture. It consists of a mosaic of various reconstitution phases and includes patches of uncleared forests and agriculture fields which cannot be realistically segregated and accounted area-wise, especially from satellite imagery. Forest fallow is an intermediate class between forest and non-forest land uses. Part of the area which is not under cultivation may have the appearance of a secondary forest. Even the part currently under cultivation sometimes has the appearance of forest, due to presence of tree cover. Accurate separation between forest and forest fallow may not always be possible.

forest mining **see** tree mining

forfaiting
forfetización
The business of **discounting** medium-term **promissory notes** or drafts related to an international trade transaction. Repayments are semiannual and **discounting** is at a fixed rate.

forgiveness (of a debt)
condonación

forgone output; foregone output
producción a que se renuncia
The use of an **input** (e.g. labor) in a project which is thereby prevented from being used elsewhere.

form of bid, tender
modelo de (presentación de) ofertas

form of contract
modelo de contrato

formal adherence
adhesión oficial

formal credit
crédito institucional

formal education
educación formal, académica

formal eligibility threshold; eligibility threshold; eligibility ceiling
límite oficial para recibir financiamiento de la AIF
The maximum limit above which a country is no longer eligible for IDA financing. In practice, only countries below the **operational cut-off**, with the exception of a few small island economies, receive IDA financing.

formal sector
sector estructurado

formal suspension of disbursements [IBRD]
suspensión oficial de los desembolsos

formal vote [ICSID]
votación formal

formation expenses; organization expenses
gastos (iniciales) de constitución

forward budgeting
presupuesto multianual
Planning tool to determine government expenditures for the next few years.

forward cover
entrega futura, a plazo
The arrangement of a forward foreign exchange contract to protect a buyer or seller of foreign currency from unexpected fluctuations in the exchange rate.

forward exchange market
mercado de divisas a término, a plazo

forward exchange rate
tipo de cambio a término, a plazo

forward integration
integración progresiva
Refers to a firm whose activities extend over more than one subsequent stage of the production process of transforming raw materials into final goods.

forward linkage of an industry
eslabonamiento descendente de una industria
The relationship between an industry or firm and other industries or firms which use its output as an **input**. A change in output or price will be transmitted forwards to users of its product.

forward-looking
de visión hacia el futuro; con visión hacia el futuro

foundation seed
semilla básica
The progeny of **breeder**, select or foundation seed handled to maintain specific genetic purity and identity.

founder's share
participación de fundador
Shares subscribed by original owners of a business.

frame agreement [IBRD]
acuerdo básico
An agreement between the World Bank and a member country on cofinancing.

framework cooperative arrangement [MIGA]
acuerdo de cooperación general

franchise
concesión; licencia; franquicia; etc.

franchising agreement
acuerdo de concesión
Agreement where the franchiser provides the franchisee with a package of resources such as trademarks, know-how and management assistance and where his remuneration depends, at least in part, on the production, revenues or profits of the investment project. Considered as a type of **non-equity direct investment** for the purposes of MIGA.

free alongside ship - FAS
franco al costado del buque - f.a.s.
Applies to goods delivered alongside a specified ship at the quay or in lighters.

free carrier (named point) - FRC
franco transportista
Applies to goods delivered into the custody of the carrier at the named point.

free-enterprise economy; free market economy
economía de libre empresa

free (foreign) exchange
divisa(s) de libre convertibilidad
Foreign exchange which is freely convertible.

free funds [IDA]
fondos de libre utilización
Funds provided to IDA in a **freely convertible currency** or in a member's currency if available for financing procurement in the territory of the member, if there is a reasonable expectation that such resources will be fully used for procurement in such territory during the disbursement period.

free in and out - fio
franco de carga y descarga - f.i.o.
A chartering term by which is meant that the owner who charters his ship is responsible for all the usual costs of ship management with the exception of loading and discharging cargo and of putting the vessel in dry dock if required to do so by the charterer.

free limit [IBRD]
límite de aprobación autónoma
The limit on a **free-limit loan**.

free-limit loan [DFCs]
préstamo de aprobación autónoma
A loan which does not exceed the amount above which **onlending** is subject to official approval.

free limit of loan [DFCs]
límite máximo de los préstamos de aprobación autónoma

free-limit subloan
subpréstamo de aprobación autónoma
A subloan which does not exceed the limit above which **onlending** is subject to Bank review.

free market economy; free-enterprise economy
economía de libre empresa

free of particular average - FPA
franco de avería particular
Type of marine insurance which does not cover partial loss and damage.

free on board - FOB
franco a bordo - f.o.b.
Applies to goods delivered and loaded onto a ship at a port of shipment specified in the sales contract.

free on board (FOB) port of shipment price
precio f.o.b. puerto de embarque

free on quay - FOQ; free on wharf - FOW
franco en muelle
Same as **free alongside ship** (FAS)

free on rail - FOR
franco vagón
Applies to goods delivered and loaded to the railway.

free on wharf **see** free on quay

free port
puerto franco, libre
Area sometimes found in large ports where provision is made for reshipping imported goods without taking them through customs.

free reserves
reservas disponibles
Total reserves held by a bank less reserves required by authorities.

free resource ratio **see** gearing ratio

free rider [economics]
que se beneficia sin asumir carga alguna
In banking, a bank that collects full interest due on outstanding loans without contributing to the **new money** loans which provide, in part, the resources to pay future interest. In other contexts, any party that benefits from the activities of others without making any contribution.

free-standing; self-contained
independiente; autónomo

free-standing loan
préstamo independiente, autónomo

free-standing project
proyecto independiente, autónomo

free-standing technical assistance - FSTA
asistencia técnica independiente
Technical assistance independent of a loan.

free trade
libre comercio; libre intercambio

free trade area
zona de libre comercio

free trade zone - FTZ; bonded area
zona franca

freely convertible currency
moneda de libre convertibilidad

freely usable currency
moneda de libre uso
1. Any currency designated as such by the International Monetary Fund from time to time.
2. Any other freely available and effectively usable currency which the Board of Directors may designate for the purposes of the Convention after consultation with the International Monetary Fund and with the approval of the country of such currency. Will normally apply to the United States dollars, Japanese yen, Deutsche marks, French francs and pound sterling.

freeze (of salaries, prices, etc.)
congelación
[see also price freeze]

freeze drying
deshidratación por congelación; liofilización

fresh fruit bunch - FFB
racimo de frutas frescas

frictional unemployment
desempleo friccional

fringe benefits
prestaciones suplementarias

front-end cost
costo inicial

front-end fee
comisión inicial
Fee levied on borrower when a loan is first made. The World Bank used to levy a front-end fee on its loans but no longer does.

frontier technology
tecnología avanzada, de vanguardia

front-loaded spending
gasto concentrado al comienzo de un período

front loading
desembolsos, gastos, reembolsos, etc., concentrados al comienzo de un período

front loading of the subscription [IBRD]
mayor pago inicial de la porción pagada de las suscripciones de capital

front office
dirección

frozen capital
capital congelado, bloqueado

fruit vegetable
hortaliza de fruta

fuel cell
célula energética; pila de combustible

fuel efficiency
eficiencia en la utilización del combustible

fuel oil
petróleo residual, combustible; fuel oil

full budgeting
presupuestación completa

full cost accounting
contabilidad de costo total
A method of accounting in the oil and gas industry in which costs of unsuccessful acquisition and exploration activities are initially recorded as assets and then amortized as expenses as the total reserves in the cost center are produced.

(full cost) nominal budget planning, budgeting
planificación presupuestaria nominal
Budget planning based on a fixed overall sum for the budget, rather than for a fixed amount of items, with allowances for cost increases.

full cost pricing
valoración a costo total

full member
miembro de pleno derecho

full development, at [project]
en pleno funcionamiento

full mission
misión general

full pay out lease **see** finance lease

fully allocated cost
costo totalmente imputado
Cost derived from the apportionment of the total costs of operating an enterprise by distributing this total among the various units or classes or service in such a manner that the sum of the costs imputed to each unit or class is made to equal the total costs.

fully funded system
sistema financiado con fondos propios

fully paid stock **see** paid-up stock

functional literacy
alfabetización funcional

funded debt
deuda consolidada
The debt of a business or government in the form of outstanding bonds and other long-term **notes**.

funding gap
brecha, déficit de financiamiento

funding latter maturities
financiamiento de los últimos vencimientos
Type of IBRD **"B" loan**, whereby IBRD would take an initial share of the loan up to about 25 percent, concentrated in the latter maturities.

funding pro rata
participación proporcional
Type of IBRD **"B" loan**, whereby IBRD takes a pro rata share of about 10 percent in each maturity of the commercial loan.

funds flow; flow of funds
flujo de fondos; corriente de fondos
The flow of purchasing power into and out of an organization. Inward flows include sales revenue, sales of fixed assets and investments, and issues of **debentures**, loans, and shares. Outward flows include purchases of fixed assets and investments, repayment of debt, payment of dividends, and taxation on profits.

funds flow statement **see** statement of changes in financial position

funds-in-trust
fondos fiduciarios
Funds held by one agency on behalf of another when the first agency is implementing a project on behalf of the other agency.

funds statement **see** statement of changes in financial position

fungible funds
fondos intercambiables, transferibles

fungible goods
bienes fungibles

funk money [UK] **see** hot money

furrow irrigation
riego por surcos

futures
futuros
An agreement to take or make delivery of a specific commodity or instrument on a particular date.

futures market
mercado de futuros
Market where **futures contracts** are bought and sold.

- G -

galloping inflation
inflación galopante

game **see** management game; negative sum game; plus sum game; zero sum game

gap
brecha; déficit; diferencia

gap theory
teoría de recuperación de los bosques
The process by which tropical forest regenerates spaces opened by windfalls.

gas flaring
quema de gas
The burning of gas in the field as a means of disposal when there is no market for the gas.

gazetted (protected) public forest
bosque público protegido
Woodlots which have been subjected to a formal act of classification or where the State has carried out **reafforestation**.

gearing [UK]; leverage
nivel de endeudamiento relativo al capital; relación endeudamiento-capital propio

gearing ratio; free resource ratio; capital gearing ratio
relación préstamos desembolsados y pendientes-capital y reservas [Banco Mundial]; relación pasivo-capital
1. [UK] [= leverage ratio in US] Ratio of debt/liabilities to equity/assets. Includes **debt** and **debt-equity ratios**.
2. [IBRD] Ratio of capital plus reserves to loans outstanding and loans disbursed.

gearing ratio [IFC]
relación pasivo-capital
Ratio of outstanding investments and guarantees to the capital base.

gender issues
cuestiones que afectan a la mujer; cuestiones relativas a las desigualdades entre los sexos, a las diferencias de roles del hombre y la mujer; *a veces:* discriminación sexual

gene bank [plants]
banco de genes

gene pool
reserva genética, génica

General Algebraic Modeling System - GAMS [IBRD]
sistema de modelos algebraicos generales

General Capital Increase - GCI
aumento general del capital

general cargo
carga general; carga mixta

general equilibrium analysis
análisis del equilibrio general

general equilibrium model **see** computable general equilibrium model

general government [national accounts]
administraciones públicas

General Loss Reserve [IFC]
Reserva general para pérdidas
Loss Reserve set up to replace Unidentified Loss Reserve. It broadens the reserve coverage to the entire disbursed portfolio, excluding the portion on which there are specific loss reserves.

general price level accounting; price level accounting
contabilidad según el nivel general de precios

general procurement notice
anuncio general de adquisiciones
A notice of bidding opportunities in a competitive bid. It should contain information concerning the recipient, amount and purpose of the loan, describe the goods and works to be procured, indicate the scheduled date for availability of documents and specify the Borrower's agency responsible for procurement. In the case of Bank loans these are normally published in the United Nations Development Forum, Business Edition.

General Reserve(s) [IBRD]
Reserva General

Generalized System of Preferences - GSP
Sistema Generalizado de Preferencias - SGP

generated traffic
tráfico generado

generic drug
producto farmacéutico genérico; medicamento genérico

geothermal deposit
yacimiento geotérmico

germplasm
germoplasma

ghost fishing
pesca fantasma
Fish killed by being caught in lost or discarded fishing nets, traps and other fishing gear.

ghost worker
empleado "fantasma"
Worker who is drawing pay but is not actually doing any work, e.g. because he is dead, does not exist or is doing another job.

gill fishing
pesca por enmalle
Fishing using a flat net suspended vertically in the water with meshes that allow the head of a fish to pass but entangles its gill covers as it seeks to withdraw.

gilt-edged securities
valores de primer orden; bonos del gobierno británico

ginning [cotton]
desmotado

Global Cap Authority [IFC]
facultad de adquisición de contratos con interés tope
Authority given by the Board to IFC to purchase contracts with interest rate ceilings (**caps**) and then sell to its borrowers. It reflects the total amount of **caps**, in dollars, that IFC is authorized to make.

global commons
patrimonio natural de la humanidad; bienes comunes de la humanidad
The elements of the Earth and atmosphere, comprising the oceans and sea bed, the atmosphere and outer space, which are not the property of any one nation or individual and are therefore deemed to the property of all.

global depositary receipt - GDR
certificado internacional de depósito
Instrument that allows trading of stocks on foreign exchanges when the country concerned will not allow foreign ownership of the stock of domestic firms. The shares are deposited with a bank in the country of incorporation and an affiliate or correspondent bank in other countries issues depositary receipts for the securities. They can then be traded on stock exchanges in the same way as other securities. Used, for example, in Korea.

Global Swap Authority [IFC]
facultad para efectuar *swaps*
Authority given to IFC by the Board to borrow from the markets up to a level of US$250 million equivalent through private placements and direct institutional loans.

global warming
recalentamiento atmosférico, de la Tierra; calentamiento de la Tierra; aumento de la temperatura mundial
The predicted excessive warming of the atmosphere, as a result of the accumulation of atmospheric carbon-based and other heat absorbing gases.

global warming potential - GWP
potencial de recalentamiento atmosférico, de la Tierra
The extent to which individual emissions contribute to global warming.

globalization
globalización

glued-together household
unidad familiar con intereses en común

GNP price deflator
deflactor de precios del PNB

going concern
empresa en plena actividad y crecimiento

going price
precio corriente, vigente

gold content (e.g. of US dollar)
contenido de oro
The amount of gold formally maintained in the legal tender of a currency. From January 1934 to May 1972, the gold content of the United States dollar was 0.888671 gram of fine gold. This dollar was used as the common denominator of the value of capital subscriptions for the Bank and Fund. Because the US changed the value of the US dollar, partially because of the abolition of the official price of gold, the Fund (in 1978) and the Bank (in 1986) ceased to used the US dollar for this purpose and adopted the Special Drawing Right in its place.

gold holdings
tenencias en oro; reservas de oro

gold-pegged currency
moneda vinculada al oro

gold value
valor oro

golden share
acción con derecho de veto
Single share in a privatized company which gives the holder (usually the government) the right to block certain key decisions.

good practice project
proyecto modelo
Project using good project design and a good approach to a special operational emphasis area, such as **women in development**.

goods and services
bienes y servicios

goodwill
fondo de comercio; *a veces*: **"derecho de llave"**

goodwill clause
cláusula de buena voluntad
A clause in a Paris Club loan agreement that commits the creditors to consider debt relief after the end of the stipulated consolidation period. In return, creditor countries ask the debtor country to meet two conditions. Firstly, the debtor country must have secured debt relief from creditors not covered by the Paris Club agreement and secondly at the time the creditors agree to review the need for further debt relief, the country remains eligible for use of upper credit tranche IMF resources.

governance
gobierno; buen gobierno; buen ejercicio del poder; buena gestión de la cosa pública; dirección; conducción
The exercise of political power to manage a nation's affairs. Public service that is efficient, a judicial system that is reliable and an administration that is accountable to its public.

governing law
derecho, ley aplicable

government
gobierno; autoridades; Estado

government bond
bono público, del Estado

government expenditure
gasto(s) público(s)

government-owned programs
programas preparados por el gobierno mismo

government paper
efectos públicos

government receipts, revenues
ingresos públicos; rentas públicas

government securities
efectos, valores públicos, del Estado

government services
administración pública

grace period
período de gracia
The period allowed in a loan schedule during which repayments of loan principal need not be made.

grade creep
tendencia hacia categorías más altas de clasificación del personal
Tendency for the employees of an organization to be in a higher average classification as people rise up the scale but do not leave the organization.

grade ratio; retention rate [education]
tasa de retención
Ratio between enrolment in a given grade and enrolment in the previous grade the previous school year.

grading **see** land grading

graduate, to [Bank, IDA]
"graduarse"; pasar de las condiciones de asistencia de la AIF a las del Banco; dejar de reunir las condiciones para recibir financiamiento del Banco

graduated tax
impuesto progresivo

graduation [IBRD]
graduación (paso de las condiciones de la AIF a las del Banco; terminación del derecho a financiamiento del Banco)

graduation mission [IBRD]
misión de finalización (previa a la terminación de un proyecto)

grandfather clause
cláusula de exención por derechos adquiridos

grant basis, on a
a título de donación

grant element
factor, elemento concesionario, de donación

grant equivalent
equivalente en donación

grant-in-aid
donación; subvención

grant-like contribution
aportación con características de donación

graphical user interface - GUI
interfaz gráfica para el usuario

grass root plant; greenfield plant
planta totalmente nueva

grass root(s) level, at the
a nivel popular, comunitario, local; de base

grass roots organization
organización de base, comunitaria

graveling; regraveling
recubrimiento, aplicación de grava

gravel road
camino de grava

gravity check irrigation **see** bordercheck irrigation

gravity irrigation
riego por gravedad

gray cotton; light gray cotton; blue stained cotton
algodón gris claro
A discolored cotton which has been stained to a gray color by exposure.

gray market **see** grey market

green projects
proyectos verdes
Projects concerned with the promotion of sustainable natural-resource management and the reduction of resource degradation, including agriculture and land management, forest management, water-resource and **watershed management**, marine and coastal-zone management, and biodiversity conservation. Cf. **blue projects, brown projects**.

greenfield investment
inversión de tipo totalmente nuevo

greenfield plant; grass root plant
planta totalmente nueva

greenfield project
proyecto totalmente nuevo

greenhouse effect
efecto de invernadero
Increased retention of heat energy by the Earth's atmosphere as a result of increased emissions of carbon-based and other heat absorbing gases, including **chlorofluorocarbon** and carbon dioxide.

greenhouse gas - GHG
gas que produce el efecto de invernadero
Gas that helps cause the **greenhouse effect**. Includes carbon dioxide, methane and **chlorofluorocarbons**.

greenhouse index
índice de invernadero
Net emissions of three major **greenhouse gases** (carbon dioxide, methane and **chloro-fluorocarbons**), with each gas weighted according to its heat trapping quality, in carbon dioxide equivalents and expressed in metric tons of carbon per capita.

green labeling
etiquetas verdes
Labeling goods that are considered environmentally sound. Has been proposed for wood grown under sustainable conditions.

green manure
abono verde

grey market; gray market
mercado gris
Market in bonds that have not been given a firm price.

gross budget
presupuesto bruto
Bank budget including non-Bank resources (e.g. from Trust funds and reimbursable programs).

gross calorific value - GCV; gross heating value - GHV; higher heating value
poder calorífico bruto - PCB
Total amount of heat produced by combustion.

gross domestic income - GDY
ingreso interno bruto - YIB
Gross income from domestic as opposed to foreign sources.

gross domestic investment - GDI
inversión interna bruta - IIB
Outlays for additions to the fixed assets of the economy plus the net value of **inventory** changes.

gross domestic product - GDP
producto interno bruto - PIB; producto geográfico bruto - PGB [Chile]; producto territorial bruto [Perú]
[see also commercial, commercialized GDP; monetized GDP]

gross domestic product at factor cost
producto interno bruto al costo de los factores
The **gross domestic product at market prices** minus the difference between indirect taxes and subsidies.

gross domestic product at market prices
producto interno bruto a precios de mercado
The sum of the income accruing from production, i.e. the provision for consumption of fixed assets, compensation of employees, operating surplus and the excess of indirect taxes over subsidies.

gross earnings margin [banks]; gross margin; banker's spread; banker's markup
margen (bancario) bruto
Interest received on loans less interest paid on deposits plus other income (interest received on investments, gains or losses in foreign exchange operations and commissions and fees received and paid).

gross enrollment ratio **see** gross (primary) enrollment ratio

gross fixed capital expenditure; gross fixed investment
inversión bruta en capital fijo; gasto bruto de capital fijo
The addition during a period of time - usually a year - to a country's stock of fixed capital without making any allowance for the depreciation of the existing fixed capital.

gross fixed capital formation - GFCF
formación bruta de capital fijo
The outlays of industries, producers of government services and producers of private non-profit services to households, on additions of new durable goods to their stocks of fixed assets less their net sales of similar second-hand and scrapped goods. Excludes government outlays on military goods.

gross fixed investment; gross fixed capital expenditure
inversión bruta en capital fijo; gasto bruto de capital fijo
The addition during a period of time - usually a year - to a country's stock of fixed capital without making any allowance for the depreciation of the existing fixed capital.

gross heating value - GHV; gross calorific value - GCV; higher heating value
poder calorífico bruto - PCB
Total amount of heat produced by combustion.

gross margin; banker's spread; banker's markup; gross earnings margin [banks]
margen (bancario) bruto
Interest received on loans less interest paid on deposits plus other income (interest received on investments, gains or losses in foreign exchange operations and commissions and fees received and paid).

gross material product - GMP
producto material bruto - PMB
Corresponds to gross domestic product less output of certain services, such as public administration, defense, education, health and social insurance. Used instead of GNP in state-trading countries.

gross national income - GNY
ingreso nacional bruto - YNB
Gross national product and a **terms of trade** adjustment. The **terms of trade** adjustment reflects changes in the capacity of exports to buy imports.

gross national investment - GNI
inversión nacional bruta - INB
The total of new capital goods built with allowing for wear and tear on existing capital.

gross national product - GNP
producto nacional bruto - PNB

gross operating profit
utilidad bruta de operación, de explotación
Difference between total output per period and the costs of goods and services purchased to produce this output less cost of labor and taxes (excluding income tax). The English term is invented as the concept does not exist in US and UK accounting.

gross (primary) enrollment ratio - GER
tasa bruta de matrícula (primaria)
Total number of children enrolled in school as a percentage of the school-age population.

gross (register) tonnage - GRT [shipping]
tonelaje (de registro) bruto
A measure of the total space of a vessel in terms of 100 cubic feet (equivalent tons) including mid-deck, between deck and the closed-in spaces above the upper deck, less certain exemptions.

gross value product - GVP
producto agrícola bruto
The total value of all agricultural production for a given country in a given year, expressed in constant dollars.

groundwater table
nivel freático; capa freática

group credit
crédito colectivo

Group of Fifteen
Grupo de los Quince
Created in September 1989 to promote South-South cooperation, it consists of Algeria, Argentina, Brazil, Egypt, India, Indonesia, Jamaica, Malaysia, Mexico, Nigeria, Peru, Senegal, Venezuela, the former Yugoslavia and Zimbabwe. Chile joined in 1993.

Group of Five
Grupo de los Cinco
Informal meeting of senior officials (usually ministers of finance or heads of state) of the five most industrialized nations (France, Germany, Japan, UK, US).

Group of Seven
Grupo de los Siete
Informal meetings of senior officials (usually ministers of finance or heads of state) of the seven most industrialized countries (Canada, France, Germany, Italy, Japan, UK, US). Cf **Group of Five**.

Group of Seventy-Seven
Grupo de los 77
Set up in 1967, it is an informal meeting of senior officials/ministers/heads of state of the developing countries. It currently has 128 members plus the PLO.

Group of Ten
Grupo de los Diez
Also known as the Paris Club, it consists of the wealthiest members of the IMF that provide most of the money for lending. It currently has eleven members: Belgium, Canada, France, Germany, Italy, Japan, Netherlands, Sweden, Switzerland, UK, US.

Group of Twenty-Four
Grupo de los Veinticuatro
Set up in 1972, it exists to promote the interests of developing countries in the IMF. Current membership: Algeria, Argentina, Brazil, Colombia, Côte d'Ivoire, Egypt, Ethiopia. Gabon, Ghana, Guatemala, India, Iran, Lebanon, Mexico, Nigeria, Pakistan, Peru, Philippines, Sri Lanka, Syria, Trinidad and Tobago, Venezuela, former Yugoslavia, Zaire.

group travel [World Bank]
viaje en grupo
Travel by Executive Directors to member countries outside their constituencies.

growing concern
empresa en plena actividad y crecimiento

growing period
período vegetativo, de crecimiento
Period during the year roughly between spring and autumn when crops grow, usually from seed to full maturity and ripen for harvesting. It corresponds to the period when mean daily temperatures are above 6 degrees C.

growth accounting [econometry]
análisis del crecimiento
Decomposition of the observed rate of economic growth of a given country into components corresponding to factors of production responsible for growth.

guarantee authority
facultad de otorgar garantías

guarantee capacity [MIGA]
capacidad de garantía

guarantee commission, fee [IBRD]
comisión de garantía
Commission payable periodically (e.g. to IBRD) as compensation for the risk in guaranteeing a loan.

guarantee currency
moneda de la garantía
The currency designated as the currency for the guarantee in the contract.

guarantee holder [MIGA]
tenedor de la garantía
Holder of a guarantee issued by MIGA.

guarantee leverage
capacidad de endeudamiento en, por concepto de garantías

guaranteed percentage
porcentaje garantizado
The percentage of each loss for which the **guarantee holder** is entitled to compensation under the contract.

Guaranteed Recovery of Investment Principal -
GRIP [IFC]
**Recuperación Garantizada del Principal de las
Inversiones - GRIP**
A financial service offered by IFC, involving the
structuring of IFC and co-investor equity
exposures in such a way as to take advantage of
differences in their risk-preferences and
perceptions, generating benefits which can be
shared by both. An investor making an investment
in the equity of a developing country enterprise,
instead of making the investment directly, gives
the money to IFC in return for a U.S. dollar debt
instrument. IFC makes the investment in its own
name but has a contractual agreement with the
investor regarding voting of shares, management
and long-term strategy for the enterprise.

guidance **see** vocational guidance

guidelines
directrices; pautas, normas generales

guiding price
precio indicativo

- H -

hairy cotton; upland cotton
algodón velloso; algodón upland; algodón americano

halfway country
país medianamente industrializado; país parcialmente industrializado
A country that is on the way to being industrialized but is not yet fully industrialized.

handles see tax handles

handling charges
cargos por manipulación, tramitación, etc.

harbor dues, fees; port dues
derechos portuarios
Charged for the use of the port by the ship and its cargo.

hard-blend countries
países que reciben financiamiento en condiciones predominantemente gravosas
Country receiving more loans from IBRD than credits from IDA.

hard coal; anthracite
antracita; carbón antracitoso

hard component [projects]
componente físico

hard copy
copia impresa; salida impresa

hard core [projects]
núcleo; base; básico; mínimo

hard currency; strong currency
moneda fuerte

hard loan
préstamo en condiciones ordinarias, de mercado

hard loan window
servicio, entidad de préstamos en condiciones ordinarias, no concesionarias

hard technical assistance see engineering-related technical assistance

hardening of loan terms
tendencia a condiciones de préstamo más gravosas

hardship allowance
subsidio por lugar de destino difícil

hardware
componentes físicos; equipo de computación

harmonic mean [statistics]
media armónica
A special kind of mean which is determined by calculating the mean of the reciprocals of the values concerned and then calculating the reciprocal of this quantity.

harnessing
captación; movilización; aprovechamiento; etc.

harvest fishery see capture fishery

hardwood forest
bosque de especies frondosas, no coníferas

head gate structure [irrigation]
estructura de cabecera

head hunting
búsqueda de personal calificado

head tax; poll tax; capitation tax
impuesto de capitación

headcount index (measure) of poverty; headcount ratio - HCR
índice de recuento de la pobreza
A useful way to measure poverty by expressing the number of poor as a proportion of the population although it ignores the extent to which the poor fall below the poverty line.

headroom [World Bank]
margen de maniobra
The difference between the **statutory lending limit** and the value of loans that are disbursed and outstanding.

health delivery system
sistema de prestación de servicios de salud

health maintenance organization - HMO
organización de medicina preventiva; centro integral de salud
An organized health care delivery system where participants pay a fixed, regular sum and receive an agreed range of health services from an approved set of health care providers. Health system where medical care is provided directly by salaried employees in facilities owned by the HMO.

health post
puesto de salud; dispensario

health screening
reconocimiento, examen médico

heating oil
petróleo, combustible para calefacción

heat rate
rendimiento térmico; consumo calorífico

heat trapping
retención térmica
The ability of a gas to prevent heat escaping from the Earth's atmosphere.

heat trapping gas
gas que produce retención térmica
Gases, such as carbon dioxide and methane, that trap heat in the **ozone layer**.

heat value
poder calorífico

heavy commodities
productos pesados

heavy engineering industry
industria metalmecánica

heavy fuel oil
petróleo combustible pesado

heavy industry
industria pesada

heavy oil
aceite, petróleo pesado

hedge [securities market]
valor de protección
Security acquired to cover possible loss on speculative investments.

hedge clause
cláusula de salvaguardia

hedging
operaciones de cobertura, de protección cambiaria

hedonic price analysis
análisis del valor hedónico; análisis hedónico de los precios
Economic analysis technique which takes into account the implicit prices of specific characteristics of properties. For example, in the environment field, it places value on improvements or deterioration in environmental quality.

herbaceous cotton; Levant cotton; American short staple cotton; Arabian cotton
algodón herbáceo

hidden hunger
hambre oculta, encubierta

hidden inflation
inflación latente, oculta

hidden reserves
reservas ocultas

hidden unemployment; concealed, covert, disguised unemployment
desempleo oculto, encubierto, disfrazado

high absorber [oil exporter]
país de elevada absorción, de gran capacidad de absorción
Oil exporting **capital surplus country** which is a net importer of capital and has been able to make full use of revenues from oil production for domestic development. Includes Algeria, Ecuador, Gabon, Indonesia, Nigeria and Venezuela.

high-flow diversion **see** floodway

high fructose corn syrup - HFCS
sirope, jarabe de maíz de alto contenido en fructosa

high income countries
países de ingreso alto

high performing economy
país de gran crecimiento económico

high school **see** junior high school

high-power(ed) money
dinero de alta potencia [teoría monetarista]; base monetaria; dinero primario; dinero de la Reserva Federal de los EE.UU. para uso de los bancos comerciales

higher heating value; gross heating value - GHV; gross calorific value - GCV
poder calorífico bruto - PCB
Total amount of heat produced by combustion.

higher income brackets
grupos de ingresos más elevados

higher level staff
personal, funcionarios de nivel profesional

higher training
estudios avanzados

highest bidder
licitante que presenta la oferta más alta

highland rice; upland rice; mountain rice
arroz de montaña, de tierras altas, de secano

highly indebted country
país muy endeudado, sumamente endeudado, fuertemente endeudado

highly leveraged
con alto coeficiente de endeudamiento; con gran endeudamiento

Highways Design and Maintenance Model - HDM [IBRD]
modelo de normas de diseño y mantenimiento de carreteras
A mathematical model based on two earlier models developed by the Massachusetts Institute of Technology and the Transport and Road Research Laboratory, UK, used to determine the total life-cycle transportation cost, provide economic comparisons for large numbers of alternative designs and maintenance policies and search for the lowest total cost alternative.

hillside farming
cultivo en pendiente

hire purchase [UK]
compra a plazos

historical cost
valor inicial; precio de compra, de adquisición

historically valued assets
activos a su valor de adquisición

hit-and-run project
proyecto de muy corto plazo, relámpago
Project where an investor takes advantage of local tax laws to operate a project (e.g. mining, textiles) under a tax-free regime and then withdraws as soon as he is liable for taxation, often leaving severely depreciated equipment or exhausted mineral reserves.

holding company
sociedad de cartera, de inversiones

holdings [foreign exchange, gold]
tenencias [en, de divisas, oro]

home country [MIGA]
país de origen
The country or countries whose membership in MIGA made the **Guarantee Holder** eligible under Article 12 of the Convention Establishing MIGA to receive the guarantee provided for in a contract.

home leave allowance [World Bank]
asignación para vacaciones en el país de origen

hoof **see** cattle on the hoof

horizontal equity
equidad horizontal
Treating taxpayers with the same amount of income equally irrespective of the source of income.

horizontal integration
integración horizontal

host country [MIGA]
país receptor [inversiones]; país beneficiario, anfitrión
A member, its government or any public authority of a member in whose territories, as defined in article 66 of the Convention, an investment which has been guaranteed or reinsured, or is considered for guarantee or reinsurance by MIGA is to be located.

Host Organization [ICSID]
Organismo Anfitrión

hot money; funk money [UK]
capitales itinerantes
Short-term international capital movements, motivated by interest rate differentials or revaluation hopes/devaluation fears.

house connection
conexión domiciliaria

household expenditure survey - HES
encuesta de gastos familiares

household goods
enseres domésticos

household survey
encuesta por, de hogares

household waste collection charge
tarifa de recolección de basura(s)
Charge levied for removal of household waste.

housing expenses/income ratio; affordability ratio
relación gastos de vivienda-ingresos
The ratio of expenditure on housing to total income.

housing stock
disponibilidades de viviendas

hub and spoke system
sistema radial

human immunodeficiency virus - HIV
virus de la inmunodeficiencia humana - VIH

human resource development
perfeccionamiento de los recursos humanos

human settlements
asentamientos humanos

hurdle rate
tasa crítica de rentabilidad
A somewhat arbitrary **rate of return**, related to the current cost of borrowing money, set by a government or company to guide investment decisions. Below this limit, investment is normally considered inadvisable.

husbandry **see** animal husbandry

husk, to; dehusk, to
descascarar; deshojar

hybrid capital base [IFC]
base de capital híbrida
Capital base consisting of current paid-in capital and **retained earnings** to support growth in operations with the debt-equity ratio not exceeding 2.5:1, combined with new **callable** capital to support investment growth in a 1:1 **gearing ratio**.

hydrant; standpipe; standpost
toma de agua

hydrocracking
hidrocraqueo

hydrodevelopment
aprovechamiento de la energía hidroeléctrica

hydroelectric power; hydropower
energía hidroeléctrica

hydrofluoroalkane - HFA
hidrofluoroalcano - HFA
An alternative name for **chlorofluorocarbons**, thought up by the wily manufacturers of **chlorofluorocarbons**, to avoid the bad press.

hydrochlorofluorocarbon - HCFC
hidroclorofluorocarbono - HCFC
A substitute for **chlorofluorocarbons**.

hydrofluorocarbon - HFC
hidrofluorocarbono - HFC
A substitute for **chlorofluorocarbons**.

hydropower; hydroelectric power
energía hidroeléctrica

- I -

ICSID clauses
cláusulas contractuales que estipulan someter las diferencias al CIADI; cláusulas del CIADI

IDA-eligible country
país que puede recibir créditos, financiamiento de la AIF; país habilitado para recibir créditos de la AIF
Developing country which is entitled to receive IDA credits because its per capita income is below the IDA norm.

IDA management fee
comisión por administración de la AIF

IDA recipient
país prestatario de la AIF; receptor de créditos de la AIF

IDA reflows
reembolsos de los créditos de la AIF; reflujos de los créditos de la AIF
Payments received by IDA in the form of reimbursements for credits made.

IDA's "free-funds"
fondos de libre utilización de la AIF
Funds provided to IDA in a **freely convertible currency** or in a member's currency if available for financing procurement in the territory of the member, if there is a reasonable expectation that such resources will be fully used for procurement in such territory during the disbursement period.

idle cash
dinero inactivo

IFC Global Indexes (IFCG Indexes)
Indices de Cobertura Amplia de la CFI (Indices IFCG)
The IFCG Indexes are neutral and reliable benchmarks of emerging markets' performance, calculated in a uniform manner. They include price and total return indexes for 20 emerging markets, as well as a composite index for those 20 markets and regional indexes for Latin America and Asia. Stocks are selected for inclusion in each index on the basis of three criteria: market capitalization, liquidity, and industry classification.

IFC Investable Indexes (IFCI Indexes)
Indices de la CFI de Valores para Inversión (Indices IFCI)
These Indexes are calculated using the same factors as the **IFC Global Indexes** but also take into account the extent to which national laws, regulations, or company statutes prohibit or limit foreign ownership. They thus provide global investors with a definitive benchmark of the performance of stocks in emerging markets in which they can invest.

IFC risk assets-equity ratio
relación activos de riesgo-patrimonio
Ratio calculated by measuring the risk content of IFC's assets in relation to the sum of paid-in capital and **retained earnings**.

illegal housing
vivienda ilegal

illegality clause
cláusula de ilegalidad
Clause in a loan agreement which allows the lender to ask for repayment of his funds if a change in national legislation obliges him to withdraw from the loan.

illiteracy rate
tasa de analfabetismo
Proportion of population 15 years and older who cannot, with understanding, both read and write a short simple statement on every day life.

immunity from taxation
inmunidad tributaria

impact (evaluation) report
informe de evaluación de los efectos; informe sobre las repercusiones (de un proyecto)

Implementation Completion Report - ICR
informe final de ejecución - IFE

implementing agency
organismo de ejecución

implementing agreement
acuerdo de ejecución

implicit deflator
deflactor implícito
Obtained by taking each component of **gross national product** in as fine detail as possible and deflating it from current data. Once deflated the components are again aggregated to obtain GNP in constant dollars.

implicit gross domestic product deflator
deflactor implícito del producto interno bruto
A **deflator** calculated by dividing, for each year of the period, the value of GDP in current market prices by the value of GDP in constant market prices, both in national currency.

implied money control theory
teoría del control del dinero implícito

import coefficient
coeficiente de importaciones (importaciones/producción total)

import component
componente importado, de importación

import coverage index
índice de cobertura de las importaciones

import coverage ratio
coeficiente, relación de cobertura de las importaciones
The rate at which imports are covered by exports.

import growth rate
tasa de aumento, crecimiento de las importaciones

import-intensive
con gran intensidad de importaciones; con alto contenido de importaciones

import levy
gravamen a las importaciones

import licensing
sistema, régimen de licencias de importación

import parity price
precio paritario de importación
The estimated price at the farm gate or project boundary derived by adjusting the cif or fob prices by all the relevant charges between the farm gate and the project boundary and the point where the cif or fob price is quoted.

import quota
cuota, cupo de importación

import subsidy
subvención, subsidio a las importaciones

import substitution
sustitución de importaciones

import surcharge
recargo a la(s) importación(es)

importing power of exports
capacidad de importación derivada de las exportaciones

imprest account, fund
cuenta de anticipos; fondo de anticipos
An account or fund maintained for payments made in cash, commonly used as a petty cash fund. A fixed maximum sum is kept in the fund and, as the fund is depleted, this sum is periodically brought up to the maximum.

imputed costs
costos imputados
Generally used to mean costs that do not involve at any time actual cash outlay and which do not, therefore, appear in the accounting records but are relevant to the decision at hand.

imputed value
valor imputado

inactive borrower, nonactive borrower
prestatario inactivo
Country that is not currently seeking new borrowings from the Bank.

inactive loan
préstamo inactivo
A loan which is in force but not being disbursed.

Inaugural Meeting [ICSID]
Reunión Inaugural

in-bond industries
empresas, industrias maquiladoras; industrias de zona franca

incentive
incentivo; estímulo

incentive payment
incentivo en dinero; prima; bonificación

incentive price
precio de incentivo

inception report
informe inicial

incidence [medicine]
incidencia

incidental services
servicios conexos
Additional services required of the supplier as specified in the **Special Conditions of Contract**, including on-site assembly, startup, provision of tools required for assembly, provision of manuals, etc.

income
ingreso(s); renta

income (and expenditure) account
cuenta de ingresos y gastos, de pérdidas y ganancias

income and outlay accounts [national accounts]
cuentas de ingresos y gastos
Accounts showing the receipt and disbursement of incomes by resident institutional units.

income bracket
grupo, categoría, nivel de ingreso(s)

income effect
efecto de ingreso, de renta

income elasticity
elasticidad-ingreso; elasticidad con respecto al ingreso
A measure of the change in supply and/or demand as income changes.

income elasticity of demand
elasticidad-ingreso de la demanda; elasticidad de la demanda en función del ingreso
A measure of the percentage change in the demand for a commodity or service as induced by a given percentage change in the income of the individual.

income note
bono, pagaré participatorio
Note where the income is wholly or partially dependent on the earnings of the issuing corporation.

income shortfall
insuficiencia de ingresos
[see also poverty gap]

income statement [US]; profit and loss account [UK]
estado de ingresos y gastos, de pérdidas y ganancias
[see also consolidated income statement]

income tax
impuesto sobre, a la renta

income tax [corporations]
impuesto sobre, a las utilidades, los beneficios

income tax return
declaración del impuesto sobre la renta

income terms of trade
relación de intercambio de ingresos
The net **barter terms of trade** weighted by the volume of exports. It gives an indication of the purchasing power of exports.

incremental benefits
beneficios adicionales

incremental budgeting
presupuestación incremental
A budget process in which justification is generally required only for increments (or decrements) to previous budgeting levels.

incremental building, housing
construcción progresiva de viviendas
Building, usually from a core where additional features are gradually added.

incremental capital-output ratio - ICOR
relación incremental capital-producto
Ratio of the change in capital investment (net of gross investment minus **capital consumption allowances**) to the change in output. If a certain industry adds $2.5 million net to its capital equipment and its yearly output increases by $1 million then its ICOR is 2.5:1.

incremental cost
costo incremental
[**see also** average incremental cost]

incremental housing, building
construcción progresiva de viviendas
Building, usually from a core where additional features are gradually added.

incremental rate of return
tasa diferencial de rentabilidad
The **discount rate** which equalizes the **present value** of incremental costs with the incremental benefits of the project.

indefinite quantity contract
contrato por cantidades indeterminadas
Contract which provides for the provision of an indefinite quantity of specific goods or services, within stated limits and during a specified period.

independent variable; predictor
variable independiente, predictiva

indexed, index-linked bond
bono ajustable, indizado
Bond where the **coupon rate** or redemption value is indexed (to other currencies, gold, or fuel prices).

indexed, index-linked, index-tied loan
préstamo indizado, reajustado según un índice

Indicative Planning Figures - IPF [UNDP]
cifras indicativas de planificación - CIP
UNDP target expenditures for technical cooperation.

indicator **see** concurrent indicator; convergent indicator; economic indicator; lagging indicator; leading indicator; performance indicators

indifference curve
curva de indiferencia

A graphical representation of different bundles of, say, two commodities, from the consumption of which the individual derives the same amount of total utility. If we assume an individual obtains the same utility from a bundle of 5 bananas and 6 mangoes or 4 bananas and 8 mangoes or 3 bananas and 11 mangoes, we can plot a graph with bananas as the x-axis and mangoes as the y-axis. We get three points for the three different bundles. The curve we obtain by joining these points is the indifference curve, so called because the individual is indifferent about his choice as regards total utility.

indigenization
reemplazo de personal extranjero por personal nacional

indigenous NGO
ONG autóctona

indirect costs; on-costs [UK]
costos indirectos

induced-by benefit
beneficio inducido indirecto
A form of indirect benefit that accrues to suppliers of project **inputs**. Includes the direct and indirect value added to national income generated by the investment and recurrent expenditures of a project. Equivalent to using a shadow price for a project **input** for which an adjustment is made for **opportunity cost** in the estimates of direct and indirect value added. Sometimes estimated using specialized forms of **input**-output multipliers.

induced development effect; boomtown effect
efecto secundario de urbanización
The secondary growth of settlements and infrastructure, resulting from a project.

industrial and trade policy adjustment - ITPA
ajuste de la(s) política(s) industrial y comercial

industrial and trade policy adjustment loan - ITPAL [World Bank]
préstamo para ajuste de la(s) política(s) industrial y comercial
World Bank loan made to assist adjustment of a country's industrial and trade policy.

industrial deepening
intensificación industrial
Increasing the amount of the industrial sector compared with other sectors.

industrial estate [UK], park [USA]
zona, parque, polígono industrial

industrial goods
bienes, productos industriales

industrial market economy
país industrial con economía de mercado

industrial park [USA], estate [UK]
zona, parque, polígono industrial

industrial relations; labor-management relations; labor relations
relaciones entre empleados y empleadores; relaciones obrero-patronales

ineligible
inadmisible; carente de derecho a; no habilitado; que no cumple los requisitos

inertial inflation
inflación inercial
Inflation caused by spiraling wage and price increases.

infant industry
industria naciente, incipiente

infant mortality
mortalidad infantil; mortalidad de niños menores de un año
[**see also** child mortality]

infected area
zona infestada, de infestación

inflation accounting
contabilidad en períodos de inflación
Accounting for dealing with the impact of inflation. Includes the current purchasing power method whereby accounts are expressed in terms of purchasing units employing a retail price index; value accounting whereby assets are measured by reference to their value and not cost; **replacement cost** accounting whereby assets are revalued from historic to current costs.

inflationary expectations
expectativas, previsiones inflacionarias

inflationary gap
brecha inflacionaria
A condition of excess aggregate spending (for consumer, investment and government goods and services) relative to the spending that would be consistent with a full-employment stable economy. The gap is actually the amount of change in spending which would lead to stability.

inflation premium
prima de inflación
A **premium** added to a **security** to allow for inflation.

inflation tax
impuesto de la inflación; impuesto que significa la inflación
Increased income tax paid as wages rise with inflation but tax thresholds remain constant.

inflow see capital inflow; cash inflows; flow

inflow of capital
entrada, afluencia de capital

informal credit
crédito no institucional

informal education
educación informal

informal meeting
reunión oficiosa

informal sector
sector no estructurado; sector informal
The sector of the economy which is not organized and which, therefore, does not appear in official economic statistics. Sometimes used for the underground economy.

informal suspension of disbursements [IBRD]
suspensión no oficial de los desembolsos

infrastructure developer
empresa de obras y servicios de infraestructura

in-house training
capacitación, formación en la empresa

initial expenses
gastos iniciales, de instalación

initial operation
actividades iniciales; explotación inicial

initial subscription [IDA]
suscripción inicial

initiating memorandum - IM [World Bank]
primer memorando oficial

in-kind costs
costos de, en servicios

inland fisheries, fishing
pesca en aguas interiores

input
insumo; aportación
[see also cash input; noncash input]

input mix
combinación de insumos

input-output coefficient
coeficiente de insumo-producto

input-output model
modelo de insumo-producto
A mathematical model of **inputs** and outputs to a system. In econometrics it refers to a model representation of an **input-output table**.

input-output ratio
relación insumo-producto

input-output table
tabla de insumo-producto
A matrix which shows the way in which industries or sectors interact. It generally shows, for each industry, the amount of that industry's output that goes to each other industry as **input** (as raw materials or as semifinished products), as well as the amount that goes to the final markets of the economy.

input shifting
sustitución de recursos para reducir costos
Reducing costs by using lower priced **inputs**, e.g. using contractors instead of permanent staff, communications instead of travel.

input subsidy
subvención para insumos

input switching
reasignación de fondos presupuestarios
Budget term which means managers can change budget allocations as a result of changing cost pressures over the range of expense accounts.

in-service training
capacitación, formación, adiestramiento en el servicio

insider dealer, trader
especulador (en la Bolsa) que aprovecha información interna

insider dealing, trading
especulación (en la Bolsa) aprovechando información interna

instability index
índice de variación
An index which measures the variability of world prices for selected agricultural commodities.

installed capacity [electricity]
capacidad instalada
The maximum runoff of a hydroelectricity facility that can be constantly maintained and utilized by equipment.

institutional framework
marco, estructura institucional

institutional investors
instituciones inversionistas

institutional performance
desempeño de las instituciones; actuación de las instituciones

institutional programs [IBRD]
programas de fortalecimiento institucional
Programs undertaken that are required to further the institution itself, as opposed to being part of its operations. These would include production of the Annual Report, Annual Meetings and the like.

institutional ratio
coeficiente interinstitucional
The ratio between Bank subscriptions authorized solely in **general capital increases** and IMF quotas obtained solely from general quota increases. Used to determine the initial share allocation of countries joining the Bank during the period of the 1979 **General Capital Increase**.

institution building
desarrollo, fortalecimiento institucional

instructional aid
material didáctico, pedagógico

institution-related technical assistance; soft technical assistance
asistencia técnica relacionada con los componentes no físicos o de servicios; asistencia técnica para desarrollo institucional
Technical assistance geared towards institutional development as opposed to **engineering-related technical assistance**.

Institution Rules [ICSID]
Reglas de Iniciación
[see Rules of Procedure for the Institution of Conciliation and Arbitration Proceedings]

instrument [ICSID]
instrumento (oficial)

instrument of acceptance
instrumento de aceptación
A legal document indicating that a state has accepted the rules and regulations of an organization it is joining.

insurance see social insurance

intake
toma (de agua); ingesta; ingestión; admisión; contingente; entrada
[see also calorie intake]

intangible assets, property
activos, bienes intangibles, inmateriales
Items or rights lacking physical existence, their value being mainly in their income generation potential and the rights and benefits that possession confers.

integrated conservation-development project - ICDP
proyecto integrado de conservación y desarrollo
A new type of experimental project that attempts to link the conservation of biological diversity in protected areas with local economic and social development.

integrated management training program
programa integrado de capacitación y perfeccionamiento de funcionarios que ocupan cargos de dirección

integrated pest management - IPM
lucha integrada contra las plagas
Growing farm crops with fewer chemical pesticides and more natural pest controls. Monitoring for pests and rotating plantings, the use of pesticides can be virtually eliminated on crops such as potatoes, corn and apples.

integrated rural development project
proyecto de desarrollo rural integrado

integration see backward-forward integration; backward integration

interchange see course interchange

intercompany pricing
fijación de precios de transferencia entre empresas

intercropping
cultivo intercalado
Growing two or more crops simultaneously as in alternate rows in the same field or single tract of land.

interest see beneficial interest; controlling interest; covered interest arbitrage; depositor rate of interest; effective interest rate; working interest

interest bearing note
pagaré que devenga intereses

interest charges
intereses (cobrados, pagados)

interest coverage ratio - ICR; times interest earned ratio
relación de cobertura de intereses
Net income before interest expenses divided by interest expenses. IFC's definition is "The number of times income, after deducting all expenses except borrowing charges and provision for losses, covers borrowing charges."

interest during construction - IDC
intereses durante la construcción
Interest payable on long-term or short-term debt incurred to finance capital works (e.g. plant or road construction in progress) in a fiscal year. Financing charges, including **commitment fees**, should also be included. IDC is frequently capitalized (or charged to the project cost) until the asset is commissioned or as a capital expenditure item it is transferred to a deferred charges or deferred capital expenditure account. For Bank projects IDC should be computed as part of project costs to determine total financing requirements.

interest earnings, income
ingresos por intereses

interest equalization tax
impuesto de igualación, de equiparación de intereses
A tax on foreign investments for the purpose of curtailing the outflow of private funds.

interest income, earnings
ingresos por intereses

interest leakage
fluctuación de los tipos de interés debida a la fuga de capitales
Changes in U.S. interest rates due to movement of funds from the U.S. to the **Eurodollar** markets.

interest rate cap [IBRD]
tope de los tipos de interés
A limit on the amount of interest that can be levied on a variable rate loan. Proposed for IBRD.

interest-rate differential
margen, diferencia entre tipos, tasas de interés

interest rate risk
riesgo de pérdida en, por concepto de intereses
Risk due to difference in interest rates.

interest (rate) sensitivity
sensibilidad a las tasas de interés
Rate-sensitive assets as a percentage of rate-sensitive liabilities

interest (rate) swap
intercambio, *swap* de tipos de interés
An agreement to exchange floating rate payments for fixed-rate payments in the same currency.

interest rebate
rebaja de intereses

interest service ratio
coeficiente del servicio de los intereses
Ratio of payment of interest on debt to exports of goods and services.

interest subsidy, subsidization
subvención de intereses

Interest Subsidy Fund [= Third Window]
Fondo de Subvención de Intereses [= Tercera Ventanilla]
A lending facility to extend loans to the developing countries on terms intermediate between those charged by the Bank and IDA. Now discontinued.

interest support
apoyo de los intereses

interfuel substitution
sustitución de combustibles

Interim Committee [IMF]
Comité Provisional

interim financial statement
estado financiero intermedio

interindustry linkages
eslabonamientos interindustriales, entre industrias

interlocking debt
deuda(s) recíproca(s)

intermediate goods
bienes intermedios
Those goods used as an **input** for further transformation by some other production activity, not for consumption or as an addition to the stock of fixed capital.

intermediation
intermediación
Process whereby a financial institution interposes its names and trustworthiness between a lender and a borrower. For example, instead of buying an issue directly from a corporation, an investor may deposit funds with a bank which, in turn, invests in the issue.
[**see also** market intermediation]

intermediation rate
tasa de intermediación

intermediative borrowing
préstamos obtenidos de intermediarios financieros
Borrowing from financial intermediaries.

internal audit
auditoría interna; control interno

internal cash generation; internally generated funds; cash generation
recursos propios; recursos provenientes de las operaciones
The gross income from all sources less all operating and administrative expenses, excluding depreciation, interest, other non-cash charges and other charges on debt, and taxes.

internal cross subsidy
subvención, subsidio cruzada(o) interna(o)

internal exchange rate; modified Bruno ratio
tipo de cambio interno; coeficiente modificado de Bruno
As for the **Bruno ratio** but using for the entire project life instead of for just one year.

internal importing costs
costos internos de importación

internal rate of financial return **see** financial rate of return

internal rate of return - IRR
tasa de rentabilidad interna
The **rate of return** on an asset investment. It is the **discount rate** that equates the **present value** of future net revenue streams (over the economic life of the asset) to the cost of the investment.
[**see also** economic rate of return; financial rate of return]

internally generated funds; cash generation; internal cash generation
recursos propios; recursos provenientes de las operaciones

international agricultural research centers - IARC
centros internacionales de investigaciones agrícolas

international banking facility - IBF
servicio bancario internacional
International branch of a bank in a kind of internal **free trade zone** in the U.S., which allows banks to engage in international banking without some of the usual restrictions facing domestic banks. Those restrictions from which IBFs are exempt include reserve requirements, payment of certain insurance premiums, and special relief from state tax.

international commodity agreements, arrangements
convenios, acuerdos internacionales sobre productos básicos
Any intergovernmental agreement or arrangement to promote international cooperation in a commodity, the parties to which include produces and consumers covering the bulk of world trade in the commodity concerned.

international commodity bodies - ICBs
organismos internacionales de productos básicos
An international body concerned on a continuiing basis with the trade, production and consumption aspects of a commodity.

international commodity organizations - ICOs
organizaciones internacionales de productos básicos
An organization established by an international commodity agreement to implement the provisions of the agreement.

International Comparison Project, Programme -
ICP
**Proyecto, Programa de Comparación
Internacional - PCI**
A project supported by the World Bank and the
United Nations which enables incomes to be
compared in terms of the prices of a common set
of consumer goods, which reflect real purchasing
power. When outside financing dried up in 1987,
the Project became a Programme, which is what it
is now.

international competitive bidding - ICB
licitación pública internacional
Bidding open to all eligible suppliers and
contractors.

international competitiveness margin - ICM
margen de competitividad internacional
The percentage by which the Bank/Fund payline
should exceed the combined French/German
market paylines to provide adequate international
competitiveness.

International Compilers Working Group on
External Debt Statistics
[WB/IMF/BIS/OECD/Berne Union]
**Grupo de Trabajo Internacional de
Compiladores de Estadísticas sobre la Deuda
Externa**

international credit guarantee fund
fondo internacional de garantías de crédito

international credit guarantee system
sistema internacional de garantías de crédito

international financial institutions - IFIs
instituciones financieras internacionales

international liquidity
liquidez internacional

international payments position
situación de pagos internacionales

international reserves
reservas internacionales

international shopping
comparación internacional de precios
Procurement based on comparing price quotations
from at least three foreign suppliers.

internship
pasantía; internado; práctica(s)

intervention currency
moneda de intervención
Currency used by central bank for official
intervention in the foreign exchange market. This
currency is often not the same as the home
currency, which may not be a convertible currency.

intervention price
precio de intervención
The minimum price set by an agency at which a
producer is guaranteed to sell his product.

intra-day settlement
pago en el día
Trading settlement within less than one day.

inventory; inventories
existencias; inventario(s)
Raw materials and supplies, goods finished and
being manufactured and stock on hand, in transit,
in storage or consigned to others at the end of the
accounting period.

inventory control
control de existencias, inventario(s)

inventory investment
inversión en existencias

inventory turnover
**movimiento, rotación del inventario, de las
existencias**

inverted rates [electricity tariffs]
tarifas progresivas
Rate where the lowest block is the cheapest, in
order to subsidize low income groups.

investment agreement [IFC]
convenio de inversión [CFI]

investment bank [US]; merchant bank [UK]
banco de inversiones
Institution that accepts new issues of stocks from a
corporation and attempts to sell them to the public
at a profit. In the U.S., they have a separate legal
status from commercial banks.

investment budget
presupuesto de inversiones

investment center [accounting]
centro de inversión
A responsibility unit whose performance is measured in terms of resources committed (capital invested) relative to monetary costs and returns.

investment commitment [IFC]
compromiso de inversión [CFI]

investment company, fund
compañía de inversiones; sociedad de inversiones; fondo de inversiones
Company that uses its capital to invest in other companies. The two kinds are **open-end investment company** and **closed-end investment company**, the former being by far the most frequent.
[**see also** closed end investment company, fund; open end investment company, fund]

investment gap
déficit de inversiones

investment goods
bienes de inversión, de equipo, de capital

investment grant
subvención para inversión

investment incentives
incentivos para la inversión

investment income
ingresos por (concepto de) inversiones, derivados de inversiones

investment insurance
seguro de inversión
[**see also** multilateral investment insurance]

investment loan
préstamo para proyecto de inversión

investment portfolio
cartera de inversiones (a largo plazo)
Portfolio of longer-term investments. Cf. **trading portfolio.**

investment project
proyecto de inversión

investment return, yield
rentabilidad, rendimiento de la inversión

investment review mission [IBRD]
misión de estudio de oportunidades de inversión

investment tax credit
crédito impositivo por inversiones

investment trust **see** closed-end investment company, fund

invisible transactions
operaciones, transacciones invisibles
Exports and imports of services. Includes insurance, shipping charges and tourist expenditures.
[**see also** surplus on invisibles]

invitation to bid, to tender
llamada a licitación
A notice issued under competitive bidding procedures calling on **bidders** to submit bids for contracts.

invitation to prequalify [contracts]
invitación a la precalificación
A notice issued under competitive bidding procedures calling on **bidders** to prequalify prior to bidding on a contract.

involuntary lending
préstamos no voluntarios
Lending by banks as long as the resulting reduction in probability of default, multiplied by the existing exposure, exceeds the amount of **new money** multiplied by the remaining probability of default even after the new assistance.

involuntary resettlement
reasentamiento involuntario
Movement of peoples away from their normal place of abode against their will.

inward-looking; inward-oriented [country; policy]
orientado hacia el interior; aislacionista

irrevocable agreement to reimburse
garantía irrevocable de reembolso
An agreement given e.g. by the Bank to a commercial Bank that it will reimburse any part of a cofinancing loan on which a borrower defaults.

irrevocable letter of credit
carta de crédito irrevocable
Form of **letter of credit** whereby the issuing bank gives an undertaking to the beneficiary that payment will be made, provided that the beneficiary complies with the terms of the credit. Sometimes used as **performance security**.

irrigation **see** basin irrigation; border check irrigation; border ditch irrigation; border irrigation; center pivot sprinkle irrigation; corrugation irrigation; drip irrigation; flood control irrigation; flood irrigation; gravity irrigation; micro-sprayer irrigation; runoff irrigation; small-scale irrigation; sprinkle irrigation; strip irrigation; subirrigation; surface irrigation; trickle irrigation; wild flooding

island developing country
país insular en desarrollo

issued share capital
capital accionario emitido

issues on tap; tap issue
emisión continua
An issue of a security made available on an as required basis. Used primarily in the British market, where the British Government issues Treasury stock and seeks subscriptions. As the stock is rarely fully subscribed, the remainder is sold to Stock Exchange jobbers as demand requires

issues paper
documento de exposición de problemas; Temas del Banco Mundial [IBRD]

issuing bank; bank of issue
banco emisor, de emisión

item [budget]
partida
[see **also** tariff item]

- J -

jeopardy clause; escape clause; break clause
cláusula de salvaguardia, de elusión, de escape
A clause in a Eurocurrency agreement specifying that, if certain events curtail the lender's activity or the operation of the Euromarkets, other designated actions will come into effect.

jeopardy loan
préstamo con riesgo de posibles pérdidas
Term used by IFC to indicate that a loan has serious problems. IFC expects to make a loss (though not necessarily a 100% loss) on a jeopardy loan.

jitney
colectivo

jobbing
trabajo a destajo

job description
descripción de cargo, puesto

job order accounting
contabilidad por órdenes de trabajo, por pedidos
A cost accounting method which accumulates the costs of doing a separately identifiable job.

job-related training
formación, capacitación para el puesto, cargo

joint and several
mancomunado y solidario

joint committee
comité conjunto; comisión conjunta

joint monitoring committees
comités conjuntos de fiscalización

joint stock company
sociedad en comandita por acciones

joint venture
sociedad en participación; empresa, operación conjunta

jumbo borrowing(s)
(obtención de) empréstitos gigantescos
Borrowing or lending in large quantities; usually refers to amounts in excess of US $250,000.

junior creditor
acreedor no prioritario

junior debt; subordinated debt
deuda subordinada
Debt which, in case of liquidation, cannot be paid till payments on other obligations have been made. Opposite of **senior debt**.

junior high school
escuela secundaria de primer ciclo

juridical personality; legal existence
personalidad jurídica

justification
documentos justificativos; documentación de apoyo

just in time (JIT) manufacturing
fabricación "justo a tiempo"
Production and **inventory** control systems designed to produce small lots and to produce the right items in the quantities needed by subsequent production processes at the right time.

- K -

key data
datos clave, básicos

key interest rates
tipos, tasas de interés clave
The main market interest rates - includes **LIBOR**, U.S. **prime rate**, U.S. **federal funds rate** and certain others, depending on where it is used.

key money rate; central rate
tipo, tasa central
The term used to describe the main interest rate set by the central bank (or equivalent) and which effectively governs other market interest rates. In the U.S., it is the **federal funds rate**.

keynote address, speech
discurso principal

keynote speaker; keynoter
orador principal

key species
especies esenciales
Species that have a more profound impact on their ecosystem than other species. They are organisms which provide critical support through webs of interactions to the existence of other species.

kidney cotton; West Indian cotton; Sea Island cotton; Egyptian cotton;
algodón de las Indias Occidentales; algodón de Barbados; algodón egipcio

knapsack spraying
rociado, fumigación con tanque llevado a la espalda

know-how
conocimientos técnicos, tecnológicos

- L -

labor costs
costos de mano de obra; costos del factor trabajo; costos laborales

labor force
fuerza de trabajo, laboral; mano de obra; *a veces:* **población activa**

labor force penetration; labor force participation rate
tasa de actividad
The extent to which those of working age are actually working.

labor-intensive
con gran intensidad de mano de obra; de uso intensivo de mano de obra; de alto coeficiente de mano de obra

labor-intensive industry
industria con gran intensidad de mano de obra

labor-management relations; labor relations; industrial relations
relaciones entre empleados y empleadores; relaciones obrero-patronales

labor market
mercado de trabajo, laboral

labor relations; industrial relations; labor-management relations
relaciones entre empleados y empleadores; relaciones obrero-patronales

labor shed
zona de contratación de mano de obra

laboratory school **see demonstration school**

lag; slippage
retraso; demora; desfase
A delayed climatic effect.

lagged inflation
inflación desfasada

lagging indicator
indicador retrospectivo
A statistic that does not change till after the economy in general has changed, e.g. the value of construction completed.

lamplight fishing; fishing by lamplight
pesca con luz (artificial), al encandilado

land betterment tax
impuesto de valorización, sobre la plusvalía

land consolidation
concentración parcelaria

land development
aprovechamiento, habilitación, acondicionamiento de tierras; urbanización

land equivalent, equivalency ratio - LER
coeficiente de la tierra de cultivo equivalente
Area needed under sole cropping to give as much produce as 1 hectare of **intercropping** or mixed cropping at the same management level, expressed as a ratio.

landfill
vertedero

land improvement
mejoramiento de tierras

landlocked country
país sin litoral, mediterráneo

land reclamation
bonificación, recuperación, saneamiento de tierras

land reform
reforma de la tenencia de la tierra

land register
registro catastral; catastro

land resilience
capacidad de recuperación de la tierra
A measure of the ability of the land to withstand and recover from shock, i.e. a sudden impact such as drought, overgrazing, change in specified land use.

land settlement
asentamiento; colonización

land tax
contribución, impuesto territorial

land tenure rights
derecho de tenencia de la tierra

land tenure system
régimen de tenencia de la tierra

land use plan
plan de utilización de tierras

land use planning
planificación de tierras

land use ratio
coeficiente de utilización de tierras

landed price
precio al desembarque
The quoted or invoiced price of a commodity, including costs of loading, shipping and unloading at destination.

lapse-of-time decision
decisión tácita por vencimiento de un plazo
A decision which is deemed to be approved if no objection is received by a specific date.

last in, first out - LIFO
salida en orden inverso al de adquisición, fabricación, etc.

late bid
oferta fuera de plazo, tardía
Bid submitted after the deadline specified for bid submission.

late maturing [crop]
de maduración tardía

latrine **see** bucket latrine; cistern flush latrine; pit latrine; pour flush latrine; vault toilet; ventilated improved pit latrine

law of diminishing marginal utility
ley de utilidad marginal decreciente
Law which states that although total utility increases, the marginal utility received from consuming each additional unit of a commodity decreases.

law of diminishing returns
ley de rendimientos decrecientes

laydays; laytime
estadía
The period of time agreed between the parties during which the owner shall make and keep the ship available for loading/discharging without payment additional to the freight.

layout
diseño; planos generales (de un proyecto); distribución

layout plan
plan de distribución

laytime **see** laydays

lead agency
organismo director, principal

lead bank; lead manager
banco director
Bank with main responsibility for arranging a bond issue or international **Eurocredit**. Lead manager is also used in the sense of **agent bank**.

lead donor
donante principal

lead economist
economista principal (de un departamento geográfico)

lead manager **see** lead bank

lead time of a project
período de gestación de un proyecto

leading indicator
indicador anticipado
A statistic valued for predicting purposes because its movement is generally followed by a certain movement of the economy in general, e.g. building permits, average weekly work hours, unemployment claims and corporate profits.

leads and lags
adelantos y atrasos
A term referring to changes in the pattern of international payments terms. At any one time a country is extending and receiving trade credit via its exporters and imports. If a devaluation of its currency is feared, its importers with foreign currency obligations may hurry to pay, otherwise their debts will be greater after devaluation, i.e. they "lead" payments. Conversely, exporters will benefit by not hurrying to convert export receipts in foreign currency - they "lag" payments.

leakage
utilidades encubiertas
In investment, benefits to selected parterns by means other than declared financial returns, such as distorted transfer pricing, non-arms length royalties or **management fees** and inflated equipment costs.

learning by doing
aprender sobre la marcha; aprender con la práctica
A method of learning involving practical experience.

learning curve
curva de aprendizaje
An imaginary graph which describes the rate at which people learn something new. Initially, they will normally pick up a lot of information quickly but then will gradually take more time to learn less.

learning materials
materiales didácticos

learning rate
tasa de asimilación de conocimientos

lease **see** finance lease; operating lease; true lease

leaseback
retroarriendo; retrocesión en arrendamiento

leasing
arrendamiento; arrendamiento financiero;
a veces: **leasing financiero**

least cost analysis
análisis de costo mínimo
A type of analysis commonly used to compare alternative projects or project designs when value of output (benefits) cannot be measured adequately (e.g. certain transport projects). If it can be assumed that the (unquantifiable) benefits exceed the cost and if appropriate adjustments are made for any differences in benefits among the alternatives, the task is then to minimize the cost of obtaining them through least-cost analysis.

least developed countries - LLDCs
países (en desarrollo) menos adelantados - PMA

least squares method
método de mínimos cuadrados
An econometric estimation technique involving minimizing the sum of the squares of the vertical distance between the observed data points and the regression line.

legal authority
autorización legal; facultad legal

legal entity, person
persona jurídica

legal existence; juridical personality
personalidad jurídica

legal force
fuerza de ley

legal instruments [agreements, etc.]
instrumentos jurídicos, legales

legal opinion
dictamen jurídico; opinión jurídica

legal person, entity
persona jurídica

legal remedy
recurso (legal)

legal reserve
reserva obligatoria; encaje legal

legal status
condición jurídica

legal tender
moneda de curso legal

lender of last resort
prestamista en última instancia
One of the functions and a major raison d'être of a modern central bank whereby the bank has to provide liquid assets to the banking system when the existing liquid assets of the banking system threaten to deplete.

lending agency, institution
organismo de crédito, crediticio; institución de crédito, crediticia

lending authority
facultad para conceder préstamos
The amount of money that the Bank can lend, based on its paid-in capital.

lending commitment
compromiso de préstamo

lending limit
límite de crédito, de préstamos

lending pipeline; pipeline of projects
proyectos en tramitación, en reserva
Projects which have advanced beyond the stage of appraisal mission departure, i.e. which are expected to be in the forthcoming year's lending program.

lending program
programa de operaciones crediticias; programa de financiamiento

lending rate
tipo, tasa de interés sobre los préstamos; tipo, tasa activo(a)

lengthman [highway maintenance]
peón caminero
A man appointed to maintain a certain length of road.

less developed country - LDC
país en desarrollo; país menos desarrollado - PMD

less than carload freight - LCL
tráfico, mercancías de detalle
A shipment that occupies less than a full railroad car, that may moved from car to car as economy of shipment dictates and on which higher rates than full carload lot rates apply.

letter of acceptance
carta de aceptación
Written notification by the **employer** to the **contractor** of acceptance of his bid.

letter of comfort
carta de seguridades
A written instrument issued by A, where A agrees to make every effort to assure B's compliance with the terms of a contract, but without committing A to perform B's obligation in the event that B is unable to fulfil his obligation. Usually issued by a parent company on behalf of a subsidiary in another country.

letter of credit (L/C)
carta de crédito
Form of documentary credit whereby a bank promises to honor drafts payable to one party, drawn on it by another party.

letter of development policy - LDP [IBRD]
carta de intenciones sobre la política de desarrollo
Letter from the Government of a country receiving a structural adjustment loan to the President of the Bank, setting out the Government's medium-term objectives for structural change and the range of measures that it intends to take over several years to achieve these objectives.

letter of intent - LOI
carta, declaración de intención, de intenciones
Used to put in writing a preliminary understanding of parties who intend to enter into a contract.

letter of no objection - LNO [imports]
consulta sobre posibles objeciones
In some countries, a letter sent by the Government
to a domestic company, asking that company if it
has any objection to specific items being imported.
The company may make an objection, thereby
preventing the goods from being imported.

letter of sectoral policy [IBRD]
carta de intenciones sobre la política sectorial
Letter from the Government of a country receiving
a **sectoral adjustment loan** to the President of the
Bank, setting out the Government's medium-term
objectives for sectoral change and the range of
measures that it intends to take over several years
to achieve these objectives.

letter of understanding
carta de entendimiento

Levant cotton; herbaceous cotton; American short
staple cotton; Arabian cotton
algodón herbáceo

leveling off
nivelación; estabilización

level annuity system
**sistema de pagos totales iguales (de principal e
intereses)**
The level annuity system entails equal aggregate
payments of principal and interest (i.e. with
principal repayments made in gradually ascending
amounts). This system was used by the World
Bank prior to 1975.

level border irrigation **see** basin irrigation

level repayment
reembolso en cuotas iguales
Repayment scheme where repayments are at a
fixed level, even though the interest rate may
change.

leverage (ratio) [US]; gearing (ratio) [UK]
**nivel de endeudamiento relativo al capital;
relación endeudamiento-capital propio; relación
pasivo-capital**
Ratio of debt/liabilities to equity/assets. Includes
debt and **debt-equity ratios.** [See also guarantee
leverage]

leverage, to
**ejercer influencia; ejercer, producir efecto
multiplicador [finanzas] [diferentes contextos
pueden requerir distintas traducciones]**
[See also highly leveraged; underleveraged]

leveraged buyout - LBO
**compra de una empresa con fondos tomados en
préstamo**
Purchase of a company by a small group of
investors, often including management, mostly
with borrowed funds. The debt is usually repaid
from the company's cash flow or from the sale of
assets.

levy
gravamen (tributario)
[see also betterment levy]

liabilities
pasivo; obligaciones
The credit half of a balance sheet.
[see also accrued liabilities; contingent liability;
currency liabilities; current liabilities; deposit
liabilities; long-term liabiliaties; sight liabilities;
sundry liabilities; tax liability; temporary
liabilities; unfunded liabilities]

liability management
gestión de pasivos
[see also asset and liability management]

LIBOR [London interbank offered rate]
**LIBOR [tipo, tasa de oferta interbancaria de
Londres]**
The interest rate at which banks in London are
prepared to lend funds to first-class banks. It is
used to determine the interest rate payable on most
Eurocredits.

licensing agreement
**acuerdo, convenio de licencia, de concesión de
licencia**

lien; charge [legal]
gravamen; embargo preventivo; cargo

life (of a project)
duración, vida útil

life cycle cost evaluation
evaluación de los costos durante la vida útil (de equipos)
Evaluation of equipment over its whole life, including initial purchase, maintenance and operation.

life expectancy
esperanza de vida

lifeline tariff
tarifa mínima, vital
A special low tariff for a commodity (e.g. gas or electricity) made available to disadvantaged groups (e.g. poor or elderly) or to all consumers but only up to a certain amount.

lifelong education; continuing education; recurrent education
educación permanente

life of a loan
vigencia de un préstamo

light Arabian crude; Saudi Arabian light crude
(petróleo) crudo liviano, ligero de Arabia Saudita
The world's most prolific crude oil, frequently used as a **marker crude** in establishing the prices of other crudes.

light gray cotton **see** gray cotton

light industry
industria ligera, liviana

light spotted cotton
algodón ligeramente manchado

limited international bidding - LIB
licitación internacional limitada
International competitive bidding by direct invitation without open advertisement.

limited liability company
sociedad de responsabilidad limitada

limited recourse finance
financiamiento con recurso limitado
Finance arranged on the basis of the lender having recourse to the borrower only in certain circumstances (e.g. the loan to British Petroleum (BP) to finance the Forties oil field in the North Sea, where the lenders had no recourse to BP if there was insufficient oil).

line breeding
cruzamiento continuo; cruzamiento absorbente
Special form of inbreeding to maintain a high genetic relationship to a desirable ancestor.

line department
departamento ejecutivo, de ejecución, de operaciones
[see also line ministry]

line-haul [transportation]
transporte, acarreo entre terminales

line item [budget]
partida (presupuestaria)
A specific revenue or expenditure separately detailed in a budget.

line kilometer [surveying]
kilómetro lineal
A kilometer as measured by the line of flight of an aircraft. Used to measure the distance covered by an aircraft when taking remote sensing images.

line management
dirección; supervisión

line management position
cargo ejecutivo, de dirección, de supervisión

line manager
supervisor directo, inmediato

line ministry, department
ministerio, departamento de operaciones, sectorial, de ejecución
A Government ministry responsible for implementing a program or group of programs as opposed to one responsible for general planning and administration, e.g. would include Agriculture, Social Security but exclude Finance, Planning.

line position
cargo, puesto ejecutivo, de operaciones

line staff
personal ejecutivo, de operaciones

linear programming
programación lineal
A mathematical procedure to obtain an optimal answer to a series of equations that usually specify resources available; technological relationships of the production process; goals of the society; relevant constraints to any solution that is found.

liner (shipping) conference
conferencia marítima
A combination of shipping companies or owners which sets common liner freight rates on a particular route and which regulates the provision of services.

link **see** UHF link; VHF link

linkage **see** backward-forward integration, linkage; backward integration, linkage

liquefied natural gas - LNG
gas natural licuado - GNL

liquefied petroleum gas - LPG
gas de petróleo licuado - GPL

liquid assets; quick assets
activos líquidos, disponibles; disponibilidades
Cash in banks and on hand and marketable securities.

liquid assets portofolio; liquidity portfolio [IFC]
cartera de activos líquidos

liquid ratio **see** acid test ratio

liquidated damages
cláusulas penales; penalidades; multa; daños y perjuicios previstos en un contrato
A sum of damages agreed upon in advance between parties to a contract, to be paid by the party who breaches the contract, as opposed to **unliquidated damages**, which are not fixed in advance, and are liable to be overturned by the courts.

liquidation value; forced sale value
valor de venta forzosa
The price obtainable from an immediate sale, where the seller is under either legal or voluntary compulsion to sell.

liquidity management; liquidity portfolio management
gestión de la liquidez

liquidity portfolio [IFC]; liquid assets portfolio
cartera de activos líquidos

liquidity position
situación de liquidez

liquidity ratio
coeficiente de liquidez
The ratio of the actual level of liquidity to projected three year **net cash requirements**.

liquidity shortage
insuficiencia de liquidez

liquidity squeeze
crisis de liquidez

listing (of securities)
cotización (de valores en la bolsa)
The process of public quotation on a Stock Exchange of a share or bond.

literacy; literacy education
alfabetización

literacy level
nivel de alfabetización

live fencing
setos, cercos vivos
The use of live trees as boundary markers for the production of fruit, fodder or other products, instead of wooden fences.

live storage, capacity
capacidad útil

living area
área, superficie habitable

load **see** peak load

load, base
carga de base, fundamental

load bearing capacity; traffic bearing capacity
capacidad de tráfico

load factor [electricity]
factor de carga
The ratio of the average load over a designated period of time to the peak load occurring in that period.
[see also system load factor]

load fund
fondo mutuo que cobra comisión
Mutual fund which charges a handling fee.

loan account
cuenta del préstamo

loan agreement
convenio de préstamo

loan application
solicitud de préstamo

loan assumption agreement
convenio de asunción de préstamo

loan capital
capital en préstamo; empréstito

loan commitment
compromiso de préstamo

loan costing see loan pricing

loan equivalency pricing
fijación de precios equivalentes en operaciones de cofinanciamiento
Pricing procedure adopted in Bank cofinancing, whereby credit alternatives offered by the Bank, such as loans and guarantees, are all priced comparably and do not compete among themselves.

loan investment
inversión en forma de préstamo

loan officer
oficial del préstamo, de préstamos

loan origination fee
comisión por tramitación de solicitud
The fee typically charged by a DFI to recover the cost of investigating and granting a request by a borrower for a loan.

loan portfolio
cartera de préstamos
The unpaid loans of a lending organization.

loan pricing, costing
fijación, determinación del costo de un préstamo
Establishing the interest rate of a loan.

loan processing
tramitación del (de un) préstamo

loan proceeds see allocation of loan proceeds

loan recovery
recuperación de un préstamo, de préstamos

local area network - LAN
red de área local - LAN

local authority; local government
administración local; autoridades municipales, provinciales, etc.

local competitive bidding - LCB see competitive bidding in accordance with local procedures

local cost; onshore cost
costo en moneda nacional

local currency
moneda nacional

local employee [IBRD]
funcionario, empleado contratado localmente

local government; local authority
administración local; autoridades municipales, provinciales, etc.

local shopping
comparación nacional de precios
Procurement based on comparing price quotations obtained from several local suppliers.

localization
autoctonización
Use of local staff.

localization economies
economías de ubicación
Agglomeration economies which are external to a specific company but internal to a specific industry. They commonly result from the increased demand for goods and services from specific industries. Increased demand leads to increased competition and efficiencies among firms intending to provide **inputs** to production. It also includes vertical and horizontal integration of specific industries, where ancillary industries within the same area provide **inputs** or complementary services to other industries and firms. Cf. **urbanization economies**.

locked in capital gains
ganancias de capital realizadas

locked in interest rate
tipo, tasa de interés inmodificable

locked-up capital
capital inmovilizado
Capital that is unavailable as it is committed to other uses.

lock gate price; sluice price; sluice gate price
precio de compuerta
A theoretical cif price used in calculating European Communities supplementary levies on imports of pork, poultry and eggs.

logging [forestry]
corte y extracción de madera en trozas; explotación forestal; extracción de madera

long form audit report
informe largo de auditoría
A detailed report or letter prepared by an auditor following an audit. It is addressed to the management or directors.

long-run average incremental cost - LRAIC
costo incremental medio a largo plazo

long-run marginal cost - LRMC; efficiency price; efficient price [electricity tariffs]
costo marginal a largo plazo
The cost of meeting an increase in consumption, sustained indefinitely into the future, when needed capacity adjustments are possible.

long staple cotton
algodón de fibra larga
Cotton with fibers of 1 1/8 inches long or more.

long-term blended cost rate - LTB [IFC]
coeficiente de costos combinados a largo plazo
A rate used by IFC to assist in determining the performance of its loan portfolio, it is based on three parts of average costs of borrowed funds and one part capital resources.

long-term debt ratio
relación de endeudamiento a largo plazo
Ratio of long-term debt to total assets.

Long-term Facility for Financing Purchases of Capital Goods by Developing Countries [IBRD]
Servicio de financiamiento a largo plazo para la compra de bienes de capital por los países en desarrollo

long-term liabilities
pasivos a largo plazo
Liabilities that will become due in the future, usually more than one year.

long-term prime rate - LTPR
tipo, tasa preferencial a largo plazo
Prime rate used in Japan.

longitudinal survey
encuesta longitudinal
Surveys of limited populations in purposively selected areas, recording events as they actually occur (as opposed to making estimates).

loss in weight; waste [commerce]
pérdida; desperdicio

loss leader
artículo de propaganda, de cebo, de reclamo

loss of load probability - LOLP
probabilidad de pérdida de carga
A measurement of the probability of power outages.

loss payee
beneficiario
In insurance, a third party suffering the actual loss named as beneficiary of the policy.

loss provision; provision for losses; reserve for losses
reserva para pérdidas

low absorber [country]
país de baja capacidad de absorción
Oil exporting **capital surplus country** that has been able to make very limited use of oil revenues for domestic development. Includes Saudi Arabia and Kuwait.

lower heating value; net heating value - NHV; net calorific value - NCV
poder calorífico neto - PCN

lower middle income country - LMIC
país de ingreso mediano bajo
Developing country with a per capita income in 1980 exceeding $600 but below $1200. Include some Latin American countries, some South-East Asian ones (such as Philippines and Thailand), Mediterranean countries (such as Morocco and Tunisia) and some sub-Saharan African countries (such as Côte d'Ivoire and Nigeria).

lower quality old debt
deudas anteriores con condiciones menos favorables

lower secondary education
educación secundaria de primer ciclo, de ciclo básico

lowest bidder
licitante que presenta la oferta más baja
[see also second lowest bidder]

lowest evaluated bid
oferta evaluada como la más baja
Bid which is considered to have the lowest price, taking into account factors such as time of performance, reliability of construction methods or efficiency of equipment, availability of maintenance services and other criteria disclosed to the **bidder**. The relative factors should be stated in the **bidding documents** and should be expressed in monetary terms or given a relative weight.

lowest priced bidder
licitante que presenta la oferta de menor precio
The **bidder** who offers a bid at the lowest price.

low income country
país de ingreso bajo

low load factor consumer [electricity]
consumidor de bajo factor de carga
A consumer using a low amount of electricity.

low standard road
camino, carretera de normas reducidas, bajas

low voltage consumer [electricity]
consumidor de bajo voltaje

lump sum borrowing [IFC]
empréstito de suma global
A currency-specific borrowing made in a lump sum by IFC from IBRD for its short-term future needs.

lump sum contract [consultants]
contrato a suma alzada
Contract where payments are based on an agreed lump sum with no matching of **inputs** to payment being made once the figure has been agreed.

lump sum loan
préstamo de suma global
One of two types of fixed rate loan made by the Bank to IFC involving currency-specific lump sum amounts to meet net cash requirements for the following six to twelve months.

lump sum price
tanto alzado; monto global; suma alzada; precio global

- M -

macro-level accountability
responsabilidad macroeconómica
Macroeconomic accountability (including financial accountability and accountability for overall economic performance), e.g. congruence between public policy and actual implementation, the efficient allocation and use of public resources and external auditing and follow-up to this auditing.

macromanagement
macrogestión

main contractor; prime, principal contractor
contratista principal, primario

mainframe computer
gran computadora; gran ordenador [España]

main power grid [electricity]
red principal

mainstream, to
incorporar a las actividades habituales (del Banco)

maintenance of value - MOV (of IBRD capital)
mantenimiento del valor
The provision in the Bank's Articles of Agreement requiring members to maintain the value of that portion of their paid-in capital that is subscribed in their own currency in terms of the subscription price (i.e. 100,000 gold dollars).

maintenance of value settlement; settlement of maintenance of value
liquidación por concepto de mantenimiento del valor

major currency
moneda importante

malnourished
malnutrido

malnutrition
malnutrición

manageable
controlable; manejable; gobernable; etc.

managed costs
gastos generales directos
Discretionary and direct overhead expenses for which budget units are responsible.

managed economy
economía dirigida

management **see** asset and liability management; cash management; collegial management; comanagement; corporate management; country assistance management; demand management; economic management; IDA management fee; labor-management relations; liability management; line management; liquidity management; participative management; project management; range management; risk management; supply management; water management; watershed management

Management [World Bank]
la administración

management accounting
contabilidad de gestión
The design, installation and operation of financial planning, budgeting and financial accounting systems with the use of appropriate methods and techniques to monitor and control all aspects of financial operations and the coordination of these systems, methods and techniques with the primary activities of an entity.

management audit
evaluación administrativa
A review and appraisal of any or all parts of management activity.

management auditor
inspector administrativo

management by objectives - MBO
gestión, administración por objetivos

management chart; performance chart; working table
diagrama, gráfico de situación

management company
**compañía administradora, de administración,
de gestión**

management consultant
**consultor en dirección de empresas, en
administración de empresas**

management contract
contrato de administración, gestión
Contract where the contractor assumes
responsibility for the management of the
investment project or a significant part of its
operations and where his remuneration
substantially depends on the production, revenues
or profits of the investment project.

management development
**perfeccionamiento del personal directivo;
perfeccionamiento de la función de gestión**

management fee
comisión de administración; comisión de gestión
Fee payable to **lead bank** for handling bonds.

management game
juego de gestión

management group; managing group
consorcio, grupo de dirección, directivo

management information system - MIS
sistema de información para la administración
System, usually computerized, designed to provide
the management of a particular organization with
the key information needed for decision-making.

management letter [auditing]
carta a la administración
A formal letter from auditors to the management
concerning the accounts. It will discuss any
deficiencies or weaknesses which the entity should
remedy for its own protection.

management participation system;
codetermination; comanagement
**cogestión; coadministración; sistema de
participación en la gestión; administración**
System which gives employees the right to be
represented in the decisions of a corporation.

management succession planning
plan de sucesión para cargos de dirección

managerial accounting
contabilidad gerencial
That portion of accounting which attempts to
supply management with quantitative information
as a basis for decisions, as opposed to
management accounting which is accounting
designed for or adapted to the needs of information
and control at the various administrative levels of
an organization.

managers
administradores; gerentes; directivos; etc.

managing group
consorcio, grupo de dirección, directivo

managing unit
unidad directiva

mandatory planning
planificación obligatoria, preceptiva

man-day
día-hombre

man-made capital
capital creado por el hombre

man-made disaster
desastre provocado por el hombre

man-month contract
contrato por meses-hombre
Contract where payment is based on agreed time-
based rates (usually the man-month rate),
subsistence allowance for staff and reimbursable
items.

manpower development
**perfeccionamiento, formación de recursos
humanos, de la mano de obra**

manpower planning
**planificación de recursos humanos, de la mano
de obra**

manufacturing grade [meat]
calidad para elaboración

Manufacturing Unit Value Index [World Bank]
índice del valor unitario de las manufacturas - VUM
Industrial countries' indices of US dollar unit values of manufactured exports to developing countries. There are two indices - the cif index which combines a 90% weight of FOB export prices with a 10% weight of transport costs and a FOB index.

mapping see school mapping

marginal benefit
beneficio marginal

marginal capacity cost - MCC
costo marginal de mantenimiento de la capacidad
Present worth of the least-cost investment stream divided by **present worth** of the stream of incremental output resulting from the investment.

marginal cost
costo marginal
[**see also** long-run marginal cost]

marginal cost pricing
fijación de precios al costo marginal
A policy used to minimize selling price or to lower costs to keep a business operating during a period of poor sales, by which the firm charges for each unit sold only the addition to total costs which results from manufacturing that unit, usually just material and direct labor.

marginal disutility
desutilidad marginal
The extra disutility resulting from a small change in some variable.

marginal effective tax rate - METR
tasa impositiva efectiva marginal
A measurement of the effect of taxes on investors' **rate of return** for an incremental addition to their activities.

marginal efficiency of capital
eficiencia, productividad marginal del capital
In popular terms, the expected rate of profit. More rigourously, it is a **discount rate** at which the perpetual annual yields of an asset are expressed in **present value** terms. The **present value** is obtained such that it is equal to the **replacement cost** of the asset or its supply price. For example if the supply or **replacement cost** of an asset is $ 80 and it yields a perpetual annuity of $5 then the **present value** of the perpetual annuity is equal to $80 if the rate of discount applied is .0625 or 6.25%. This 6.25% is the marginal efficiency of capital.

marginal national savings rate
tasa marginal de ahorro nacional

marginal propensity (to consume, to save, etc.)
propensión marginal (al consumo, al ahorro, etc.)
An induced increase (in consumption or saving) as a proportion of the increase in income. If income increases by $10 and consumption or saving by $5 then the marginal propensity is 0.5.

marginal physical product - MPP
producto físico marginal
The change in total product that results from employing one additional unit of a variable resource together with other fixed resources.

marginal reserve requirement
encaje legal adicional; reserva obligatoria marginal
Additional deposits that by law depository institutions (e.g. banks) must set aside in their vaults or with the central bank. In the U.S., this applies to additional reserve requirements on increased managed liabilities imposed by the Federal Reserve, in order to curtail the expansion of bank lending.

marginal revenue product - MRP
ingreso marginal
The change in the firm's total revenue from selling the marginal physical product that results from employing one additional unit of a resource together with other fixed resources.

marginal soil(s)
suelo(s) de fertilidad marginal, de baja fertilidad

marginal utility
utilidad marginal
The utility derived by an individual from his consumption of an additional unit of a commodity or service at a given time. It may also be regarded as the utility of a unit of the commodity or service the consumption of which an individual may decide to forego.

marginal value product
valor del producto marginal

margin of preference; preference, preferential margin
preferencia; margen de preferencia
[see also domestic preference]

marker crude; benchmark crude [oil]
crudo de referencia
Saudi Arabian light crude oil (gravity API 34 degrees) employed as the standard on which OPEC price changes have been based.

marker price; benchmark price [oil]
precio de referencia
The reference price used by OPEC for oil price changes, based on the price of **Saudi Arabian light crude oil**.

market-clearing prices
precios de equilibrio del mercado
A price for an item which attracts just enough buyers as there are buyers. If prices are lower demand will be too high; if higher demand will be too low.

market-clearing quotations
cotizaciones de precios de equilibrio del mercado

market-clearing returns
rentabilidad de equilibrio del mercado

market-eligible countries
países que tienen acceso al mercado financiero
Countries that have access to financial markets.

market-friendly
en armonía con, que armonice con el mercado; de conformidad con las leyes del mercado

"market-in-hand" agreement
contrato "mercado en mano"
Turnkey contract requiring **contractor** to assist in sales.

market intermediation
intermediación del mercado
Acting on the market (i.e. buying and/or selling of **securities**) on behalf of someone else.

market power
influencia en el mercado

market-related lending
financiamiento en condiciones de mercado
Lending at market rate and under market conditions (Cf. **commercial lending**).

market timing
distribución óptima de los vencimientos
Taking advantage of securities of different maturities.

market value
valor comercial, de mercado

marketable securities
valores negociables
Equity **securities** or debt securities that are actively traded or which can be otherwise bought or sold.

marketability
posibilidad de comercialización, de colocación; comerciabilidad

marketing
comercialización [productos]; colocación [valores]

marketing arrangement
acuerdo de comercialización

marketing board
junta de comercialización

mark-up
margen de utilidad; aumento de precio

marshal evidence, to [ICSID]
presentar y ofrecer pruebas

marshalling yard
patio de maniobra, de clasificación

mass media
medios de información, difusión, comunicación

mass production
producción en gran escala, en serie

master plan
plan maestro

Master Loan Agreement
convenio de préstamo entre el Banco y la CFI
Agreement between the Bank and IFC on Bank lending to IFC. First issued 1971 and periodically updated as the Bank makes further loans to IFC.

matched funding [IFC]; matching funds
financiamiento, fondos de contrapartida
Funding needed by the IFC to commit a loan. It must match the loan in terms of amount and maturity.

matching contribution
contribución de contrapartida
A contribution that is conditional on a similar amount of funds being contributed by another party.

matching credit
crédito de contrapartida
[**see also** tax sparing]

matching funds **see** matched funding

matching grant
donación de contrapartida
A grant given when an equal sum is provided by the recipient or a third party.

matching payment
pago de contrapartida

mathematical expectation [mathematics]
esperanza matemática
The mean value of single observations drawn from a finite or infinite universe in repeated samplings.

matrix reporting
responsabilidad ante más de una autoridad, entidad, jefe
Staff or offices reporting to more than one agency.

maturation (of borrowers from IDA to IBRD loans)
maduración

mature investments [IFC]
inversiones que han alcanzado su madurez, su fase productiva
Investments which are just at the beginning of the stage at which they will start to become profitable.

mature markets [securities]
mercados bien establecidos

mature project
proyecto en avanzado estado de ejecución, próximo a terminarse

maturity (of a loan, bond, etc.)
vencimiento (de un préstamo, obligación, etc.); plazo de vencimiento

maturity mismatch
discordancia entre los vencimientos
Having borrowings and loans with different maturities. This could mean, for example in the case of the Bank, that borrowings the Bank had made on the capital market to finance certain loans it had made were due before it had received the money from the loans.

maturity transformation
modificación de los vencimientos
Reborrowing, in order to extend the maturity of a loan.

maximum aggregate liability [MIGA]
responsabilidad global máxima
The maximum liability of MIGA for all claims arising from coverage for one project enterprise.

maximum amount of guarantee
monto máximo de garantía
The maximum amount of guarantee coverage provided under all forms of coverage.

maximum likelihood method
método de máxima verosimilitud
An econometric estimation technique which involves the maximization of the likelihood function of the sample observations with respect to the values of the parameters of the equation(s) being estimated. It chooses those values of the parameters which are "most likely" to have generated the sample observations.

McNamara Fellow
becario McNamara

McNamara Fellowship
beca McNamara

mean annual increment - MAI [forestry]
incremento anual medio
The total growth of a stand of trees divided by the total age.

means-tested pension plan
plan de pensiones según, conforme a las necesidades, con comprobación previa de medios de vida

measured production
producción medida, efectiva
The actual production of a farmer as measured, as opposed to the estimated production.

meat processing
elaboración de carne

mechanical completion [projects]
terminación de las instalaciones
The final stage of a project where the actual physical equipment has been installed.

medium absorber [oil exporter]
país de mediana capacidad de absorción
Oil exporting **capital surplus country** which has only been able to make some use of oil revenues for domestic development. Includes Iran, Iraq and Libya.

medium staple cotton
algodón de fibra mediana
Cotton with fibers of 1 to 1 1/8 inches long.

membership [IFC]
calidad de miembro; *a veces*: **ingreso; miembros**

membership application
solicitud de ingreso

membership shares [World Bank]
acciones de adhesión
These were introduced in connection with the 1979 **General Capital Increase** in order to ensure that the voting power of small members was not eroded by the Capital Increase. A special allocation of 250 shares, known as membership shares, was made to each member in addition to the pro rata allocation. No payment was required for these shares nor were they included in the Bank's lending authority.

membership votes
votos de adhesión

memo item; memorandum entry, item
partida de memorando; partida pro memoria
An explanatory notation in a book of accounts which does not change the balance in any account.

memorandum account
cuenta de orden
A temporary account used to store accounting data prior to actual receipt or disbursement of the sums concerned.

memorandum entry, item; memo item
partida de memorando; partida pro memoria; partida informativa
An explanatory notation in a book of accounts which does not change the balance in any account.

Memorandum of Administrative Arrangements [ICSID]
Memorando sobre Arreglos Administrativos

memorandum of law
memorando jurídico; dictamen legal
A legal opinion signed by a legal officer of a government authorized to give legal opinions on his Government's behalf.

memorandum of understanding
memorando de acuerdo
A written document detailing the points upon which two or more parties agree.

memorial [ICSID]
memorial

menu approach
método de la lista de opciones

merchandise balance **see** trade balance

merchandising
comercialización; ventas

merchant bank [UK] **see** investment bank [US]

merger
fusión

merit goods
bienes preferentes, deseables; bienes de interés social
Goods the consumption of which is deemed to be intrinsically desirable. In the case of such goods it is argued that consumer sovereignty does not hold and that if consumers are unwilling to purchase adequate quantities of such goods they should be compelled or encouraged to do so. Examples are education and health services.

merit increase
aumento por mérito

merit point system
sistema de puntos
In procurement, a system whereby points are given to each bid in respect to a number of factors. These points are then correlated with the **bid price** and the contract awarded on the basis of the best points/price combination.

message front-end system
sistema múltiple de mensajes financieros

messages [agricultural extension]
contenido técnico
The basic information that an **agricultural extension** scheme wishes to impart to farmers.

metal works
estructuras metálicas

Metals and Minerals Price Index [IBRD]
índice de precios de los metales y minerales

meter rent [electricity]
cargo por medidor, por contador
The income received from electricity metering.

mezzanine financing
financiamiento "mezzanine"
Financing using medium-risk capital, as opposed to pure debt financing. The risk is intermediate - between secured or senior debt and equity. It differs from venture capital lending in that owners surrender only a low amount of equity.

MIBOR [= Madrid Interbank Offered Rate]
MIBOR (tipo, tasa de oferta interbancaria de Madrid)

microdata
microdatos; datos detallados

micro-level accountability
responsabilidad microeconómica
Microeconomic accountability, e.g. ensuring efficiency in investment and in the production and delivery of goods and services.

micromanagement
microgestión

micro-sprayer irrigation
riego por microaspersión

microteaching
microenseñanza
Scaled-down version of teaching, planned to develop new teaching skills and analyse existing ones. The technique provides teaching practice in a situation in which the complexities of the classroom are minimized by restricting the number of pupils and length of lesson and by focusing on specific teaching skills.

middle income country
país de ingreso mediano
Developing country with per capita income of $400 or more.

midterm project review mission [World Bank]
misión de supervisión general del proyecto a mediados del período de ejecución

Midterm Review - MTR [IDA]
examen de mediados del período (de una reposición)
Review of IDA resources in the middle of a replenishment period.

midyear review
examen de mitad del ejercicio, de mitad de año

milling yield
rendimiento en la fabricación, la molienda, el maquinado

millions of barrels per day oil equivalent - mbdoe
millones de barriles diarios de equivalente en petróleo - mbdep

minehead price
valor en boca de mina
The price of a mineral as it comes out of the mine, i.e. excluding transportation and processing.

mineral lick; salt lick
salegar

mine run coal; run-of-mine coal
carbón sin clasificar, tal como sale, en bruto
Ungraded coal of various sizes as it comes from the mine.

minimum cash ratio
encaje legal; coeficiente mínimo de encaje

minimum cash requirement
(porcentaje de) reserva mínima obligatoria; encaje legal

minimum package project
proyecto de contenido mínimo

minimum tillage
labranza mínima
Planting crops through a sod of dead weeds or stubble.

minority threshold [IBRD]
umbral de veto de una minoría
Situation whereby a minority has an effective veto because a certain majority is required to effect a change and the minority holds enough votes to prevent this majority being obtained, e.g. in the World Bank, the US could block changes requiring 80% majority when it had a 20% shareholding.

misalignment (of rates of exchange)
desajuste, divergencia entre tipos de cambio

misallocation of resources
asignación desacertada de los recursos

misprocurement [IBRD]
adquisición no conforme con los procedimientos reglamentarios
Procurement not in accordance with agreed procedures.

mission see appraisal mission; audit mission; composite mission; end-of-mission document; external review mission; field mission; full mission; investment review mission; midterm project review mission; post appraisal mission; preappraisal mission; review mission; supervision mission

mission statement [EDI]
declaración de objetivos

mitigation plan; environmental management plan; action plan
plan preventivo; plan de ordenación ambiental
Part of a formal project environmental assessment, this plan outlines feasible and cost-effective measures which may reduce potentially significant adverse environmental impacts to acceptable levels. It should provide details of proposed work programs and schedules to ensure that the proposed environmental actions are in phase with engineering activities throughout preparation. The Bank uses all three terms.

mixed enterprise
empresa mixta

mixed farming project
proyecto agropecuario; *a veces*: **proyecto de cultivos múltiples**

mixed fertilizer see compound fertilizer

mixed financing; blend financing
financiamiento combinado (del BIRF y la AIF)

mixed forest
bosque mixto
Type of temperate forest, consisting of trees of different species.

mixed-use forest
bosque de usos múltiples
Forest which has uses other than timber production.

mobile training unit
unidad móvil de formación, de capacitación

mobilization advance [contracts]
anticipo para movilización
Advance payment to a contractor to enable him to start work.

mobilization costs
costos de movilización
In a construction project, the initial costs needed to get a project under way, including advance payments, bonds, etc.

mobilization ratio [IFC]
coeficiente de movilización
Ratio of project cost net of IFC financing to IFC financing.

model bid documents
modelos de documentos de licitación

model school **see** demonstration school

modified Bruno ratio; internal exchange rate
coeficiente modificado de Bruno; tipo de cambio interno
As for the **Bruno ratio** but using for the entire project life instead of for just one year.

moisture stress
estrés por falta de humedad

monetary aggregates
agregados monetarios
The main indicators of the monetary status. Include such features as monetary base and **money supply**.

monetary correction
corrección monetaria
Macroeconomic changes to the **money supply**, e.g. by adjusting interest rates or altering the amount of money in circulation.

monetary ease
relajación monetaria; flexibilidad monetaria

Policy of reducing restrictions on the availability of money, e.g. by easing credit restrictions.

monetary expansion
expansión monetaria; expansión de la masa monetaria

monetary restraint
austeridad monetaria
Holding down the rate of growth of the **money supply**.

monetary stringency
constricción monetaria

monetization
monetización

monetized GDP
PIB monetizado

money at call **see** call money

money center banks
bancos establecidos en las principales plazas financieras
Bank based in a large financial center (e.g. New York or London).

money income
ingreso monetario

money-losing operation
operación deficitaria

money market
mercado monetario, de dinero
The market for short-term debt instruments, such as **certificates of deposit, commercial paper, bankers' acceptances, Treasury bills, discount notes** and others. These instruments are all liquid and tend to be safe. [**see** note to **capital market, financial market**].

money market (mutual) fund - MMF; mutual fund
fondo común de inversiones; fondo mutuo
A mutual fund specializing in high yield short-term instruments of credit such as **Treasury Bills, certificates of deposit, commercial paper, bankers' acceptances** and **repurchase agreements**. For the difference between FCP and SICAV, see mutual fund.

money market paper
títulos, valores del mercado monetario

money market rate
tasa del mercado monetario; tasa de los fondos comunes de inversiones
The rate of interest in the **money market**. In the U.S., there is no single rate but a series of rates, including the **prime rate**, the Federal Reserve **discount rate**, the **Federal Funds rate**, the 1 month **commercial paper** rate and the 3 and 6 month **Treasury Bill** rate.

money stock, supply
oferta monetaria; medio circulante

money wage
salario monetario, nominal

moneyness
liquidez
Closeness to being money; ease with which an asset can be spent; liquidity.

monitoring
observación; verificación; seguimiento; vigilancia; supervisión

monitoring and evaluation - M & E
seguimiento y evaluación

monoculture; sole cropping
monocultivo

monocyclic management
ordenación monocíclica
Forest management system which provides for the removal of all merchantable trees down to a specific diameter at breast height in a single operation, followed by a poison - girdling of remaining large noncommercial stems. Silvicultural treatment is continued at intervals to promote the growth of desirable species.

monopoly rent
renta de monopolio

moral hazard
riesgo moral
Irresponsible conduct by the insured which is likely to increase the possibility of loss.

mortgage bank
banco hipotecario

mortgage financing
préstamos, créditos hipotecarios

most-favored-nation clause
cláusula de la nación más favorecida
A clause in an international trade agreement which states that contracting parties to an agreement are bound to grant to each other treatment as favorable as they extend to any other country regarding the application of import and export duties and other trade regulations. First put forward at Geneva Trade Conference, 1947 and became a part of GATT regulations.

most immediately impacted (MII) countries
países inmediatamente afectados

most seriously affected countries - MSA
países más gravemente afectados

mother and child health (MCH) center
centro de salud maternoinfantil

motivator [family planning]
promotor

motor octane number - MON
índice de octano; octanaje
A measurement of the octane quality of gasoline relating to part throttle operation.

mountain forest
bosque de altura

mountain rice; upland rice; highland rice
arroz de montaña, de tierras altas, de secano

moving average **see** running average

multiattribute decision analysis
técnica de análisis de decisiones tomando en cuenta múltiples atributos
Technique of decision analysis which allows tradeoffs between objectives to be analysed.

multicropping; multiple cropping
cultivos múltiples

multicurrency clause [loan contract]
cláusula de, sobre múltiples monedas
A clause in a loan agreement stating that more than one currency may be used in paying or redeeming the loan.

multidwelling houses
viviendas multifamiliares

Multifibre Arrangement
Acuerdo Multifibras

multigrade teaching
enseñanza simultánea de varios grados
Teaching where more than one grade is taught in the same class due to shortage of teachers and/or low amount of pupils.

multilateral investment insurance
seguro multilateral de inversiones

multilateral trade negotiations - MTN
negociaciones comerciales multilaterales

multilevel farming **see** multistory farming

multimedia training modules [EDI]
módulos audiovisuales de capacitación

multimodal transport
transporte multimodal

multiple cropping; multicropping
cultivos múltiples
Growing two or more crops in the same year on the same field.

(multiple) (currency) option bond
bono con opción de cambio de divisas
Bond (usually **Eurobond**) which gives the lender the right to opt to receive interest and/or capital in a currency other than that in which the bond is denominated.

multiple stage tax
impuesto por etapas, en cascada
A tax which has more than one rate such as income tax in most countries.

multiple trading approaches
sistema de múltiples procedimientos para las transacciones

multiplier **see** credit multiplier

multiproduct agency credit line [IFC]
línea de crédito para productos múltiples a través de agentes

multipurpose berth
puesto de atraque de fines múltiples

multipurpose project
proyecto de fines múltiples

multisectoral general equilibrium model
modelo multisectorial de equilibrio general
A **computable general equilibrium model** which covers several sectors.

multishift teaching
enseñanza en múltiples turnos, jornadas

multistory farming; multilevel farming
cultivos mixtos silvoagropecuarios
Intercropping trees, shrubs and crops of various heights for total ground cover.

multivariate technique
técnica de variables múltiples
A technique of analysis (normally of a statistical nature) which involves more than two variables.

multiyear rescheduling arrangement; multiyear restructuring agreement - MYRA
acuerdo de reprogramación multianual de la deuda
Agreement in **commercial bank** negotiations which allowed for restructuring over a period of years rather than annually, to reduce the burden imposed by annual restructurings.

mutual fund; money market (mutual) fund
fondo común de inversiones; fondo mutuo

mutually offsetting entries
partidas que se compensan mutuamente
In accounts, two entries which cancel each other out.

- N -

narrow money
dinero en el sentido estricto
Easily available money, i.e. cash, checking accounts, very short-term liquid funds, etc. Equivalent to M1.

national agricultural research system - NARS
sistema nacional de investigaciones agronómicas

national environmental action plan - NEAP
plan nacional de protección ambiental - PNPA
Environmental action plan at the level of an individual country. They are intended to ensure that decision-makers take environmental issues into consideration in policy formulation and are closely linked to World Bank projects.

natural capital
capital natural
The natural environment. Includes land, watercourses, the oceans, the air, etc.

natural gas liquids - NGL
líquidos de gas natural

near cash instruments
instrumentos cuasimonetarios
Instrument that can be converted to cash in a very short time.

near money; quasi-money
cuasidinero
Assets which have properties resembling those of money in the strict sense. Includes savings deposits, time deposits, **certificates of deposits**, deposits in thrift institutions, etc.

negative amortization loan
préstamo de amortización negativa
Installment loan having the annuity principal as a basis for computation, whose fixed periodic payments increase from time to time, e.g. annually, bi-annually. Initial installments typically are insufficient to meet the interest accruing on the loan principal and unpaid balances of interest are added to the principal outstanding. As the periodic installments increase in value they become sufficient to meet the interest due and commence reducing the principal outstanding.

negative pledge clause
cláusula de obligación negativa, de abstención
Clause in loan agreement obligating the borrower not to grant security without equally securing the loan in question.

negative rate of interest
tipo de interés negativo; tasa de interés negativa

negative sum game
juego de suma negativa

net beneficial product
producto útil neto

net benefit investment ratio
relación beneficio neto-inversión
The ratio between the **present worth** of net benefits and the **present worth** of an investment; alternatively, the sum of **present worths** after the incremental net benefit stream has become positive, divided by the sum of **present worths** in the earlier years of the project.

net book value; current equity investment; net investment
valor contable neto; inversión en capital social corriente; inversión neta
The **contribution value** plus covered **retained earnings**, less remitted earnings, less depreciation of assets or other commercial losses. Used by some countries as a basis for computing the amount of compensation.

net calorific value - NCV; lower heating value; net heating value - NHV
poder calorífico neto - PCN
Total amount of heat produced by combustion less the latent heat of evaporation of any water present in fuel before combustion.

net cash requirements - NCR
necesidades netas de efectivo
Gross disbursements plus outstanding debts due to mature, less repayments and sales of loans, less net income adjusted for non-cash items, less the increase in usable capital.

net discounted value
valor neto actualizado

net energy ratio - NER
relación de energía neta - REN
Ratio between delivered net energy demand and GDP.

net factor service income
ingreso neto por servicios de los factores
Net income derived directly from the provision of services.

net heating value - NHV; net calorific value - NCV; lower heating value
poder calorífico neto - PCN
Total amount of heat produced by combustion less the latent heat of evaporation of any water present in fuel before combustion.

net income
ingresos netos [BIRF]; utilidades netas [sociedades]
Revenues less operating costs.

net interest margin on average earning assets
margen neto de interés sobre el promedio de activos productivos
Average interest return on loans and investments less average rate of debt interest expenses. Return on investments includes realized capital gains and losses.

net investment **see** net book value

net material product - NMP
producto material neto - PMN
The total amount of material goods and services associated with production supplied by the national economy. Used in the national accounting of the socialist countries.

net of taxes
deducidos los impuestos

net out
expresar en cifras netas; obtener cifras netas

net present value in efficiency prices - ENVP
valor actual neto a precios económicos
The **present value** of net benefits measured in efficiency prices.

net present worth, value - NPW, NPV
valor neto actual, actualizado
The net value or net benefit of a project when all costs have been discounted to the present at the accounting rate of interest. May be positive or negative but for project to be acceptable must be either zero or positive.
[**see also** social net present value]

net profits interest [oil]
participación en las ganancias, utilidades netas
A share of gross production from a property, measured by net profits from operation of the property. It is carved out of the **working interest**.

net realizable value **see** current exit value

net register tonnage - NRT
tonelaje de registro neto
The **gross register tonnage** of a ship (calculated on cubic capacity at 100 cu ft per ton) less engine room, navigation, light, air, locker room spaces, etc. It represents the actual carrying capacity of the ship.

net reproduction rate - NRR
tasa de reproducción neta - TRN
Number of daughters a newborn girl is projected to bear during her lifetime, assuming fixed age-specific fertility rates and a fixed set of mortality rates.

net unrealized gain
ganancia neta no realizada
The difference between unrealized gain and specific reserves in the equity portfolio.

net worth [individuals, private corporations]
patrimonio neto
The excess of all assets over liabilities. In a company this represents the net interests of the owners, i.e. **stockholders' equity**.

net worth **see** stockholders' equity [corporations]

netback value [energy]
valor residual neto; ganancia neta
Value of oil or gas taking the price paid downstream for the product less the transportation and other costs incurred between the **wellhead** and the downstream place of sale.

network analysis
análisis de redes

network diagram
diagrama de red(es)

newly agro-industrialized economy - NAE
país de desarrollo agroindustrial reciente

newly industrialized country - NIC
país recientemente industrializado
Used in OECD classifications, this refers to those countries at a relatively advanced level of economic development with a substantial and dynamic industrial sector and with close links to the international trade, finance and investment system (Argentina, Brazil, Greece, Hong Kong, Korea, Mexico, Portugal, Singapore, Spain, Taiwan and Yugoslavia).

newly industrializing country - NIC
país de reciente industrialización, en vías de industrialización
A general term, often used synonymously with **newly industrialized country**, used by the Bank but not as one of their official classifications.

new money packages
cantidades de dinero nuevo

"new style" project [IBRD]
proyecto de "nuevo estilo"
Project geared less toward large infrastructure construction (often carried out almost entirely by foreign contractors) and more toward smaller efforts using local staff, emphasizing appropriate technology and low-cost design, using and/or strengthening local institutions, having a built-in monitoring and evaluation system and paying attention to cost recovery from beneficiaries.

next-in-line manager
supervisor inmediato

niche market
mercado especializado, para productos específicos

night soil
excretas; abono de cloaca, de letrina

NIMBY (not-in-my-backyard)
"ecología, sí; en mi barrio, no"; "sí, muy bien, pero no en mi barrio"
The idea that people favor, e.g. waste disposal sites, anywhere but in their immediate environment.

nitrogen, nitrogenous fertilizer
fertilizante nitrogenado

nitrogen oxides (NO_x)
óxidos de nitrógeno
Compounds which affect the human respiratory system and plant growth. In combination with SO_x, one of the causes of acid rain.

nitrous oxide
óxido nitroso
A **greenhouse gas**.

no load fund
fondo de inversión que no cobra comisión
Money market fund that does not charge a fixed fee commission to investors.

nominal effective exchange rate
tipo de cambio efectivo nominal
An effective exchange rate which is not adjusted for relative inflation differentials.

nominal price
precio nominal, simbólico

nominal protection coefficient - NPC
coeficiente de protección nominal
A coefficient that takes into account tariffs, quotas and **nontariff barriers** that protect farmers as well as the impact of export taxes or restrictions that penalize farmers and the over- or undervaluation of the exchange rate, when determining the incentives or disincentives farmers face in different countries.

nominal service
servicio mínimo

nominated subcontractor
subcontratista propuesto
Subcontractor approved by the **employer** or **engineer**.

nomination
propuesta de candidatura

nonaccelerating-wages rate of unemployment - NAWRU
tasa de desempleo que no modifica el nivel salarial
The level of unemployment at which wage growth might be kept stable.

nonaccrual rate [World Bank]
porcentaje de préstamos excluidos del régimen de contabilidad en valores devengados
Percentage of loans in **nonaccrual status**.

nonaccrual status
exclusión del régimen de contabilidad en valores devengados
When a borrower is placed in nonaccrual status, accrued interest is eliminated from the **financial statement** receivable balances and interest income is correspondingly reduced. During the time the borrower remains in nonaccrual status, interest income is reflected in the **financial statement** only to the extent actually received in cash. Placing a borrower in nonaccrual status in no way affects the interest payment obligations to the borrower; interest continues to be billed on the original terms of the loan.

nonaccrual trigger point, date
período previo a la exclusión del régimen de contabilidad en valores devengados
Period, usually six months, before a loan or credit is put into **nonaccrual status**.

nonaccruing loan **see** nonperforming loan

nonactive borrower **see** inactive borrower

nonassociated gas
gas no asociado
Free gas not in contact with crude oil in the reservoir.

nonbulk traffic
transporte de productos empacados
Carriage of small items, not in bulk form.

noncallable [bond]
no rescatable, no redimible antes del vencimiento
Bond or other instrument that cannot be recalled or redeemed prior to maturity.

noncash expenses
gastos, costos no monetarios
Depreciation and amortization for the year and other expenses appearing in an **income statement** which are not subject to cash drawn down, and which should be added to net income in preparing a **sources and applications of funds statement**.

noncash input
insumo no monetario
Agricultural **input** not in the form of cash.

noncash item
partida de transacción no monetaria

noncash working capital
capital de trabajo, de explotación no disponible inmediatamente
Working capital not in cash form, i.e. **receivables** and **inventories**.

nonconcessional, nonconcessionary flows
movimientos, flujos de capital en condiciones no concesionarias

noncore project
proyecto no básico
Opposite of a **core project**, i.e. a project not in one of the key designated by the Government.

non-18% currency
moneda distinta del monto del 18%
Protected **18% currency** recovered by the Bank under the **accelerated recall** procedure and exchanged for an equivalent amount of currency freely convertible and usable by the Bank.

nonequity direct investment
inversión directa distinta de las contribuciones al capital social
Any of the following forms of investment which have terms of at least three years and the other characteristics individually specified. Investments such as: **production-sharing contracts, profit-sharing contracts, management contracts,** franchising agreements, licensing agreements, **turnkey contracts, operating leasing agreements** and subordinated **debentures**.

nonexcludable, nonexcludible goods
bienes no exclusivos, no excluyentes
A good is said to be non-excludable if its provision
to any one person automatically makes it available
to others.

nonexpendable equipment
material no fungible
Used in UNDP to cover all items for which
inventory records are maintained at Agency HQ,
i.e. valued at more than $100 with a normal life
expectancy of more than 5 years.

nonfactor services - n.f.s.
servicios no atribuibles a factores
In balance of payments, all services except for
interest payments and other income from capital
and wages, salaries and other income from labor.

non-food agricultural commodity
producto básico agrícola no alimentario

Non-Food Agricultural Price Index [IBRD]
**índice de precios de los productos agrícolas no
alimentarios**

nonformal education
educación no formal
Education taking place outside of schools, colleges
and universities and aiming to develop knowledge,
skills and attitudes that are not normally given
prominence in formal educational institutions.

nonfuel minerals
minerales no combustibles

nongovernmental organization - NGO
organización no gubernamental - ONG

noninterest bearing note
pagaré sin intereses

noninterest current account deficit
**déficit en cuenta corriente (excluidos los
ingresos por concepto de intereses)**

noninterest deficit **see** primary deficit

nonmarket economy
economía no de mercado

nonmarket services [national accounts]
servicios no comerciales

Services that do not have a commercial aim.
Usually used for the services provided by local and
national government and other official bodies.

nonnegotiable note
pagaré no negociable

nonoil developing country
país en desarrollo no petrolero

nonoperating income
ingresos no provenientes de las operaciones
The revenue of an enterprise derived from sources
other than its regular activities.

nonoriginal member [MIGA]
miembro no fundador
Full member, i.e. has signed and ratified the
Convention and paid initial capital subscription as
required by Resolution No. 12. of the Council of
Governors, adopted on March 1989, since
adoption of this Resolution.

non-pension retiree medical costs
**gastos médicos del personal retirado no
cubiertos por el sistema de pensión**

nonperforming assets
activos no redituables, improductivos
Assets which have no financial return.

nonperforming debt
acreencias no redituables, improductivas
A debt which has no financial return (i.e. no interest is paid on it).

nonperforming loan; nonaccruing loan
préstamo no redituable, improductivo
Loan where payment of interest has been delayed
for more than 90 days.

nonpoint source
fuente (de contaminación) no identificable
Discharge of pollutants from a non-specific source.
Includes runoff from city streets, parking lots,
agricultural land and construction sites.

nonportfolio project [IFC]
proyecto no incluido en la cartera
Project carried out by IFC that does not form part
of its loan portfolio, e.g. providing technical
assistance.

nonprice competition
competencia no relacionada con los precios

nonprofit organization; not-for-profit organization
organización sin fines de lucro

nonproject aid
asistencia, ayuda no destinada a proyectos específicos, para fines generales

nonproprietary name
nombre genérico; denominación común

nonpurpose loan
préstamo sin finalidad específica

nonrecourse finance
financiamiento sin posibilidad de recurso
A loan where the lenders look solely to the cash flow generated by the project being financed for repayment. There is no recourse to the sponsor of the project, so that the lenders assume all the commercial and political risks of the project.

nonrecourse participation
participación sin posibilidad de recurso
Sales of participation in a company where the sale is on a "nonrecourse" basis, i.e. the buyer has no recourse against the seller if the project fails to generate money.

nonrecurring expenses
gastos extraordinarios

nonregular staff - NRS
personal no permanente

nonreporting nonmember country
país no miembro y no declarante

nonresponsive
...que no se ajusta (a las estipulaciones, normas, etc.)

nonrevenue water
agua que no produce ingresos
Water that is supplied but for which no revenue is collected (e.g. illegal extraction, leakages).

nonstock corporation
sociedad no accionaria

nontariff barrier - NTB
barrera no arancelaria
Factors other than tariffs inhibiting international trade. Include advance deposits on import payments, customs and administrative procedures and similar practices.

nontradable [noun]
bien no comerciable, no comercializable; no exportable o importable
A good that cannot be exported because its domestic cost of production is higher than the export (fob) price but lower than the import (cif) price.

nontraded goods
bienes no comerciados, no comercializados, no exportados o importados
Tradable goods that for economic or policy reasons are neither imported nor exported, or inherently **non-tradable** goods.

nontraded tradable; tradable but nontraded (good, item)
bien comerciable no comerciado (etc.)
Goods which would usually be imported were it not for an import quota or outright ban enforced against them.

"no objection" (procedure)
(procedimiento de) aprobación tácita
Procedure whereby a proposal is deemed approved if no objection is formally received by a specified date.

no recourse sale
venta sin recurso de rescisión, irrevocable
Sale where the buyer has no legal recourse against the seller.

no-return equity
capital improductivo

normal financing
financiamiento contra factura

not applicable - n.a.
no se aplica - n.a.

not available - n.a.
no disponible - n.d.

notebook computer
computadora portátil

not elsewhere specified - n.e.s.
no especificado en otra parte - n.e.p.

not-for-profit organization; nonprofit organization
organización sin fines de lucro

not included elsewhere - n.i.e.
no indicado separadamente - n.i.s.

not-in-my-backyard **see** NIMBY

note [capital markets]
pagaré
A bond with short- or medium-term maturity.
[**see also** deep discount note; demand note; discount note; floating rate note; interest bearing note; noninterest bearing note; nonnegotiable note; promissory note; Treasury note]

note deposit [IDA]
depósito de pagarés

note issuance facility - NIF **see** revolving underwriting facility

note issue
emisión fiduciaria

notice of registration
notificación de registro
Notice sent to **applicant** on receipt of **preliminary application for guarantee** to show that the investment has been registered by MIGA.

notice to proceed [contracts]
orden de proceder
A letter sent to a vendor prior to the issuance of a contract to ensure that certain basic agreements are clearly understood by both parties. When signed by both parties, this document establishes a contractual relationship and is legally binding.

nuclear housing **see** core housing

nuclearization [education]
nuclearización

nucleus estate
plantación núcleo
A central unit in the form of a processing plant or plantation that provides technical assistance, **inputs** and marketing services to its associated **outgrowers** who, in return, sell their products through the unit.

nuisance tariff
arancel de "puro estorbo"
Very low tariff established merely to cause a nuisance.

numeracy
conocimientos básicos de aritmética

numeraire
unidad de cuenta; numerario

nurse crop; cover crop
cultivo protector, de cobertura

nurse **see** practical nurse; registered nurse

nutrients
nutrientes; elementos, sustancias nutritivos(as)

nutritional dwarfing **see** stunting

- O -

objection to jurisdiction [ICSID]
excepción de incompetencia

objective function [economic analysis]
función objetivo
A function relating the objective (the variable to be optimized) to the choice variable in an optimization problem.

object-oriented programming system - OOPS
sistema de programación orientado a objetos
Type of computer programming where each object carries out specific tasks and the information passed between objects is in a standardized way. It is an extension of structured programming.

occasional earnings
ganancias ocasionales, eventuales

ocean freight rate index
índice de fletes marítimos
An index of trans-oceanic freight rates. For grains, the Bank uses US/Canada (St. Lawrence) to Antwerp/Rotterdam/Amsterdam; for sugar Queensland, Australia to UK or Japan.

octane booster
aditivo que aumenta el octanaje
Fuel additive used to boost octane level. Lead has been the main octane booster till recently but now other, more environmentally friendly substances, such as ether, are being used.

office automation
automatización de oficinas; ofimática

office occupancy fee - OOF
cargo por uso de oficinas
The fee paid by IFC to the Bank for occupying the I Building.

official capital
capital oficial, público

official debt
deuda pública

official development assistance - ODA
asistencia oficial para el desarrollo - AOD

official export credit
crédito oficial a la exportación

official flows [development]
flujos oficiales; corrientes oficiales

official holdings
tenencias oficiales

officialization (of debt)
oficialización de la deuda
Shifting of the composition of debt holdings from commercial banks to official creditors.

off-market transaction
transacción fuera de mercado

off-season, out-of-season crop
cultivos de fuera de estación, de temporada

offset agreements
acuerdos compensatorios
Countertrade in which a company agrees to buy products unrelated to its normal business to complete a sale.

offset borrowings
empréstitos compensatorios, contra depósitos
Borrowings of funds by Bank from institutions where deposits are held, prior to the maturity of the deposits.

offshore assembly, processing
elaboración, montaje de material fabricado en otro país
Production activity in a developing country involving assembling materials produced in a foreign country.

offshore bank
banco extraterritorial
Bank located outside the country in question.

offshore cost
costo extranacional
Assembly costs outside the host country.

offshore drilling
perforación submarina, mar adentro

offshore field
yacimiento submarino, mar adentro

offshore market
mercado extraterritorial
A non-domestic market, e.g. there is a domestic (US) and offshore market in US dollars.

offshore processing, assembly
elaboración, montaje de material fabricado en otro país
Production activity in a developing country involving assembling materials produced in a foreign country.

offtake [livestock]
extracción
Livestock which can be taken out of a herd (flock, etc.) and for marketing.

offtake rate [livestock]
tasa de extracción
The rate at which livestock is withdrawn from a herd (flock, etc.) for marketing.

off-the-shelf
en existencia

off-the-shelf goods
bienes, mercancías en existencia
Goods that are available ready made, i.e. that do not have to be custom made.

off-the-shelf purchases
compra de bienes en existencia en el mercado

off-the-shelf price
precio en almacén
The price of goods obtained off the shelf.

off-the-shelf technology
técnicas disponibles

oil see heating oil; heavy oil; heavy fuel oil

oil bill [national]
gastos en petróleo; costo del petróleo

oil fired power station
central eléctrica de petróleo

oil (drilling) rig, platform
equipo, torre de perforación petrolera; plataforma de perforación petrolera [mar.]

oil sands
arenas petrolíferas, asfálticas; arenas impregnadas de brea

oil shale
lutita bituminosa; esquisto bituminoso

oil shock
crisis, conmoción petrolera, producida por los precios del petróleo

oilcake
torta (de semillas) oleaginosa(s)

onchocerciasis; river blindness
oncocercosis; ceguera de los ríos

on-costs [UK]; indirect costs
costos indirectos
A cost not attributed to the production of a specified good or service but to an activity associated with production generally.

on demand guarantee
garantía pagadera a la vista
Guarantee, such as a **performance guarantee**, where the bank issuing the guarantee must pay the person or organization to whom the guarantee is given the sum guaranteed, on demand, without any reason being given.

one parent family
familia monoparental

one-shot survey
encuesta puntual

one-stop agency, shop
oficina, organismo de centralización de trámites
System whereby several bureaucratic procedures are combined into one.

on-farm consumption
consumo en la explotación agrícola

on-farm developments, improvements
mejoras en las explotaciones agrícolas; *a veces*: **adecuación predial**

on-farm research - OFR
investigación(es) en las explotaciones agrícolas

onlend, to
represtar; prestar de nuevo (el importe de un préstamo)

onlending; onward lending
represtamo
Equivalent to **relending** in connection with **new money** loans. The funds are recorded as a deposit in the central bank but the foreign bank and the contractual borrower (usually the Central Bank) agree that the loan proceeds will be made available to a third party within the country of the borrower.

onshore cost; local cost
costo en moneda nacional

on-the-job training
capacitación, formación, adiestramiento en el empleo, trabajo

onward lending **see** onlending

open cast, cut, pit, strip mining
explotación a cielo abierto, a tajo abierto [Chile]

open economy
economía abierta
An economy which engages in international trade.

open-ended commitment
compromiso sin plazo o volumen definidos

open-ended contract; open-end contract
contrato de duración indefinida
A contract providing an unspecified amount of goods or services over a period of time, which may or may not be specified.

open-ended group
grupo abierto; grupo de participación abierta

open-end (investment) fund; unit trust [UK]
sociedad de inversiones con número de acciones variable
An **investment company** that sells and reclaims its **capital stock** continuously, selling it at **book value**, adding a sales charge, and redeeming it at a slight **discount** or at **book value**.

open general licence - OGL
licencia general de importación
System where, for a previously approved list of commodities, qualified importers can automatically obtain licenses and unlimited foreign exchange from the authorities.

open-hearth steelmaking
fabricación de acero en hogar abierto, en horno Martin-Siemens

open market
mercado abierto; mercado financiero
1. The market maintained by government **securities** dealers. As regards U.S. Treasury borrowing operations, the open market is the **money market** in the case of short-term obligations or the capital market in the case of long-term obligations.
2. The general **financial market**.

open pit, open cast, open cut, strip mining
explotación a cielo abierto, a tajo abierto [Chile]

open registry flag; flag of convenience
bandera de conveniencia, de favor

open tender; public tender
licitación pública

open unemployment
desempleo evidente, manifiesto

operating account
cuenta de explotación, operación
Revenue and expense account.

operating budget
presupuesto de explotación, operación
A budget covering recurrent revenue and expense.

operating deficit
déficit de explotación, operación

operating department
departamento de operaciones
A department in an organization which is responsible for the basic operating functions of the organization (as opposed to support department).

operating expenses, costs
**gastos, costos de explotación, operación,
funcionamiento**
The expense, other than financing, of carrying on
the normal activities of an enterprise.

operating income, profit
ingresos, utilidades de explotación, de operación

operating lease
contrato de arrendamiento operativo
A lease where the asset is not wholly amortized
during the obligatory period (if any) of the lease,
and where the lessor does not rely for his profit on
the rentals in the obligatory period. In other words,
the payments received under the lease do not
necessarily cover the purchase price, and the lessor
expects to take the asset back and re-lease it or
resell it. Operating leases are often offered by
equipment manufacturers rather than finance
houses.

operating leasing agreement
**acuerdo de arrendamiento de equipo para
operaciones**
Agreement with terms of at least three years where
the lessor leases capital goods to a lessee and
where rental payments are at least in part
dependent on the production, revenues or profits of
the investment project. Considered as a type of
non-equity direct investment for the purposes of
MIGA.

operating losses
pérdidas de explotación, de operación

operating profit, income
ingresos, utilidades de explotación, de operación

operating program [IBRD]
programa de operaciones

operating ratio
**coeficiente de operación; coeficiente neto de
explotación**
The operating costs before debt service,
depreciation and other financing charges, divided
by operating revenues.

operating subsidy
**subsidio, subvención de explotación, de
operación, de funcionamiento**

operating surplus
superávit de explotación, operación

Operational Assistance - OPAS [UNDP]
asistencia operacional - ASOP

operational cut-off; effective cut-off; operational
threshold
**límite práctico para recibir financiamiento de
la AIF**
The maximum limit above which a country
normally does not receive IDA financing. In
theory, countries below the formal eligibility
threshold can receive IDA financing but, with the
exception of a few small island economies, do not.

operational department [IBRD]
departamento de operaciones

Operational Manual Statement - OMS
documento del Manual de Operaciones

operational, operations research
investigación operativa, de operaciones

operational review
estudios operacionales

operational threshold **see** operational cut-off

operational travel
viajes oficiales relacionados con operaciones

Operations & Maintenance - O & M
funcionamiento y mantenimiento

opportunity cost
costo de oportunidad, de sustitución
The value of something forgone. For example, the
direct opportunity cost of a man-day of labor is
what the man would otherwise have produced had
he not been taken away from his usual occupation
to be employed in a project.
[**see also** social opportunity cost]

option bond **see** multiple currency option bond

option value
valor de opción
The value given to keeping an asset (particularly
an environmental one) for possible future use.

oral procedure [ICSID]
actuación, procedimiento oral

oral rehydration therapy - ORT
terapia de rehidratación oral
A method of treating victims of acute diarrhoea by given them, orally, fluids containing oral rehydration salts which contain special substances to combat rehydration, such as sodium chloride, glucose, trisodium citrate or potassium chloride.

orderly marketing arrangements - OMA
disposiciones de comercialización ordenada
In international trade, a market-sharing pact that restricts competition and preserves shares in national markets for local manufacturers who would otherwise lose out to cheaper or better products from abroad.

ordinary share **see** common share

organizational fine tuning
ajuste institucional

organizational structure
estructura orgánica

organization expenses; formation expenses
gastos (iniciales) de constitución
Any cost incurred in establishing a corporation or other form of organization, such as incorporation, legal and accounting fees, promotional costs, etc. These constitute an **intangible asset**.

original issue discount (OID) bond
bono emitido con descuento
Bond with a rate of interest below that demanded by the market place and sold at a price at a significant discount to par.

original member [MIGA]
miembro fundador
Full member, i.e. has signed and ratified the Convention and paid initial capital subscription prior to adoption of Resolution No. 12.

origin tax
impuesto de origen

other official flows - OOF
otras corrientes oficiales; otros flujos oficiales
The transfer of resources from donor governments to developing countries which are not classified as

official development assistance. This concept is used by the OECD to measure flows from DAC countries to developing countries and to multilateral organizations.

outage [electricity]
interrupción del servicio; apagón

outgrower
agricultor con pequeña(s) explotación(es) satélite(s)
Smallholder who manages his own crops but is linked to a **nucleus estate** in the form of either a processing plant or a plantation. The central unit provides technical assistance, **inputs** and marketing services and the outgrowers sell their products through this unit.

outlay account **see** income and outlay account

outlier
valor atípico
Datum that is greater than five standard deviations from the mean.

outlier project
proyecto aislado
A one-off project.

out-of-school education
educación extraescolar
Education taking place outside of schools, colleges and universities and aiming to develop knowledge, skills and attitudes that are not normally given prominence in formal educational institutions.

out-of-season crop; off-season crop
cultivos de fuera de estación, de temporada

outpatient treatment
tratamiento ambulatorio

outplacement
reubicación; recolocación

output
producto; producción; egresados

outreach activities
actividades de extensión, de divulgación
Activities by a central authority (government, World Bank) to establish contact with and assist people or small business in provincial areas.

outreach post
centro fuera de la sede
Local representative for an **outreach program**.

outreach program
programa de alcance exterior, de extensión, de divulgación
Program by a central authority (central government, World Bank) to establish contact with and assist people or small business in rural areas.

outreach worker
trabajador, funcionario de extensión, de divulgación; promotor
Worker engaged in an **outreach program**.

outright sale
venta simple, al contado

outsourcing; sourcing
contratación de uno o varios servicios, adquisición de bienes, etc., fuera de la empresa, etc.
The process whereby an institution, corporation, etc. has an entire service carried out by an external company or purchases its entire needs in a specific area from an outside company.

outstanding bonds, securities, shares, stock
bonos, valores, acciones en circulación
Capital stock in the hands of the public.

outstanding drawings [IMF]
giros pendientes de reembolso; total, monto neto de los giros
In the International Monetary Fund, the total amount of credit outstanding under the different Fund policies and facilities.

outstanding external debt
deuda externa pendiente

outstanding loans
préstamos pendientes

outward-looking, outward-oriented country
país orientado hacia el exterior

overaccruals
cargos contables excesivos
Recording more money than was actually spent in a set of accounts, for an item.

overage loan
préstamo para cubrir posibles excesos de costos
A special loan issued to cover excess costs on a project.

overdesign
diseño demasiado ambicioso; diseño excesivo para las necesidades

overdraft facilities
servicio de sobregiro

overemployment
sobreempleo; hiperempleo; exceso de empleo

overexpenditures
gastos superiores a los previstos

overexposure
concentración excesiva de riesgos de financiamiento

overflow basin
cuenca de rebalse
Swampy area between river levees and valley sides, set aside for the diversion of floodwater.

overgeared
endeudado en exceso

overgrazing
pastoreo excesivo

overhang
exceso de oferta; excedente; sobrante; saldos pendientes
Excess, normally of supply over demand.
[see also debt overhang]

overhaul [equipment]
reparación general de equipo

overhead capital
capital social fijo; capital nacional fijo
[see also social overhead capital]

overhead costs; overheads
gastos generales
An actual cost of doing business that cannot be associated directly with the production of a certain product.

overinvestment
exceso de inversiones; inversión excesiva

overlay [highways]
recubrimiento; revestimiento

overnight funds
fondos de un día para otro
Short-term funds borrowed to be returned by the following business day.

overnight maturity
vencimiento de un día para otro

overrun **see** cost overrun; time overrun

overseas allowance
bonificación, prima por trabajo en el exterior

overshoot
exceder el objetivo

overshooting
ajuste excesivo

overstaffed
con exceso de personal

oversubscription [capital markets]
suscripción en exceso de la emisión

oversupply
oferta excesiva

over-the-counter market; curb market
mercado extrabursátil, fuera de bolsa
Market for **securities** not listed in any of the exchanges (about 80 percent of total **securities** in the U.S.). In the U.S. includes U.S. Government and agency issues, state and local government bonds, railroad bonds and shares, many public utility bonds and shares, and most corporation and bank shares.

over-the-counter securities
valores extrabursátiles, fuera de bolsa

own, to
asumir como propio
E.g. the Government must own the program.

owners' equity **see** stockholders' equity

ownership (of a corporation)
los propietarios de las acciones; control mayoritario
[**see also** equity ownership]

ownership (of programs)
autoría; identificación

ownership structure (of a company)
estructura, composición del capital social

own price elasticity; price elasticity
elasticidad-precio; elasticidad con respecto al precio
The change in quantity (demanded or supplied) which results from a given change in price.

ozone-depleting potential - ODP
potencial de agotamiento de la capa de ozono - PAO
A measurement of the potential harm of the **ozone layer** of each **chlorofluorocarbon**, based on the life span of the CFC and the number of chlorine atoms it contains.

ozone-depleting substance - ODS
sustancia que agota la capa de ozono
Substance that contributes to destruction of the **ozone layer**. Cf. **greenhouse gas**; **ozone depletion**.

ozone depletion
agotamiento de la capa de ozono
The destruction of ozone molecules in the **ozone layer** by chemical reaction with materials released from human activities, including **chlorofluoro-carbons** and halons.

ozone hole
agujero en la capa de ozono; adelgazamiento de la capa de ozono
A large area over Antarctica discovered to have a seasonal reduction of some 50% in **stratospheric ozone** as a result of the release of **ozone-depleting substances**. Subsequent discoveries suggest an ozone hole may be forming in the Northern Hemisphere.

ozone layer
capa de ozono
An area of the **stratospheric ozone** about 12 to 30 miles in altitude where the intensity of short wavelength ultraviolet light from the sun is high enough to convert normal oxygen (0_2) to ozone (0_3).

ozone sink
pozo de ozono
Atmospheric zone where ozone reacts with nitric oxide to form nitrogen dioxide and oxygen.

- P -

Pacific Rim countries
países del arco del Pacífico

package
conjunto, serie de disposiciones, equipos, proyectos, actividades, financiamiento; programa de medidas, etc.
[see also bid package; financial package; minimum package project; new money packages; policy package; rescue package; slice and package]

package coverage [MIGA]
cobertura global
Coverage of a combination of types of risk.

package deal contract
contrato global
A variant of the **turnkey contract**.

paid-in (share) capital; called up (share) capital
capital pagado
The total amount of cash, property and services contributed to a corporation by its stockholders and constituting a major balance-sheet item.

paid-in capital subscriptions [IBRD]
monto pagado de las suscripciones de capital [BIRF]

paid-up capital
capital pagado, totalmente pagado
That part of the issued capital of a company which the subscribers have been required to pay.

paid-up stock; fully paid stock
acciones pagadas
Stock fully paid for (i.e. upon which no further subscription installments are due).

panel data set
tabla de conexiones de datos
Set of survey respondent data, obtained from the same group of respondents over a period of time.

Panel member [ICSID]
integrante de la Lista (de Conciliadores o de Arbitros)

Panel of Conciliators, Arbitrators [ICSID]
Lista de Conciliadores, de Arbitros

panel of experts
grupo de expertos

paper [financial]
efectos; valores
[see also commercial paper; eligible paper; financial paper; government paper; money market paper]

paper profit
utilidades en libros

parallel economy; black economy; underground economy; submerged economy
economía subterránea, paralela
Transactions for goods and services not declared to the tax authorities and not appearing in the **gross national product**.

parallel financing
financiamiento paralelo
Cofinancing, but with the partners financing different parts of the project.

parastatal [noun]
entidad, institución, organismo, servicio paraestatal

parchment coffee
café pergamino
Coffee which is dried but unhulled.

parent body
órgano, organismo principal

parent company
sociedad, empresa matriz

Pareto optimum
óptimo de Pareto
A state of the economy in which all economic resources are allocated and used efficiently, such that it is impossible to make anyone economically better off without making someone else economically worse off.

pari passu clause
cláusula *pari passu*
Clause in loan agreement precluding subordination of the loan to other debt. In the issue of new shares, it states that the new shares will rank equally for dividend with an existing similar issue.

parity price
precio de paridad
A price which is sought or maintained. For an agricultural product, quantity of the goods and services which could have been purchased with the proceeds of a given amount of the product in a reference period is determined. Parity exists today if the proceeds from the same amount of that product can purchase the same goods and services.

Part I countries [IBRD]
países de la Parte I
In the World Bank, those member countries who are considered as developed countries and no longer entitled to Bank lending.

Part II countries [IBRD]
países de la Parte II
In the World Bank, those member countries that are considered as developing and therefore entitled to borrow from the Bank.

partial budget
presupuesto parcial
A budget that addresses itself to only part of an enterprise.

participation certificate; pass-through certificate
certificado de transferencia de préstamos
Certificate representing an interest in a pool of funds or in other instruments.

participation rate; labor force penetration
tasa de actividad
The extent to which those of working age are actually working.

participative management
administración, gestión participatoria

participatory development
desarrollo participatorio, con participación
Development where people influence development decisions that affect them.

participatory poverty assessment - PPA
evaluación de la pobreza con la participación de los afectados

participatory rural appraisal, analysis - PRA
evaluación con la participación de los habitantes de las zonas rurales

particulate matter - PM
partículas
In water, solid matter, in either solid or dissolved states. In air pollution, solid particles or drops of liquid carried by air or other gases.

partly knocked down - PKD
parcialmente montado
Components of a piece of machinery that have only been partially assembled.

partner countries
países asociados, que mantienen relaciones comerciales

partnership
sociedad simple, colectiva; asociación

party (to proceeding or to the dispute) [ICSID]
parte (en el procedimiento o en la diferencia)

par value
paridad; valor a la par (monedas); valor nominal (valores)
When applied to **capital stock**, a stated amount of money by which the stock is known for accounting and tax purposes. The market value of the stock seldom bears any relationship to its par value. When applied to bonds sometimes used interchangeably with maturity value.

pass rate; promotion rate [education]
tasa de promoción

pass-through audit [IBRD]
evaluación *ex post* **abreviada de un proyecto**

pass-through certificate **see** participation certificate

pass-through effect
efecto secundario

pastoral association - PA
asociación de pastoreo comunitario
A legally recognized, voluntary association of pastoral livestock owners who use a common area for grazing and frequent the same water points for the purpose of managing natural resources (water, graze and other vegetation), for the procurement of **inputs** and services and the selling of products.

pastoralist
pastor nómada

patching; spot improvement, patching; road, surface patching [highways]
bacheo; reparación de baches

pattern farm plan
plan modelo de presupuesto de finca

payable on demand
pagadero a la vista, contra presentación

pay-as-you-earn - PAYE; pay-as-you-go [taxation]
retención (de impuestos) en la fuente

pay-as-you-go system [social security]
sistema (o planes) de reparto; régimen de pagos con cargo a los ingresos corrientes
A method of accounting for an unfunded pension plan in which payments to the pension plan beneficiaries are made from current receipts and not from previous contributions.

payback period
plazo de amortización, de reembolso; plazo de recuperación (de inversiones)

paying agency fee
comisión del agente pagador
Fee paid by borrower in the financial markets, representing costs incurred in having the borrowing serviced by an agent.

payline
curva salarial
The line connecting the midpoints of a given salary structure. Also used for the line connecting market pay data for several grades, at a given level.

payload
carga útil

payment arrears
atraso(s) en los pagos; pagos en mora

payment basis, on a
a título oneroso

payment bond [US]
fianza de pago
A bond executed in connection with a contract to assure payment as required by law of all persons supplying labor and material under the contract.

payment-in-kind - PIK
pago en especie

payment guarantee
garantía de pago
A guarantee executed in connection with a contract to assure payment as required by law of all persons supplying labor and material under the contract.

payment schedule
plan de pagos
Timetable for payment by the purchaser to the supplier/**contractor**.

payments position (of a country)
situación de pagos (de un país)

payout date
fecha de desembolso
Date on which a due periodic payment, such as payment on a bond or a stock dividend, is made.

payout price
precio neto
Difference between the **face value** of a bond and the net value received by the **bondholder**, after deducting commission.

payroll
nómina

payroll contributions
aportes

payroll tax
impuesto sobre nóminas

peak load
carga de punta

peak (load) shaving [electricity]
recorte de la demanda de punta

peer monitoring
fiscalización por los pares
Having neighbors who are in a good position to monitor the borrower be required to pay a penalty if the borrower goes bankrupt.

peg, to (prices, interest rates)
vincular; fijar

peg out, to [surveying]
marcar; trazar; piquetear

penalty clause
cláusula penal, punitiva
A clause in a legal instrument providing for the assessment of a penalty under certain stated conditions.

penstock [hydroelectricity]
tubería, canal de presión, de carga
A closed conduit which supplies water under pressure to a turbine.

pent-up demand
demanda reprimida

P/E ratio; price/earning ratio
relación precio-utilidades

per capita income
ingreso, renta per cápita, por habitante

percentage (fee) contract [consultants]
contrato a porcentaje, de honorario porcentual
A contract where the cost of consulting services are directly related to project construction costs or a ceiling thereof. A percentage of the approved construction costs is paid and, once approved, no matching of **inputs** to payment is required.

percentage point
punto (porcentual)

perfect competition; pure competition
competencia perfecta

perfection (of security)
inscripción; registro (de valores)
Registration of a security.

performance
actuación; desempeño; resultados; comportamiento; rendimiento; eficacia; etc.
[**see also** economic performance; financial performance; institutional performance; project performance (audit) report; tax performance ratio]

performance audit
evaluación de resultados

performance bond
fianza de cumplimiento
A bond put up by a **contractor** to protect the **employer** from any **breach of contract**. This practice is particularly prevalent in the United States, where performance bonds are provided by insurance companies. The bond usually gives the guarantor the option of remedying a specific default by the **contractor**, performing the contract in his place or paying the beneficiary what it costs to have the contract performed, up to a certain limit of money.

performance budget
presupuesto por funciones
A budget of outputs, as in a **planning, programming, budgeting system (PPBS)** but often without the accompanying relations to longer range accomplishments that form an integral part of most PPBS budgets.

performance chart; working table; management chart
diagrama, gráfico de situación
A chart comprising numerical data which indicates the current performance of an organization or part of an organization or an individual.

performance contract
contrato-plan; contrato con fines específicos celebrado entre el gobierno y el sector privado

performance evaluation [personnel]
evaluación; calificación

performance guarantee [consultants]
garantía de cumplimiento
A security in the form of a **performance** bond, bank guarantee, cashier's check, certified check or cash at an amount specified in the **bidding documents** required in a contract to protect the owner in case of **breach of contract** by the **contractor**.

performance indicators
indicadores del desempeño, de la actuación

Performance Management Process - PMP
proceso de evaluación del desempeño (del funcionario)
World Bank personnel evaluation system.

performance monitoring
fiscalización, seguimiento, observación del desempeño, de los resultados

performance period
período de cumplimiento de obligaciones
During a **workout** program for a country with protracted arrears, the period prior to clearance of arrears when the country's performance, including compliance with a Bank-approved structural adjustment program, is monitored by the Bank. This performance period must be satisfactorily completed before the country is eligible for regular Bank lending.

Performance Planning and Review - PPR [IBRD]
(sistema de) planificación y evaluación del desempeño (del funcionario)
System set up by the Bank for evaluating staff performance. An individual performance plan is set up every year and reviewed at the end of that year. Now replaced by the **Performance Management Process** (PMP).

performance requirements [contracts]
requisitos de desempeño, cumplimiento, funcionamiento

performance security [contracts]
garantía de cumplimiento, contra el riesgo de incumplimiento
A security in the form of a **performance** bond or bank guarantee at an amount specified in the **bidding documents** required in a contract to protect the owner in case of **breach of contract** by the contractor.

performance specifications
especificaciones de funcionamiento

performance work statement - PWS
(documento de) especificación de servicios laborales
Statement defining the contractual performance required of a vendor providing labor service requirements such as custodial services, construction trades, etc.

performing assets
activos redituables, productivos

periodic health assessment - PHA
evaluación médica periódica

(periodic) review clause
cláusula de examen (periódico)
A clause in a loan agreement, particularly **policy-based lending**, which gives the lender the right to determine periodically whether the stated objectives are being met and whether any problems have been encountered. If problems occur, further disbursement may be withheld.

permanent assets **see** capital assets

perpetual bond
bono perpetuo
A bond which pays agreed-upon interest indefinitely. It has no maturity date.

personal history [medicine]
historia clínica

personal stock **see** registered share, stock

Personnel Manual Statement
documento del Manual del Personal

pest and disease control
lucha contra plagas y enfermedades

phase out, to
eliminar, suspender por etapas,
progresivamente

phase out period [IBRD]
período de eliminación gradual de los préstamos
del Banco
Gradual period by which a country is graduated
from the Bank.

phase out program [IBRD]
programa de eliminación gradual de los
préstamos del Banco
Gradual program by which a country is graduated
from the Bank.

Philippines formula [MOV]
fórmula de Filipinas
A formula (named after the first country to use it)
whereby under the **maintenance of value** system a
country may repurchase the local currency value of
its capital subscription with a currency acceptable
to the Bank.

phosphate rock; rock phosphate
fosforita; roca fosfatada

physical contingencies
asignación para excesos de cantidades físicas

physical facilities
instalaciones

physical infrastructure
infraestructura física

physical investment
inversión en activos fijos

physical planner
planificador de obras, de instalaciones

physical planning
planificación del espacio físico

Physical Quality of Life Index - PQLI
índice de la calidad material de la vida
Indexes which attempts to evaluate quality of life
by combining life expectancy at age one, infant
mortality rate and literacy rate, each with equal
weight.

piggyback financing
financiamiento concatenado
Financing studies for a future project as part of a
loan to finance another project usually in the same
sector.

piggyback project
proyecto concatenado

pioneer industry
industria pionera, de vanguardia

pioneering research
investigación inicial, de avanzada

piped water
agua corriente, por tubería

pipeline loan, credit
préstamo, crédito en tramitación

pipeline of projects; lending pipeline; project
pipeline
proyectos en tramitación, en reserva
Projects which have advanced beyond the stage of
appraisal mission departure, i.e which are
expected to be in the forthcoming year's lending
program.

pipeline project
proyecto en tramitación, en reserva
Project in **pipeline of projects**.

pipeline ratio, lending
coeficiente de proyectos en reserva
Projects past appraisal as a percentage of next
year's lending program.

pit latrine
letrina de pozo

pit privy
letrina de pozo

pithead power plant
central eléctrica en la zona de una bocamina

planning **see** aggregative planning; blueprint
planning; comprehensive planning; development
planning; family planning; indicative planning
figures; land use planning; mandatory planning;
manpower planning; Performance Planning and
Review; physical planning; planning forecasts

planning forecasts
previsiones para fines de planificación

planning, programming, budgeting system - PPBS
sistema de planificación, programación y presupuestación - SPPP
A budget, usually for a government agency, in which the budget items are grouped under various programs.

plant see base load station; biogas plant; biomass (power) plant; coal fired power station; diesel (fired) power plant; oil fired power station; pithead power plant; steam plant; step-down power station; step-up power station

plant and equipment
instalaciones y bienes de equipo

plant breeder see breeder

plant breeding
fitogenética

plant cover
cubierta vegetal

plant population
densidad de siembra

planting material
material vegetativo; material de propagación

pleadings [ICSID]
presentaciones [demandas, alegatos, etc.]

pledge (of shares) [IFC]
promesa de participación en el capital accionario

pledging
promesa de contribuciones

plot servicing
instalación de servicios en los lotes; urbanización de lotes

plowed-back profits
utilidades reinvertidas

plus sum game; positive sum game
juego de suma positiva

point see basis point

point source [environment]
fuente puntual
An identifiable and confined source of discharge of pollutants.

policy-based assistance
(medidas de) política; políticas; asistencia en apoyo de políticas

policy-based lending; policy loans [IBRD]
préstamos, financiamiento en apoyo de reformas de políticas
Loans made in support of policy and institutional changes, rather than for specific projects. Normally given under the structural adjustment and sector adjustment lending programs.

policy framework
marco normativo; marco de políticas; normativa

policy package
conjunto de medidas de política

policy paper
documento de política (sectorial, financiera, etc.)

political entrepreneurship
iniciativa, motivación (política)
Having a "political entrepreneur" who motivates others, engenders trust, and mobilizes tangible benefits to cooperation in the interest of collective action. It is a key element in common property management.

poll tax; head tax; capitation tax
(impuesto de) capitación

polluter
contaminadores (personas, industrias)

polluter-pays principle - PPP
principio de quién contamina paga
Principle whereby a polluter has to pay to clean up the damage his pollution causes.

pollution haven
país que permite la contaminación sin restricciones
Country which allows companies to pollute with few or no restrictions.

polychlorinated biphenyl - PCB
bifenilo policlorinado - BPC
Aromatic compounds used as insulating and cooling agents, plasticizers and in paper and ink manufacture. They are very stable and are found extensively in the environment.

polycyclic aromatic hydrocarbons - PAH
hidrocarburos aromáticos policíclicos - HAP
Aromatic ring compounds found in coal, tar and petroleum. They are emitted by combustion-related activities, including cigarette smoking.

polycyclic management
ordenación policíclica
Forest management system which is designed to limit the damage to advanced regeneration of commercial species that will become the final timber crop after 20-30 years. It relies on efficient monitoring of stand development, with thinning where necessary to favor the growth of promising individual timber trees.

pool **see also** borrowing pool; currency pool

Pool-Based Lending Rate System [IBRD]
sistema de tipos de interés basados en una cesta de empréstitos pendientes
Lending rate system using the **pool-based variable lending rate**.

pool-based variable lending rate [IBRD]
tipo de interés variable basado en una cesta de empréstitos pendientes
IBRD **lending rate** where the **lending rate** on all outstanding balances is adjusted every six months to achieve a given spread above the average cost of outstanding borrowings.

pooled loan
préstamo incluido en el sistema de fondo común de monedas
A loan included in the **currency pooling system**.

pooling
unión; centralización

pool unit
numerario del fondo común de monedas
A synthetic currency unit used as the numeraire for the **currency pool**. In practice, it is the constant 1980 dollar.

port authority
dirección, administración, autoridad portuaria

port charges, tariffs
tarifas portuarias

port dues; harbor dues, fees
derechos portuarios
Charges for the use of the port by the ship and its cargo.

port of entry price **see** cost, insurance and freight port of entry/border point price

port of shipment price **see** free on board port of shipment price

port tariffs, charges
tarifas portuarias
Specific charges for port services such as berth occupancy, aids to navigation, pilotage, towage, cargo handling, power and water supply, etc.

portfolio cleanup
saneamiento de la cartera

portfolio equity
inversiones de cartera

portfolio equity investments
inversiones de cartera en capital social, accionario
Investment in **money market funds**, depository receipts, and direct purchases of shares by foreign investors.

portfolio income
ingreso(s) de los valores en cartera

portfolio sale
venta de valores en cartera

portfolio securities
valores en cartera

positive list
lista positiva
List of imports defined as critical to a specific program.

positive sum game; plus sum game
juego de suma positiva

post appraisal mission
misión de evaluación complementaria

posted price [oil]
precio de lista, cotizado, de cotización
A written statement of crude petroleum prices circulated publicly among sellers and buyers of crude petroleum in a particular field in accordance with historic practices and generally known by sellers and buyers within the field.

posted values
precios en plaza (lista de)

postgraduate studies
estudios de posgrado; estudios posteriores al primer título universitario

postqualification of bidders
poscalificación de licitantes
Determination of capability and financial resources of a **successful bidder** who has not been prequalified.

pour flush latrine
letrina de sifón

poverty gap
brecha de pobreza
It measures the transfer that would bring the income of every poor person exactly up to the poverty line, thereby eliminating poverty.

poverty income threshold; poverty line
línea de pobreza; umbral de pobreza
The minimum acceptable level of standard of living in a given country or region.

power plant, station **see** base load station; biogas plant; biomass (power) plant; coal fired power station; dendrothermal power plant; diesel (fired) power plant; oil fired power station; pithead power plant; steam plant; step-down power station; step-up power station

power system
red de energía eléctrica

power takeoff - PTO
toma de fuerza
An attachment, usually consisting of a shaft and two or more universal joints, which is used to transmit power from a tractor to an attached unit such as a combine or hay baler.

practical nurse
enfermero(a) auxiliar, no diplomado(a)

practice school **see** demonstration school

preamble to an agreement; recital of an agreement
preámbulo de un convenio

preappraisal
evaluación preliminar

preappraisal mission
misión de evaluación preliminar

precedent conditions [legal]
condiciones previas
Conditions which must occur for a subsequent event to take place. Frequently found in international contracts.

precipitator; dust collector; dust separator
precipitador
An air pollution control device usually using mechanical/electrical means to collect particulates from an emission.

predatory price
precio desleal

predevelopment work [oil]
actividades previas a la explotación

predicated variable; predictor
variable independiente, predictiva

predictor; predicated, independent, explanatory variable; fixed variate; regressor [statistics]
variable independiente, predictiva
If a relationship between two variables x and y is interpreted in a causal way such that changes in y are said to be caused or explained by changes in x, then x is the predictor.

166

preemptive rights **see** first refusal rights

preference, preferential margin; margin of preference
preferencia; margen de preferencia
Preference given to certain goods and services of local origin in a contract.
[**see also** domestic preference]

preferred provider organization (PPO) system
sistema de prestador preferido - SPP
Health care system where care is provided by allowing participants to choose among participating professional, who are paid on either a fee for service or capitation (fixed amount per participant per year) basis.

preferred stock
acciones preferenciales, preferentes, preferidas
Stock which has a claim upon the earnings (and sometimes upon the assets and control) of a corporation prior to the common or other class stock.

prefinancing
prefinanciamiento; financiamiento previo

preinvestment study, survey
estudio de preinversión

preliminary application for guarantee [MIGA]
solicitud preliminar de garantía
An initial application for a MIGA guarantee, to be made before the investment is made or irrevocably committed. It sets forth the information MIGA needs to make a provisional determination that the investor and the investment appear eligible for MIGA guarantees. *See* **notice of registration, definitive application for guarantee.**

preliminary design, engineering
planos preliminares; estudios técnicos preliminares

preliminary estimates of quantities
estimaciones cuantitativas preliminares

preliminary question [ICSID]
cuestión previa

prematured loan
préstamo cuyo vencimiento se ha anticipado
Loan that matures before time initially specified.

prematuring
anticipación del vencimiento

premier borrower **see** prime borrower

premium
[**see also** inflation premium; price premium; quality premium; standby premium]

premium
recargo; bonificación

premium, at a
con recargo

premium [MIGA]
prima
Sum charged by MIGA for each guarantee, calculated on an annual basis as a percentage of the amount of guarantee.

premium [securities]
prima; agio
The difference between the **par value** and the higher market value of a **security** expressed as a percentage of the **par value**.

premium [stocks]
prima de emisión
Difference between the **face value** and the selling price of the share when the selling price is higher.

premium on prepayment [IBRD]
prima por reembolso anticipado

premium sale
venta con prima

preparatory school; feeder school; contributory school
escuela preparatoria

prepayment [IBRD]
reembolso anticipado

prepool loan
préstamo anterior al sistema del fondo común de monedas
Loan made before the introduction of the **currency pool** (prior to 1980).

prequalification documents
documentos de precalificación

prequalification of bidders
precalificación de licitantes
In procurement, determination of the technical and financial capacity of potential **bidders** to perform the contract.

pre-reading
prelectura
Learning about the nature and function of print, reading commons signs and labels, learning letters and some sounds and writing one's name.

present value, worth
valor actual, actualizado
An amount which, taking into account the earning power of capital over time and the difference in time between the present and some future date, would be equivalent today to an expenditure or receipt at such a future date; the result of discounting a future value to the present by the appropriate **discount rate**.

present worth of an annuity factor
valor actual de una anualidad constante
How much 1 received or paid annually is worth today.

preservation forest
bosque totalmente protegido
Forest designated for total protection of representative forest ecosystems in which all forms of extraction are prohibited.

pre-shipment inspection
inspección previa al embarque
Inspection of procured goods before they are shipped.

pre-shipment price inspection
verificación de precios previo al embarque
A new Bank requirement in **international competitive bidding**, whereby prices are checked, prior to shipping, by a third party inspection company, to ensure that they are accurate and competitive.

President's Contingency
reserva del Presidente
A fund, usually one percent of the Budget, used to meet resource demands during the budget year that were not and could not have been fully anticipated at the time of budget preparation.

presumptive taxation
impuestos sobre la renta presuntiva, presunta
Lump sum taxation paid in advance.

prevailing market rate
tipo, tasa vigente en el mercado

prevalence [disease]
prevalencia

price adjustment clause; price escalation clause; escalation clause
cláusula de ajuste de precios
Clause in a contract that states that price adjustments will be made in the event changes occur in major cost components of the contract such as fuel, labor, equipment and materials.

price contingencies
asignación para alzas de precios

price differential, spread
margen, diferencia entre los precios

price-earning ratio; P/E ratio - PER
relación precio-utilidades
Market price per ordinary share divided by earnings per ordinary share after tax. It expresses the market value placed on the expectation of future earnings.

price effect
efecto en, sobre los precios

price elasticity; own price elasticity
elasticidad-precio; elasticidad con respecto al precio
The change in quantity (demanded or supplied) which results from a given change in price.

price escalation clause **see** price adjustment clause

price ex factory **see** ex factory price

price fixing
fijación de precios; fijación ilícita de precios (entre productores)

price freeze
congelación de precios

price incentives
incentivos de precios

price inelasticity
inelasticidad con respecto al precio
When there is no change in quantity (demanded or supplied) as a result of a change in price.

price leader, setter, maker
que impone los precios

price level accounting; general price level accounting
contabilidad según el nivel general de precios

price maintenance **see** resale price maintenance

price maker, setter, leader
que impone los precios
A seller who dominates to the extent that when it changes prices, its competitors make similar changes.

price premium
sobreprecio

price quotations [contracts]
cotizaciones

price range
escala, gama de precios

price schedule [procurement]
lista de precios
A document containing an itemized breakdown of the goods or services to be provided with a statement of the **unit prices** applicable.

price setter, maker, leader
que impone los precios

price spread, differential
margen, diferencia entre los precios

price support
sostén, apoyo de precios

price swing
fluctuación, oscilación de precios

price taker
país que no influye en los precios internacionales
A party to a transaction in which the price was determined by natural forces of competition. The seller wanted a higher price, while the buyer wanted a lower price; neither could influence the price because it was determined by the market.

price to factory
precio puesto en fábrica

priced bill of quantities
estimación cuantitativa con precios
Detailed list of the work to be done, as priced by the **contractor**, based on quantities estimated by employer and engineer.

pricing policy
política de precios; política tarifaria

pricing system [financial markets]
sistema de fijación de tipos, tasas de interés

primal city
ciudad principal

primary commodity, product
producto primario, básico
A commodity which has not yet undergone any significant degree of processing, e.g. natural rubber, raw wool, etc.

primary deficit; noninterest deficit
déficit primario; déficit excluido el pago de intereses
Deficit which excludes all interest payments and which therefore only measures current deficit rather than current and past deficits.

primary exporting country
país exportador de productos primarios

primary health care
atención primaria de (la) salud
Health care based on practical, scientifically sound and socially acceptable methods and technology, made universally accessible to individuals and families in the community through their full participation and at a cost that the community and the country can afford to maintain.

primary producing country
país de producción primaria

primary product, commodity
producto primario, básico

primary reserves
reservas primarias
Funds which a bank keeps for immediate use as opposed to secondary reserves which are not for immediate use but can be quickly converted to money.

prime bill
valor, efecto de primera clase
A **bill of exchange** in which the parties have high credit ratings.

prime borrower; premier borrower
prestatario preferencial, preferente, de primera clase
The most creditworthy type of borrower.

prime contractor; principal, main contractor
contratista principal, primario

prime rate
tipo preferencial; tasa preferencial

prime underwriting facility (PUF) **see** revolving underwriting facility

principal
principal; capital (de un préstamo)

principal contractor; prime, main contractor
contratista principal, primario

principal (income) earner
principal sostén económico

principal economist
economista principal

principal exchange rate linked securities notes
pagarés con pago del principal vinculado a los tipos de cambio de diversas monedas

Principles of Staff Employment [World Bank]
principios relativos al empleo del personal

printout
impresión, impreso (de computadora)

prisoner's dilemma [economics]
dilema del prisionero
Theory which compares naked self-interest with cooperation.

private benefit-cost ratio - PBC
relación costos-beneficios privados

private final consumption expenditure - PFCE
gasto de consumo final privado
Discretionary expenditure by individuals.

private sector assessment - PSA
estudio (de evaluación) del sector privado
Assessment carried out by the Bank to identify opportunities and obstacles facing private sector development.

private voluntary organization - PVO
organización privada de voluntarios

privatization vouchers
cupones para la privatización
Vouchers used in the **voucher privatization** system.

privy **see** aqua privy; pit privy

privity [legal]
relación contractual (bipartita)
The principle whereby only the two parties to a contract have a contractual relationship and no third party is involved in this relationship.

problem loan [IFC]
préstamo problemático

procedural law; adjective law
derecho procesal, adjetivo, de forma
The bodies of principles and rules of law other than the substantive law dealing not with the rights and duties of persons but with the means whereby those rights and duties may be declared, vindicated or enforced, or remedies for their infraction ensured. Includes court procedure, rules relating to the jurisdiction of different courts, pleading, evidence, appeal, execution of judgements, legal aid, conveyancing, costs, etc.

procedural orders [ICSID]
disposiciones procesales

proceedings
deliberaciones, acta de sesión(es); actuaciones (jurídicas)

proceeds
importe, fondos de un préstamo o crédito; producto

process chart **see** flow chart

process control
control de procesos industriales

process engineering
ingeniería de procesos

processed
multicopiado
Refers to a document that has been distributed in an unpublished form.

processing of a loan
tramitación del (de un) préstamo

processing
elaboración; transformación; tramitación; tratamiento; etc.

procurement **see** bulk procurement

procurement agent
agente de adquisiciones
Firm which specializes in handling international procurement and acts on behalf of contract awarding authority in a bid.

Procurement Manual Statement - PMS
documento del Manual de Adquisiciones

procurement (procedures)
procedimientos de adquisición

producer gas
gas pobre
A low-energy gaseous fuel, generally produced from coal, whose principal combustible components (carbon monoxide and hydrogen) are generally diluted by air.

producer goods
bienes de producción
Goods manufactured for use in making other goods but which do not themselves continue through the manufacturing stream and are not used directly by consumers.

producer price
precio al productor; precio recibido por el productor
The price of a unit of output of some commodity as it leaves the establishment of the producer. It includes any indirect tax or subsidy levied on that output before it leaves the establishment.

producer price equivalent - PPE
equivalente de subvención de precios al productor
The value of transfers to farmers generated by agricultural policy. These are paid either by consumers in the form of market price support or by taxpayers via direct payments and other support. Measures the aggregate assistance to producers before deduction of farm feed adjustment.

producers' values [national accounts]
valor a precio de productor
The value in the market of the gross output on commodities, industries, etc at the establishment of the producers; or the sum of the values of direct **inputs**, intermediate **inputs** at **purchasers' values** and indirect taxes less subsidies in respect of the commodities, industries, etc.

product in hand contract
contrato "producto en mano"
Turnkey contract which determines the characteristics of the final product to be manufactured.

production build up
aumento de la producción

production forest
bosque de producción
Forest designated for sustainable production of forest products.

production possibility curve; transformation curve
curva de posibilidades de producción; curva de transformación
A graphic representation of the various output combinations of two commodities which can be produced from a given quantity of resources.

production-sharing contract
contrato de participación en la producción
Contract where the contractor makes contributions to the investment project and his remuneration substantially (but not necessarily wholly) depends on a share of the production of the investment project, including his right to purchase such share at a predetermined price or a price to be determined under an agreed formula. Considered as a type of **nonequity direct investment** for the purposes of MIGA.

productive capacity
capacidad de producción

product mix
combinación de productos; composición de la producción; estructura de la producción

product wage
salario-producto

profit and loss account [UK]; income statement [US]
estado de ingresos y gastos, de pérdidas y ganancias

profit center [accounting]
centro de utilidades
A **responsibility center** which accumulates revenues as well as costs.

profit making
con fines de lucro

profit margin
margen de utilidad, de beneficios

profit on sales of investments
utilidad sobre la venta de inversiones

profit sharing
participación en las utilidades

profit-sharing contract [MIGA]
contrato de participación en las utilidades
Contract where the contractor makes contributions to the investment project and his remuneration substantially depends on the revenues or profits of the investment project.

profit squeeze
reducción de los márgenes de utilidad

profits tax
impuesto sobre las utilidades, los beneficios

program aid
asistencia, ayuda para programas

program budget
presupuesto por programas
A **PPBS** budget which emphasizes long-range planning and associated accomplishments and resource requirements.

program contract
plan contractual
A concept developed in France and now used in Senegal, Cameroon and other former French colonies. They are **performance contracts** between Government and companies generally covering a period of three years, which set annual targets for the company (covering physical production, operating efficiency, billing recovery, employee training, etc.) and establish reciprocal commitments by the Government (e.g. agreement on tariff levels, investment support, increased managerial autonomy, etc.). They are indicative rather than legally binding.

program evaluation and review technique - PERT
técnica de evaluación y revisión de programas - PERT
A tool of managerial economics used both in planning a project and in monitoring it. A PERT chart shows each task to be performed, the time each will require, the prerequisites and other information.

program loan, lending
préstamo, financiamiento para programas
Bank loan given not for a specific project but to help a country overcome unforeseen temporary difficulties which would otherwise result in inappropriate long-term policy adjustments to correct short-term balance of payments problems.

program objective category - POC
categorías principales del programa de operaciones
The main areas covered by the Bank's operation program. Currently they are poverty reduction, adjustment and debt, human resources development, private and public sector development, environment and forestry, financial intermediation, natural resources, infrastructure and urban development and economic management.

program of special emphasis - PSE
programa de atención especial
Program that the Bank is giving special priority to, covering such areas as debt management, human resources, **women in development**, environment, food security, poverty alleviation and private sector development.

Program of Targeted Interventions - PTI
Programa de intervenciones dirigidas

progress certificate [IBRD]
estado de pagos (certificado)

progress chart
gráfico de ejecución
[**see also** construction progress chart]

progress payment
pago parcial; pago a cuenta
Payment made as work progresses under a contract on the basis of costs incurred, percentage of **completion** or a particular stage of **completion**.

progress report; status report
informe sobre la marcha (de un proyecto), sobre la labor realizada, sobre las actividades

project advance account
cuenta de anticipos para la preparación de un proyecto

project agency
organismo del proyecto; organismo responsable del proyecto

project agreement
convenio sobre el proyecto

project aid
asistencia, ayuda para proyectos

project appraisal
evaluación (inicial) de un proyecto, de proyectos

project area
zona del proyecto

project audit, evaluation
evaluación *ex post* de un proyecto, de proyectos

project brief
datos básicos de un proyecto
In Bank projects, the basic issues-oriented operational document relating to the early part of the project cycle. It is short (2-6 pages) and focuses on a project's development objectives, policy or other issues and the preparation work required.

project completion report - PCR
informe de terminación del proyecto, de proyectos - ITP
A report prepared within six months of the completion of loan/credit disbursements which highlights strengths and weaknesses of the project and draws appropriate lessons for the Bank for future projects.

project cycle
ciclo del proyecto, de los proyectos
The sequence of analytical phases through which a project passes.

project design
diseño, formulación, preparación de un proyecto, de proyectos

project enterprise [MIGA]
empresa del proyecto; empresa receptora del proyecto
A corporation, association, partnership or any other entity which holds title to, or the power to dispose of, the assets contributed to the Investment Project.

project evaluation, audit
evaluación *ex post* de un proyecto, de proyectos

project fund agreement
convenio sobre financiamiento para el proyecto
Agreement whereby a lender agrees to lend funds for a specific project.

project identification
identificación, determinación de un proyecto, de proyectos

project implementation review - PIR
examen de la ejecución del (de un) proyecto
Semi-annual Bank-wide report on how projects have been implemented.

Project Information Brief - PIB
documento de información sobre el proyecto

project life
duración, vida útil, de un proyecto

project loan, lending
préstamo, financiamiento para un proyecto, para proyectos

project management
administración de proyectos

project management unit - PMU [IBRD]
unidad de administración del proyecto

project manager
director, administrador del proyecto

project officer
oficial del proyecto, de proyectos

project performance audit memorandum - PPAM
memorando de evaluación *ex post* de un proyecto

project performance audit report - PPAR
informe de evaluación *ex post* de un proyecto
A report which provides a preliminary review and evaluation of a project at the end of the execution phase.

project pipeline; pipeline of projects; lending pipeline
proyectos en tramitación, en reserva

project preparation
preparación, elaboración de un proyecto, de proyectos

project rent
utilidades netas derivadas de un proyecto
Income derived from a project.

project supervision
supervisión de un proyecto, de proyectos

project unit
unidad del proyecto

promissory note
pagaré
An unconditional promise in writing made by one person to another signed by the maker, engaging to pay, on demand or at a fixed or determinable future time, a sum of money to or to the order of a specified person, or to bearer.

promotion rate; pass rate [education]
tasa de promoción
Rate at which students pass to the next higher grade.

property income [government]
ingreso(s), renta(s) proveniente(s) de propiedades públicas

property income [individuals, corporations]
ingreso(s) de la propiedad, del patrimonio

proprietary good, item
artículo patentado o de marca registrada

proprietary interest
interés mayoritario
An ownership interest, as in the interest held by an equity holder in a company or a patent holder who licenses use of the patent by others.

proprietary rights
derechos de propiedad

proprietary training
enseñanza privada con método(s) patentado(s)
Training offered by private, for-profit firms.

pro rata commitment authority limitations
límites a la facultad para contraer compromisos impuestos por el principio de proporcionalidad

pro rata recall
reintegro a pro rata, proporcional
Currency recalls for outstanding loans whereby major currencies would be recalled in proportion to the amounts that remain outstanding on each of these loans (as opposed to the previous system where the order of the currency recalled was determined by the Bank). This new system was introduced in January 1990.

pro rata rules [IDA]
principio de proporcionalidad
Rules which state that other donors may maintain proportionality vis-à-vis the US in the amount of contribution released for commitment.

prospectus [financial markets]
prospecto
A document containing all the pertinent information about a **public offering** of **securities** and about the borrower. It is made available to the appropriate legal authorities, stock exchanges, and the prospective investors by the **lead manager**.

protected forest
bosque protegido; bosque de protección

provision [accounting]
reserva; asignación

provision for losses; reserve for losses; loss provision
reserva para pérdidas

provisional measure [ICSID]
medida provisional

proxy
sustituto; sustitutivo; representativo; poder (jurídico)

proxy [IBRD lending rates]
cantidad representativa (de los empréstitos del BIRF contraídos antes del inicio del sistema de tipos de interés basados en una cesta de empréstitos pendientes)

prudential constraints
limitaciones por razones de prudencia

prudential supervision and regulation
normas de disciplina y control; supervisión y reglamentación

prudent man rule
normas de prudente discreción
In a trust arrangement, one of the frequent limitations of the trustee's actions; it states that the trustee may make investments "only in such securities as would be acquired by prudent men of discretion and intelligence in such matters who are seeking a reasonable income and the preservation of their capital."

prudent shopping
comparación de precios; obtención de cotizaciones

public borrowing, offering
oferta pública; emisión ofrecida al público

public (capital) expenditure
gastos públicos de capital

public corporation
empresa, sociedad pública

public debt
deuda pública

public economics
economía del sector público

public enterprise rationalization loan - PERL
préstamo para racionalización de empresas públicas
World Bank loan to help rationalize the finances of a public enterprise.

public enterprise reform loan - PERL
préstamo para reforma de empresas públicas
World Bank loan to help reform the finances of a public enterprise.

public enterprise rehabilitation loan - PERL
préstamo para rehabilitación de empresas públicas
World Bank loan to help rehabilitate the finances of a public enterprise.

public offering, borrowing
oferta pública; emisión ofrecida al público

public sector borrowing requirement - PSBR
necesidades de financiamiento del sector
público
The total excess of expenditure over revenue for
all government entities, which must be financed by
new borrowing net of repayment of previous debts.

public tender; open tender
licitación pública

public utilities
servicios públicos

public utility corporation
empresa de servicios públicos

public works; civil works
obras civiles

publicly guaranteed debt
deuda con garantía pública

publicly held government debt
deuda pública del Estado, en poder de
particulares

publicly issued (bonds, etc.)
(bonos, etc.) emitidos mediante oferta pública

publicly traded company
sociedad cuyas acciones se cotizan en bolsa

pull-down menu
menú desplegable

pull inflation **see** demand-pull inflation

pump priming policy [economics]
política de reactivación
Government policy of spending during a recession
in order to put money into the economic stream so
that spending power will continue and economic
expansion will follow.

pumping station **see** booster pumping station

pupil-teacher ratio - PTR; student-teacher ratio -
STR; teacher-pupil ratio
relación, coeficiente alumnos-profesor, alumnos
por profesor
Total students enrolled in primary and secondary
levels divided by number of teachers in the
corresponding levels.

purchasing power parity - PPP
paridad del poder adquisitivo
An exchange rate adjustment that changes a
currency's foreign purchasing power after there
has been a change in that currency's domestic
purchasing power.

purchasers' values [national accounts]
valor a precio de comprador
The cost of goods and services in the market to the
point of delivery to the purchaser. Equals
producers' values plus the trade and transport
margins appropriate to the purchaser in question.

pure competition; perfect competition
competencia perfecta

pure IDA countries
países que sólo reciben financiamiento de la AIF

pure stand
cultivo único, de un solo tipo o especie
A stand of trees in which at least 80 percent of the
trees in the main crown canopy are of a single
species.

pure time preference **see** rate of pure time
preference

pure variety; true to type variety [agriculture]
variedad pura
A variety that is like the parental type, without
change.

push inflation **see** cost-push inflation

put option
opción de venta
A contract which entitles one party to it, at his
option, to sell a specified amount of **securities** or
commodities to the other party, at the price fixed
in the contract, during the life of the contract.

"put right" guarantee
garantía de funcionamiento de acuerdo con las
especificaciones garantizadas

- Q -

qualified agreement to reimburse
acuerdo, convenio condicional de reembolso
Agreement given by the Bank to a commercial bank to enable a borrower to make purchases under a loan agreement prior to disbursement of the funds. The guarantee is qualified and the Bank has the right to cancel its guarantee should the loan be suspended or cancelled.
[See also **irrevocable agreement to reimburse**.]

qualified bidder
licitante calificado
A **bidder** for a contract who has prequalified, i.e. who has been deemed capable of performing a particular contract satisfactorily based on past performance, quality of staff and equipment and financial position.

qualified borrowing(s) [currency pool]
empréstitos calificados
Originally, borrowings by IBRD after July 1, 1982 (i.e. based on the **pool-based variable lending rate**), using **proxy borrowings**. Under the current system (May 1989), they are defined to exclude borrowings that are determined by the Bank to fund investments and any new differentiated loan product should the Bank wish to offer one in the future. The extraction of borrowings that fund investments would be made separately for each currency. The term *Qualified Borrowings 1982* is used to describe the old system.

qualified guarantee
garantía condicional

qualified instrument of commitment
instrumento de compromiso condicionado
Agreement by a member country to pay its subscription and contribution in part, with the remainder subject to enactment by its legislature of the necessary legislation.

qualified majority
mayoría calificada

qualified opinion [auditing]
dictamen con reservas
An auditor's opinion that indicates that the auditor has found deficiencies in the **financial statements**, as regards the accounting (e.g. reservations on acceptability of the accounting policies and their consistent application) or auditing (e.g. timing of appointment after valuation of **inventories** or other assets) or there is significant uncertainty due, e.g. to the outcome of major lawsuits or other **contingent liabilities**.

qualifying shares
acciones habilitantes
Stock, possession of which enables the holder to buy further stock at a predetermined (reduced) price.

qualitative coinsurance
coaseguro cualitativo
Insurance involving two or more **underwriters** with the different **underwriters** underwriting different risks pertaining to the same project.

quality loan [IBRD]
préstamo de calidad
A Bank loan which has been carefully prepared and is financially viable.

quality premium
prima de, por calidad

quantitative coinsurance
coaseguro cuantitativo
Insurance involving two or more **underwriters** with the different **underwriters** underwriting separate tranches of a single large risk.

quantity surveyor
estimador, medidor de materiales

quantity theory of money
teoría cuantitativa del dinero
Theory holding that the overall level of prices is proportional to the size of the **money supply**. A key monetarist theory.

quantum index
índice de volumen

quasi-equity
cuasicapital
Includes **equity-like instruments** and other forms of loans that have the form of equity or equity that has the form of loans. An example is equity with a **put** agreement, i.e. unlike normal equity, the investor requires return of the equity, for example, in five years at ten percent interest.

quasi-money **see** near money

quayage; wharfage; wharfage charges; dockage
muellaje

queuing theory, problem
teoría, problema de las colas
Mathematical techniques including probability theory used in operations research to identify, illustrate and, it is hoped, influence the characteristics of queues, whether of people, materials, work-in-progress, etc.

quick assets **see** liquid assets

quick disbursing (loan); fast disbursing (loan)
(préstamo) de rápido desembolso

quick ratio **see** acid-test ratio

quick yielding project [IBRD]
proyecto de rápido rendimiento
A project which brings a more rapid return than usual, i.e. after only a few years, and often means faster disbursements.

quiet emergency **see** slow onset emergency

- R -

radial reductions
reducciones arancelarias radiales
Method of reducing a tariff structure whereby at each stage all tariffs are reduced to an equal fraction of their previous levels.

radiative forcing
forzamiento radiativo; variaciones climáticas inducidas por la radiación solar
Changes in the climate due to changes in solar radiation. Solar sunspots and the **greenhouse effect** are examples.

rainfed
de secano; de temporal [México]; de rulo [Chile]

rain forest
bosque húmedo, pluvial; selva pluvial
[see also tropical rain forest]

raise, to (funds, etc.)
obtener, movilizar (fondos, etc.)

random sample
muestra aleatoria, al azar

rangeland
tierra de pastoreo

range management
ordenación de tierras de pastoreo

rank correlation coefficient see Spearman's rank correlation coefficient

ratchet effect
efecto de trinquete
The idea that at the beginning of a recession consumers try to maintain the same level of spending and investment.

ratcheting up
alza, subida por efecto de trinquete

rate basis conversion
conversión de la clase de interés
Option in IFC loan that allows the borrower to convert from a variable rate to a fixed rate loan or vice versa.

rate contract
contrato a precios unitarios
A contract for the supply of goods at specified rates during the period of the contract.

rate of exchange see buying rate of exchange

rate of pure time preference
tasa de preferencia pura en el tiempo
The interest rate at which consumers are willing to forgo present consumption in order to save, presumably for future consumption.

rate of return
tasa de rentabilidad, de rendimiento
[see also economic rate of return; equalizing rate of return; financial rate of return; incremental rate of return; internal rate of return; required rate of return; social rate of return]

rated capacity
capacidad de diseño, nominal, de régimen

rating agency
organismo de clasificación de valores
Organization that evaluates the credit **rating** of prospective borrowers on the **securities** markets.

ratio see accounting ratio; acid-test ratio; affordability ratio; Bruno ratio; capital-labor ratio; capital-output ratio; capital-service ratio; cost-benefit ratio; current ratio; debt-equity ratio; debt-to-capital ratio; debt-to-equity ratio; debt ratio; debt-service ratio; dependency ratio; enrollment ratio; entrepreneurial benefit-cost ratio; equity ratio; feed conversion ratio; fill ratio; financial ratios; gearing ratio; grade ratio; gross (primary) enrollment ratio; housing expenses/income ratio; import coverage ratio; incremental capital-output ratio; input-output ratio; interest coverage ratio; interest service ratio; land equivalent, equivalency ratio; land use ratio; leverage (ratio); liquidity ratio; liquid ratio; long-term debt ratio; minimum cash ratio; modified Bruno ratio; net energy ratio;

operating ratio; price-earning ratio; private benefit-cost ratio; pupil-teacher ratio; quick ratio; reserve ratio; risk asset ratio; smoothness ratio; staffing ratio; stripping ratio; tax/GDP ratio; tax performance ratio; tax ratio; teacher-pupil ratio; volatility ratio; working capital ratio; working ratio

rational expectations
expectativas racionales
A theory based, first, on the assumption that individuals and companies will try to maximize their own welfare -- that is, they will try to make their own economic and other circumstances as desirable as possible -- and, second, that, as individuals and companies make economic decisions in their own interest, they do so in such a way that markets move towards equilibrium, easing inflation.

raw data
datos brutos, sin elaborar

raw water
agua bruta, cruda, sin tratar

reafforestation; reforestation
reforestación; repoblación forestal

real assets
bienes inmuebles, raíces; activos reales

real effective exchange rate
tipo de cambio efectivo real
Nominal effective foreign exchange value of the dollar (a trade-weighted exchange rate) multiplied by the ratio of the US consumer price index to the foreign consumer price index. Below 100 the dollar depreciates in real terms; above 100 it appreciates in real terms.

real estate developer
promotor inmobiliario; urbanizador

real estate equity
participación en inversiones inmobiliarias

real sectors
sectores productivos
The nonfinancial sector.

real terms, in
en términos, cifras reales

realized price [oil]
precio efectivo, de realización
The price actually obtained on the world market for sales concluded.

rebar [= reinforcing bar]
barra de refuerzo
Bar used for reinforcing concrete.

recall [MOV]
reintegro

recall installments [MOV]
pagos parciales por concepto de reintegro

recall under loans [MOV]
reintegro de los montos en préstamo

recapture clause
cláusula de recuperación
Clause in a loan agreement that allows a lender to recover part or all of his previously lent assets if economic circumstances improve.

receivables; accounts receivables
cuentas por cobrar

received energy
energía recibida

recession
recesión

recession crop
cultivo de decrecida
Crop planted on land which has recently been flooded.

recession, recessive cultivation
cultivo en recesión
Cultivation in an area where the amount of land available for cultivations is being reduced due, e.g. to desertification.

recipient country
país receptor, beneficiario

reciprocal debt
deuda recíproca

recital of an agreement; preamble to an agreement
preámbulo de un convenio

reclaim
bonificar; recuperar; sanear

reclamation see land reclamation

recognition and enforcement (of award) [ICSID]
reconocimiento y ejecución (de un laudo)

recommendation domain
ámbito de aplicación de las recomendaciones

reconciliation account
cuenta de reconciliación
Account which shows any difference between two
or more accounts.

reconciliation item [accounting]
partida de reconciliación
Item in account that reconciles the differences
between two or more accounts.

reconcile
conciliar; reconciliar

reconnaissance survey
estudio preliminar

reconstitution
conversión inmediata
Immediate conversion of interest payments
received in a currency other than a pool currency
into a pool currency.

reconstruction import credit - RIC
**crédito para importaciones con fines de
reconstrucción**

record owner
propietario registrado
A person who has title to a property, though not
necessarily beneficial use of it.   Cf. **beneficial
owner**.

recoupment [insurance]
resarcimiento

recovery
recuperación; reactivación

recurrent costs, expenditures
**gastos, costos ordinarios (en presupuestos);
gastos periódicos**
Costs for items consumed immediately or used up
in a comparatively short period, usually a year.

recurrent education; lifelong education; continuing
edcation
educación permanente

recycling (of capital)
reciclaje; recirculación (de capital)

redeemable
rescatable; redimible; amortizable

redemption
rescate; redención; amortización

redeployment cost
costo de conversión, de modificación
The cost of switching one type of loan to another,
e.g. from a fixed rate loan to a variable rate loan.

redeployment cost [IFC]
cargo por reinversión
The cost levied by IFC and representing its cost of
reinvesting a prepaid loan at a lower interest rate.

redeployment (of funds)
reasignación, redistribución (de fondos)

red herring issue
emisión exploratoria
An issue of bonds made on an experimental basis.

rediscount
redescontar; redescuento
Resale of instruments such as **banker's
acceptances** already **discounted** by lender, usually
with central bank or **discount house**, at a price less
than the **face value**.

rediscount ceiling
límite de redescuento

reducing charge method see declining balance
method

redundancy [staffing]
exceso de personal; reducción de personal; prescindencia; supresión de puestos

reference rate of exchange [MIGA]
tipo de cambio de referencia
The effective average rate of exchange applied by the central bank or other foreign exchange regulatory authority of the **host country** for the exchange rate category concerned on the date of loss to conversion of the local currency into **guarantee currency**.

reference zone; target zone [foreign exchange]
zona de referencia
A wide zone of exchange rates, perhaps plus or minus 10 per cent, within which a currency can freely move against other currencies. Suggested at the New York Plaza Agreement at the **Group of Five** meeting, 9/85 and proposed by the French Treasury 2/86, as a way to reduce major currency swings.

referral
remisión; envío

refinancing
refinanciación; refinanciamiento

reflation
reflación

reflecting pool
fondo indicativo [fondo común de monedas]
Concept of movements in the **currency pool** reflecting movements in the three main currencies constituting the pool (US dollar, yen, mark). This concept enables borrowers to predict changes in the **currency pool** by watching changes in these three currencies on the world markets.

reforestation; reafforestation
reforestación; repoblación forestal
Establishment of trees on ground that has been cleared of trees.

reform see land reform

refresher course
curso de repaso; curso de actualización (para refrescar los conocimientos)

refunding
reembolso; refinanciación

regional integration arrangements
acuerdos regionales de integración

register see land register

Register [ICSID]
Registro

registered [vehicle]
matriculado; inscrito

registered (e.g. tradesmen)
inscrito; registrado; autorizado

registered bond
bono nominativo
A bond whose ownership is recorded by the issuer.

registered capital; share capital
capital social, accionario, en acciones

registered nurse
enfermero(a) diplomado(a)

registered security
valor, título nominativo
A security whose ownership is determined by the name in which it is registered as opposed to a bearer security whose ownership is determined by who possesses it.

registered seed
semilla registrada
The progeny of **foundation** or registered seed.

registered share, stock; personal stock
acciones nominativas
Stock which cannot be transferred without placing the signature of the owner upon the **books** of the issuing corporation and delivery of the certificate.

registrar [ICSID]
registrador

registration [Stock Exchange]
inscripción

regrading [highways]
renivelación

regrading [personnel]
reclasificación

regraveling; graveling
recubrimiento, aplicación de grava

regress **see** economics of regress

regression equation
ecuación de regresión
An equation expressing average relationships between two or more variables.

regressor; predictor
variable independiente, predictiva
An independent variable in a regression analysis.

regrowth
rebrote

regular appointment [IBRD]
nombramiento ordinario, permanente

regular budget
presupuesto ordinario
One of three Bank budgets, it is for funds used to cover the administrative expenses of the Bank.

regular lending program [IBRD]
programa ordinario de financiamiento
The Bank lending program that includes the **base lending program** and the **standby program**.

regular share
acción ordinaria
Share of IBRD **capital stock** other than those allocated as **membership shares**.

regular staff
personal permanente

Regulations and Rules (of the Centre) [ICSID]
Reglamento y Reglas (del Centro)

regulatory agency
organismo regulador

rehabilitation
rehabilitación; reorganización; modernización; etc.

rehabilitation import credit, loan - RIC, RIL
crédito, préstamo para importaciones con fines de rehabilitación
Loan, credit to support policies to stabilize the economy and reactivate growth, following a period of economic decline caused inter alia by inappropriate policies.

reimbursable budget
presupuesto para programas reembolsables
One of three Bank budgets, it is for funds used to cover costs on behalf of outside agencies under billing agreements.

reinforcing bar; rebar
barra de refuerzo
Bar used for reinforcing concrete.

reinsurance
reaseguros
Form of insurance used by insurance companies for their own protection, whereby they share insurance risk with other insurance companies. The risk they share may either be in the form of an individual risk (**facultative reinsurance**) or a large number of risks (**treaty reinsurance**).

release **see** block release

release [ICSID]
fascículo

release, to [capital]
entregar; liberar

relend, to
represtar; prestar de nuevo (el importe de un préstamo)

relief
socorro; auxilio; alivio; etc.; desgravación (fiscal)

relocation grant
asignación, subsidio por traslado

remeasurement contract **see** unit price contract

remedy **see** legal remedy

remittances
transferencias [empresas]; remesas
[**see also** workers' remittance]

remote sensing
teledetección; teleobservación

renewable energy
energía, energéticos renovable(s); energía, energéticos de fuentes renovables

rent **see** economic rent; project rent

rent recovery index [projects]
índice de recuperación de la renta económica
The proportion of the economic rent created by a project that accrues to project beneficiaries and is recovered from them.

rent-seeking
(sistema de) captación de rentas

repayment bond
fianza de reembolso
Form of **performance** bond issued by a bank as a **repayment guarantee**.

repayment guarantee
garantía de reembolso
Form of guarantee whereby the guarantor undertakes, in the event of default by the principal, to pay the beneficiary an amount advanced or paid by the beneficiary to the principal in accordance with the contract between them. They are generally issued by banks.

repayment schedule
plan de amortización

repeater loan
préstamo complementario

repeater project
proyecto complementario
Project in the same sector and same country as a previous project.

repeater rate [education]
tasa de repetición
The rate at which students repeat a grade.

repeat financing
financiamiento complementario

rephasing of a debt; debt rephasing; rescheduling of debt
reprogramación (del servicio) de la deuda

replacement cost
costo de reposición, de sustitución

replacement level [population]
nivel de reemplazo, de renovación

replacement value **see** current (entry) value

replenish (an account), to
reponer; reconstituir

replenishment of resources
reposición de los recursos [AIF]; reconstitución de los recursos
The addition of funds to IDA. The Eleventh Replenishment starts fiscal year 1997.

replicability
posibilidad de repetición, de duplicación

report (of Commission) [ICSID]
acta (de la Comisión)

reported debt
deuda notificada

reporting country
país declarante, informante

reporting requirement(s)
requisito(s) en materia de informes

reporting system [projects]
sistema de presentación de informes

representations
declaraciones

representative office [bank]
representación

repression **see** financial repression

repurchase agreement
acuerdo de recompra
Arrangement by banks and other institutions to borrow short-term (usually one day) money by transferring **securities** to the lender, with the agreement that they will buy them back.

request for proposal - RFP
solicitud de propuestas

Requesting Organization [ICSID]
organismo solicitante

required rate of return - RRR
tasa de rentabilidad requerida, exigida

requited transfer
transferencia con, de contrapartida
Transfer of resource or financial item between two countries that is counterbalanced with a similar transfer in the other direction.

resale price maintenance - RPM
imposición de precios por el fabricante
Agreement whereby manufacturers independently or collectively specify minimum prices at which their products could be resold by wholesalers and retailers.

rescheduling of debt; rephasing of a debt; debt rephasing; debt rescheduling
reprogramación (del servicio) de la deuda

rescue package
programa, conjunto de medidas de rescate, de salvamento

resealing [highways]
resellado

research and development - R & D
investigación y desarrollo

research-push innovations; upstream innovations
innovaciones inducidas por la investigación

reservation price (of labor)
precio de reserva
The minimum price at which an individual is willing to offer a good or service. Often applied to labor, it is the lowest wage at which an individual is willing to offer his or her services.

reservation salary, wage
salario de reserva
The minimum wage at which a worker will accept work.

reserve **see** legal reserve

reserve against losses
reserva para pérdidas

reserve asset
activo de reserva
Those funds which constitute reserves in a bank.

reserve center
centro de reserva
Country or area where significant financial reserves are held.

reserve currency
moneda, divisa de reserva
The name given to a foreign currency which a government is prepared to hold as part of its foreign exchange reserves. This is used for financing international trade.

reserve for contingencies; allowance for contingencies; contingency allowance
reserva para imprevistos, contingencias
An amount of **retained earnings** earmarked for general undetermined contingencies or for any indefinite possible future losses.

reserve for depreciation; allowance for depreciation; depreciation allowance
asignación, reserva para depreciación
A valuation account set up to allow for the depreciation in an asset.

reserve for losses; provision for losses; loss provision
reserva para pérdidas
An amount of **retained earnings** earmarked for any indefinite future losses.

reserve money; base money
base monetaria; dinero primario

reserve operations [lending program]
operaciones "en reserva"
Lending operations on which initial preparation is being undertaken but which have not been appraised.

reserve position
posición de reserva(s); situación de las reservas

reserve ratio [banking]
coeficiente de reservas, de liquidez
The fraction of demand deposit money which a **commercial bank** must keep in its reserve account. This ratio determines the maximum amount of money a bank may loan out. In the United States, the **legal reserve** requirement is imposed by the Federal Reserve on depository institutions. The reserves (*cash maintained in a bank's own vault or claims on cash on deposit with compulsory or optional depositories*) for transaction accounts are 3% on $25 million or less and 12% for larger sums.

reserve requirement
encaje legal; reserva obligatoria

reserved procurement
adquisición reservada (a proveedores, contratistas nacionales)
Under the Bank's procurement guidelines, procurement that the client wishes to reserve for local suppliers or **contractors**, where it would have been attractive to international competition.

resettlement grant
asignación, subsidio por reasentamiento, por reinstalación

resident mission
misión residente

resident office
oficina del representante residente

resource balance
balanza de recursos
The difference between exports of goods and **nonfactor services** and imports of goods and **nonfactor services**.

resource based industries
industria basada en recursos naturales

resource envelope
presupuesto
In budgeting, an overall expenditure limit for a unit. The unit can then decide how it allocates individual expenditures within this envelope.

resource(s) gap
déficit, insuficiencia, brecha de recursos
Imports of goods and **nonfactor services** minus exports of goods and **nonfactor services**, or the **resource balance** with the opposite sign.

resource-neutral
sin efecto sobre los recursos

responsibility center [accounting]
centro de responsabilidad
Any organizational unit accountable to higher authority for performance of assigned functions, usually including its incurrence of specific costs under budget limitations and control.

responsive
...que se ajusta (a las estipulaciones), normas, etc.; que tiene en cuenta...

restocking
reposición de existencias

restraint policy
política de austeridad

restricted currency
moneda de uso restringido
The portion of capital subscriptions paid in the currencies of members and usable by IBRD in its lending operations only with the consent of the respective members.

restricted distribution
distribución reservada

restricted release (of 18% currency)
liberación restringida (de los montos del 18%)
Release by Bank member of its **18% currency** for lending or relending, with some restrictions, such as the requirement that the funds only be used in the currency concerned without being converted or are only used for initial lending and not indefinite lending and relending.

Restricted Toxic Materials List - RTML
Lista de Sustancias Tóxicas Prohibidas
A list of toxic materials that may not be used in Bank projects.

restrictive trade policy
política comercial restrictiva

resubmission [ICSID]
resometimiento (en el sentido del Art. 52[6] del Convenio)

resurfacing [highways]
renovación de la superficie

retail banking
servicios bancarios para consumidores
Traditional banking operations conducted with the general public.

retail training
formación en el propio país
Training of officials directly in the country by their compatriots rather than abroad by EDI or others.

retained earnings
utilidades no distribuidas
Accumulated net income, less distributions to stockholders and transfers to **paid-in capital** accounts.

retainer
honorario anticipado

retention money
retención en, como garantía; montos retenidos en garantía
Percentage of each payment retained until the contract has been completed and the **contractor** has fulfilled his performance (and maintenance) obligations.

retention rate; grade ratio [education]
tasa de retención
Percentage of students that pass from one grade to next grade.

retired debt
deuda amortizada
A debt that has been paid off.

retirement (of a fixed asset)
baja (de activos fijos)
Removal of an asset from service, following its sale or the end of its productive life, accompanied by the necessary adjustment of fixed asset and depreciation-reserve accounts.

retirement benefits
pensión; jubilación

retirement of outstanding debt
reembolso, rescate (anticipado) de la deuda
[see also debt retirement]

retraining
readiestramiento

retrieval
recuperación

retroactive financing; retrofinancing
financiamiento retroactivo
... of expenditures made ... date of signing a loan ... to normal financing. ... **off date**, before which ... for Bank financing.

... e financing

... ndustrial
]

... to capital
recuperación del capital
The purchase ... the investor ... of part or all of the initial investment of capital ... in a project.

return of investment
recuperación de la inversión

return of labor
(lista de) efectivos laborales
A detailed list of the staff and labor employed.

return on, to capital
rentabilidad, rendimiento del capital
1. The **internal rate of return** of the incremental net benefit after financing.
2. Net income divided by equity.

return on, to investment
rentabilidad, rendimiento de la inversión

returns; revenues
ingresos; rentas; entradas

returns to scale
rendimiento a escala; rendimiento en función de la escala

revaluation
revaluación; revalorización

revaluation factor [currency pool]
factor de revaluación
A ratio establishing the appreciation or depreciation due to exchange rate changes in the U.S. dollar value of currencies in the pool from one date to another. It is calculated by dividing, as of any day, the total U.S. dollar value at the exchange rates of that day of the balances of currencies in the pool brought forward from the previous day, by their total U.S. dollar value at the exchange rates of the previous day.

revealed comparative advantage - RCA
ventaja comparativa manifiesta, explícita, evidente, etc.
Concept developed by Bela Balassa, it is measured by an item's share in the country's exports relative to its share in world trade. If the share of the item in the country's exports is more than the corresponding world share, then the country has a revealed comparative advantage; if less, it has a revealed comparative disadvantage.

revenue see current revenues; fiscal revenue; government revenues

revenue account [national accounts]
cuenta de ingresos

revenue-earning enterprise
empresa productiva, que produce ingresos

revenue recognition
registro de ingresos
In accounting, when income is deemed to have been received. IFC records dividends, profit participations and fees (other than **commitment fees**) as income when received. Income and **commitment fees** are recorded as income on an accrual basis. It does not recognize income on loans where collectibility is in doubt and payments of principal or interest are past due more than sixty days.

revenue sharing
participación en los ingresos (fiscales)

revenue stamp
timbre fiscal

revenues; returns
ingresos; rentas; entradas

reverse charge call; collect call; transfer charge call
llamada de cobro revertido

reverse transfer of technology
transferencia inversa de tecnología
Transfer of technology from the developing to the developed countries.

review clause; (periodic) review clause
cláusula de examen (periódico)
Clause in a loan agreement which allows the lender to determine periodically whether stated objectives are being met.

review mission
misión de examen

revised minimum standard model - RMSM
modelo estándar mínimo modificado
An IBRD mathematical model of **monetary aggregates**, covering a few basic economic factors.

revolving credit
crédito renovable, rotatorio, refinanciable
Any line of credit that be borrowed against up to a stated credit limit and into which repayments go for crediting.

revolving fund
fondo rotatorio
A fund for project-related expenditure.

revolving underwriting facility - RUF; note issuance facility - NIF; prime underwriting facility - PUF
servicio de emisión de pagarés - SEP
A medium-term arrangement under which a borrower can issue short-term paper (Euronotes) backed up by **commercial bank** underwriting commitments.

rhizomes; rootstock crops
rizomas; cultivos de rizomas

ribbon check irrigation see border check irrigation

rice see floating rice; floded rice; upland rice

rig see oil (drilling) rig

right of first refusal see first refusal right

right of way
derecho de vía; zona expropiada; servidumbre de paso

rights issue, offering
emisión, oferta de acciones (con derecho preferencial de suscripción)

riot [MIGA]
motín
An assemblage of individuals who commit public acts of violence in defiance of local authority. Covered by MIGA under the **war and civil disturbance** category. Cf. **civil commotion**.

ripple price effects
repercusiones de las alzas de precios

risk allowance [projects]
margen (de precio) en concepto de riesgos
An allowance made when funding a project for risks that might occur.

risk-asset ratio
relación riesgo-activos
Ratio between assets held and amount of risk. MIGA's risk-asset ratio may not exceed one-to-five.

risk capital; venture capital
capital de riesgo
Capital invested in high-risk or relatively high-risk **securities** and enterprises, in expectation of commensurately high returns. It is sometimes used of equities or ordinary stock, the dividend of which varies with the profits earned by the corporation.

risk contract [oil]
contrato de riesgo
Contract that typically places all risk and investment on the **contractor**, who provides capital for exploration and production.

risk management
gestión de (los) riesgos

risk of expropriation [MIGA]
riesgo de expropiación

risk pooling [MIGA]
cobertura conjunta de riesgos
Sharing of risks among members of an insurance pool.

risk posture
posición de riesgo
The degree of risk of an investment.

risk spread
margen

risk transformation guarantees
garantías relativas a la transformación de riesgos

river blindness; onchocerciasis
ceguera de los ríos; oncocercosis

river channel
cauce, lecho, canal de un río

ro/ro [= roll-on/roll-off]
autotransbordo; embarque, desembarque por propulsión propia

road base see base [highways]

road, surface patching; spot improvement, patching; patching [highways]
bacheo; reparación de baches

road pricing
fijación de cargos por el uso de las carreteras

road user charges
cargos a los usuarios de las carreteras

rock phosphate; phosphate rock
roca fosfatada, fosforita

rollback
desmantelamiento
In GATT, the progressive dismantling of all trade restrictions which are inconsistent with GATT.

rolled (costs)
(costos) promediados

rolling back
reducción

rolling plan
plan renovable

roll-on/roll-off - ro/ro
autotransbordo; embarque, desembarque por propulsión propia

rollover
refinanciamiento continuo; renovación
1. Reinvestment of money received from a maturing **security** in a similar **security**.
2. Term used for a delay allowed by a lender to borrower in making a principal payment on a loan. With governments, rollovers in the form of refundings or refinancings are routine.

rollover credit **see** revolving credit

rollover of gains
reutilización de las ganancias

rollover project, program
repetición de un proyecto, programa

root crops
raíces alimentarias; cultivos de raíces alimentarias; tubérculos alimentarios

rootstock crops; rhizomes
rizomas; cultivos de rizomas

rotating savings and credit association - ROSCA
asociación de ahorro y crédito rotatorio
Type of savings institution whereby each member contributes a certain sum each month and the entire proceeds for that month are given to one individual. Each member takes it in turn to be the recipient.

roundwood
madera redonda

routine maintenance
mantenimiento de rutina, rutinario

row crops
cultivos en hileras

Rules of Procedure for Arbitration Proceedings (Arbitration Rules) [ICSID]
Reglas Procesales Aplicables a los Procedimientos de Arbitraje (Reglas de Arbitraje)

Rules of Procedure for Conciliation Proceedings (Conciliation Rules) [ICSID]
Reglas Procesales Aplicables a los Procedimientos de Conciliación (Reglas de Conciliación)

Rules of Procedure for the Institution of Conciliation and Arbitration Proceedings (Institution Rules) [ICSID]
Reglas Procesales Aplicables a la Iniciación de los Procedimientos de Conciliación y Arbitraje (Reglas de Iniciación)

Rules of Procedure for Meetings of the Executive Directors
Reglamento Interno para las Reuniones del Directorio

runaway inflation
inflación desenfrenada, galopante

running average; moving average
media, promedio móvil
The average rate of interest applied to an outstanding loan, based on the rates applied on all previous disbursements, weighted, where necessary, to allow for different levels of disbursement.

running contract
contrato por cantidades aproximadas
A contract for the supply of an approximate quantity over or below the approximate quantity mentioned in the contract. This reduces the holding cost and is normally applied to goods for which prices are not subject to appreciable market fluctuations.

running costs
gastos de explotación

run-of-mine coal; mine run coal
carbón sin clasificar, tal como sale, en bruto
Ungraded coal of various sizes as it comes from the mine.

run-of-the-river hydroelectric power plant
central hidroeléctrica de agua corriente
Hydroelectric power plant that uses water flow as
it comes in the river, with little or no storage to
allow for modifications in demand or water flow.

runoff [water]
escorrentía; escurrimiento

runoff irrigation
riego por escorrentía, por escurrimiento

- S -

safe drinking water **see** safe water

Safe Motherhood Fund [IBRD/WHO]
Fondo para la Maternidad sin Riesgos

Safe Motherhood Initiative [IBRD/WHO]
Programa para la Maternidad sin Riesgos

safe water; drinking water; safe drinking water
agua potable
Drinking water. The terms **drinking water, safe water** and safe **drinking water** are used interchangeably.

safety net
medidas de protección social
[**see also** social safety net]

salaries and wages
sueldos y salarios

saleability [securities]
posibilidad de colocación

saleable assets
activos vendibles

sale from portfolio
venta de valores en cartera

sale of loan maturities
venta de vencimientos de préstamos

sales tax
impuesto sobre, a la(s) venta(s)

salt lick; mineral lick
salegar

salt water intrusion
intrusión de agua salada
Salt water entering fresh water, thereby destroying freshwater sources.

salvage value
valor de recuperación, de rescate

sample survey [statistics]
encuesta muestral, por muestreo

sanitation
saneamiento

Saudi Arabian light (crude oil); light Arabian crude
(petróleo) crudo liviano; ligero de Arabia Saudita
The world's most prolific crude oil, frequently used as a **marker crude** in establishing the prices of other crudes.

savings and loan association
sociedad de ahorro y crédito; sociedad de ahorro y préstamo

scarcity value
valor en razón de la escasez

scatter chart, diagram; scattergram
diagrama de dispersión

scattered plotting
gráfico de dispersión

schedular tax; scheduled tax
impuesto cedular

schedule
anexo [convenios de préstamo o crédito]; cuadro; programa; calendario; etc.

schedule contract
contrato con base en una lista oficial de precios

schedule of rates contract
contrato basado en una lista de tarifas
A type of **unit price contract**, paid on the basis of a schedule of rates. It is similar to a **bill of quantities contract** but used where the quantity of work to be performed is difficult or impossible to estimate in advance, such as maintenance, drilling or dredging.

scheduled tax; schedular tax
impuesto celular

school mapping
levantamiento del mapa escolar, de mapas escolares

scrap, to
desechar; dar de baja; desguazar

scrap value
valor residual, de desecho

SDR currencies
monedas que integran la cesta del DEG

Sea Island cotton; West Indian cotton; Egyptian cotton; kidney cotton
algodón de Barbados; algodón de las Indias Occidendales; algodón egipcio

seasonal credit
crédito estacional

seasonally adjusted
ajustado para tomar en cuenta las variaciones estacionales; desestacionalizado

seasonal movements
variaciones estacionales

seasonal peak
máxima estacional; punto máximo estacional

seasoned securities
valores acreditados

second-best optimum
subóptimo; segunda alternativa
If one of the conditions for Pareto optimality cannot be fulfilled, then the best attainable situation (the second-best optimum) can, in general, only be achieved by departing from all the other Paretian conditions.

second-best policy
política subóptima

second generation special account - SGSA
cuenta especial secundaria
Special account set up for use by a specific implementation unit that cannot readily access the special account to meet eligible expenditures as they occur.

second lowest bidder
licitante que presenta la oferta clasificada en segundo lugar
[**see also** lowest bidder]

second tier bank
1. **banco de segunda instancia**
2. **banco de importancia secundaria**
1. Bank used as secondary source for funds.
2. Smaller lenders, i.e. banks other than the main **commercial banks**. Used particularly in Latin America.

second tier country
país de nivel intermedio
A classification proposed by OECD which covers those countries below the newly industrialized countries but above other developing countries. They are exporters of between $100 million and $2 billion worth of manufactured goods. Include Chile, Cyprus, Haiti, Indonesia, Jordan, Macau, Malaysia, Malta, Mauritius, Morocco,, Peru, Philippines, Sri Lanka, Thailand, Tunisia and Uruguay.

secondary education **see** lower secondary education; upper secondary education

secondary energy; final energy
energía secundaria, final

secondary market
mercado secundario

secondary market mortgage institution
institución de transferencia de hipotecas

secondary recovery
recuperación secundaria

secondary reserves
segunda línea de reservas

secondary securities
valores de segundo orden

secondary transmission line; subtransmission line
línea de transmisión secundaria, subtransmisión
Transmission line in a subtransmission system, i.e. one which supplies distribution substations from bulk power sources, such as large transmission substations or generating stations.

secondment
adscripción; envío en comisión de servicio

sector adjustment loan - SECAL; SAD
préstamo para (fines de) ajuste sectorial
A loan aiming at major policy improvements in a sector.

sector GDP
PIB sectorial
The contribution to GDP generated by a particular sector.

sector implementation review - SIR
examen de la ejecución de proyectos sectoriales

sector investment and maintenance loan - SIM
préstamo para inversión y mantenimiento sectoriales
Loan aimed at investing in a particular sector maintaining the level of activity in that sector.

sector loan
préstamo sectorial, para un sector
A loan geared towards a particular sector.

secular trend
tendencia a muy largo plazo
Long-term average of a statistical series, usually understood to cover at least three or four generations.

secure a loan, to
garantizar un préstamo; obtener un préstamo

secured loan
préstamo garantizado

securities (custody) account
cuenta de valores (en custodia)

securities dealer; securities firm
corredor de valores; sociedad de valores
Firm acting as a principal rather than an agent in the **securities market**.

securities market
mercado de valores
The primary and secondary market for negotiable equity (stocks) and long-term debt instruments (bonds).

securitization
conversión de activos financieros en valores
1.   Issue of **securities** in exchange for debt. The Bank has used it to specifically refer to "the packaging and selling of a pool of creditor risks in the form of a **security**".
2.   The tendency on **financial markets** to make greater use of **securities**, i.e. firms issue **securities** rather than borrow directly from banks.

security
seguridad; título; valor; garantía
1.   Document giving title to property or claim on income.
2.   Income-yielding paper traded on the stock exchange or secondary market.
[**see also** bid security; blue chip security; gilt-edged securities; government securities; marketable securities; outstanding securities; over-the-counter securities; performance security; portfolio securities; seasoned securities; secondary securities; social security]

security agreement
acuerdo de garantía

security lending
préstamo en valores; financiamiento en valores
Lending of **securities** which the IBRD owns (typically a U.S. Government obligation) against receipt of cash or similar **securities** as collateral in amounts equal to or higher than the market value of the **security** lent.

security of tenure
seguridad de tenencia; seguridad en el cargo; inamovilidad

sedimentation ponds
estanques de sedimentación
Pond where waste water is temporarily stored to allow the solids to settle out.

seed **see** breeder seed; certified seed; field seeds; foundation seed; registered seed

seed capital; seed money
capital simiente, generador

seed farm
finca, granja (de producción) de semillas

seed garden
huerta (de producción) de semillas

seed money; seed capital
capital simiente, generador

seed plant
planta de simiente; planta para semilla

seedling
plántula; plantón (de árboles); planta de semillero, vivero

seine fishing
pesca (con redes) de tiro

seismic survey
estudio, reconocimiento sísmico

seizure [legal]
secuestro
Act or process of seizing property by virtue of a writ or other legal order to satisfy a judgment made by a court under the authority of a legal order.

selection felling, cutting
tala selectiva
Harvesting of only a small proportion of the standing crop.

Selective Capital Increase - SCI
aumento selectivo del capital
An increase in the Bank's capital which does not apply equally to all shareholders. The most recent one was in 1984. Though always referred to as *Selective Capital Increase*, the legal document calls it *Special Capital Increase*.

self-adjustment
autocorrección; autorregulación

self-care; self-treatment
autotratamiento; autoterapia

self-contained; free standing
independiente; autónomo

self-determination
autodeterminación; libre determinación

self-employed person
trabajador por cuenta propia, independiente, autónomo

self-financing
autofinanciamiento

self-financing-ratio - SFR
coeficiente de autofinanciamiento
The rate at which a project is financed from internal resources.

self-help
autoayuda; esfuerzo propio

self-help housing scheme
plan de vivienda por el sistema de esfuerzo propio y ayuda mutua

self-insurance
autoaseguro

self-liquidating assets
activos autoliquidables, autoamortizables
Assets that will pay for themselves over a period of time.

self-liquidating project
proyecto que se autofinancia
Credit reimbursed by the income from the operation for which it was lent.

self-reliance
confianza en sí mismo; capacidad para valerse por sí mismo
[see also collective self-reliance]

self-restraint
autolimitación; moderación; autocontrol

self-sufficiency
autosuficiencia; autonomía; autoabastecimiento

self-sustaining growth
crecimiento autosostenido

self-sustaining state
situación de autosostenimiento

self-targeting (commodity)
(producto) destinado por su propia índole a determinados grupos de la población
Basic foodstuffs that are mainly consumed by the poor. So-called because their target is obvious.

self-treatment; self-care
autotratamiento; autoterapia

self-weighting sample
muestra autoponderada

sell down
venta de un crédito fuera del consorcio
The transfer of a credit from a bank within a
syndicate to a bank outside the **syndicate**.

seller's market
**mercado de vendedores; mercado favorable al
vendedor**

selling consortium, group, syndicate
**consorcio (bancario); grupo de colocación;
grupo vendedor**
A group of bank or **securities** dealers involved in
placing a **security** as sellers.

selling rate
precio vendedor; precio de venta
Price proposed (for a **security**).

selling value
valor, precio de liquidación, de realización

semiannual coupon equivalent basis, on a [bonds]
sobre una base semestral

semiknocked down - SKD
semimontado

seminar **see** Board seminar

seminar paper
documento para un seminario

semipermanent housing
vivienda semipermanente

semipublic company
empresa mixta, semipública, paraestatal

semiskilled manpower
mano de obra semicalificada

semiskilled worker
trabajador semicalificado

senior debt, loan
deuda prioritaria; préstamo prioritario
Debt for which claims on the assets of the
borrower rank ahead of other debts in case of
liquidation.

senior economist
economista superior

senior level staff
funcionarios superiores

senior management
administración superior

senior manager
**directivo principal; alto funcionario;
funcionario superior**

Senior Policy Seminar [EDI]
Seminario de políticas generales

Senior Policy Seminar on... [EDI]
Seminario de políticas de...

sensitive product
producto sensible a la coyuntura

sensitivity analysis
análisis de sensibilidad
A study of the impact that changes in costs and
benefits would have on the profitability or **present
value** of a project.

separation [employment]
separación del servicio

septic tank
tanque séptico; foso séptico

sequential cropping **see** double cropping

serial bond, loan
**bono, préstamo de vencimiento escalonado;
bono, préstamo con vencimiento elegido a la
suerte**
1.   Bond issues split into a series of maturities.
2.   Special type of serial bonds where
reimbursement is decided by drawing in lots (used
in France).

service see debt service; fee-for-services basis

service; service line; supply line; connection [electricity]
conexión de servicio

service a loan, to
atender el servicio de un préstamo

service and support fee [IFC]
cargo por servicios
Fee paid by IFC to the World Bank for the services it receives from the Bank.

service charge
cargo, comisión por servicios

service industry
industria de servicios

service line; service; supply line; connection [electricity]
conexión de servicio

service road
vía, calzada de servicio

service station [livestock]
puesto de monta

serviceable [highways]
transitable

serviced area, lot, site
zona urbanizada; lote con servicios
Site having essential services.

servicing [plots]
instalación de servicios en los lotes; urbanización de lotes

serving chairman
presidente en funciones

session [ICSID]
período de sesiones

set aside agreement
acuerdo, convenio de destinación especial
Agreement for payment receipts from a project to be designated for a specific purpose.

settlement (of a dispute) [ICSID]
arreglo (de una diferencia)

settlement date
fecha de cierre, de liquidación
The date on which payment for a transaction must be made.

settlement of maintenance of value; maintenance of value settlement
liquidación por concepto de mantenimiento del valor

settling-in grant [IBRD]
subsidio, asignación para instalación
Grant provided to assist new staff members in meeting additional expenses (electrical appliances, furniture, car, etc.) associated with relocation to the Greater Washington Metropolitan Area.

severance pay
indemnización por despido; prestación, pago de cesantía

sewage disposal
eliminación de aguas negras, servidas

sewage (treatment) plant
planta de tratamiento de aguas negras, servidas

sewerage project
proyecto de alcantarillado

shadow discount rate
tipo, tasa de descuento sombra, de cuenta
The opportunity cost of capital.

shadow exchange rate - SER; shadow pricing of the exchange rate
tipo de cambio sombra; tipo de cambio de cuenta
The exchange rate that reflects the value of an additional unit of foreign exchange in terms of the domestic currency as used for domestic consumption.

shadow price
precio sombra; precio de cuenta
The value used in economic analysis for a cost or a benefit when the market price is felt to be a poor estimate of economic value.

shadow pricing of the exchange rate see shadow exchange rate

shadow project
proyecto compensatorio
Project that would provide substitute environmental services to compensate for the loss of the original assets.

shadow rate of interest
tipo, tasa de interés sombra; tipo, tasa de interés de cuenta
Rate of interest used as the **discount rate** in project analysis. Include **consumption rate of interest** and **accounting rate of interest**.

shadow wages
salario sombra; salario de cuenta
A wage rate that is used for measuring the **opportunity cost** of labor in project analysis. Three components are used to establish it: forgone marginal product, changes in consumption and savings and changes in leisure.

shakeout (of the market)
asentamiento; sacudimiento
1. A moderate stock market or business recession, usually corrective of an inflationary condition.
2. Any movement in the market prices of **securities** that forces speculators to sell their holdings.

share see also bonus share; common share; founder's share; membership shares; outstanding shares; publicly traded share; qualifying shares; registered share; stock

share capital; registered capital
capital social, accionario, en acciones
Capital represented by shares of **capital stock**.
[**see also** authorized share capital]

share capital, to supply
participar en el capital social

share premium account [IFC]
cuenta de primas de emisión
Account of a corporation, in which IFC has a holding and in which the premiums obtained on new shares are deposited.

share retention agreement [IFC]
acuerdo de retención de acciones
Agreement, under which a company agrees not to sell the stock of another company in which IFC has an interest, until the loan has been reimbursed.

sharecropping
aparcería; mediería

shareholders' equity see stockholders' equity

sharing clause
cláusula en que se estipula que se han de compartir los reembolsos
Clause in loan agreement that states that if one participant fails to receive payment, the others will share receipts with the participant(s) not receiving payments.

shell (of a building)
obra gruesa

shell company
sociedad ficticia; compañía de papel
Company which exists on paper but does not apparently trade or operate, possibly being used as a cover for illegal or unethical activities.

shifting cultivation
cultivo migratorio

shifting of tax
traslación del impuesto
Changing the tax burden so that someone other than the person or firm on whom the tax is levied pays all or part of it.

shift parameter
parámetro de cambio
Parameter leading to a movement to the left or right of a curve, e.g. a demand curve.

shipping
transporte marítimo; embarque; envío; etc.

shipping conference see liner (shipping) conference

shopping [procurement]
comparación de precios
A procurement method based on comparing price quotations obtained from several foreign or local suppliers, usually at least three, to ensure competitive prices. It requires no formal **bidding documents** and is an appropriate method for procuring readily available **off-the-shelf goods** or standard specification commodities that are small in value.

shortfall
deficiencia; disminución; insuficiencia; déficit

short form audit report
informe corto de auditoría
A succinct report or letter prepared by an auditor following an audit. It is addressed to the management or directors. The short form is standard. Cf. **long form audit report.**

short list
lista final de selección

short season (crop)
(cultivo de) temporada corta

short staple cotton
algodón de fibra corta
Cotton with fibers of 3/8 to 1 inches long.

Short Term Economic Monitor [IBRD]
indicadores de las perspectivas económicas a corto plazo

showcase project
proyecto de exposición
Project designed for prestige, with high unit and/or recurrent costs. The Bank does not normally support such projects.

Siam cotton; tree cotton; Ceylon cotton; China cotton
algodón arbóreo

SIBOR [= Singapore Interbank Offered Rate]
SIBOR (tasa de oferta interbancaria de Singapur)

side letter; supplemental letter
carta complementaria

sight assets
activos a la vista

sight deposit
depósito a la vista
Deposits held in banks and similar deposit-taking institutions which are transferable by check or withdrawable in cash without notice.

sight liabilities
obligaciones a la vista

simplified sewerage
sistemas simplificados de alcantarillado
A modified design of sewer so that the sewers are smaller, shallower and flatter, with fewer manholes, with no decline in performance but with cost savings of about 30 percent over the costs of conventional sewerage.

single-crop economy
economía de monocultivo

single currency loans, [IBRD]
préstamos en moneda única; préstamo en una sola moneda
IBRD program where selected borrowers are offered a choice of currencies on their loans as an alternative to the existing standard multicurrency loan product. The program offers United States dollars, yen, deutschmarks, French francs, and pounds sterling. Its interest rate will be tied to six-month **LIBOR** in each loan currency (PIBOR in the case of French francs).

single-entry accounting
contabilidad por partida simple
A system of accounting in which only records of cash and of personal accounts are maintained.

single factorial terms of trade
relación de intercambio de un solo factor
Terms of trade incorporating productivity changes in the exporting country. Provides a useful indicator of changes in the amount of real resources, in the form of capital and labor services, which a country must give up in order to purchase a given volume of imports.

single fertilizer
fertilizante, abono simple
A fertilizer containing only one nutrient.

single parent family, household
familia monoparental

sink (e.g. of greenhouse gases)
sumidero; medio receptor; zona de absorción, de disipación
Receptacle, or receiving area, for materials translocated through a system (e.g. the oceans are the sink into which many water-borne pollutants are drained; the seed of a plant is the sink in which nutrients are stored).

sinking fund
fondo de amortización
A fund created by a borrower for the purpose of redeeming bonds. The borrower is obliged to redeem specified amounts of the bond within specified periods.

sinking fund factor
factor de fondo de amortización
The level deposit required each year to reach 1 by a given year. The reciprocal of the **compounding factor** for 1 per annum. Generally obtained from a set of compounding and discounting tables. This factor permits calculating the equal installment that must be set aside each year, to be invested at compound interest, in order to have a predetermined sum at a given time. It is primarily used to determine how much must be put into a fund in order to have recovered the amount of an investment at the end of its useful life.

sister companies
empresas asociadas, pertenecientes al mismo grupo; afiliadas

site
lugar, emplazamiento (de un proyecto)

site coverage
terreno comprendido, cubierto

site development
preparación del terreno; trabajos de urbanización

site plan
plano del emplazamiento, del lugar

sites and services
lotes y servicios
The provision of land and basic public services, to enable housing projects to get off the ground.

sitting [ICSID]
sesión

sketch plan [architecture]
boceto; croquis

skidding
arrastre, deslizamiento de troncos

skilled manpower
mano de obra calificada

skilled worker
trabajador calificado

skills
conocimientos; experiencia; competencia

skills development
capacitación; adiestramiento; formación

skills mix
combinación de especialidades

skill training center
centro de desarrollo de aptitudes; centro de capacitación especializada; centro de perfeccionamiento

slack [economy] [noun]
capacidad no utilizada

slash-and-burn cultivation
método de roza y quema
Agricultural method involving slashing undergrowth at ground level and felling trees with axes at any convenient height. The area is then thoroughly burned and crops planted.

slice [contracts]
porción; componente; etc.
In contracts, an individual contract for which a **contractor** or a manufacturer may bid, rather than having to bid for the whole project.

200

slice and package [procurement]
fraccionamiento de adquisiciones
Project where **contractors** and manufacturers may bid for an individual contract (**slice**) or group of similar contracts (**package**) rather than the whole project.

"slice and package" contract
contrato fraccionado
Contract allowing use of **slice and package** technique.

sliding-scale clause
cláusula de escala móvil

slippage; lag
retraso; demora; desfase

slow onset emergency; quiet emergency
situación de emergencia latente
Emergency which occurs over a period of time, such as a drought, and which rarely causes much destruction of physical assets.

sluggish growth
crecimiento lento

sluice price; sluice gate price; lock gate
precio de compuerta [avicultura]
A theoretical cif price used in calculating European Communities supplementary levies on imports of pork, poultry and eggs.

slum
barrio de tugurios

slum clearance
eliminación de tugurios, de zonas de tugurios

slump
contracción; recesión

slumpflation
recesión con inflación
Harsh economic conditions created by a combination of simultaneous recession and growing unemployment as well as rapid price inflation.

slum upgrading
mejoramiento de zonas, barrios de tugurios

small and medium enterprises - SME; small- and medium-scale enterprises - SMSE
pequeña y mediana empresa - PYME

small and medium industries - SMI; small- and medium-scale industries - SMSI
pequeña y mediana industria

small-bore sewerage **see** effluent sewerage

smallholder
pequeño agricultor

smallholding
pequeña explotación agrícola

small-scale enterprise - SSE
pequeña empresa

small-scale industry - SSI
pequeña industria

small-scale irrigation
pequeña zona, pequeño proyecto de riego

smoothness ratio
coeficiente de uniformidad

snatching effect
efecto de captación incidental de beneficiarios
The effect of creating incidental beneficiaries to a project as well as those intended.

social accounting matrix - SAM
matriz de contabilidad social
A system of accounts in which the various incomings of each and every account are represented by an ordered row and the corresponding outgoings by a similarly ordered column. They describe the financial flows that take place within and among various institutions and sectors of the economy, each of which is disaggregated according to local conditions and policy relevance. They integrate data on income distribution and production and are suitable vehicles for studying the impact of macroeconomic policy action on the level of living of different household groups.

social accounts
cuentas sociales; contabilidad social
The systematized treatment of social indicators which represent quality of life conditions in a country, region or other geographical unit.

social advantages
ventajas sociales, colectivas

social benefit-cost ratio - SBC
relación costos-beneficios sociales

social benefits
prestaciones sociales

social costs
costos sociales, colectivos

social dimensions of adjustment - SDA
aspectos sociales del ajuste

social discount rate; social rate of discount
tasa de actualización social

social forestry
plantación de bosques comunitarios
Forestry used for community use as opposed to private sector forestry.

social impact assessment - SIA
evaluación de los efectos sociales
A kind of ex ante evaluation of a project, where a sociologist examines a development project prepared by a group of other experts and is asked to make an assessment about whether or not it will have positive or adverse social repercussions.

social infrastructure; community facilities
infraestructura social; instalaciones comunitarias

social insurance
seguro, previsión social; seguridad social

social marketing program [population]
programa de ventas subvencionadas
A program of sales of goods with reduced prices for special groups.

social net present value - SNPV
valor social neto actual, actualizado
The net **present value** of a project after incremental income flows generated by the project

have been weighted to reflect social income-distribution priorities.

social opportunity cost
costo de oportunidad social
The **opportunity cost** to society of diverting resources from marginal private sector projects to public sector ones.

social overhead capital
infraestructura social

social overhead investment
inversión en infraestructura social
Investment in social facilities.

social price
precio social
The price that reflects the value to the country of **inputs** and outputs and takes into consideration "non-efficiency" but socially important goals such as reduction of consumption of alcohol, tobacco and fancy cars or expanded production of goods to meet basic needs, etc.

social pricing
fijación, determinación, cálculo de precios sociales
A method of economic analysis which takes into account savings and consumption.

social rate of discount; social discount rate
tasa de actualización social

social rate of return - SRR
tasa de rentabilidad social
The **economic rate of return** in social prices. Social prices are shadow prices which incorporate social factors such as scarcity of savings, income inequality and poverty.

social returns [projects]
beneficios sociales

social safety net
red de seguridad social; medidas de protección social

social security benefits
prestaciones de (la) seguridad social

social security fund
fondo, caja de seguridad social

social security scheme
plan, sistema de seguridad social

social shadow wage rate - SSWR
salario de cuenta social
Shadow wage rate (= shadow price for labor, generally set by estimating the marginal value product of labor) in **social prices**.

social time preference rate
tasa de preferencia social en el tiempo
A rate, usually expressed in the form of a percentage, that expresses the preference of a society as a whole for present returns rather than future returns and that sometimes is proposed as a **discount rate** for project analysis.

social wants
necesidades sociales

social welfare
bienestar, asistencia social

social welfare function
función de bienestar social

socioeconomic status - SES
situación socioeconómica; condiciones socioeconómicas

soft component [projects]
componente no físico, de servicios

soft currency
moneda débil
A currency with a falling exchange rate due to continuing balance of payments deficits.

soft loan
préstamo en condiciones concesionarias, blando, liberal
A loan with no rate of interest or a rate of interest below the cost of the capital being lent.

soft loan affiliate
institución afiliada que otorga el financiamiento en condiciones concesionarias

soft loan window
servicio, ventanilla para préstamos concesionarios

soft project
proyecto de carácter social
A project of a social nature.

soft technical assistance **see** institution-related technical assistance

software
componentes lógicos; programas; instrucciones; elementos no físicos

softwood forest
bosque de coníferas

soil conservation
conservación del suelo

soil study, survey
estudio de suelos, edafológico

sole cropping; monoculture
monocultivo
Cultivation of a single crop as wheat or cotton to the exclusion of other possible uses of the land.

sole source procurement
adquisición de un solo proveedor
Procurement from a single vendor, without benefit of competitive bidding.

solids-free sewerage **see** effluent sewerage

solid state technology
tecnología de estado sólido, de semiconductores, de transistores

sound loan
préstamo sólido, seguro

sour gas discharge
descarga de gases ácidos, ricos en productos azufrados

source and use of funds statement **see** statement of changes in financial position

sources and application of funds statement **see**
statement of changes in financial position

sourcing; outsourcing
**contratación de uno o varios servicios,
adquisición de bienes, etc., fuera de la empresa,
etc.**
The process whereby an institution, corporation,
etc. has an entire service carried out by an external
company or purchases its entire needs in a specific
area from an outside company.

Southern Cone
Cono Sur

sovereign act doctrine
acto de gobierno
Legal theory according to which the courts of one
country should abstain from passing judgment
about the legality of a sovereign act by a foreign
state.

sovereign credit, loan
crédito garantizado por el Estado
A borrowing guaranteed by the state.

sovereign creditor
Estado acreedor

sovereign risk
**riesgo soberano; riesgo que plantea el Estado
prestatario**
The risk of changes in a borrowing country's
overall foreign exchange position, which might
affect its ability to repay a loan.

sovereign risk loan
préstamo que entraña un riesgo soberano
Loan to a State or loan where the State takes the
responsibility for the loan.

spate irrigation **see** flood irrigation

Spearman's rank correlation coefficient
**coeficiente de correlación por rangos de
Spearman**
A measure of the degree to which two variables
are associated with each other, not necessarily in
value but in rank. The coefficient will be between
+1 (high association) and -1.

special budget; extraordinary budget
presupuesto extraordinario

Special Joint Financing
financiamiento conjunto especial
Special financing made by several countries
(Germany, Japan, Switzerland and the United
Kingdom initially) in addition to contributions
made directly to the Special Facility for
Sub-Saharan Africa using arrangements
negotiated directly between IDA and the
contributors to be used in countries meeting the
eligibility requirements of the Facility with
repayment terms at least equivalent to IDA terms
and with procurement open at least to those
countries under the Facility.

special majority
mayoría especial

special operational emphasis - SOE
campo de atención especial de las operaciones
Concept introduced in FY88 which provided for
attention to be focused on priority development
objectives. Currently includes such areas as the
environment, debt and adjustment, poverty
reduction, food security and private sector
development.

Special Reserve [World Bank]
reserva especial
A reserve set aside by the Bank to meet liabilities
such as defaulting loans, liabilities on borrowings
or guarantees, contractual payments of interest,
other charges or amortization on the Bank's own
borrowings or similar payments on loans
guaranteed by the Bank.

specialized agency [UN]
organismo especializado

specific (customs) duty
derecho (aduanero) específico

specific investment loan - SIL [IBRD]
préstamo para una inversión específica
World Bank loan for a specific investment project.

specific performance
ejecución de un contrato según sus términos

specimen of signature **see** authenticated specimen of signature

spending ministry
ministerio que efectúa gastos; ministerio de ejecución

spillover effect, impact; spinoff effect
efecto secundario, derivado
An effect that occurs when an economic unit not directly involved benefits from a transaction, project, etc.

spillover exports
exportaciones de excedentes del mercado interno
Goods normally consumed by the domestic market but available for export because of low domestic demand.

spillway chute; tailrace
canal de descarga

spinning reserve [electricity]
capacidad de reserva inmediatamente disponible
That reserve generating capacity connected to the bus and ready to take load.

spinoff [financial market]
cesión, transferencia de activos (de una sociedad) a cambio de acciones (de otra sociedad nueva)
The transfer by a corporation of a portion of its assets to a newly formed corporation in exchange for the latter's **capital stock**, which is thereupon distributed as a dividend to the stockholders of the first corporation.

spinoff effect; spillover effect, impact
efecto secundario, derivado
An effect that occurs when an economic unit not directly involved benefits from a transaction, project, etc.

splicing
empalme; enlace
Linking different series of data based on slightly different definitions into a single series.

split degree
título otorgado por dos universidades
Higher education degree split between a local university and top-rated international university or other educational institution.

sponsor
patrocinador; promotor

spontaneous lending **see** voluntary lending

spot exchange rate
tipo de cambio al contado
The exchange rate prevailing under a spot contract, i.e. delivery in one or two business days or less.

spot improvement, patching; road, surface patching; patching [highways]
bacheo; reparación de baches

spot market; cash market [foreign exchange]
mercado al contado
Foreign exchange market where currency is sold for immediate delivery. *See* **futures market.**

spot market [commodities]
mercado de productos disponibles, de entrega inmediata
Market where goods are sold for cash, for immediate delivery.

spot patching, improvement; road, surface patching; patching [highways]
bacheo, reparación de baches

spot price
precio al contado, para entrega inmediata
The price of a commodity available for immediate sale and delivery, the commodity being referred to as a "spot" commodity.

spot quotation
cotización al contado

spotted cotton
algodón manchado
Cotton that has been changed in color to a brown, écru or yellow cast by unfavorable weather, wet bolls, stems, leaves or rainstorms. The spots affect the grading.

spray irrigation
riego por aspersión
Sprinkling water over land to be used for crops. Often used to dispose of wastewater from sewage treatment plants.

spraying **see** knapsack spraying

spread (e.g. between borrowing cost and lending rates)
margen (p.ej., entre el costo de los empréstitos y el interés sobre los préstamos)
Difference between rate at which bank borrows money and rate at which it onlends funds to its customers.

spread (between spot and forward quotations)
margen (entre las cotizaciones al contado y a término)

spread of spreads
diferencia entre los márgenes

spreadsheet
planilla de cálculo electrónica; hoja electrónica de cálculo

sprinkle irrigation
riego por aspersión
A method of irrigation in which water (under adequate pressure) is sprinkled over the land through nozzle lines, perforated pipes or sprinklers.

squat, to
ocupar terrenos ilegalmente, sin tener derecho

squatter
ocupante sin título, ilegal, precario

squatter area, settlement
zona de ocupantes ilegales, sin título

squeeze **see** credit squeeze

Stabex (System for the stabilization of ACP and OCT mining products) [European Communities]
STABEX (Sistema de estabilización de los ingresos de exportación de los Estados ACP y PTUM)

stabilization fund
fondo de estabilización

stabilizers **see** built-in stabilizers

staff
personal; funcionarios
[**see also** counterpart staff; field staff; fixed term staff; higher level staff; line staff; overstaffed; Principles of Staff Employment; supervisory staff; support staff]

staff, to
dotar de personal

staff appraisal report - SAR
informe de evaluación inicial preparado por el personal

staff assistant
auxiliar especial

staff audit
evaluación de funciones directivas
Check by Personnel on staff management functions, e.g. performance reviews to see that they are being carried out properly.

staff department
departamento de servicio, de asesoramiento

staff development
perfeccionamiento del personal

staff house
alojamiento para el personal

staff-month
mes-funcionario

staff rule
norma (del Manual de Personal)

Staff Rules [IBRD]
Reglamento del Personal

staffing
dotación de personal

staffing ratio
relación personal-población; coeficiente de ocupación de cargos [administración de personal]

staffyear equivalent - SYE
equivalente en años-personal

stagflation
estanflación

stagnation (of the economy)
estancamiento

stakeholders
partes interesadas; interesados

stall feeding
engorde en establo

stand [forest]
rodal

stand-alone project
proyecto independiente

standard charge section
sección estándar (del presupuesto)
The basis of the Bank's budgetary system, it comprises five basic attributes of all administrative expenditures (managing unit, source of funds, expense category (type of goods or services), task category (Bank function) and product. All administrative commitments and expenditures are related to the standard charge section.

standard conversion factor - SCF
factor de conversión estándar
A number, usually less than 1 that can be multiplied by the domestic market price, **opportunity cost**, or value in use of a nontraded item to convert it to an equivalent **border price** that reflects the effect of trade distortions on domestic prices of that good or service. A standard conversion factor is the reciprocal of 1 plus the foreign exchange premium stated in decimal form.

standard cost accounting
contabilidad de costos estándar
A method of accounting whereby standard costs (i.e. forecast costs under projected conditions) are the basis for credits to work-in-process accounts

standard deduction [taxation]
deducción estándar

standard deviation
desviación estándar
A commonly used measure of the degree to which a variable is dispersed around its mean value.

Standard International Trade Classification - SITC
Clasificación Uniforme para el Comercio Internacional - CUCI

standard of living
nivel de vida

standard rate (of interest)
tipo, tasa (de interés) vigente

standard recovery
recuperación estándar
Recovery of currency used in lending operations subject to maintenance of value. Recovery takes place on the first recall date of the Bank's fiscal year following the ninth anniversary of the disbursement of the currency by the Bank and every ten years thereafter.

standard values [trade]
valores normales, corrientes, estándar

standardized occupational streams
perfiles ocupacionales normalizados

standby agreement [IFC]
acuerdo de compromiso contingente

standby amount of guarantee
monto de la garantía contingente
The amount of guarantee provided under **standby coverage**. Cf. **maximum amount of guarantee**.

standby arrangement [IMF]
acuerdo de derecho de giro

standby commitment [IFC]
operación de compromiso de compra

standby coverage [MIGA]
cobertura contingente
An option to obtain coverage for additional contributions to the investment project. Under MIGA rules, this standby coverage may not exceed fifty percent of the initial amount of the guarantee and shall in no case exceed one hundred percent.

standby equity [investment]
compromiso contingente de participación en el capital social
In investment an agreement that is conditional on stock purchase.

standby loan
préstamo contingente
Loan which is not part of the current schedule but which can be presented to the Board if other projects slip.

standby (lending) program [IBRD]
programa (de financiamiento) de reserva
Lending operations that are under preparation and are likely to be ready for the fiscal year following the fiscal year in question but may be ready sooner and which could substitute for projects in the fiscal year in question.

standby premium [MIGA]
prima contingente
Additional **premium** charged for **standby coverage**.

standby underwriting commitment [IFC]
compromiso contingente de garantía de suscripción

standing, financial **see** creditworthiness

standing instructions, orders
instrucciones permanentes

standpipe; standpost; hydrant
toma de agua

standstill
statu quo
In GATT, means no new trade restrictions inconsistent with GATT, no new trade restrictions which go further than necessary to remedy specific situations provided for in GATT and no trade measures taken to improve negotiating positions.

standstill agreement
acuerdo de mantenimiento de la situación existente

staple (food)
alimento básico

staple (food crop)
cultivo alimentario básico

staple (good)
artículo básico

starchy root crop
tubérculo feculento, raíz feculenta

start-up cost
costo de puesta en marcha

State eligible to sign (the Convention) [ICSID]
Estado que puede adherirse

statement
declaración; intervención; exposición
[see also financial statement; income statement; summary statement]

statement of account
estado de cuenta; extracto de cuenta

statement of changes in financial position; sources and application of funds statement; funds statement; working capital statement; source and use of funds statement; funds flow statement; changes in working capital statement; statement of sources and applications of funds; statement of cash flows [World Bank]
estado de flujo de fondos; estado de fuentes y utilización de fondos
A statement used in conventional accounting which summarizes the financing and investing activities of an entity, including the extent to which the enterprise has generated funds from operations during the period and for completing the disclosure of changes in financial position during the period. The first English term is the one recommended by the U.S. Accounting Principles Board (APB) since 1971; the second and last terms are the ones found most frequently in the World Bank and IFC; and the third is the most common one used in the U.S. prior to the APB recommendation. The other terms are also found.

statement of condition [IDA]
estado de situación financiera
A statement of IDA's financial situation.

statement of expenditure - SOE
declaración, estado, relación de gastos

statement of sources and applications of funds **see** statement of changes in financial position

state-owned enterprise - SOE
empresa estatal

state-trading countries
países de comercio estatal

static efficiency
eficiencia estática
The efficiency with which current outputs are produced.

Static Life Index [commodities]
índice estático de las reservas (años)
Index in years of reserves of a commodity assuming no growth in rate of production.

status
estado; situación; categoría; condición social

status report; progress report
informe sobre la marcha (de un proyecto), sobre la labor realizada, sobre las actividades

statutory body
organismo de derecho público

statutory ceiling
límite estatutario, legal, reglamentario

statutory lending limit - SLL
límite estatutario de los préstamos
The maximum amount of total outstanding guarantees, participations in loans and direct loans, equal to one hundred percent of the unimpaired subscribed capital, reserves and surplus of the Bank.

stay of enforcement [ICSID]
suspensión de la ejecución (del laudo)

steady state lending
nivel estable de préstamos

Lending position whereby the total amount disbursed and outstanding equals the sum of the annual amounts disbursed and outstanding.

steam coal
carbón de alto poder calorífico; carbón térmico
Coal intermediate in rank between bituminous coal and anthracite. Typical steam coals have a carbon/hydrogen ratio of about 20% (more = anthracite less = bituminous coals). Some steam coals are used for smelting and coke making while others are specifically suitable for steam generation.

steam plant
central de vapor

steelmaking **see** open-hearth steelmaking

steepness (of a curve)
grado de inclinación; pendiente (de una curva)

stemming-from benefit
beneficio derivado indirecto
A form of indirect benefit that accrues to purchasers of project outputs that are themselves intermediate products. The direct and indirect value added generated in forward-linked industries. For example, cotton that is produced by an agricultural project and that would be used in existing cotton gins having unused production capacity might allow those gins to create additional value added that would not exist without the project. Stemming-from benefits sometimes are calculated using specialized input-output multipliers. Would not normally exist where project outputs are traded, since the same stemming-from benefits could be had by increasing imports of the intermediate product or by diverting exports to local use.

step-down power station
estación reductora
Power station where the outgoing power from the transformers is at a lower voltage than the incoming power.

step-down, step-up interest rates
tasas de interés crecientes
Interest rates which are below market rates in the early period of the loan and above market rate in the latter part of the loan.

stepped tariff structure
estructura tarifaria escalonada

step-up power station
estación elevadora

stock see capital stock; closing stock; common stock; corporate stocks; outstanding stocks; paid-up stock; preferred stock; publicly traded stock; registered stock; share; volatile stock; voting stock

stock accounting; stores accounting
contabilidad de existencias

stock carrying capacity [livestock]
capacidad de carga

stock corporation
sociedad anónima

stock dilution, watering; dilution
dilución del capital (accionario)
The lessening of an ownership share's earnings and assets equity, caused by the issue of more ownership shares without corresponding increases in earnings and assets.

stock dividend
dividendo en acciones

stock exchange transaction
operación bursátil

stock option
opción de compra de acciones

stock ownership
cartera de acciones

stock rights [IFC]
derechos de suscripción

stock watering see stock dilution

stock watering [livestock]
abrevado [ganado]

stockholders' equity; shareholders' equity; owners' equity; equity; net worth
patrimonio; patrimonio neto; activo neto
The value of assets less liabilities of a corporation. All the terms given here are generally synonymous, but accountants tend to give different slants to these terms in certain circumstances, so they may, on occasion, have slightly different meanings.

stocking rate [livestock]
tasa, densidad de carga; carga ganadera
The relative number of livestock per unit area for a specific time.

stockpiling
acumulación de existencias

stop and go growth
crecimiento intermitente

stopgap measure
medida temporal, de transición; recurso provisional

stop-go, stop and go policy
alternancia rápida (de medidas) de expansión y contracción; política de avance intermitente
Action on the part of the government to curtail aggregate demand due to, for example, a balance of payments deficit, soon followed by action with the opposite effect to ameliorate the rise in unemployment caused by the first action.

storage dam
presa, represa de almacenamiento

store-of-value
reserva de valor
One of the functions of money in that it stores wealth or value. An individual can sell a good or a service and store the money until he needs something and can then use the money to purchase what he needs.

stores accounting; stock accounting
contabilidad de existencias

storm water drainage system
drenaje de aguas lluvias, pluviales

straight bond
bono clásico, ordinario
Bond with unquestioned right to repayment of principal at a specified future date, unquestioned right to fixed interest payments on stated dates, and no right to any additional interest, principal, or conversion privilege.

straight-line depreciation; depreciation on a straight line
amortización (depreciación) lineal, constante, de cuotas fijas
Assignment of the service cost of any item to the benefits to be yielded by the item. In practice, a period charge for depreciation is usually substituted for a more exact measurement of benefits yielded.

strategic investors
inversionistas que se estimen adecuados, apropiados; inversionistas estratégicos
Major investors who have a significant equity investment in a company and, by virtue of their specialized knowledge, play an active role in the management of the company.

stratospheric ozone
ozono estratosférico

stream, to go on
entrar en producción; iniciar (sus) actividades

streamed school
escuela organizada por secciones

streamlined project procedure
procedimiento simplificado (para proyectos...)
A procedure adopted by IFC for more rapid review of investment projects. Projects must be for less than $25 million in loans or $10 million in equity, have no novel features and must be to countries in which IFC has invested in the last five years.

streamlining
agilización; simplificación; racionalización

streams of costs and benefits
corrientes, flujos de costos y beneficios

strength charge
cargo (aplicado) según la concentración de los contaminantes
Charge levied for water pollution, based on concentration of pollutants in the water, rather than on volume of wastewater discharged. Cf. **volumetric charge.**

strip check irrigation **see** border check irrigation

strip cropping **see** alley cropping

strip irrigation **see** border check irrigation

strip mining; open pit, open cast, open cut mining
explotación a cielo abierto, a tajo abierto [Chile]

strip of maturities
porción de cada uno de los vencimientos de un préstamo
A time portion of each of the maturities of a multi-maturity loan.

strip participation
participación en cada uno de los vencimientos (de un préstamo)
Participation in each of the maturities of a multimaturity loan.

strip planting
plantación en franjas

stripping **see** asset stripping

stripping ratio [mining]
relación de desmonte
Unit amount of spoil or waste that must be removed to gain access to a similar unit amount of ore or mineral material.

strong currency; hard currency
moneda fuerte

Structural Adjustment Facility (SAF) within the Special Disbursement Account [IMF]
servicio financiero de ajuste estructural (SAE) dentro del marco de la Cuenta Especial de Desembolso
Facility created by the International Monetary Fund in March 1986 to provide balance of payments assistance on concessional terms to low income developing countries. The resources will consist of assets received in the Special Disbursement Account as a result of the termination of the Trust Fund.

structural adjustment lending - SAL
préstamos para (fines de) ajuste estructural

structural unemployment
desempleo estructural

structural work
estructura; obra gruesa

structured financing
financiamiento estructurado
Financing using **structured securities**.

structured security
título, valor híbrido, estructurado
Security that is a combination of derivatives and standard cash securities, with its reimbursement and risk terms structured according to the client's needs.

stubble mulch farming
abonado con rastrojo

student flow
movimiento, flujo de estudiantes, alumnos

student placement
orientación

student-teacher ratio - STR; pupil-teacher ratio - PTR; teacher-pupil ratio
relación, coeficiente profesor-alumnos; alumnos por profesor

stumpage fee
canon, derecho por pie

stumpage price
precio por pie

stunting; nutritional dwarfing
enanismo nutricional; cortedad de talla; crecimiento insuficiente
Being smaller than the standard height based on a height-for-age formula, as developed by WHO. Below minus two standard deviations from median weight for height for age of reference population.

stylized fact
hecho estilizado, de ocurrencia frecuente; generalización
A generalization about economic trends extrapolated from data or an individual or group of individual countries.

subborrower
subprestatario
A smaller loan which is a part of a larger loan, often one provided for **onlending**.

subcontract
subcontrato

subcontractor
subcontratista

subgrade [highways]
subrasante

subirrigation; subsoil irrigation
riego subterráneo

subject matter [education]
materia; asignatura

subject matter specialist - SMS [agricultural extension]
técnico especializado

subloan
subpréstamo
A loan that has been onlent.

submerged bridge
vado pavimentado; badén

submerged economy **see** parallel economy

subordinated debt **see** junior debt

subordinated loan
préstamo subordinado
A loan where repayment is made subject to other conditions being met, normally repayment of other loans which are deemed to be "senior" (often because they are secured).

subordinate lender
prestamista subordinado
Lender holding a **subordinated loan**.

subordination fee
cargo por subordinación
A fee IFC receives because its debt is subordinated to other debts.

subproject
subproyecto

subscriber trunk dialing - STD
selección automática interurbana

subsidiarity
subsidiariedad; complementariedad
Principle according to which the higher levels of government should be as limited as possible and should be subsidiary to those of lower levels.

subsidiary account
cuenta subsidiaria, auxiliar
An account maintained in a separate record and controlled by an account in the general ledger.

Subsidiary Agreement [IBRD]
convenio de préstamo subsidiario

subsidiary loan
préstamo subsidiario

subsistence allowance
dieta; viático

subsistence economy
economía de subsistencia

subsistence farming
agricultura de subsistencia

subsoil irigation; subirrigation
riego subterráneo

substantive law
derecho sustantivo, de fondo
The major part of any legal system, concerned with the legal rights attributed to and legal duties imposed on particular legal persons in particular circumstances. Includes both primary or antecedent rights.

substitution effect
efecto de sustitución
The effect on the demand for a good of a change in price of that good assuming real income is held constant.

subtractability
posibilidad de extracción

How much one user's consumption of a good or service subtracts from the ability of others to consume the good or service.

subtransmission line; secondary transmission line
línea de subtransmisión, de transmisión secundaria
Transmission line in a subtransmission system, i.e. one which supplies distribution substations from bulk power sources, such as large transmission substations or generating stations.

subunderwriter [IFC]
subgarante [CFI]

success fee
comisión por captación de fondos
Fee paid that is proportional to amount of funds obtained.

successful bidder
licitante cuya oferta ha sido aceptada; adjudicatario; licitante favorecido

summary account
cuenta de resumen; cuenta de cierre

summary of project information
síntesis informativa sobre un (el) proyecto

Summary Proceedings
Actas Resumidas

summary statement
estado resumido

sundry assets
activos varios

sundry cash accounts
cuentas diversas de caja

sundry liabilities
pasivos varios

sunk cost
costo no recurrente de capital, no recuperable
A cost incurred in the past that cannot be retrieved as a residual value from an earlier investment.

sunset clause
cláusula con fecha de expiración

superannuation
jubilación

superintendency (of banks)
superintendencia bancaria, de bancos

supervision mission
misión de supervisión

supervisory grades
niveles, categorías de supervisión; niveles medios

supervisory staff
personal de supervisión

supplemental letter; side letter
carta complementaria

Supplemental Reserve against Losses on Loans and from Currency Devaluations (Supplemental Reserve)
Reserva Suplementaria para pérdidas en préstamos y por devaluaciones de monedas (Reserva Suplementaria)
A reserve established by the Bank in 1950, into which the Bank maintained a policy of automatically allocating all of its net income until FY64. It was renamed **General Reserve** in FY76.

supplementary contributions [IDA]
aportaciones suplementarias

supplier industry
industria auxiliar, abastecedora

supplier credit; supplier's credit
crédito de proveedores
Export finance made available to the supplier of the goods (as distinct from credits to the overseas buyer under **buyer's credits**)).

supply curve
curva de la oferta
A graphical representation of the relationship between the supply of a commodity and its price (usually with price on the vertical axis and quantity supplied measured along the horizontal axis). The positive relationship between these two variables is reflected by the fact that the supply curve slopes upwards from left to right.

supply line; service; service line; connection [electricity]
conexión de servicio

supply management
regulación de la oferta

supply-push factors
factores de rechazo (del lugar de origen) relacionados con la oferta
Factors that encourage migrants to leave their own country.

supply side economics
economía de la oferta, basada en la oferta
Economic policies and actions that will have long-term benefits even though they may be contractionary in the short-term. Supports the theory that money injected anywhere into the financial system expands the entire economy.

supply side politics
política favorable a la economía de la oferta
Political point of view favoring **supply side economics**.

supply system; delivery system
sistema de prestación, de suministro (de un servicio); sistema, red de distribución, de reparto

support department [IBRD]
departamento de (servicios de) apoyo

support price
precio de sostén, de apoyo, de sustentación

surface course; wearing course [highways]
capa superficial, de rodadura

surface dressing [highways]
sellado superficial, de superficie; tratamiento superficial

surface irrigation
riego superficial, de superficie

surface, road patching; spot improvement, patching; patching [highways]
bacheo; reparación de baches

surfacing [highways]
revestimiento
[**see also** resurfacing]

surplus country
país superavitario

surplus dividend
dividendo extraordinario
Dividend paid over and above statutorily required dividend.

surplus on invisibles
superávit de las transacciones invisibles

surrogate market
mercado sustitutivo
Similar markets to the target market that can be used for study purposes. For example, in assessing environmental damage, the property value of the target and similar, surrogate markets can be assessed to determine how much property values have been reduced as a result of environmental degradation.

survey
estudio; encuesta; levantamiento topográfico
[**see also** reconnaissance survey; soil survey]

survey mission
misión de estudio

survey of resources
inventario de recursos

survival rate [education]
tasa de supervivencia escolar
The percentage of pupils enrolled in the first grade who reach subsequent grades.

suspended matter
sólidos en suspensión

suspended particulate matter - SPM
partículas en suspensión
Particulate matter suspended in a fluid.

suspense account
cuenta transitoria
A temporary account for funds which have not yet been identified.

sustainability
continuidad; mantenimiento; sostenibilidad

sustainable development
desarrollo sostenible
Economic growth conducted in an environmentally responsible manner.

sustainable forestry
silvicultura sostenible; ordenación forestal sostenible
Forestry which aims at replacing trees that have been cut down.

sustainable level of lending - SLL
nivel sostenible de préstamos

sustainable net national product - SNNP
producto nacional neto sostenible - PNNS
A measure of a country's economic performance, it differs from GNP and GDP in that investments to maintain the integrity of the environment are excluded from the computation as is income generated from harvesting a resource stock over and beyond its capacity to be replenished. It therefore differs from GNP in that it can be used to demonstrate to policymakers the monetary value (loss) associated with policies that allow unsustainable use of a country's resources.

sustained growth
crecimiento (económico) sostenido

swap
swap; **intercambio de monedas; crédito recíproco [FMI]; operaciones de pase [Argentina]**
A spot purchase of foreign exchange (**currency swaps**), fixed or floating rate funds (**interest rate swaps**) or assets (**asset swaps**) with simultaneous forward sale or vice versa. *Pase financiero* is an Argentinian system, related to the **swap** system, whereby persons or institutions making capital investments are given an "exchange guarantee," which guarantees that the funds can be reexchanged at a predetermined exchange rate on a specific date.
[**see also** currency swap; debt-equity swap; debt-for-health swaps; Global Swap Authority; interest (rate) swap]

swap, to [finance]
efectuar una operación de *swap*, **de intercambio**
de monedas, de crédito recíproco
To carry out a **swap** transaction.

swap market
mercado de *swaps*
[**see also** currency swap; interest (rate) swap]

sweat equity
aportación en mano de obra propia
A share or interest in a building obtained as a result of contributing labor to its construction and/or maintenance.

swing producer
productor compensador, de compensación
In oil production, a country that varies its production to ensure that a previously agreed cartel price remains fixed. In practice, OPEC uses Saudi Arabia as the swing producer to keep a certain fixed price.

swing space
oficinas provisionales
Temporary space used to provide office space for staff whose current offices are being remodeled or demolished but for whom new office space is not yet available.

switching equipment [telephone]
equipo de conmutación

switching policies
políticas de reasignación de recursos

switching value [sensitivity analysis]
valor crítico
The value that reverses the ranking of two alternative projects. For example, Farm A will produce beef with high technology equipment and few workers, while Farm B will consist of a low-technology operation employing many farm workers. Up to a weight of 1.5 on income going to the poor, Farm A has a higher **rate of return**. However, if a weight greater than 1.5 is given, Farm B will have a higher **rate of return**. The switching value, therefore, is 1.5.

syndicate [banking]
consorcio (bancario, de financiamiento)
A group of bankers and/or brokers who underwrite and distribute a new issue of **securities** or a large block of an outstanding issue. By extension, can also refer to a group of banks or **securities firms** who are involved in a **Eurocredit** or **Eurobond** issue.

syndicate a loan, to
concertar un préstamo a través de un consorcio
(bancario, de financiamiento)
To arrange for a loan using a **syndicate**.

syndicated loan
préstamo de un consorcio, concedido por un
consorcio
Loan made by a **syndicate**.

synfuel; synthetic fuel
combustible sintético

Sysmin (= Special financing facility for ACP and OCT mining products) [European Communities]
Sysmin (Servicio especial de financiamiento
para productos mineros de los países ACP y
PTUM)

system load factor [electricity]
coeficiente de carga de la red

Systemic Transformation Facility [IMF]
servicio para la transformación sistémica
Temporary facility to help member countries facing balance of payment difficulties.

- T -

tailing pond
depósito de decantación de residuos
Pond containing waste matter from metal ore extraction.

tailrace; spillway chute [hydroelectricity]
canal de descarga

take a straight equity position, to
(hacer) inversiones en acciones comunes
Investment in a standard, low-risk security.

take-and-pay contract
contrato de compra contra entrega
A guarantee to buy an agreed amount of a product or service provided it is delivered.

take-home pay
salario neto; remuneración neta

taken over by
absorbido(a) por

take-off
arranque; despegue; impulso
[see also power take-off]

take-or-pay agreement, contract
acuerdo, contrato firme de compra (sin derecho de rescisión)
An unconditional guarantee to buy an agreed amount of a product or service whether or not it is delivered.

take-out agreement; buy-back agreement
acuerdo de recompra

takeover bid
oferta pública de compra - OPT
An offer to acquire a controlling interest in a corporation.

take over, to
hacerse cargo; absorber; asumir

take-up problems (of means-tested pension plans)
problemas de cobertura efectiva, de incorporación al plan, de participación en el plan

tangible assets, property
bienes materiales, tangibles, corpóreos
Material property that can be seen and touched as opposed to intangible property such as a patent.

tanker
buque cisterna; buque tanque; camión cisterna; camión tanque

tap issue
emisión continua
An issue of a **security** made available on an as required basis. Used primarily in the British market, where the British Government issues Treasury stock and seeks subscriptions. As the stock is rarely fully subscribed, the remainder is sold to Stock Exchange jobbers as demand requires.

target, to
orientar a grupos específicos; usar un enfoque selectivo; etc.

target contract
contrato sobre la base de un presupuesto meta

target group
grupo beneficiario; grupo objeto de ...; grupo escogido (como meta); grupo previsto

target price
precio indicativo

target zone; reference zone
zona de referencia
A wide zone of exchange rates, perhaps plus or minus 10 per cent, within which a currency can freely move against other currencies. Suggested at the New York Plaza Agreement at the **Group of Five** meeting, 9/85 and proposed by the French Treasury 2/86, as a way to reduce major currency swings.

targeted beneficiaries
beneficiarios designados, escogidos, específicos, seleccionados

targeted grant **see** categorical grant

targeted interventions
intervenciones dirigidas

targeted programs
programas focalizados, dirigidos a grupos específicos

targeting
focalización

tariff
arancel; derecho arancelario; derecho de aduana, de importación; tarifa
[**see also** also lifeline tariff]

tariff barriers
barreras arancelarias

tariff escalation
progresividad arancelaria; escalada, alza de tarifas

tariff item
partida arancelaria

tariff jumping
elusión del pago de aranceles (mediante el establecimiento de una empresa en el país)

tariff line
renglón arancelario
The most disaggregated level of classification of international trade flows. It is the production level where the tariff is applied.

tariff negotiations, round
negociaciones arancelarias, sobre aranceles

tariff peak
cresta arancelaria

tariff position
partida arancelaria

tariff privatization
control empresarial del arancel
Situation where the main domestic producer in a given market is also the main importer (or has very close links to the main foreign producer) and is therefore able to shield itself from import competition and obtain considerable profits by controlling the volume of imports. All the revenue thus obtained accrues the producer instead of the government (in the form of tariffs).

tariff quota
cuota arancelaria; cupo, contingente arancelario
Specified volume (quota) of imports of a good for a given period defining the application of different rates of duty (tariffs), the lower are applying until the specified volume is reached, the higher rate thereafter.

tariff rates
tasas, derechos arancelarios

tariff round, negotiations
negociaciones arancelarias, sobre aranceles

tariff schedule
arancel; tarifa [precios]

tariff wedges
diferencias arancelarias
Difference between the tariff at a particular stage of processing and at the preceding stage.

tariffication
conversión en arancel
The conversion of quotas or other **nontariff barriers** to tariffs.

tar sands
arenas impregnadas de brea; arenas asfálticas

task force
grupo de estudio; grupo de trabajo

tax **see also** benefit taxes; betterment levy, tax; border taxes; business (profit) tax; capital gains tax; cascade tax; corporate tax; delinquent taxes; destination tax; earmarked tax; end use tax; foreign tax credit; income tax; inflation tax; interest equalization tax; investment tax credit; land betterment tax; land tax; multiple stage tax; net of taxes; origin tax; pay-as-you-earn; payroll tax; poll tax; presumptive taxation; profits tax; sales tax; schedular tax; shifting of tax; turnover tax; value-added tax; withholding tax

tax allowance
exención tributaria; desgravación; deducción
Amount deducted from gross income to arrive at taxable income.

tax amnesty
amnistía tributaria

tax arbitrage
arbitraje impositivo

tax assessment; assessment for tax
avalúo, tasación para fines impositivos; estimación de la base impositiva

tax audit
auditoría impositiva, tributaria

tax avoidance
evitación, elusión, evasión legal de impuestos
The legal minimization of taxes due government by application of tax planning devices.

tax base
base imponible
The amount that forms the basis for calculating a taxpayers' liability. In income tax it is a person's earnings while in property tax, the value of the property.

tax bill, demand
liquidación, notificación de impuestos
A document sent to a taxpayer, telling him/her how much s/he owes in taxes.

tax bracket
grupo, nivel, tramo impositivo

tax buoyancy
elasticidad tributaria global
Total elasticity of the tax system (built-in elasticity plus elasticity due to discretionary changes in the tax system). Measured by the annual mean growth in receipts divided by the annual mean growth in gross domestic product (GDP).

tax burden
carga impositiva, tributaria, fiscal; presión fiscal
The actual effect of a tax. For example, the tax burden of income tax falls on the income-earner; however, the burden of indirect taxes such as sales taxes is generally passed on to the consumer.

tax clearance
certificado de pago de impuestos

tax credit
descuento, crédito impositivo, tributario
A 100% offset against tax liability.

tax deduction
deducción tributaria, de impuestos
An expenditure that may legally be deducted from taxable income by taxpayers

tax deferral
aplazamiento, diferimiento impositivo; moratoria

tax demand, bill
liquidación, notificación de impuestos

tax effort
esfuerzo tributario
The total amount of tax due from a country, sector, enterprise, etc.

tax elasticity
elasticidad del impuesto

tax evasion
evasión (ilegal) tributaria, fiscal, de impuestos
Avoidance of taxes by illegal means.

tax exemption
exención de impuestos
A specific sum that a taxpayer may deduct from taxable income for him- or herself and for each dependent. Also refers to certain kinds of income not subject to tax such as social security payments, monies received by certain diplomats, etc.

tax expenditures
gastos fiscales

tax/GDP ratio
relación impuestos-PIB
Ratio of tax receipts to gross domestic product.

tax handles
sujetos (potenciales) del impuesto
The means by which the tax authorities can raise (or lower) revenues through taxation. For example, in an economy where income is typically derived from self-employment and the wage income that does exist is from small establishments, the government has only a limited tax handle on income compared with a modern economy where earned income is largely in the form of wages and salaries from large organizations.

tax haven
paraíso tributario
A country which offers permanent tax incentives in order to attract multinational enterprises.

tax holiday
tregua tributaria; exoneración temporal (parcial o total) de impuestos
Tax relief or exemption granted temporarily, e.g. to encourage industrial development.

tax incentive
incentivo tributario

tax incidence analysis
análisis de la incidencia fiscal
Analysis of the redistributive effects of taxation.

tax liability
obligación tributaria

tax loophole
escapatoria, laguna tributaria; resquicio tributario

tax mitigation
atenuación, reducción de los impuestos

tax net
sujetos, bienes y actividades imponibles

tax office
oficina, dirección, administración de impuestos

tax on value added; value added tax - VAT
impuesto al, sobre el valor agregado, añadido - IVA

tax-paid cost - TPC
costo incluidos los impuestos

tax-paying capacity
capacidad tributaria

tax performance ratio
relación, coeficiente de recaudación de impuestos

tax ratio
relación impuestos-ingresos; coeficiente tributario
The ratio of income tax expense to net income before taxes.

tax rebate
desgravación tributaria; reducción de impuestos
A partial refund to taxpayers of taxes already paid.

tax refund
reembolso, devolución, reintegro de impuestos

tax relief
desgravación fiscal

tax reference price [oil]
precio de referencia para fines tributarios [petróleo]
An arbitrary posted price for hydrocarbons utilized in a number of countries for the purpose of calculating taxes and other payments due the State from an operator.

tax return
declaración de ingresos; declaración de impuestos

tax sharing
participación en los impuestos
The practice of a state or central government levying a tax and sharing its proceeds with a local government.

tax shelter
refugio tributario
Any of a number of investments which generate losses, usually due to noncash deductions such as depreciation or depletion, or due to accelerated payments which flow through to individual taxpayers and can be used to offset other income, thereby lowering the individual taxable income.

tax sparing
descuento del impuesto potencial

tax surcharge
recargo tributario; sobretasa

tax technology
técnicas de administración tributaria
The tools used to administrate tax policy, e.g.
management information systems.

tax wedge
discrepancia impositiva
The difference between wages or labor income and
the same wages or income plus government taxes
on them. It is called a wedge because it is like a
wedge which the tax drives between the value of a
worker to the firm and the amount received by the
worker for working one more hour. A Bank
document defined it as "the difference between a
given (arbitrary) after-tax **rate of return** to an
individual investor and the pre-tax real **rate of
return** on investment that the firm would need to
generate in order to fund the investment."

tax withholding
retención del impuesto

tax write off
deducción tributaria (por pérdida, etc.)

tax yield
recaudación tributaria

teacher-pupil ratio; pupil-teacher ratio - PTR;
student-teacher ratio - STR
**relación, coeficiente profesor-alumnos, alumnos
por profesor**

teacher's guide
**guía del maestro; libro del maestro; manual del
instructor**

teacher's kit
material pedagógico básico

teaching aids
materiales didácticos; auxiliares de enseñanza

teaching load
carga docente

Technical Advisory Committee - TAC [CGIAR]
Comité Asesor Técnico - CAT

technical assistance loan - TAL
préstamo para asistencia técnica
World Bank loan for technical assistance purposes.

technical assistant
**funcionario de asistencia técnica; asistente
técnico**

technical background
formación técnica; preparación técnica

technical cooperation among developing countries
- TCDC
**cooperación técnica entre países en desarrollo -
CTPD**

technical-efficiency index - TEI
índice de eficiencia técnica

technical note
nota técnica

technical package
conjunto de medidas prácticas

teething problems
problemas iniciales

temperate hardwood forest
bosque de especies frondosas

temporary assets
activos transitorios

temporary liabilities
pasivos transitorios

tender
oferta; propuesta

tender documents **see** bidding documents

tenure **see** land tenure; security of tenure

tenure [education]
permanencia (en el cargo)

term deposit
depósito a plazo

term financing
financiamiento a mediano o largo plazo

term loan
préstamo a mediano o largo plazo

term sheet
hoja de plazos y condiciones

terminate
terminar; dar por terminado; rescindir [nombramiento]

termination
terminación; rescisión; cese de funciones; despido

termination grant
indemnización por terminación, rescisión, cese de funciones, despido

terms and conditions (of a contract)
condiciones

terms of reference [e.g. consultants]
términos de referencia; mandato

terms of reference [study]
términos de referencia, parámetros (de un estudio)

terms of trade
relación, términos de intercambio
A relationship between the prices of exports and the prices of imports. When the concept is not further qualified, reference is being made to the net **barter terms of trade**, which is the quotient between an index of export prices and an index of import prices.
[**see also** barter terms of trade; double factorial terms of trade; income terms of trade; single factorial terms of trade]

tertiary (oil) recovery
recuperación terciaria
Enhanced recovery methods for the production of crude oil or natural gas. It requires a means for displacing oil from the reservoir rock, modifying the properties of the fluids in the reservoir and/or the reservoir rock to cause movement of crude oil in an efficient manner, and providing the energy and drive mechanism to force its flow to a production well.

test check [accounting]
verificación de prueba

test plot
lote, parcela de prueba

thematic team
grupo de expertos
Team of technical specialists working in a specific area of the Bank's activities, which monitors Bankwide activities in a specific area, e.g. technical assistance.

theory of public choice
teoría de la elección social
Study of the problems involved in decision-making by governments and the factors that influence their decision-making.

think tank
grupo de expertos

Third Window
Tercera Ventanilla

33-Commodity Aggregate Price Index [IBRD]
índice global de precios de 33 productos básicos

threshold countries
países que se encuentran "en el umbral"
Countries on the threshold between IDA and IBRD status or between IBRD and graduation status.

threshold limit value - TLV
concentración máxima admisible
The maximum allowed amount of exposure to a given hazard in a given time frame.

threshold price
precio umbral

through bill of lading
conocimiento de embarque directo
Bill of lading for cargo shipped between two specified ports plus inland portion of transit.

throughput
volumen de material elaborado [manufacturas]; número de estudiantes que pasan por el sistema escolar [educación]
[**see also** berth throughput]

through traffic
tráfico en tránsito; tráfico directo

tied aid
ayuda condicionada, vinculada

tied currency
moneda vinculada

tied resources
recursos reservados (para un determinado proyecto)

tight credit policy
política de restricción crediticia; política crediticia restrictiva

tightening of credit
restricciones crediticias; contracción del crédito

tight money
dinero escaso, caro
Contractionary monetary policy. In taking steps to decrease the rate of growth of the **money supply**, monetary authorities are said to be following a tight money policy.

timber
madera; madera en pie

time-adjusted [project analysis]
actualizado a partir del segundo año
An accounting convention in which the first year of an investment analysis is used solely for investment and in which incremental benefits appear only from year 2 or later.

time-based contract [consultants]
contrato por tiempo
A contract for consultants where payment is made according to time expended.

time deposit
depósito a plazo, a término

time frame
marco temporal, cronológico

time lag
desfase (cronológico); retraso; intervalo

time limit [ICSID]
plazo

time-of-use (TOU) rates [electricity tariffs]
tarifas según hora de consumo

time overrun
demora respecto del plazo previsto

time pattern
pauta cronológica; cronología

time series
serie cronológica

time sharing [computers]
tiempo compartido; multipropiedad

time sheet
hoja de asistencia

time-slice loan
préstamo por etapas
Loan where the lender only finances the loan a part of the time.

time underrun
adelanto respecto del plazo previsto

time value of money
valor temporal del dinero
An expression referring to the concept that values received earlier are worth more than values received later. The concept underlying discounting.

times interest earned ratio **see** interest coverage ratio - ICR

tinged cotton
algodón tintado
A discolored cotton graded between **spotted** and stained cotton.

tissue culture
cultivo de tejidos

titling (land)
adjudicación (de títulos de propiedad) de la tierra

Round Agreement
do de la Ronda de Tokio

tombstone
anuncio de emisión efectuada; esquela
Advertisement which announces that a credit has been arranged or a bond issue made.

ton of coal equivalent - tce
tonelada de equivalente en carbón - tec
A common accounting unit used to define energy usage. Actual definitions differ. The European Communities, for example, define it as yielding 7 Gcal net calorific value while the United Kingdom defines it as the average gross calorific of all grades of coal and the UN as the gross calorific value.

ton of oil equivalent - toe
tonelada de equivalente en petróleo - tep
A common accounting unit for energy usage. Definitions differ. OECD/IEA define it as having a net calorific value of 10 Gcal (= 41.9 GJ) while the United Kingdom defines it as the weighted average gross calorific value of all petroleum products.

top-down (approach) [projects]
vertical

top dressing [agriculture]
abono, estercoladura, fertilizante de superficie

top-rated bank loan
préstamo bancario de primera categoría

top-up scheme; minimum pension guarantee
plan de jubilación mínima
System whereby the government brings up a pension to a specified minimum level.

Toronto terms
condiciones de Toronto
Terms for debt relief (rescheduling for low-income countries) agreed upon at the **Group of Seven** meeting in Toronto in 1988.

total dissolved solids - TDS
total de sólidos disueltos - tsd
Total weight of dissolved mineral constituents in water per unit volume or weight of water in the sample.

total external debt - EDT
deuda externa total

total factor productivity - TFP
productividad total de los factores
A measurement of changes in outputs per unit of all **inputs** combined.

total fertility rate - TFR
tasa de fecundidad total
The average number of children that would be born live to a woman (or group of women) during her lifetime if she were to pass through her childbearing years conforming to the age-specific fertility rates of a given year.

total loss cover
cobertura contra pérdida total
Insurance against all losses.

Total Return Index [IFC]
índice de rendimiento total; índice de rentabilidad total
Index devised by IFC to measure the US dollar return on developing country equity markets, taking into account both domestic price changes and exchange rate fluctuations.

total suspended particulates - TSP
total de partículas en suspensión
Any solid or liquid particles dispersed in the atmosphere, such as dust, pollen, ash, soot, metals and various chemicals.

total suspended solids - TSS
total de sólidos en suspensión
The amount of particulate matter suspended in a water sample.

tracer study [education]
estudio de seguimiento de egresados
A follow-up study of students after they have left school to see what they have become.

tradable [adj.]
comerciable; exportable o importable; comercializable

tradable [noun]
bien comerciable, comercializable, exportable o importable
A good that could be traded internationally in the absence of restrictive trade policies. Depending on national and world costs of production and transport, tradables may be importables, exportables or, in some cases, both.

tradable but nontraded (good, item); nontraded tradable
bien comerciable no comerciado (etc.)

tradable emissions permit
permiso negociable de contaminación
Permit to emit a specified quantity of a pollutant. This permit may be traded. Cf. **emissions trading, bubble concept.**

trade adjustment
ajuste del régimen comercial
Adjustment of **terms of trade**, e.g. by reducing import tariffs.

trade adjustment loan
préstamo (para fines de) ajuste de la política de comercio exterior
Loan to assist a country in liberalization of its trade policy.

trade balance; balance of trade; merchandise balance
balanza comercial
The difference in a given time period between a country's imports and exports of goods and services valued in current monetary units.

trade coverage ratio
proporción de importaciones sujetas a barreras no arancelarias; tasa de importaciones afectadas
The amount of imports affected by para-tariff, price and volume control measures expressed as a percentage of total imports of the same product group.

trade cycle; business cycle
ciclo económico; coyuntura

trade deficit
déficit comercial

trade-off
compensación (de factores, de ventajas y desventajas); ventaja relativa; solución de compromiso; transacción; concesión recíproca; disyuntiva; opción; alternativa, etc.

trade organization
organización gremial, patronal

trade pattern
estructura, modalidad del comercio

trade promotion
fomento, promoción del comercio

trade publication
publicación especializada para determinada industria, negocio o profesión

trade receivables
efectos de comercio por cobrar

trade-related investment measures - TRIMS
medidas en materia de inversiones relacionadas con el comercio

traded goods
bienes comerciados, comercializados, exportados o importados

trading see block trading

trading currency
moneda de intercambio

trading partners
países que mantienen relaciones comerciales

trading portfolio
cartera de inversiones a corto plazo
Portfolio of short-term investments. Cf. **investment portfolio.**

trading ticket [capital market]
orden de compra; orden de venta
Purchase/sales order for a **security.**

traffic-bearing capacity; load-bearing capacity
capacidad de tráfico

traffic count
cuenta, conteo, recuento de tráfico

train **see** block train; unit trains

trainability [EDI-World Bank]
susceptibilidad, posibilidad de capacitación

trainee
**persona que recibe adiestramiento; participante
en un curso o programa de capacitación;
principiante**

trainer
instructor

training **see** advanced training; higher training;
in-house training; in-service training; job-related
training; mobile training unit; multimedia training
module; on-the-job training; retail training;
retraining; skill training center; vocational
training; wholesale training

training and visit [T & V] system
sistema de capacitación y visitas
System of **agricultural extension** which involves
training **village-level workers** so that they can,
through **contact farmers**, pass on new agricultural
techniques.

training production unit
unidad de capacitación práctica

trammel fishing
pesca con trasmallos
Type of fishing using a set net, where the fish
entangle themselves in net pockets, which are
made by the pushing movement of the fish through
the three - occasionally two - walls of the net.

tranching [loans]
repartición en porciones, tramos
Division of a loan (specifically adjustment loans)
into several tranches. Release of tranches is
conditional on specific agreed actions being
carried out.

transfer charge call; collect call; reverse charge
call
llamada de cobro revertido

transfer payments
pagos de transferencia

transfer price
precio de transferencia
Price between a corporation and its subsidiary or
within a corporation (opposite of **arm's length
price**).

transformation curve; production possibility curve
**curva de transformación; curva de posibilidades
de producción**
A graphic representation of the various output
combinations of two commodities which can be
produced from a given quantity of resources.

transient climate change
cambio climático circunstancial
The path of realized climate change which takes
into account the lags in the climate system, as
opposed to **equilibrium change**.

translation (of currency)
**traducción de monedas; conversión contable de
monedas**
Recording in accounts of assets (or liabilities) in
one currency when they are actually in another.
No actual exchange of funds takes place. The
World Bank and IFC, for example, translate all
their assets and liabilities into U.S. dollar
amounts, regardless of the actual currency in
which they are denominated.

translation adjustment [accounting]
ajuste de traducción (de monedas)
Adjustment in accounts to reflect movements in
the rate of exchange between the currency of the
accounts and the currency of the transaction.

transparency
diafanidad; transparencia
[see also fiscal transparency]

transterritorial; cross-border
transnacional; transterritorial fronterizo; *a
veces*: **internacional**

trashy farming
laboreo con abrigo vegetal
Tillage which leaves the major portion of crop
residues on the soil surface

trawl fishing
pesca de arrastre

Treasury bill
pagaré del Tesoro a corto plazo
Bill issued by U.S. Treasury with short maturity (less than one year).

Treasury bond
bono del Tesoro
Long-term (more than ten years) fixed **coupon** paper issued by the Federal Reserve on behalf of the U.S. Treasury.

Treasury note
pagaré del Tesoro
A medium-term (normally from two to ten years) coupon **security** issued by the U.S. Treasury.

treaty reinsurance
reaseguro contractual
Form of **reinsurance**, whereby an insurance company shares a large number of risks with other insurance companies.

tree cotton; Ceylon cotton; Siam cotton; China cotton
algodón arbóreo

tree crop
cultivo arbóreo

tree farming
arboricultura

tree fodder
forraje arbóreo

tree mining; forest mining
extracción excesiva de árboles
Clear-felling of large wooded areas.

tree tenure
tenencia comunitaria de bosques
Ownership of a wood, forest or other collection of trees, usually by a group. The term is used in **social forestry**.

trend rate
tasa tendencial

triage
triaje; selección

tribal peoples
pueblos tribales; poblaciones indígenas

trickle-down effect
efecto de (la) filtración; chorreo
The idea that stimulants applied to a lagging economy are best given to business to induce economic growth that will benefit citizens directly rather than being given directly to consumers to spur purchasing power.

trickle irrigation **see** drip irrigation

trigger clause
cláusula de revisión, de activación
Clause in IBRD loan agreement requiring review after a certain number of years to determine whether changes in the country's economic condition warrant harder or softer loans.

trigger date [IBRD]
fecha de activación
Date on which a loan is placed in **nonaccrual status**. This is normally when service payments are overdue by more than six months.

Trigger Price Mechanism - TPM [US]
mecanismo de precios de intervención
System set up by the US to prevent unfair competition for steel imports. Costs of production in the world's lowest cost producer, Japan, would be determined and publicly announced. These would be the trigger prices. If the price charged for an import shipment were below the trigger price, the US Government would launch an antidumping investigation against the foreign supplier.

Trinidad terms
condiciones de Trinidad
Terms for debt relief to replace the **Toronto terms**, proposed by the United Kingdom at a conference in Trinidad. They propose writing off $18 billion of the debt of the world's nineteen poorest countries (mainly Sub-Saharan African countries plus Bolivia and Guyana), extending repayment periods to 25 years and capitalizing interest.

triple superphosphate - TSP [fertilizer]
superfosfato triple
A commercial fertilizer which contains 2.5 to 3 times as much available phosphoric acid as superphosphate. The phosphate rock is treated with phosphoric acid and, in the manufacturing process, the gypsum is removed.

tropical cattle unit - TCU; tropical animal unit - TAU; tropical livestock unit - TLU
unidad de ganado tropical
A standard unit of measurement, equivalent to 250 kg, the weight of a standard cow, for calculating the impact of animals on the land.

tropical rain forest
bosque (húmedo) tropical; selva (pluvial) tropical
[**see also** rain forest]

trucking industry
industria del transporte por carretera

true lease
contrato de arrendamiento verdadero
Lease where the lessee has no right to a share of the proceeds of the sale of the leased asset to third parties at the end of the non-cancelable lease period and no bargain renewal option.

true to type variety; pure variety [agriculture]
variedad pura
A variety which is like the parental type, without change.

trunk infrastructure
infraestructura primaria

trunk network
red interurbana

trunk roads
carreteras troncales, principales

trunk sewer
alcantarilla colectora, maestra

trust fund
fondo fiduciario; fideicomiso

Trustee [GEF]
Depositario

tubewell
pozo entubado
Strictly speaking a circular well consisting of tubes or pipes bored into the ground but often used synonymously with **drilled well**.

tuition fees
derechos de matrícula

turnaround (time)
tiempo de rotación, del viaje de ida y vuelta; tiempo necesario para un servicio

turnkey contract, project
contrato, proyecto llave en mano
A contract where a firm will undertake all the activities to deliver a complete project, including the provision of professional services, the supply of goods and civil works construction.

turnover
movimiento; rotación; volumen de negocios
[**see also** inventory turnover]

turnover tax
impuesto sobre el volumen, la cifra de negocios

twenty equivalent units - TEU [containers]
unidades de 20 pies (de contenedores) - TEU
Standard unit for counting (equivalent) containers of various dimensions.

twinning arrangements
acuerdos de "hermanamiento"
Arrangement whereby two organizations (or a group of organizations) work jointly on a project. In the Bank, it is generally used to refer to a situation where an organization (or a group of organizations) from an industrial country works with an organization (or a group of organizations) from a developing country, providing assistance as well as being involved in the project.

two digit inflation; double digit inflation
(tasa de) inflación de dos dígitos, de 10% o más

two-envelope procedure [consultants]
procedimiento de dos sobres
A procedure for selecting bids whereby each **bidder** is required to submit simultaneously his qualifications in one envelope and his bid in a second.

two-gap model
modelo de las dos brechas
A mathematical model of the economy of a country using two-gap analysis, i.e. adjustments in accumulation and trade in response to a unit change in the available supply of foreign resources.

2% currency [IBRD]
monto del 2%
The portion of capital subscriptions payable in US dollars.

two-stage, two-step procedure [IBRD]
tratamiento por separado; procedimientos separados
Procedure whereby technical and financial proposals are submitted and evaluated separately.

two-tier market
mercado de dos niveles
An exchange rate regime which normally insulates a country from the balance of payments effects of capital flows while it maintains a stable exchange rate for current account transactions. Capital transactions are normally required to pass through a "financial" market while current transactions go through an "official" market, though other arrangements are possible. Examples are found in Belgium and the United Kingdom, though France and Italy have experimented with such systems.

two-tier meeting
reunión en dos niveles
Meeting arranged for public officials, where one meeting is for top-level officials and another, overlapping meeting, for middle-level officials.

two-track development
dos ritmos, trayectorias de desarrollo
Development where one group develops at a much faster rate than another, e.g. the Asian countries develop more rapidly than Latin America and Sub-Saharan Africa.

two-year trigger rule
regla de los dos años
Rule whereby provisions are made against countries placed by the Bank in **nonaccrual status** that do not resume loan payments within two years.

- U -

UHF link [telecommunications]
enlace UHF, en frecuencia ultraalta

ultimate model
modelo exhaustivo
A model which contains all the information needed for its operation.

ultimate recoverable reserves - URR
reservas recuperables definitivas - RRD
The total amount of oil and gas recovered and believed to be recoverable from both discovered and undiscovered reservoirs, in the light of probable improvements in technology and based on a geological evaluation of a particular area or territory.

ultra low volume (ULV) spraying
rociado de muy bajo volumen

umbrella (agreement)
acuerdo global; *a veces*: **acuerdo marco**
Agreement whereby MIGA and a member government provide the framework for MIGA's cooperation with the public and private insurers of that member.

umbrella project
**proyecto que sirve de marco para otros;
proyecto global**
A UNDP project under which an allocation from a country's indicative planning figures funding is provided for a specific period of time to finance a flexible package of preinvestment studies or other technical assistance activities, all of which may not be identified before approval by UNDP.

umpire [legal]
árbitro dirimente

unaccounted [e.g. water, electricity]
no contabilizado; perdido

unallocatable expenditure
gasto no asignable

unappropriated (earned) surplus
utilidades no distribuidas y no asignadas
That part of **retained earnings** which has not been transferred to a subordinate account or otherwise earmarked for any specific purpose, thus remaining available for the absorption of dividends.

unbundling
desagregación; desglose; descomposición

unbundling of financial risks
desagregación, separación de riesgos financieros
The separation and separate evaluation of financial risks.

uncalled capital
capital suscrito y no desembolsado
The amount of capital by which the total capital authorized by the stockholders exceeds the paid-up capital.

uncovered interest rate parity model
modelo de paridad de los tipos de interés sin cobertura

underaccruals
suma, diferencia por la cual las cantidades devengadas son inferiores a las previstas

undercapitalized
subcapitalizado

undercollection [taxation]
deficiencia de recaudación

underemployment
subempleo; subocupación

undergraduate
estudiante (que no ha recibido el primer título universitario)

undergraduate studies
estudios universitarios para obtener el primer título

underground economy **see** parallel economy

underinvestment
subinversión; inversión insuficiente

underinsurance
infraseguro
Failure to maintain adequate coverage for a specific loss or damage.

underinvoicing of exports
subfacturación de exportaciones; subvaloración de las facturas de exportación

underleveraged
con bajo coeficiente de endeudamiento

underlying costs
costos implícitos

underlying inflation
inflación subyacente

undernourished
desnutrido

undernutrition
desnutrición

underprivileged
desfavorecido; marginado

underrun cost
costos inferiores a los previstos; infracostos

underwriter [securities]
suscriptor; asegurador; garante
The middleman for selling and distributing **securities** to investors or the public.

underwriting **see also** equity underwriting

underwriting authority [MIGA]
autoridad emisora
The President or any official or officials of MIGA designated by the President to make the decision on the issuance of a guarantee and on related matters.

underwriting commitment [IFC]
operación de garantía de emisión

underwriting costs
costos de garantía de emisión

underwriting syndicate
consorcio garante

undeveloped plot
lote sin servicios, no urbanizado

undrawn balance
saldo no utilizado

undrawn borrowings
empréstitos pendientes de utilización

unearned income
ingreso(s) no proveniente(s) del trabajo; *a veces*: **ingreso(s) no salarial(es)**

unearned interest
intereses cobrados anticipadamente
Interest on a loan that has already been collected but has not yet been earned because the principal has not been outstanding long enough.

uneconomic production
producción antieconómica

unemployment compensation, benefit
seguro de desempleo

unfunded interest
interés no financiado

unfunded liabilities
obligaciones sin financiamiento previsto
Any short-term liabilities as opposed to long-term obligations such as bonds.

unfunded system [insurance; social security]
sistema financiado con aportaciones

unified cross rates
tipos de cambio concordantes

uniform votes [IBRD]
votos básicos más votos de adhesión
Basic votes plus votes derived from **membership shares**.

unimpaired capital
capital libre de gravámenes
Capital which has no liens against it. MIGA's unimpaired capital is used as a basis for calculating its guarantee capacity.

unit activity (crop) budget
presupuesto por unidad de actividad
In farm investment analysis, a farm budget based on an easily segregated activity such as planting a single hectare of a crop or raising a particular group of animals. It is difficult to prepare a unit activity budget on a with and without basis; rather, it is generally prepared on an incremental basis, with all costs and all benefits included at the incremental value. For both financial analysis and economic analysis, this means that for some elements the **opportunity cost** must be estimated directly, often especially difficult for land and for family labor. As a result, unit activity budgets are most appropriate in project analyses where the **opportunity cost** of land and family labor can be taken to be zero.

unit budget envelope
presupuesto (de una unidad del Banco)
The budget for a specific unit in the Bank.

unit cost
costo unitario; precio unitario

unit(ary) elasticity
elasticidad igual a la unidad
A schedule in which the coefficient of elasticity is 1, that is, a change of x percent in the price will cause a change of x percent in the quantity demanded or supplied.

unit-managed costs
costos, gastos descentralizados
Costs which are the responsibility, for budgetary purposes, of individual units, as opposed to those that are **centrally-managed**.

unit of account - UA
unidad de cuenta
An artificial concept designed to provide a consistent reference value against varying exchange rates, e.g. **European Currency Unit**, Special Drawing Rights

unit of output
unidad de producción

unit price contract; admeasurement contract; remeasurement contract
contrato a, de precio(s) unitario(s)
A contract based on **unit prices**. Includes a **bill of quantities**, which is a statement of all the items of work included in the contract together with the estimated quantity of each item. **See** bill of quantities contract, schedule of rates contract.

unit trains
trenes unidades
A complete train loaded with one product or material (such as coal) that is shipped from one specific point to another on a closely scheduled and controlled basis.

unit trust **see** open end (investment) fund

unit value
valor unitario

unit value export index
índice del valor unitario de las exportaciones
An index of the exports for the developing countries and the industrial market economies based on amount and value of total exports, calculated on an annual basis. Used to show changes over a period of time.

unlocated worker
trabajador ambulante
Worker not employed in one place.

unorganized worker
trabajador no sindicado

unpeg (a rate), to
desvincular (el tipo)

unrealized gains
ganancias no realizadas
Profits that have not become actual. The gains are realized when the security or other instrument on which there has been a gain is sold for a profit.

unregulated housing
(construcción de) viviendas no sujeta(s) a reglamentaciones

unreleased funds
fondos no disponibles para préstamos

unrequited transfer
transferencia sin contrapartida [cuentas nacionales]; transferencia unilateral [balanza de pagos]
Transfer of income that does not a involve a quid pro quo and which is non-contractual in character, for example, direct taxes, social security benefits and contributions, social assistance grants and grants between governments to finance the military or other consumption expenditure or budgetary deficit of a government.

unrestricted currency
moneda de libre uso
The portion of capital subscriptions paid in gold or US dollars and freely usable by IBRD in its lending operations.

unrestricted subscription [IDA]
suscripción no sujeta a restricciones

unseasoned investment
inversión que no ha alcanzado su pleno rendimiento
An investment that is not yet fully producing.

unsecured (note, loan, etc.)
sin garantía; no garantizado

unskilled labor
mano de obra no calificada

unsmoothed data
datos antes del análisis de regresión
Data which has not been subject to regression analysis.

unspent credit balance
saldo acreedor no utilizado

unsubdivided plot
terreno no parcelado

unsuccessful bid
oferta no favorecida (con la adjudicación)

untapped resources
recursos inexplotados

untied aid
ayuda no condicionada, desvinculada

untying of aid
desvinculación de la ayuda

upgrade, to [oil]
refinar

upgrading of skills
perfeccionamiento

upkeep costs
gastos de mantenimiento, conservación

upland cotton; hairy cotton
algodón upland; algodón americano; algodón velloso

upland crops
cultivos de montaña, de tierras altas

upland rice; mountain rice; highland rice
arroz de montaña, de tierras altas, de secano

uploading [computers]
transferencia hacia el sistema principal

upper secondary education
educación secundaria de ciclo superior

upstream innovations; research-push innovations
innovaciones inducidas por la investigación

upstream process
primeros procesos

upswing
movimiento ascendente; fase ascendente, de expansión

upturn (economic)
cambio favorable de la coyuntura; iniciación de la fase ascendente; recuperación; reactivación

upward trend
tendencia alcista, ascendente

urbanization economies
economías de urbanización
Economies of scale external to both individual firms and industries. They reflect the sum of private and public investments in specific locations, as well as the pools of labor and capital and financial, legal and public services.

urban sprawl
crecimiento urbano (no planificado)

urban sprinkling
proliferación de asentamientos urbanos
Development of small but swiftly growing urban areas in a generally undeveloped region.

Uruguay Round [GATT]
Ronda Uruguay

useful life
vida útil

useful farm space - UFS
superficie agrícola útil
The total area of a farm less the woods and nonagricultural area.

user friendly
de uso fácil

utilities
(empresas de) servicios públicos
[**see also** public utilities]

utility function **see** welfare function

- V -

vaccination yard
corral de vacunación

valuable consideration
a título oneroso
A right, interest, profit or benefit accruing to one party or some forebearance, detriment, loss or responsibility given, suffered or undertaken by the other. *See* **consideration**.

valuations for customs purposes
aforo; valoración aduanera

valuable consideration, for; for a consideration
a título oneroso

value-added tax - VAT; tax on value added
impuesto al, sobre el valor agregado, añadido - IVA

value based accounting **see** current cost (value) accounting

value date
fecha de valor
The calendar date on which a transaction takes place.

value engineering
análisis, ingeniería del valor
An objective appraisal of all the elements of the design, construction, procurement, installation and maintenance of equipment, including the specifications, to achieve the necessary functions, maintainability and reliability at the lowest cost. It entails a detailed review of product designs and specifications, placing a total dollar value on the costs of production and maintenance and relating these costs to the functional value of each part and assembly.

value for money
optimización de los recursos

value recovery clause
cláusula de recuperación económica
In **debt rescheduling** agreement, clause which states that if economic conditions improve beyond a predefined threshold, creditors will be entitled to increased reimbursement.

variety trial
prueba, ensayo de variedad(es)

vault toilet
letrina de pozo negro

vectorborne disease
enfermedad de transmisión vectorial

vehicle currency
moneda "vehículo"
Currency used in a **swap** or similar transaction, even though it may not be the target currency.

ventilated improved pit (VIP) latrine; VIP latrine
letrina de pozo mejorada con ventilación
A **pit latrine** (i.e. a latrine consisting of a pit, a squatting plate (or seat and riser) and foundation, and a superstructure) where the pit is slightly offset to make room for an external vent pipe, painted black and located on the sunny side of the latrine superstructure so that the air in the vent pipe will heat up and create an updraft with a corresponding down draft through the squatting plate.

venture [IFC]
operación

venture capital **see** risk capital

venture capital company
compañía de capital de riesgo
Company specializing in providing **venture capital** finance.

vertical cofinancing
cofinanciamiento vertical

vertical equity
equidad vertical
Distributing the tax burden among the nonpoor in line with their ability to pay.

vetiver
vetiver
Type of fodder grass, common in Africa. Also used for erosion control.

VHF link [telecommunications]
enlace VHF, en frecuencia muy alta

village extension worker - VEW
agente de extensión de poblado - AEP
The same as a **village level worker**.

village level operation and maintenance (VLOM) pump
bomba de operación y mantenimiento a nivel del poblado - BOMPO
Pump for use in small villages. It is used in areas where there is no power so it is a hand pump and must be maintained by villagers with no mechanical skills. It must also be cheap.

village level worker - VLW
trabajador a nivel de poblado
A worker with comparatively low-level education who has received training in production methods which he disseminates through selected farmers and others who adopt the new methods and compare the results with that part of their fields cultivated by normal practices.

village woodlot
bosque comunal

VIP latrine; ventilated improved pit (VIP) latrine
letrina de pozo mejorada con ventilación
A **pit latrine** (i.e. a latrine consisting of a pit, a squatting plate (or seat and riser) and foundation, and a superstructure) where the pit is slightly offset to make room for an external vent pipe, painted black and located on the sunny side of the latrine superstructure so that the air in the vent pipe will heat up and create an updraft with a corresponding down draft through the squatting plate.

vital statistics
estadísticas del estado civil, vitales

vitamin deficiency
avitaminosis

vocational guidance
orientación profesional

vocational training
formación profesional

voice mechanism
mecanismo de participación
Procedures to allow users to comment on the volume or quality of a service. In public sector management, these include dissemination of information about services, periodic evaluation, complaints procedures, participation of public representatives in decision-making or regulatory bodies and legal action by consumer action groups. This concept was developed by Albert Hirschman in *Exit, Voice and Loyalty* and adapted by Samuel Paul to the issue of accountability.

volatile capital
capital fugaz, inestable

volatile organic compounds - VOC
compuestos orgánicos volátiles
Organic compounds which are capable of producing photo-chemical oxidants by sunlight-driven reactions in the presence of **nitrogen oxides**. Include emissions such as hydrocarbon vapor emissions.

volatile stock
acciones de valor inestable
A stock that changes in a manner inconsistent with changes in the rest of the market.

volatility
inestabilidad

volatility ratio [stocks]
relación, coeficiente de inestabilidad
The ratio by which overall changes in the stock market influence changes in a specific stock.

volume driven program
programa cuya magnitud depende del volumen de actividad

volumetric charge
cargo (aplicado) según volumen de descarga
Charge levied for water pollution, based on volume of wastewater discharged rather than on concentration of pollutants in the water. Cf. **strength charge**.

voluntary export restraints - VER
limitación voluntaria de las exportaciones
An agreement by a country not to export certain goods to another country or to limit those exports to prevent them from gaining too large a share of the domestic market.

voluntary lending; spontaneous lending
préstamos voluntarios
Lending that is made willingly, as opposed to lending where the lender has some sort of obligation to lend or else the borrower will not reimburse previous loans.

voluntary restraints (on trade)
limitación voluntaria (del comercio)

vote without meeting
votación sin convocar a reunión

voting power
derechos de voto

voting right
derecho de voto

voting stock
acciones que confieren derecho de voto

voucher privatization
privatización mediante cupones
Method of privatization used primarily in the former Soviet Union whereby, prior to privatization, vouchers are distributed to eligible parties (e.g. employees, local residents). Voucher-holders exchange their vouchers for stock in the corporation, shares in an investment fund (which invests in one or more corporations to be privatized) or sell them on the open market for cash.

- W -

wage agreement
convenio salarial

wage bill
costos salariales; masa salarial

wage claim
reivindicación, reclamación salarial

wage control
ordenación, regulación salarial

wage costs
costos salariales

wage drift
desviación de los salarios
An increase in the effective rate of pay per unit of labor **input** by arrangements that lie outside the control of the recognized procedures for scheduling rates. In practice this is frequently interpreted to mean a rise in standard weekly earnings in excess of the rise in nationally negotiated wage rates.

wage goods
bienes salariales
Goods normally bought out of current salary.

wage pressure
presión de los salarios

wage-price indexing
vinculación de los salarios con los precios
System whereby wage and salary increases are indexed to price increases.

wage-price spiral
espiral salarios-precios

wage pull inflation
inflación producida por los salarios

wage rate
salario

wage restraint
restricción, austeridad salarial

waive, to
renunciar (a un derecho); dispensar, eximir (de una obligación)

waiver
renuncia (a un derecho); dispensa, exención (de una obligación); *a veces*: **exención parcial**

waiver (of a right) [ICSID]
renuncia

waiver (of immunity) [ICSID]
renuncia

war and civil disturbance [MIGA]
guerra y disturbios civiles
One of the MIGA covered risks. Defined as "any military action or civil disturbance in any territory of the host country to which the Convention shall be applicable as provided in Article 66." Cf. **riot** and **civil commotion**.

warehousing (of financial assets)
inmovilización de activos
Keeping financial assets in an investment for purposes other than making an immediate profitable investment. IFC does this to encourage other investors to invest in the project, while commercial banks are doing it with developing country assets in order to keep a presence in the country concerned.

warning signal
señal de alerta, de prevención

warrant [finance]
certificado para la compra de acciones, bonos
Option to purchase ordinary share or bond of a particular company, usually purchased by **bondholder** wanting to participate in profit growth of that company. Often attached to new bond issue as inducement for investors to take up the bond.

warrant bond
bono con certificado
Bond with **warrant** attached. This may be a bond with bond **warrant** or a bond with equity **warrant**.

wastage; waste [education]
volumen, tasa de deserción

waste; loss in weight [commerce]
desperdicio; pérdida

waste disposal
eliminación de desechos

wastewater
aguas residuales, de desecho, servidas, negras

water balance
balance hídrico
Balance of input and output of water within a given defined hydrological area such as a basin, lake, etc., taking into account net changes of storage.

water-based disease
enfermedad con base en el agua
Disease where a necessary part of the life cycle of the infecting agent takes place in an aquatic animal. Includes urinary schistosomiasis and dracunculosis.

waterborne disease
enfermedad transmitida por el agua
Disease where water acts only as a passive vehicle for the infecting agent. Includes cholera, typhoid and infectious hepatitis.

waterborne sewage system
alcantarillado de arrastre hidráulico

water charges
tarifas de agua

water control
regulación de (las) aguas

water effluent charges
cargo por contaminación del agua
Charges to users for polluting water.

water engineer
ingeniero hidrólogo, hidráulico

water harvesting
aprovechamiento de aguas
Directing runoff from a broad area by earth or stone bunds and canals onto smaller areas growing crops or trees.

waterlogging
anegamiento

waterman **see** ditch rider

water management
ordenación de las aguas

waterspreading
distribución de aguas
Diverting water from gullies onto cultivated fields for irrigation purposes.

water supply
abastecimiento, suministro de agua

water-washed disease
enfermedad vinculada con la falta de higiene
Disease caused by lack of water, poor personal hygiene and lack of proper human waste disposal. Includes scabies, skin sepsis, yaws, leprosy, trachoma and conjunctivitis.

watering **see** stock watering

watering place
aguada; aguadero; abrevadero

watershed management
ordenación de cuencas hidrográficas, de vertientes

waterway
vía navegable

ways and means
medios y arbitrios

weaning foods
alimentos para el período de destete
Foods for weaning babies.

wear and tear (fair)
desgaste (normal o natural)

wearing course; surface course [highways]
capa superficial, de rodadura

weighbridge
puente-báscula

weighted average
media ponderada; promedio ponderado

weighted average tariff rate - WATR
tasa arancelaria media ponderada
The average of all tariffs paid on imported goods
and all subsidies paid on exported goods, each
weighted by the proportion that the good
represents in the value of total trade of the country.

weighted voting system
sistema de votación ponderada

welfare costs of protectionism
costos económicos del proteccionismo
Amount of money that exporters would need to
receive to be as well off with protectionism against
them in industrial countries as they would be
without protectionism against them.

welfare economy
economía del bienestar

welfare function; utility function
función bienestar; función utilidad
For an individual, the relationship between his
level of wellbeing, welfare or utility and the things
that contribute to it. For society, the relationship
between the welfare of society as a whole and all
the variables affecting the state of the economy
and quality of life.

welfare State
Estado benefactor, providente

welfare payments
subsidios de asistencia social

wellhead
boca de(l) pozo; cabeza de(l) pozo

wellhead price
precio en la boca, en la cabeza del pozo
The price paid at the wellhead for gas or oil
produced.

West Indian cotton; Sea Island cotton; Egyptian
cotton; kidney cotton
**algodón de las Indias Occidentales; algodón de
Barbados; algodón egipcio**

wetcore
instalación sanitaria mínima

The minimum structure for sanitary facilities on a
lot.

wet gas
gas húmedo
Natural gas containing liquid hydrocarbons in
solution, which may be removed by a reduction of
temperature and pressure or by a relatively simple
extraction process.

wetlands
tierras húmedas
Estuaries, lakes, mangroves, marshes and swamps.

wet process [cement manufacture]
elaboración, fabricación por vía húmeda
Process of manufacturing cement used when the
raw material contains a quantity of water. It is
mixed in water and the paste obtained is treated.
See also dry and semidry process.

wharfage; wharfage charges; dockage; quayage
muellaje

wheeling
servicio de transmisión
Energy transported by an intervening party
between a supplier and a receiver.

wheeling charge
cargo por transmisión
Charges levied by an intermediary who allows the
producer to use his equipment to transmit
electricity to the consumer.

whole farm budget
presupuesto global de la explotación agrícola
A budget for activities on a farm.

whole farm development
desarrollo integral de la explotación agrícola

wholesale banking
**transacciones entre grandes bancos y entre
éstos y otras instituciones financieras;
transacciones interbancarias**
1. Large-scale dealings in money deposits
centered in the closely-interrelated group of
money markets which have developed strongly
since the mid-1960s.
2. Banking facilities offering a limited number
of services to select clients (generally large
corporations). *See* **retail banking**.

wholesale mechanism; wholesaling
mecanismo de préstamos a intermediarios
Bank procedure whereby loans are made to an intermediary, which in turn onlends them to the beneficiaries.

wholesale training
capacitación, formación de instructores
Training trainers for subsequent training.

wholly owned subsidiary
subsidiaria en propiedad absoluta

widening **see** capital widening

wildcat (drilling)
perforación exploratoria
Exploratory drilling for oil and/or gas on a geologic feature not yet proven to be productive, in an unproven territory or in a zone that has never produced or is not known to productive in the general area.

wildcat well
pozo exploratorio

wild flooding
riego por desbordamiento natural
Method of irrigation which consists of spilling water at frequent intervals from a grade ditch constructed along the high edge of a sloping field. The water is allowed to flow freely down the slope, irrigating the soils the water moves across. Interceptor ditches are placed at intervals down the slopes to collect the water. Used primarily for irrigating low-income crops on steep lands where uniformity of water distribution is not a major consideration.

wildland management area - WMA
zonas silvestres administradas
Area where wildlands are protected and managed to retain a relatively unmodified state.

wildland management unit - WMU
zona silvestre protegida

wildlands
zonas silvestres

willingness to pay - WTP
voluntad de pagar; disposición para pagar

The amount consumers are prepared to pay for a final good or service. An estimate of the value in use.

wind pump
bomba eólica

windbreak
(plantación) cortavientos; barrera contra vientos

windfall profit
utilidad imprevista, extraordinaria

window [computers]
ventana

window (in a market)
resquicio
Short-lived opportunity to issue **securities** that may be taken up by any of a significant number of highly rated borrowers.
[**see also** discount window; Third Window]

window dressing
alteración del balance; manipulación de la contabilidad (para aparentar una mejor situación)
Financial actions such as stock market trading, whose purpose is to make a corporation's financial situation seem better than it really is, just before the publication of a balance sheet or other **financial statement**.

window guidance [central bank]
restricción oficiosa del crédito
Unofficial control of interest rates by central bank.

"with-and-without" test [projects]
prueba, método de "con y sin"
A test of the net benefit with and without the project.

withholding tax
impuesto retenido en la fuente

women in development - WID
participación de la mujer en el proceso de desarrollo

woodfuel
leña; combustible de biomasa leñosa

word processor
operador(a) de tratamiento de textos; máquina de tratamiento de textos

workers' remittances
remesas de los trabajadores (emigrados, expatriados)

working account
cuenta de explotación
A normal revenue and expense account.

working age population
población en edad de trabajar

working agreement
acuerdo provisional (para facilitar ulteriores labores)

working capital
capital de trabajo, de explotación
The capital necessary to purchase goods and services that are used for the production activities of an enterprise and that are turned over during the production cycle.
[**see also** noncash working capital]

working capital loan
préstamo para capital de trabajo; crédito de avío

working capital ratio **see** current ratio

working capital statement **see** statement of changes in financial position

working funds
fondos de explotación

working interest [oils, minerals]
participación del concesionario; interés económico directo
The fractional interest of the lessee of a tract of land in the production of crude oil and gas from the tract. Costs are borne at the same rate as the interest held.

working population
población activa

working ratio
coeficiente de explotación
Cash working expenses divided by operating revenues, expressed as a percentage.

working table; performance chart; management chart
diagrama, gráfico de situación

workmen's compensation
indemnización por accidentes de trabajo

workout [financial]
reestructuración financiera
Arrangements between borrowers and debtors (usually at international level) to extend repayment schedules and provide new credit at reduced interest rates.

workout arrangements; workouts [IFC]
arreglos
Arrangements between borrowers and debtors (usually at international level) to extend repayment schedules and provide new credit at reduced interest rates.

workshop [training]
cursillo

World Bank's Bank
Banco del Banco Mundial
Proposed organization to help raise and channel additional money for use in developing countries. Would probably had a greater lending-to-assets ratio than one-to-one as observed by the Bank itself. Would have had more flexibility in raising money than the Bank. The project has been abandoned.

World Bank Group
Grupo del Banco Mundial

(World Bank) Manufacturing Unit Value (MUV) Index
índice del valor unitario de las manufacturas - VUM
Industrial countries' indices of US dollar unit values of manufactured exports to developing countries. There are two indices - the cif index which combines a 90% weight of FOB export prices with a 10% weight of transport costs and a FOB index.

World Development Indicators - WDIs
Indicadores del desarrollo mundial
List of key economic indicators (e.g. population, labor force, urbanization, health-related indicators) given in the Annex to the World Development Report.

"wrap-up" insurance arrangement
plan de seguro global

wrap-up insurance policy
póliza de seguro global
Insurance policy covering several **contractors** all working on the same project.

wrap-up meeting
reunión de conclusiones

write down, to; expense, to
castigar; rebajar el valor en libros; amortizar parcialmente en libros
To transfer a portion of the balance of an account previously regarded as an asset to an expense account or to profit and loss.

write off [noun]
anulación, cancelación en libros
When an asset or a portion of an asset is recognized as worthless, it is removed from the books of a corporation and a corresponding loss in the corporation's capital is recognized.
[see also cumulative write-offs; tax write-off]

write off, to
anular; eliminar en libros; amortizar totalmente en libros

writing down
castigo, reducción del valor en libros; amortización en libros

write up [USA]
aumento del valor en libros

- X -

x-efficiency
eficiencia x
A situation in which a firm's total costs are not minimized because the actual output from given inputs is less than the maximum feasible level.

xenocurrencies
xenomonedas; xenodivisas
A deposit or loan denominated in a currency other than that of the country in which the bank is located.

- Y -

yellow stained cotton
algodón amarillento
Cotton almost entirely discolored to a slightly mottled tan color.

yield curve
curva de rendimiento
Graph relating rates of return to maturity.

yield rate
tasa de rendimiento

yield test of projects
prueba del rendimiento de los proyectos

yield to maturity - YTM
rendimiento al vencimiento
The return a security earns assuming that it is held until a certain date and put to the borrower at the specified put price.

- Z -

zero base budgeting - ZBB
presupuestación a partir de cero
A budget process which requires managers to justify each requested budgetary expenditure anew each year.

zero coupon bond
bono sin cupón
Bond that pays no interest but is sold at a steep discount and paid off at par.

zero fee policy
política de servicios gratuitos

zero population growth - ZPG
crecimiento cero de la población

zero sum game
juego de suma cero, nula

zero tillage system
sistema de cultivo sin laboreo, de cero labranza
Cultivation involving zero plowing, i.e. by planting directly on the soil surface, usually using manure, hay or some other substance to aid growing.

zone extension officer - ZEO [agricultural extension]
oficial de extensión de zona - OEZ
Senior extension officer, at the highest level.

Spanish-English Glossary

Glosario español-inglés

a granel
bulk, in

a nivel popular, comunitario, local
grass root(s) level, at the

a título de donación
grant basis, on a

a título oneroso
consideration, for a; valuable consideration, for

a título oneroso
payment basis, on a

abandono
droppage [IFC]

abastecimiento de agua
water supply

abogado
advocate [ICSID]

abonado
consumer [telecommunications]

abonado con rastrojo
stubble mulch farming

abono de base
basal dressing; bottom dressing

abono de cloaca, de letrina
night soil

abono de superficie
top dressing [agriculture]

abono simple
single fertilizer

abono verde
green manure

abrevadero
watering place

abrevado [ganado]
stock watering [livestock]

absorber
take over, to

absorbido(a) por
taken over by

acarreo entre terminales
line-haul [transportation]

accesibilidad financiera
affordability

accesión
accession

acción ajustable y convertible
convertible adjustable stock

acción con derecho de veto
golden share

acción de primera clase
blue chip; blue chip security

acción ordinaria
common share; common stock; ordinary share; equity

acción ordinaria
equity; common share; regular share [stock exchange]

acción recibida como dividendo
bonus share

acciones
corporate stocks; equity

acciones de adhesión
membership shares [World Bank]

acciones de valor inestable
volatile stock

acciones en circulación
outstanding shares, stock

acciones habilitantes
qualifying shares

acciones nominativas
registered share, stock; personal stock

acciones pagadas
paid-up stock; fully paid stock

acciones preferenciales, preferentes, preferidas
preferred stock

acciones que confieren derecho de voto
voting stock

aceite pesado
heavy oil

aceleración del vencimiento
acceleration of maturity (of a loan) [IBRD]

aceptación bancaria
acceptance; bank acceptance; banker's acceptance

acondicionamiento de tierras
land development

acontecimiento
development

acreedor no prioritario
junior creditor

acreencia
financial claim

acreencia [banca]
claim

acreencias no redituables, improductivas
nonperforming debt

acta (de la Comisión)
report (of Commission) [ICSID]

acta de sesión(es)
proceedings

Actas Resumidas
Summary Proceedings

actividad básica
core process [IBRD]

actividad comercial
business line

actividad de demostración
demonstration activity

actividades con fines de lucro directamente improductivas
directly unproductive profit seeking (DUP) activities

actividades de extensión, de divulgación
outreach activities

actividades iniciales
initial operation

actividades previas a la explotación
predevelopment work [oil]

activo(s)
assets

activo contingente
contingent asset

activo corriente
current assets

activo de reserva
reserve asset

activo disponible y realizable a corto plazo
current assets

activo financiero
financial claim

activo neto
stockholders' equity; shareholders' equity; owners' equity; equity; net worth

activos a la vista
sight assets

activos a su valor de adquisición
historically valued assets

activos autoliquidables, autoamortizables
self-liquidating assets

activos en el exterior
foreign assets

activos fijos
capital assets; fixed assets; permanent assets; fixed capital [accounting]

activos intangibles, inmateriales
intangible assets, property

activos líquidos, disponibles
liquid assets; quick assets

activos no redituables, improductivos
nonperforming assets

activos productivos
earning assets

activos reales
real assets

activos redituables, productivos
performing assets

activos sobre el exterior
foreign assets

activos transitorios
temporary assets

activos varios
sundry assets

activos vendibles
saleable assets

acto de gobierno
act of state; sovereign act doctrine

actuación
performance

actuación de las instituciones
institutional performance

actuación financiera
financial performance, results

actuación oral
oral procedure [ICSID]

actuaciones (jurídicas)
proceedings

actualizado a partir del segundo año
time-adjusted [project analysis]

actualizar
discount, to [finance]

acuerdo básico
frame agreement [IBRD]

acuerdo condicional de reembolso
qualified agreement to reimburse

acuerdo de arrendamiento de equipo para operaciones
operating leasing agreement

acuerdo de cesión
assignment agreement

acuerdo de comercialización
marketing arrangement

acuerdo de compromiso contingente
standby agreement [IFC]

acuerdo de concesión
franchising agreement

acuerdo de cooperación general
framework cooperative arrangement [MIGA]

acuerdo de derecho de giro
standby arrangement [IMF]

acuerdo de destinación especial
set aside agreement

acuerdo de ejecución
implementing agreement

acuerdo de garantía
security agreement

Acuerdo de la Ronda de Tokio
Tokyo Round Agreement

acuerdo de licencia, de concesión de licencia
licensing agreement

acuerdo de mantenimiento de la situación existente
standstill agreement

acuerdo de recompra
buy-back agreement; take-out agreement; repurchase agreement

acuerdo de reprogramación multianual de la deuda
multiyear rescheduling arrangement; multiyear restructuring agreement - MYRA

acuerdo de retención de acciones
share retention agreement [IFC]

acuerdo firme de compra (sin derecho de rescisión)
take-or-pay agreement, contract

acuerdo global; acuerdo marco
umbrella (agreement)

Acuerdo Multifibras
Multifibre Arrangement

acuerdo provisional (para facilitar ulteriores labores)
working agreement

acuerdo sobre un producto básico, primario
commodity agreement

acuerdos compensatorios
offset agreements

acuerdos de crédito
credit arrangements

acuerdos de "hermanamiento"
twinning arrangements

acuerdos internacionales sobre productos básicos
international commodity agreements, arrangements

acuerdos regionales de integración
regional integration arrangements

acumulación
bunching

acumulación de existencias
stockpiling

acumulación de vencimientos
bunching of maturities

acumulación de vencimientos
debt bunching

acumulaciones
accruals

adelanto
development

adelanto del vencimiento
acceleration of maturity (of a loan) [IBRD]

adelanto respecto del plazo previsto
time underrun

adelantos y atrasos
leads and lags

adelgazamiento de la capa de ozono
ozone hole

adhesión
accession

adhesión oficial
formal adherence

adicionalidad
additionality

adiestramiento
skills development

adiestramiento en el empleo, trabajo
on-the-job training

adiestramiento en el servicio
in-service training

aditivo que aumenta el octanaje
octane booster

aditivo (que aumenta la cantidad)
extender [gasoline]

adjudicación
award [contracts]

adjudicación (de títulos de propiedad) de la tierra
titling (land)

adjudicatario
successful bidder

administración, la
Management [World Bank]

administración colegiada
collegial management

administración de activos y pasivos
asset and liability management

administración de impuestos
tax office

administración de la ayuda a los países
country assistance management - CAM

administración de proyectos
project management

administración local
local authority; local government

administración participatoria
participative management

administración por objetivos
management by objectives - MBO

administración portuaria
port authority

administración pública
civil service; government services

administración superior
senior management

administraciones públicas
general government [national accounts]

administrador del proyecto
project manager

administradores
managers

admisión
intake

adopción (por el prestatario) de un programa como propio
borrower ownership

adquisición de un solo proveedor
sole source procurement

adquisición en grandes cantidades, en grueso
bulk procurement

adquisición no conforme con los procedimientos reglamentarios
misprocurement [IBRD]

adquisición reservada (a proveedores, contratistas nacionales)
reserved procurement

adscripción
secondment

afiliada
affiliate

afiliadas
sister companies

afinamiento (de la economía)
fine tuning (of the economy)

afirmación
claim

afluencia de capital
capital inflow

afluencia de fondos
cash inflows

aforo
valuations for customs purposes

agente
agent [bank syndicate]

agente (de cambio y bolsa)
broker

agente comprador
buying agent [commodities]

agente de adquisiciones
procurement agent

agente de compras
buying agent [commodities]

agente de extensión, de divulgación agrícola
extension agent, worker

agente de extensión a nivel de poblado
field-level extension worker

agente de extensión agrícola
agricultural extension officer - AEO

agente de extensión de poblado - AEP
village extension worker - VEW

agente de salud comunitaria
community health worker - CHW

agente en el terreno
field agent

agente financiero
fiscal agent

agilización
streamlining

agio
premium [securities]

agotamiento de la capa de ozono
ozone depletion

agotamiento previo de las vías administrativas o judiciales (de un Estado)
exhaustion of local administrative or juridical remedies [ICSID]

agregado
aggregate

agregados monetarios
monetary aggregates

agricultor con pequeña(s) explotación(es) satélite(s)
outgrower

agricultor de enlace
contact farmer [agricultural extension]

agricultor innovador
advanced farmer

agricultura de subsistencia
subsistence farming

agricultura en tierras de aluvión
floodplain agriculture, cultivation

agricultura industrial
factory farming

agroeconomista
agro-economist

agroindustrias
agribusiness; agroindustries; agro-based industry; agroprocessing industries

agrónomo
agriculturist

agrosilvicultura
agroforestry; farm forestry

agua bruta, cruda, sin tratar
raw water

agua corriente, por tubería
piped water

agua potable
safe water; drinking water; safe drinking water

agua que no produce ingresos
nonrevenue water

aguada
watering place

aguadero
watering place

aguas residuales, de desecho, servidas, negras
wastewater

agujero en la capa de ozono
ozone hole

ahorrador negativo
dissaver

ahorro de energía
energy conservation

ahorro forzoso
compulsory saving; forced savings

ahorro interno
domestic savings

ahorro negativo
dissaving

aislacionista
inward-looking; inward-oriented [country; policy]

ajustado para tomar en cuenta las variaciones estacionales
seasonally adjusted

ajuste
adjustment

ajuste cambiario
exchange adjustment

ajuste de la(s) política(s) industrial y comercial
industrial and trade policy adjustment - ITPA

ajuste de traducción (de monedas)
translation adjustment [accounting]

ajuste del régimen comercial
trade adjustment

ajuste excesivo
overshooting

ajuste financiero
financial adjustment

ajuste gradual del tipo de cambio
crawling peg [rate of exchange]

ajuste institucional
organizational fine tuning

al costo de los factores
factor cost, at - f.c.

alcance
coverage

alcantarilla colectora, maestra
trunk sewer

alcantarillado de arrastre hidráulico
waterborne sewage system

alfabetización
literacy; literacy education

alfabetización funcional
functional literacy

algodón amarillento
yellow stained cotton

algodón americano
hairy cotton; upland cotton

algodón arbóreo
tree cotton; Ceylon cotton; Siam cotton; China cotton

algodón de Barbados
kidney cotton; West Indian cotton; Sea Island cotton; Egyptian cotton;

algodón de fibra corta
short staple cotton

algodón de fibra extra larga
extra long staple cotton

algodón de fibra larga
long staple cotton

algodón de fibra mediana
medium staple cotton

algodón de las Indias Occidendales
Sea Island cotton; West Indian cotton; Egyptian cotton; kidney cotton

algodón de las Islas Occidentales
Egyptian cotton; kidney cotton; Sea Island cotton; West Indian cotton

algodón egipcio
West Indian cotton; Sea Island cotton; Egyptian cotton; kidney cotton

algodón gris claro
gray cotton; light gray cotton; blue stained cotton

algodón herbáceo
American short staple cotton; Arabian cotton; herbaceous cotton; Levant cotton

algodón ligeramente manchado
light spotted cotton

algodón manchado
spotted cotton

algodón tintado
tinged cotton

algodón upland
upland cotton; hairy cotton

algodón velloso
hairy cotton; upland cotton

alimento básico
staple (food)

alimentos ingeridos
food intake

alimentos para el período de destete
weaning foods

alivio
relief

alivio de la carga de la deuda
debt relief

almacén de aduanas
bonded warehouse

alojamiento para el personal
staff house

alteración del balance
window dressing

alternancia rápida (de medidas) de expansión y contracción
stop-go, stop and go policy

alternativa
alternative [projects]; trade-off

alto funcionario
senior manager

alumnos por profesor
student-teacher ratio - STR; pupil-teacher ratio - PTR; teacher-pupil ratio

alza de tarifas
tariff escalation

alza por efecto de trinquete
ratcheting up

ambiente propicio, favorable
enabling environment

ámbito de aplicación de las recomendaciones
recommendation domain

amiguismo
cronyism

amnistía tributaria
tax amnesty

amortizable
redeemable

amortización
redemption

amortización (depreciación) lineal, constante, de cuotas fijas
depreciation on a straight line; straight line depreciation

amortización en libros
writing down

amortizar parcialmente en libros
write down, to; expense, to

amortizar totalmente en libros
write off, to

ampliación
extension [building]

ampliación del capital
capital widening

análisis de costo mínimo
least cost analysis

análisis de costos-beneficios
cost-benefit analysis

análisis de la capacidad limitante
bottleneck analysis

análisis de la incidencia fiscal
tax incidence analysis

análisis de las ofertas
examination of bids

análisis de punto muerto, de equilibrio
breakeven analysis

análisis de redes
network analysis

análisis de sensibilidad
sensitivity analysis

análisis del crecimiento
growth accounting [econometry]

análisis del equilibrio general
general equilibrium analysis

análisis del valor
value engineering

análisis del valor hedónico
hedonic price analysis

análisis hedónico de los precios
hedonic price analysis

análisis por conglomerados, grupos
cluster analysis

análisis transversal
cross-sectional analysis

Andropogon gayanus
andropogon

anegamiento
waterlogging

anegamiento controlado
controlled flooding

anexo [convenios de préstamo o crédito]
schedule

animales de cruza
cross-bred progeny [livestock]

animales reproductores
breeding stock

antecedentes (profesionales)
background [education]

antecedentes académicos
educational background

anticipación del vencimiento
prematuring

anticipo de caja
cash advance

anticipo para movilización
mobilization advance [contracts]

antiselección de riesgo
adverse selection [MIGA]

antracita
anthracite; hard coal

antracita
hard coal; anthracite

anualización
annualization

anulación
cancellation

anulación de una deuda
debt cancellation

anulación en libros
write off [noun]

anulaciones acumuladas en libros
cumulative write offs

anular
write off, to

anuncio de emisión efectuada
tombstone

anuncio general de adquisiciones
general procurement notice

año agrícola
crop year

año base
base year

apagón
outage [electricity]

aparcería
sharecropping

apertura de ofertas
bid opening

aplanamiento de una curva
flattening out

aplazamiento impositivo
tax deferral

aplicación de fertilizantes a voleo
broadcasting (seed, fertilizer)

aplicación de grava
gravelling; regravelling

apoderado
agent [ICSID]

aportación
input

aportación con características de donación
grant-like contribution

aportación en efectivo
cash input [accounting]

aportación en mano de obra propia
sweat equity

aportaciones suplementarias
supplementary contributions [IDA]

aporte en efectivo
cash input [accounting]

aportes
payroll contributions

apoyo
backstopping

apoyo de los intereses
interest support

apoyo de precios
price support

aprender con la práctica
learning by doing

aprender sobre la marcha
learning by doing

aprobación
clearance

aprobación tácita
"no objection" (procedure)

aprovechamiento
development; harnessing

aprovechamiento de aguas
water harvesting

aprovechamiento de la energía hidroeléctrica
hydrodevelopment

aprovechamiento de tierras
land development

aprovisionamiento de combustible [barcos]
bunkering

arancel
tariff; tariff schedule

arancel de "puro estorbo"
nuisance tariff

arbitraje de cambios
exchange arbitrage

arbitraje de intereses con cobertura
covered interest arbitrage

arbitraje impositivo
tax arbitrage

árbitro
arbitrator [ICSID]

árbitro dirimente
umpire [legal]

árbol de cultivo, aprovechable
crop tree

árbol forrajero
forage tree

arboricultura
tree farming

área habitable
living area

arenas asfálticas
tar sands

arenas impregnadas de brea
oil sands; tar sands

arenas petrolíferas, asfálticas
oil sands

arranque
take-off

arrastre de troncos
skidding

arreglo (de una diferencia)
settlement (of a dispute) [ICSID]

arreglos
work-out arrangements; work-outs [IFC]

arrendamiento
leasing

arrendamiento financiero
finance lease; financial, full pay out lease; leasing

arroz acuático
flooded rice

arroz de montaña, de tierras altas, de secano
upland rice; mountain rice; highland rice

arroz flotante
floating rice

artículo básico
staple (good)

artículo de propaganda, de cebo, de reclamo
loss leader

artículo patentado o de marca registrada
proprietary good, item

artiga
ash farming; burn-beating; burning

asegurador
underwriter [securities]

asentamiento
land settlement; shakeout (of the market)

asentamientos humanos
human settlements

asientos (contables)
accounting entries; entries

asignación
provision [accounting]

asignación de divisas
exchange allocation

asignación de las utilidades
allocation of profits; appropriation of profits

asignación de los fondos del préstamo
allocation of loan proceeds

asignación de los ingresos netos
allocation of net income

asignación de los recursos
allocation of resources

asignación desacertada de los recursos
misallocation of resources

asignación para alzas de precios
price contingencies

asignación para depreciación
reserve for depreciation; allowance for
depreciation; depreciation allowance

asignación para excesos de cantidades físicas
physical contingencies

asignación para instalación
settling-in grant [IBRD]

asignación para vacaciones en el país de origen
home leave allowance [World Bank]

asignación por agotamiento
depletion allowance, reserve

asignación por cargas familiares, por persona a cargo
dependency allowance

asignación por construcción
construction allowance

asignación por reasentamiento, por reinstalación
resettlement grant

asignación por traslado
relocation grant

asignación presupuestaria
allotmen; appropriation [budget]; budget
appropriation

asignatura
subject matter [education]

asistencia en apoyo de políticas
policy-based assistance

asistencia en condiciones concesionarias, muy favorables
concessional, concessionary aid

asistencia en especie
commodity assistance

asistencia no destinada a proyectos específicos, para fines generales
nonproject aid

asistencia oficial para el desarrollo - AOD
official development assistance - ODA

asistencia operacional - ASOP
Operational Assistance - OPAS [UNDP]

asistencia para fines de ajuste
adjustment aid

asistencia para programas
program aid

asistencia para proyectos
project aid

asistencia social
social welfare

asistencia técnica independiente
free-standing technical assistance - FSTA

asistencia técnica para desarrollo institucional
institution-related technical assistance; soft
technical assistance

asistencia técnica relacionada con las inversiones en activos físicos
engineering-related technical assistance; hard technical assistance

asistencia técnica relacionada con los componentes físicos
engineering-related technical assistance; hard technical assistance

asistencia técnica relacionada con los componentes no físicos o de servicios
institution-related technical assistance; soft technical assistance

asistente técnico
technical assistant

asociación
partnership

asociación de ahorro y crédito rotatorio
rotating savings and credit association - ROSCA

asociación de pastoreo comunitario
pastoral association - PA

aspectos complementarios
complementarity

aspectos económicos del retroceso
economics of regress

aspectos sociales del ajuste
social dimensions of adjustment - SDA

asumir
take over, to

asumir como propio
own, to

atención básica de salud
basic health care

atención primaria de (la) salud
primary health care

atender el servicio de un préstamo
service a loan, to

atenuación de los impuestos
tax mitigation

atracción
crowding in

atraso(s) en los pagos
payment arrears

auditar
audit, to

auditor
auditor

auditoría
audit [finance]

auditoría ambiental
environmental audit

auditoría general, integral, a fondo
comprehensive auditing

auditoría impositiva, tributaria
tax audit

auditoría interna
internal audit

auge
development

aumento de la producción
production build up

aumento de la temperatura mundial
global warming

aumento de precio
mark-up

aumento del capital
capital widening

aumento del capital con respecto al trabajo
capital deepening

aumento del componente de servicios en los productos manufacturados
dematerialization of manufactures

aumento del valor en libros
write up [USA]

aumento general del capital
General Capital Increase - GCI

aumento por mérito
merit increase

aumento selectivo del capital
Selective Capital Increase - SCI

austeridad financiera
financial restraint, stringency

austeridad monetaria
monetary restraint

austeridad salarial
wage restraint

autoabastecimiento
self-sufficiency

autoaseguro
self-insurance

autoayuda
self-help

autocontrol
self-restraint

autocorrección
self-adjustment

autoctonización
localization

autodeterminación
self-determination

autofinanciamiento
self-financing

autolimitación
self-restraint

automatización de oficinas
office automation

autonomía
self-sufficiency

autónomo
free-standing; self-contained

autoría
borrower ownership; ownership (of programs)

autoridad emisora
underwriting authority [MIGA]

autoridad portuaria
port authority

autoridad que efectúa la designación
Designating Authority (of Panel Members)
[ICSID]

autoridades
government

autoridades municipales, provinciales, etc.
local authority; local government

autoridades municipales, provinciales, etc.
local government; local authority

autorización
authority [legal]; clearance

autorización legal
legal authority

autorización legislativa
enabling legislation

autorización presupuestaria
appropriation [budget]

autorizado
registered (e.g. tradesmen)

autorregulación
self-adjustment

autosuficiencia
self-sufficiency

autosuficiencia colectiva
collective self-reliance

autoterapia
self-care; self-treatment

autotransbordo
roll-on/roll-off - ro/ro

autotratamiento
self-care; self-treatment

auxiliar especial
staff assistant

auxiliares de enseñanza
teaching aids

auxilio
relief

avalúo aduanero, de aduana
customs valuation (practices)

avalúo para fines impositivos
tax assessment; assessment for tax

avalúo pericial
expert appraisal

avance
development

aviso de desembolso
disbursement letter

avitaminosis
vitamin deficiency

ayuda condicionada, vinculada
tied aid

ayuda en condiciones concesionarias, muy favorables
concessional, concessionary aid

ayuda no condicionada, desvinculada
untied aid

ayuda no destinada a proyectos específicos, para fines generales
nonproject aid

ayuda para programas
program aid

ayuda para proyectos
project aid

ayuda presupuestaria, para el presupuesto
budgetary aid

bacheo
patching; spot improvement, patching; road, surface patching [highways]

bacheo de baches
spot patching, improvement; road, surface patching; patching [highways]

badén
submerged bridge

baja (de activos fijos)
retirement (of a fixed asset)

balance (general) consolidado
consolidated balance sheet

balance de energía
energy audit

balance forrajero
feed balance; feed estimate

balance hídrico
water balance

balanza comercial
trade balance; balance of trade; merchandise balance

balanza de recursos
resource balance

balanza en cuenta corriente
current balance of payments

banco afiliado
affiliate bank

banco agente
agent bank

banco autorizado
authorized bank

banco codirector [emisiones de bonos]
colead manager

banco comercial, privado
commercial bank

banco corresponsal
agent bank; correspondent bank

banco de crédito para la producción y las exportaciones agropecuarias
agricultural production and export (apex) bank

banco de desarrollo, de fomento
development bank

banco de genes
gene bank [plants]

banco de importancia secundaria
second tier bank

banco de inversiones
investment bank [US]; merchant bank [UK]

banco de segunda instancia
second tier bank

Banco del Banco Mundial
World Bank's Bank

banco depositario
depository bank

banco director
lead bank; lead manager

banco emisor, de emisión
issuing bank; bank of issue

banco extraterritorial
offshore bank

banco hipotecario
mortgage bank

banco principal
apex bank, institution

bancos establecidos en las principales plazas financieras
money center banks

bandera de conveniencia, de favor
flag of convenience; open registry flag

baño
dip [stockbreeding]

barbecho en maleza
bush fallow

barbecho forestal
forest fallow

barra de refuerzo
reinforcing bar; rebar

barrera contra vientos
windbreak

barrera no arancelaria
nontariff barrier - NTB

barreras arancelarias
tariff barriers

barriles de equivalente en petróleo - bep
barrels of oil equivalent - boe

barriles diarios de equivalente en petróleo - bdep
barrels per day of oil equivalent - bdoe

barrio de tugurios
slum

base
base; road base [highways]; hard core [projects]

base de cálculo acumulada
cumulative charge number [currency pool]

base de cálculo de la tasa de interés
charge number [currency pool]

base de cálculo de la tasa de interés de los desembolsos acumulados
cumulative charge number [currency pool]

base de capital
capital base

base de capital híbrida
hybrid capital base [IFC]

base imponible
tax base

base monetaria
reserve money; base money; high-power(ed)
money

bases de licitación
bidding conditions

básico
hard core [projects]

beca McNamara
McNamara Fellowship

becario McNamara
McNamara Fellow

beneficiario
loss payee

beneficiarios designados, escogidos, específicos, seleccionados
targeted beneficiaries

beneficio
beneficiation [minerals]

beneficio contractual
beneficial interest

beneficio derivado indirecto
stemming-from benefit

beneficio inducido indirecto
induced-by benefit

beneficio marginal
marginal benefit

beneficios adicionales
incremental benefits

beneficios ecológicos
environmental services

beneficios sociales
social returns [projects]

bien comerciable no comerciado
tradable but nontraded (good, item); nontraded
tradable

bien comerciable, comercializable, exportable o importable
tradable [noun]

bien no comerciable, no comercializable
nontradable [noun]

bienes
assets

bienes comerciados, comercializados, exportados o importados
traded goods

bienes comunes de la humanidad
global commons

bienes de capital, de equipo
capital equipment; capital goods

bienes de consumo
consumer goods

bienes de consumo duraderos
consumer durables

bienes de escaso interés social
demerit goods

bienes de interés social
merit goods

bienes de inversión, de equipo, de capital
investment goods

bienes de producción
producer goods

bienes duraderos
durable goods; durables

bienes en existencia
off-the-shelf goods

bienes fungibles
fungible goods

bienes fungibles, de consumo
consumables

bienes industriales
industrial goods

bienes inmuebles, raíces
real assets

bienes intangibles, inmateriales
intangible assets, property

bienes intermedios
intermediate goods

bienes materiales, tangibles, corpóreos
tangible assets, property

bienes no comerciados, no comercializados, no exportados o importados
nontraded goods

bienes no exclusivos, no excluyentes
nonexcludable, nonexcludible goods

bienes preferentes, deseables
merit goods

bienes salariales
wage goods

bienes y servicios
goods and services

bienes y servicios ecológicos, para la protección ambiental
environmental goods and services

bienestar social
social welfare

bifenilo policlorinado - BPC
polychlorinated biphenyl - PCB

biodiversidad
biodiversity

boca de(l) pozo
wellhead

boceto
sketch plan [architecture]

bomba de operación y mantenimiento a nivel del poblado - BOMPO
village level operation and maintenance (VLOM) pump

bomba de refuerzo
booster pump

bomba eólica
wind pump

bonificación
bonus; development; incentive payment

bonificación de tierras
land reclamation

bonificación por descarga rápida
despatch money; dispatch money

bonificación por trabajo en el exterior
overseas allowance

bonificar
reclaim

bono ajustable, indizado
indexed, index-linked bond

bono al portador
bearer bond

bono Brady
Brady bond

bono clásico, ordinario
straight bond

bono con certificado
warrant bond

bono con cupón
coupon bond

bono con garantía de activos [Reino Unido]
debenture (bond)

bono con interés variable, flotante
floating rate bond

bono con opción de cambio de divisas
(multiple) (currency) option bond

bono con vencimiento elegido a la suerte
serial bond

bono convertible
convertible bond

bono de desarrollo
development bond

bono de descuento intensivo
deep discount bond, note

bono de exclusión
exit bond

bono de una empresa privada, de una compañía, de una sociedad anónima
corporate bond

bono de vencimiento escalonado
serial bond

bono del Tesoro
Treasury bond

bono descontado
discount bond

bono emitido con descuento
original issue discount (OID) bond

bono nominativo
registered bond

bono participatorio
income note

bono perpetuo
perpetual bond

bono perpetuo, de renta vitalicia
annuity bond

bono público, del Estado
government bond

bono sin cupón
zero coupon bond

bono sin garantía específica
debenture (bond)

bonos del gobierno británico
gilt-edged securities

bonos en circulación
outstanding bonds

bonos, etc. emitidos mediante oferta pública
publicly issued (bonds, etc.)

bosque (húmedo) tropical
tropical rain forest

bosque comunal
village woodlot

bosque de altura
mountain forest

bosque de coníferas
softwood forest

bosque de especies frondosas
temperate hardwood forest

bosque de especies frondosas, no coníferas
hardwood forest

bosque de producción
production forest

bosque de protección
protected forest

bosque de segundo crecimiento, bosque talado
cut-over forest

bosque de usos múltiples
mixed-use forest

bosque destinado a convertirse en...
conversion forest

bosque húmedo, pluvial
rain forest

bosque mixto
mixed forest

bosque protegido
protected forest

bosque público protegido
gazetted (protected) public forest

bosque reservado
designated forest

bosque totalmente protegido
preservation forest

brecha
gap

brecha de financiamiento
funding gap

brecha de pobreza
poverty gap

brecha de recursos
resource(s) gap

brecha deflacionaria
deflationary gap

brecha financiera ex ante
ex ante financing gap

brecha inflacionaria
inflationary gap

buen ejercicio del poder
governance

buen gobierno
governance

buena gestión de la cosa pública
governance

buque cisterna
tanker

buque tanque
tanker

búsqueda de personal calificado
head hunting

cabeza de(l) pozo
wellhead

cabotaje
coastal shipping

café pergamino
parchment coffee

caja de crédito para la producción y las exportaciones agropecuarias
agricultural production and export (apex) bank

caja de seguridad social
social security fund

cálculo de costos directos
direct costing

cálculo de precios sociales
social pricing

calendario
schedule

calendario del servicio de la deuda
debt service schedule

calentamiento de la Tierra
global warming

calidad de miembro; ingreso
membership [IFC]

calidad para elaboración
manufacturing grade [meat]

calificación
performance evaluation [personnel]

calzada de servicio
service road

cámara de compensación [bancos]
clearing house

cambio climático circunstancial
transient climate change

cambio climático de equilibrio
equilibrium climate change

cambio desfavorable de la coyuntura
downturn (economic)

cambio favorable de la coyuntura
upturn (economic)

camino de acceso, secundario, vecinal
feeder road

camino de grava
gravel road

camino de normas reducidas, bajas
low standard road

camino de salida
evacuation road

camino de tierra
earth road

camino trazado técnicamente
engineered road

camión cisterna
tanker

camión tanque
tanker

campaña
crop year

campo de aplicación
coverage

campo de atención especial de las operaciones
area of operational emphasis - AOE; special
operational emphasis - SOE

canal de derivación
floodway; high-flow diversion

canal de descarga
spillway chute; tailrace

canal de presión, de carga
penstock [hydroelectricity]

canal de un río
river channel

canalero
ditch rider; waterman

cancelación
cancellation

cancelación en libros
write off [noun]

cancelaciones acumuladas en libros
cumulative write offs

canon por pie
stumpage fee

cantidad asegurada corriente
current insured amount; current amount [MIGA]

cantidad corriente
current insured amount; current amount [MIGA]

**cantidad representativa (de los empréstitos del
BIRF contraídos antes del inicio del sistema de
tipos de interés basados en una cesta de
empréstitos pendientes)**
proxy [IBRD lending rates]

cantidades de dinero nuevo
new money packages

cantidades para los planos definitivos
final design quantities

capa de base
base; road base [highways]

capa de ozono
ozone layer

capa freática
groundwater table

capa intermedia
base course [highways]

capa superficial, de rodadura
surface course; wearing course [highways]

capacidad
capability [urban development]

capacidad crediticia
creditworthiness; financial standing

capacidad de absorción
absorptive capacity; carrying capacity (of the Earth)

capacidad de acarreo
carrying capacity [transportation]

capacidad de acceso a ...
affordability

capacidad de atraque
berthing capacity

capacidad de carga
carrying capacity [pastures]; stock carrying capacity [livestock]

capacidad de despacho de buques
berth throughput

capacidad de diseño, nominal, de régimen
rated capacity

capacidad de endeudamiento
borrowing capacity; debt carrying capacity

capacidad de endeudamiento en, por concepto de garantías
guarantee leverage

capacidad de garantía
guarantee capacity [MIGA]

capacidad de importación derivada de las exportaciones
importing power of exports

capacidad de obtención de ingresos
earning power

capacidad de pago
affordability

capacidad de producción
productive capacity

capacidad de reacción
buoyancy [economics]

capacidad de recuperación de la tierra
land resilience

capacidad de reserva inmediatamente disponible
spinning reserve [electricity]

capacidad de sustento
carrying capacity [pastures]

capacidad de tráfico
load bearing capacity; traffic bearing capacity

capacidad empresarial
entrepreneurship

capacidad excedentaria
excess capacity

capacidad ganadera
carrying capacity [pastures]

capacidad instalada
installed capacity [electricity]

capacidad no utilizable
dead storage (capacity)

capacidad no utilizada
slack [economy] [noun]

capacidad nominal, de diseño
design capacity

capacidad para atender el servicio de la deuda
debt servicing capacity

capacidad para valerse por sí mismo
self-reliance

capacidad tributaria
tax-paying capacity

capacidad útil
live storage, capacity

capacidades básicas
basic skills

capacitación
skills development

capacitación de instructores
wholesale training

capacitación en el empleo, trabajo
on-the-job training

capacitación en el servicio
in-service training

capacitación en la empresa
in-house training

capacitación para el puesto, cargo
job-related training

capitación
capitation tax; poll tax; head tax

capital (de un préstamo)
principal

capital (social, accionario)
equity

capital accionario autorizado
authorized share capital

capital accionario emitido
issued share capital

capital autorizado
authorized capital stock [MIGA]

capital circulante, flotante
floating capital

capital comercial, en condiciones de mercado
commercial capital

capital congelado, bloqueado
frozen capital

capital creado por el hombre
man-made capital

capital de riesgo
risk capital; venture capital

capital de trabajo, de explotación
working capital

capital de trabajo, de explotación no disponible inmediatamente
noncash working capital

capital en préstamo
loan capital

capital extranjero, externo (oficial, privado)
foreign capital (official, private)

capital fijo
capital assets; fixed assets; permanent assets; fixed capital [accounting]

capital fugado
flight capital

capital fugaz, inestable
volatile capital

capital improductivo
no-return equity

capital improductivo, "lastre"
deadwood equities [IFC]

capital inmovilizado
locked-up capital

capital libre de gravámenes
unimpaired capital

capital nacional [para un país]
capital stock

capital nacional fijo
overhead capital

capital natural
natural capital

capital oficial, público
official capital

capital pagado
called up (share) capital; paid in (share) capital

capital pagado, totalmente pagado
paid-up capital

capital simiente, generador
seed money; seed capital

capital social básico
capital infrastructure

capital social fijo
overhead capital

capital social, accionario
equity capital; capital stock (of a corporation)

capital social, accionario, en acciones
registered capital; share capital

capital suscrito y no desembolsado
uncalled capital

capitales itinerantes
hot money; funk money [UK]

capitalización de la deuda
debt-equity conversion; debt-equity swap

capitalización de la deuda
debt-equity swap; debt equity conversion

captación
capture (e.g. of public services); harnessing

captación de rentas
rent-seeking

carbón antracitoso
anthracite; hard coal

carbón bituminoso
brown coal

carbón coquificable
coking coal

carbón de alto poder calorífico
steam coal

carbón limpio, libre de impurezas
clean coal

carbón sin clasificar, tal como sale, en bruto
mine run coal; run-of-mine coal

carbón térmico
steam coal

carbonera
bunker [coal]

carente de derecho a
ineligible

carga de base, fundamental
base load [electricity]

carga de punta
peak load

carga docente
teaching load

carga excesiva de la tributación
efficiency cost of taxation; excess burden of taxation

carga familiar
dependent

carga fraccionada
breakbulk

carga ganadera
stocking rate [livestock]

carga general
general cargo

carga impositiva, tributaria, fiscal
tax burden

carga mixta
general cargo

carga útil
payload

cargo
charge; lien [legal]

cargo
lien; charge [legal]

cargo (aplicado) según la concentración de los contaminantes
strength charge

cargo (aplicado) según volumen de descarga
volumetric charge

cargo al usuario
chargeback

cargo ejecutivo, de dirección, de supervisión
line management position

cargo ejecutivo, de operaciones
line position

cargo por contaminación del agua
water effluent charges

cargo por medidor, por contador
meter rent [electricity]

cargo por presentación de solicitudes
fee for lodging requests [ICSID]

cargo por reinversión
redeployment cost [IFC]

cargo por servicios
service and support fee [IFC]; service charge

cargo por subordinación
subordination fee

cargo por transmisión
wheeling charge

cargo por uso de oficinas
office occupancy fee - OOF

cargos
charges [utilities]

cargos a los usuarios de las carreteras
road user charges

cargos autorizados
authorized positions [personnel]

cargos contables excesivos
overaccruals

cargos diferidos
deferred charges, expenses

cargos por efluentes
effluent charges

cargos por manipulación, tramitación, etc.
handling charges

carretera de normas reducidas, bajas
low standard road

carreteras troncales, principales
trunk roads

carta a la administración
management letter [auditing]

carta complementaria
side letter; supplemental letter

carta complementaria
supplemental letter; side letter

carta de aceptación
letter of acceptance

carta de crédito
letter of credit (L/C)

carta de crédito acumulativo
cumulative letter of credit

carta de crédito confirmada
confirmed letter of credit

carta de crédito irrevocable
irrevocable letter of credit

carta de declaración de la deuda externa
debt representation letter

carta de entendimiento
letter of understanding

carta de intención, de intenciones
letter of intent - LOI

carta de intenciones sobre la política de desarrollo
letter of development policy - LDP [IBRD]

carta de intenciones sobre la política sectorial
letter of sectoral policy [IBRD]

carta de seguridades
letter of comfort

cártel
(explicitly) collusive oligopoly

cartera de acciones
stock ownership

cartera de activos líquidos
liquidity portfolio [IFC]; liquid assets portfolio

cartera de inversiones (a largo plazo)
investment portfolio

cartera de inversiones a corto plazo
trading portfolio

cartera de préstamos
loan portfolio

cartera modelo
benchmark portfolio

casa de aceptaciones
acceptance, accepting house [UK]

caso hipotético
counterfactual

castigar
write down, to; expense, to

castigo del valor en libros
writing down

catastro
land register

categoría
status

categoría de ingreso(s)
income bracket

categorías de supervisión
supervisory grades

categorías principales del programa de operaciones
program objective category - POC

cauce de comercialización
channel [trade]

cauce de un río
river channel

caudalímetro
flow meter; flowmeter

cedente
assignor

ceguera de los ríos
onchocerciasis; river blindness

celebrar un convenio, un acuerdo
execute an agreement, to

célula energética
fuel cell

centésimo de punto porcentual (0,01%)
basis point

central (generadora) de energía a partir de biomasa
biomass (power) plant, station

central (productora) de biogás
biogas plant

central de biomasa
biomass (power) plant, station

central de carga de base, fundamental
base load station [electricity]

central de vapor
steam plant

central eléctrica de carbón, que utiliza carbón como combustible
coal fired power station

central eléctrica de petróleo
oil fired power station

central eléctrica dendrotérmica
dendrothermal power plant

central eléctrica diesel
diesel (fired) power plant

central eléctrica en la zona de una bocamina
pithead power plant

central hidroeléctrica de agua corriente
run-of-the-river hydroelectric power plant

centralización
pooling

centro de capacitación especializada
skill training center

centro de comunicación
communication hub

centro de costos
cost center

centro de desarrollo de aptitudes
skill training center

centro de excelencia
excellence center [education]

centro de genética ganadera
breeding unit

centro de intercambio de información
clearing house

centro de inversión
investment center [accounting]

centro de perfeccionamiento
skill training center

centro de reserva
reserve center

centro de responsabilidad
responsibility center [accounting]

centro de salud maternoinfantil
mother and child health (MCH) center

centro de utilidades
profit center [accounting]

centro fuera de la sede
outreach post

centro integral de salud
health maintenance organization - HMO

centros internacionales de investigaciones agrícolas
international agricultural research centers - IARC

cercos vivos
live fencing

cereales alimentarios
food grains

cereales forrajeros
feed grains

cereales panificables
bread grains

cereales secundarios
coarse grain(s)

certificado de depósito
certificate of deposit

certificado de pago de impuestos
tax clearance

certificado de participación
equity security

certificado de terminación
completion certificate (of a project)

certificado de transferencia de préstamos
participation certificate; pass-through certificate

certificado internacional de depósito
global depositary receipt - GDR

certificado para la compra de acciones, bonos
warrant [finance]

cese de funciones
termination

cesión
divestiture; divestment

cesión de activos (de una sociedad) a cambio de acciones (de otra sociedad nueva)
spinoff [financial market]

cesionario
assignee

chorreo
trickle-down effect

ciclo combinado
combined cycle [energy]

ciclo del proyecto, de los proyectos
project cycle

ciclo económico
business cycle; trade cycle

cierre de las actividades
close of business - c.o.b.

cierre del presupuesto
budget closure

cifra aproximada
ballpark figure

cifras efectivas
actual figures

cifras indicativas de planificación - CIP
Indicative Planning Figures - IPF [UNDP]

circuito de información
feedback loop

círculos empresariales, comerciales
business community

ciudad principal
primal city

clasificación cruzada
cross-classification

clasificación del crédito, de créditos, crediticia
credit rating

Clasificación Uniforme para el Comercio Internacional - CUCI
Standard International Trade Classification - SITC

cláusula con fecha de expiración
sunset clause

cláusula de ajuste de precios
price adjustment clause; price escalation clause; escalation clause

cláusula de arbitraje, compromisoria
arbitration clause

cláusula de bonificación
bonus clause

cláusula de buena voluntad
goodwill clause

cláusula de condicionalidad recíproca
cross-conditionality clause

cláusula de escala móvil
escalator clause [wages]; sliding-scale clause

cláusula de examen (periódico)
(periodic) review clause

cláusula de exención por derechos adquiridos
grandfather clause

cláusula de ilegalidad
illegality clause

cláusula de la nación más favorecida
most-favored-nation clause

cláusula de modificación parcial
bisque clause

cláusula de modificación unilateral
changes clause [US]

cláusula de obligación negativa, de abstención
negative pledge clause

cláusula de reajuste (de los precios)
escalation clause [prices]

cláusula de recuperación
recapture clause

cláusula de recuperación económica
value recovery clause

cláusula de referencia
cross-reference clause

cláusula de revisión, de activación
trigger clause

cláusula de salvaguardia
hedge clause

cláusula de salvaguardia, de elusión, de escape
jeopardy clause; escape clause; break clause

cláusula de suscripción preferente
clawback provision

cláusula de, sobre múltiples monedas
multicurrency clause [loan contract]

cláusula en que se estipula que se han de compartir los reembolsos
sharing clause

cláusula *pari passu*
pari passu clause

cláusula penal, punitiva
penalty clause

cláusula recíproca de entrada en vigor
cross-effectiveness clause

cláusula recíproca en caso de incumplimiento
cross-default clause

cláusula tipo, modelo, estándar
boilerplate

cláusulas contractuales que estipulan someter las diferencias al CIADI
ICSID clauses

cláusulas del CIADI
ICSID clauses

cláusulas penales
liquidated damages

clima propicio, favorable
enabling environment

clínker [fabricación de cemento]
clinker

clínquer
clinker

clorofluorocarbono - CFC
chlorofluorocarbon - CFC

coadministración
codetermination; comanagement; management participation system

coaseguro cualitativo
qualitative coinsurance

coaseguro cuantitativo
quantitative coinsurance

coaseguro(s)
coinsurance

cobertura
coverage

cobertura conjunta de riesgos
risk pooling [MIGA]

cobertura contingente
standby coverage [MIGA]

cobertura contra pérdida total
total loss cover

cobertura de servicio de la deuda
debt service coverage

cobertura global
package coverage [MIGA]

cociente de flexibilidad
flexibility quotient

codirector [emisiones de bonos]
colead manager

coeficiente alumnos-profesor, alumnos por profesor
pupil-teacher ratio - PTR; student-teacher ratio - STR; teacher-pupil ratio

coeficiente capital-servicio
capital-service ratio

coeficiente de ajuste por diferencias del costo de vida
cost-of-living differential factor

coeficiente de autofinanciamiento
self-financing-ratio - SFR

coeficiente de carga de la red
system load factor [electricity]

coeficiente de cobertura de las importaciones
import coverage ratio

coeficiente de cobertura del gasto financiero
financial expenses coverage ratio

coeficiente de concentración
concentration ratio

coeficiente de correlación por rangos de Spearman
Spearman's rank correlation coefficient

coeficiente de costos combinados a largo plazo
long-term blended cost rate - LTB [IFC]

coeficiente de dependencia de la importación de alimentos
food import dependency ratio

coeficiente de endeudamiento
debt-equity ratio; debt-to-equity ratio; debt-to-capital ratio

coeficiente de explotación
working ratio

coeficiente de importaciones (importaciones/producción total)
import coefficient

coeficiente de inestabilidad
volatility ratio [stocks]

coeficiente de insumo-producto
input-output coefficient

coeficiente de la tierra de cultivo equivalente
land equivalent, equivalency ratio - LER

coeficiente de liquidez
liquidity ratio

coeficiente de matrícula
enrollment ratio

coeficiente de movilización
mobilization ratio [IFC]

coeficiente de ocupación de cargos [administración de personal]
staffing ratio

coeficiente de ocupación de cargos, puestos
fill ratio [staff]

coeficiente de operación
operating ratio

coeficiente de protección efectiva
effective protection coefficient - EPC

coeficiente de protección nominal
nominal protection coefficient - NPC

coeficiente de proyectos en reserva
pipeline ratio, lending

coeficiente de recaudación de impuestos
tax performance ratio

coeficiente de reservas, de liquidez
reserve ratio [banking]

coeficiente de semanas-personal hasta la aprobación del proyecto
completion coefficient

coeficiente de solvencia [España]
current ratio; working capital ratio

coeficiente de uniformidad
smoothness ratio

coeficiente de utilización de tierras
land use ratio

coeficiente del servicio de la deuda
debt-service ratio

coeficiente del servicio de los intereses
interest service ratio

coeficiente interinstitucional
institutional ratio

coeficiente mínimo de encaje
minimum cash ratio

coeficiente modificado de Bruno
modified Bruno ratio; internal exchange rate

coeficiente neto de explotación
operating ratio

coeficiente profesor-alumnos
student-teacher ratio - STR; pupil-teacher ratio - PTR; teacher-pupil ratio

coeficiente tributario
tax ratio

coeficientes de calidad de los activos
asset quality ratios

cofinanciador
cofinanc(i)er

cofinanciamiento
cofinancing

cofinanciamiento *ex post*
ex post cofinancing

cofinanciamiento vertical
vertical cofinancing

cogestión
comanagement; codetermination; management participation system

colectivo
jitney

colocación [valores]
marketing

colocaciones cruzadas
cross-placements

colonización
land settlement

combinación de especialidades
skills mix

combinación de financiamiento
blending (of flows)

combinación de insumos
input mix

combinación de monedas
currency mix

combinación de productos
product mix

combustible de biomasa leñosa
woodfuel

combustible derivado del carbón
coal-based fuel

combustible diesel
diesel fuel; diesel oil

combustible no contaminante
clean fuel

combustible para calderas, barcos
bunker; bunker oil

combustible para calefacción
heating oil

combustible sintético
synfuel; synthetic fuel

combustión en lecho fluidizado
fluidized bed combustion

comerciabilidad
marketability

comerciable
tradable [adj.]

comerciales
high-power(ed) money

comercializable
tradable [adj.]

comercialización
merchandising; marketing

comercio compensatorio
countertrade

comercio de productos básicos, primarios
commodity trade

comercio de reexportación
entrepôt trade

comercio exterior
foreign trade

comisión conjunta
joint committee

comisión de administración
management fee

comisión de disponibilidad
availability fee [IFC]

comisión de garantía
guarantee commission, fee [IBRD]

comisión de garantía de compra
backup (underwriting) facility fee

comisión de gestión
management fee

comisión de participación en los costos
cost-sharing fee [APDF]

comisión de solicitud
application fee [MIGA]

comisión del agente pagador
paying agency fee

comisión inicial
front-end fee

comisión inicial (por evaluación)
appraisal fee [IFC]

comisión por administración de la AIF
IDA management fee

comisión por captación de fondos
success fee

comisión por compromiso, por inmovilización de fondos
commitment charge, fee

comisión por servicios
service charge

comisión por tramitación de solicitud
loan origination fee

comisiones devengadas, acumuladas sobre préstamos
accrued loan commissions

Comité Asesor Técnico - CAT
Technical Advisory Committee - TAC [CGIAR]

comité conjunto
joint committee

comité de adjudicación
awarding committee [contracts]

Comité Provisional
Interim Committee [IMF]

comités conjuntos de fiscalización
joint monitoring committees

compañía administradora, de administración, de gestión
management company

compañía comisionista [emisiones de bonos]
commissioned company

compañía de capital de riesgo
venture capital company

compañía de fianzas
bonding company

compañía de inversiones
investment company, fund

compañía de papel
shell company

comparación de precios
prudent shopping; shopping [procurement]

comparación internacional de precios
international shopping

comparación nacional de precios
local shopping

comparatio (la)
comparatio [staff compensation]

compensación
clearance; compensation; consideration [legal, economic]

compensación (de factores, de ventajas y desventajas)
trade-off

competencia
skills

competencia básica
basic skills

competencia no relacionada con los precios
nonprice competition

competencia perfecta
perfect competition; pure competition

competencia por la obtención de recursos
competing claims (on resources)

compilado por
edited by

compilador (de una colección de textos)
editor

complementación
complementarity

complementariedad
subsidiarity

complemento
follow-up

completamente desmontado
completely knocked down - CKD

componente
component (of a project); slice [contracts]

componente en divisas
foreign exchange component

componente físico
hard component [projects]

componente importado, de importación
import component

componente no físico, de servicios
soft component [projects]

componentes físicos
hardware

componentes lógicos
software

comportamiento
performance

comportamiento de la economía
economic performance

composición de la producción
product mix

composición del capital social
ownership structure (of a company)

compra a plazos
hire purchase [UK]

compra de bienes en existencia en el mercado
off-the-shelf purchases

compra de una empresa con fondos tomados en préstamo
leveraged buyout - LBO

compra directa
direct shopping [procurement]

compra en grandes cantidades, en grueso
bulk procurement

comprobación de cuentas
audit [finance]

comprobante de pago
certificate of payment

comprobar cuentas
audit, to

compromiso contingente [CFI]
contingent commitment [IFC]

compromiso contingente de garantía de suscripción
standby underwriting commitment [IFC]

compromiso contingente de participación en el capital social
standby equity [investment]

compromiso de inversión [CFI]
investment commitment [IFC]

compromiso de préstamo
lending commitment; loan commitment

compromiso de suscripción de acciones
equity underwriting

compromiso sin plazo o volumen definidos
open-ended commitment

compromisos netos
exposure

compromisos por países
country exposure [IBRD]

compuestos orgánicos volátiles
volatile organic compounds - VOC

computadora portátil
notebook computer

computerizado
computerized

cómputo sobre una base anual
annualization

con alto coeficiente de capital
capital-intensive

con alto coeficiente de endeudamiento
highly leveraged

con alto contenido de importaciones
import-intensive

con bajo coeficiente de endeudamiento
underleveraged

con exceso de personal
overstaffed

con fines de lucro
profit making

con gran endeudamiento
highly leveraged

con gran intensidad de capital
capital-intensive

con gran intensidad de importaciones
import-intensive

con gran intensidad de mano de obra
labor-intensive

con recargo
premium, at a

con uso intensivo de capital
capital-intensive

con visión hacia el futuro
forward-looking

concentración excesiva de riesgos de financiamiento
overexposure

concentración máxima admisible
threshold limit value - TLV

concentración parcelaria
land consolidation

concepto
design

concertar un préstamo a través de un consorcio (bancario, de financiamiento)
syndicate a loan, to

concesión
claim [mining]; franchise

concesión recíproca
trade-off

concesionario
concessional; concessionary

conciliar
reconcile

conclusión
bottom line

conclusión de los procedimientos
closure of the proceeding [ICSID]

condición jurídica
legal status

condición social
status

condicionalidad
conditionality

condiciones
socioeconomic status - SES; terms and conditions (of a contract)

condiciones concesionarias, muy favorables
concessional terms

condiciones concesionarias, muy favorables, en
concessional; concessionary

condiciones corrientes, comerciales, de mercado
conventional terms

condiciones de entrada en vigor
conditions of effectiveness

condiciones de mercado
commercial conditions

condiciones de reembolso con pagos iguales de principal e intereses
annuity-type repayment terms

condiciones de Toronto
Toronto terms

condiciones de Trinidad
Trinidad terms

condiciones previas
precedent conditions [legal]

condiciones propicias, favorables
enabling environment

condiciones que deben cumplirse
eligibility; eligibility conditions

condonación
forgiveness (of a debt)

condonación (de una deuda)
cancellation

condonación de deudas, de la deuda
debt forgiveness

condonación de una deuda
debt cancellation

conducción
governance

conducto de comercialización
channel [trade]

conexión de servicio
service line; service; supply line; connection [electricity]

conexión domiciliaria
house connection

conferencia marítima
liner (shipping) conference

confianza de la colectividad en sí misma
collective self-reliance

confianza en sí mismo
self-reliance

configuración de las cuentas corrientes
current account pattern

congelación
freeze (of salaries, prices, etc.)

congelación de precios
price freeze

congestión
bottleneck

congestión
bunching

conjunto de bienes (obras, servicios, elementos) a licitar
bid package

conjunto de disposiciones, equipos, proyectos, actividades, financiamiento
package

conjunto de empréstitos
borrowing pool [IBRD]

conjunto de medidas de política
policy package

conjunto de medidas de rescate, de salvamento
rescue package

conjunto de medidas financieras
financial package

conjunto de medidas prácticas
technical package

conmoción civil
civil commotion

conmoción petrolera, producida por los precios del petróleo
oil shock

Cono Sur
Southern Cone

conocimiento de embarque
bill of lading

conocimiento de embarque con reservas, objeciones
claused bill of lading; dirty bill of lading

conocimiento de embarque directo
through bill of lading

conocimiento de embarque sin reservas, objeciones
clean bill of lading

conocimientos
skills

conocimientos básicos
basic skills

conocimientos básicos de aritmética
numeracy

conocimientos especializados
expertise

conocimientos técnicos, tecnológicos
know-how

consejero
counsel [ICSID]

Consejo de Gobernadores
Council of Governors [MIGA]

consentimiento (a la jurisdicción)
consent (to jurisdiction) [ICSID]

conservación de energía
energy conservation

conservación del suelo
soil conservation

considerar (una cuestión) desde el punto de vista de los roles del hombre y la mujer
engender

consignar (fondos) para un fin determinado
earmark, to (funds)

consolidaciones arancelarias
binding; bindings

consolidar los vencimientos
consolidate maturities, to

consorcio (bancario)
selling consortium, group, syndicate

consorcio (bancario, de financiamiento)
syndicate [banking]

consorcio (de coordinación de la ayuda a un país)
consortium (for a country)

consorcio de dirección, directivo
management group; managing group

consorcio garante
underwriting syndicate

constricción monetaria
monetary stringency

construcción de viviendas no sujeta(s) a reglamentaciones
unregulated housing

construcción progresiva de viviendas
incremental building, housing

construcción-operación-transferencia - COT
build-operate-transfer; build-operate-turnover - BOT

construcción-propiedad-operación
build-own operate - BOO

construcción-propiedad-operación-transferencia - CPOT
build-own-operate-transfer - BOOT

consulta sobre posibles objeciones
letter of no objection - LNO [imports]

consultor en dirección de empresas, en administración de empresas
management consultant

consumidor de bajo factor de carga
low load factor consumer [electricity]

consumidor de bajo voltaje
low voltage consumer [electricity]

consumo
consumption bundle

consumo calorífico
heat rate

consumo en la explotación agrícola
on-farm consumption

consumo suntuario, de ostentación
conspicuous consumption

contabilidad de costo total
full cost accounting

contabilidad de costos
cost accounting

contabilidad de costos estándar
standard cost accounting

contabilidad de empresa, comercial
business accounting

contabilidad de existencias
stock accounting; stores accounting

contabilidad de gestión
management accounting

contabilidad en períodos de inflación
inflation accounting

contabilidad en valores de caja
cash (basis) accounting

contabilidad en valores devengados
accrual (basis) accounting

contabilidad gerencial
managerial accounting

contabilidad por órdenes de trabajo, por pedidos
job order accounting

contabilidad por partida doble
double entry accounting

contabilidad por partida simple
single-entry accounting

contabilidad según el costo (valor) de reposición
current cost (value) accounting; current value accounting; value based accounting

contabilidad según el nivel general de precios
general price level accounting; price level accounting

contabilidad según registro de caja
cash (basis) accounting

contabilidad según registro de derechos adquiridos u obligaciones contraídas
accrual (basis) accounting

contabilidad social
social accounts

contaminadores (personas, industrias)
polluter

contenedorización
containerization

contenido de origen nacional
domestic content

contenido de oro
gold content (e.g. of US dollar)

contenido técnico
messages [agricultural extension]

conteo de tráfico
traffic count

contingente
intake

contingente arancelario
tariff quota

continuidad
sustainability

contracción
slump

contracción del crédito
tightening of credit

contralor
comptroler

contramemorial
countermemorial [ICSID]

contrapartida
balancing item, entry

contraprestación
consideration [legal, economic]

contratación anticipada
advance contracting

contratación de uno o varios servicios, adquisición de bienes, etc., fuera de la empresa, etc.
outsourcing; sourcing

contratación de uno o varios servicios, adquisición de bienes, etc., fuera de la empresa, etc.
sourcing; outsourcing

contratación directa
direct contracting [procurement]

contratar
contract out, to

contratista con fianza, afianzado
bonded contractor

contratista principal, primario
main contractor; prime, principal contractor

contrato a porcentaje, de honorario porcentual
percentage (fee) contract [consultants]

contrato a precio fijo
fixed cost contract; fixed price contract

contrato a precios unitarios
rate contract

contrato a suma alzada
lump sum contract [consultants]

contrato a, de precio(s) unitario(s)
unit price contract; admeasurement contract;
remeasurement contract

contrato al costo más honorarios (fijos)
cost-plus (fixed fee) contract - CPFF; cost and fee
contract

contrato al costo más honorarios, más porcentaje
cost-plus contract

contrato al costo más un porcentaje (honorarios)
cost-plus percentage (fee) contract; cost-plus
percentage of cost contract - CPPC

contrato basado en una estimación cuantitativa
bill of quantities contract

contrato basado en una lista de tarifas
schedule of rates contract

contrato con base en una lista oficial de precios
schedule contract

contrato con fines específicos celebrado entre el gobierno y el sector privado
performance contract

contrato con interés tope
cap

contrato con reembolso de costos
cost reimbursable contract

contrato de administración, gestión
management contract

contrato de arrendamiento con opción de compra
finance lease; financial, full pay out lease

contrato de arrendamiento operativo
operating lease

contrato de arrendamiento verdadero
true lease

contrato de compra contra entrega
take-and-pay contract

contrato de duración indefinida
open-ended contract; open-end contract

contrato de fletamento
charter party - c/p

contrato de participación en la producción
production-sharing contract

contrato de participación en las utilidades
profit-sharing contract [MIGA]

contrato de plazo fijo
fixed term contract

contrato de riesgo
risk contract [oil]

contrato de servicios ocasionales
call order contract

contrato entre iguales, entre compañías independientes
arm's length contract

contrato firme de compra (sin derecho de rescisión)
take-or-pay agreement, contract

contrato fraccionado
"slice and package" contract

contrato global
package deal contract

contrato llave en mano
turnkey contract, project

contrato "mercado en mano"
"market-in-hand" agreement

contrato-plan
performance contract

contrato por cantidades aproximadas
running contract

contrato por cantidades indeterminadas
indefinite quantity contract

contrato por meses-hombre
man-month contract

contrato por tiempo
time-based contract [consultants]

contrato "producto en mano"
product in hand contract

contrato sobre la base de un presupuesto meta
target contract

contribución de contrapartida
matching contribution

contribución territorial
land tax

control
control

control de existencias, inventario(s)
inventory control

control de la contaminación en la descarga
end of pipe pollution control

control de la dotación de personal
complement control

control de la natalidad
birth control

control de procesos industriales
process control

control empresarial del arancel
tariff privatization

control interno
internal audit

control mayoritario
ownership (of a corporation)

controlable
manageable

conurbación
conurbation

convenio básico
establishment convention; base convention

convenio condicional de reembolso
qualified agreement to reimburse
 [See also **irrevocable agreement to reimburse**.]

convenio de asunción de préstamo
loan assumption agreement

convenio de crédito de fomento
development credit agreement [IDA]

convenio de destinación especial
set aside agreement

convenio de inversión [CFI]
investment agreement [IFC]

convenio de licencia, de concesión de licencia
licensing agreement

convenio de préstamo
loan agreement

convenio de préstamo entre el Banco y la CFI
Master Loan Agreement

convenio de préstamo subsidiario
Subsidiary Agreement [IBRD]

convenio modificatorio
amendment, amending agreement

convenio salarial
wage agreement

Convenio sobre Arreglo de Diferencias Relativas a Inversiones entre Estados y Nacionales de Otros Estados
Convention on the Settlement of Investment Disputes between States and Nationals of other States [ICSID]

convenio sobre el proyecto
project agreement

convenio sobre financiamiento para el proyecto
project fund agreement

convenio sobre un producto básico, primario
commodity agreement

convenios internacionales sobre productos básicos
international commodity agreements, arrangements

conversión a la par
conversion at par

conversión contable de monedas
translation (of currency)

conversión de activos financieros en valores
securitization

conversión de deuda en programas de salud
debt-for-health swaps

conversión de empresas (públicas) en sociedades comerciales, entidades previstas en la ley de sociedades
corporatization

conversión de la clase de interés
rate basis conversion

conversión de la deuda
debt conversion

conversión de la deuda en capital
debt-equity swap; debt equity conversion

conversión en arancel
tariffication

conversión en efectivo
encashment [IDA]

conversión inmediata
reconstitution

convertidor catalítico
catalytic converter

cooperación técnica entre países en desarrollo - CTPD
technical cooperation among developing countries - TCDC

cooperativa de producción y exportaciones agropecuarias
agricultural production and export (apex) cooperative

coordinador de una edición
editor

copia autenticada
conformed copy

copia impresa
hard copy

coquería
coke oven plant

corral de engorde
feedlot

corral de vacunación
vaccination yard

corrección monetaria
monetary correction

corredor (de cambio, de bolsa)
broker

corredor de valores
securities dealer; securities firm

corretaje
brokerage

corriente (de fondos) en condiciones concesionarias
concessional flow

corriente de capital equilibradora
equilibrating capital flow

corriente de fondos
cash flow; funds flow; flow of funds

corrientes de costos y beneficios
streams of costs and benefits

corrientes financieras
financial flows

corrientes oficiales
official flows [development]

cortavientos
windbreak

corte y extracción de madera en trozas
logging [forestry]

cortedad de talla
stunting; nutritional dwarfing

cosechas
crops

costo asociado
associated cost

costo de conversión, de modificación
redeployment cost

costo de eficiencia de (los impuestos) la tributación
efficiency cost of taxation; excess burden of taxation

costo de inactividad del capital
carrying cost (of capital); charge of capital

costo de inversión
capital cost

costo de los empréstitos
borrowing cost

costo de los empréstitos con doble ponderación
double-weighted borrowing cost [IBRD]

costo de los factores, al
factor cost, at - f.c.

costo de mantenimiento en existencia
carrying costs, charges [goods]

costo de oportunidad, de sustitución
opportunity cost

costo de oportunidad social
social opportunity cost

costo de puesta en marcha
start-up cost

costo de reposición, de sustitución
replacement cost

costo del petróleo
oil bill [national]

costo en divisas
exchange cost

costo en divisas
foreign exchange cost

costo en moneda nacional
local cost; onshore cost

costo en recursos internos
domestic resource cost - DRC

costo evitable
avoidable cost

costo extranacional
offshore cost

costo incluidos los impuestos
tax-paid cost - TPC

costo incremental
incremental cost

costo incremental medio
average incremental cost - AIC

costo incremental medio a largo plazo
long-run average incremental cost - LRAIC

costo inicial
front-end cost

costo marginal
marginal cost

costo marginal a largo plazo
long-run marginal cost - LRMC; efficiency price;
efficient price [electricity tariffs]

**costo marginal de mantenimiento de la
capacidad**
marginal capacity cost - MCC

costo no recurrente de capital, no recuperable
sunk cost

costo, seguro y flete - c.i.f.
cost, insurance and freight - CIF

costo totalmente imputado
fully allocated cost

costo unitario
unit cost

costos básicos
baseline costs; base costs

costos capitalizados
capitalized expenses

costos centralizados
centrally-managed costs

**costos de explotación, operación,
funcionamiento**
operating expenses, costs

costos de garantía de emisión
underwriting costs

costos de instalación y suministros
balance-of-system costs

costos de mano de obra
labor costs

costos de movilización
mobilization costs

costos de, en servicios
in-kind costs

costos del factor trabajo
labor costs

costos descentralizados
unit-managed costs

costos económicos del proteccionismo
welfare costs of protectionism

costos efectivos, reales
actual costs

costos fijos
fixed costs

costos implícitos
underlying costs

costos imputados
allocated costs

costos imputados
imputed costs

costos indirectos
indirect costs; on-costs [UK]

costos inferiores a los previstos
cost underrun; underrun cost

costos iniciales [proyectos]
baseline costs; base costs

costos internos de importación
internal importing costs

costos laborales
labor costs

costos no monetarios
noncash expenses

costos ordinarios (en presupuestos)
recurrent costs, expenditures

costos promediados
rolled (costs)

costos relativos a monedas específicas
currency-specific costs

costos salariales
wage bill; wage costs

costos sociales, colectivos
social costs

costos superiores a los previstos
cost overrun

cotización (de valores en la bolsa)
listing (of securities)

cotización al contado
spot quotation

cotizaciones
price quotations [contracts]

cotizaciones de precios de equilibrio del mercado
market-clearing quotations

coyuntura
business cycle; trade cycle

creación
design; development

crecimiento (económico) sostenido
sustained growth

crecimiento autosostenido
self-sustaining growth

crecimiento cero de la población
zero population growth - ZPG

crecimiento insuficiente
stunting; nutritional dwarfing

crecimiento intermitente
stop and go growth

crecimiento lento
sluggish growth

crecimiento urbano (no planificado)
urban sprawl

crédito
credit standing

crédito [finanzas]
claim

crédito a los consumidores
consumer credit

crédito acumulativo
cumulative letter of credit

crédito colectivo
group credit

crédito con garantía de otro crédito
back-to-back credit

crédito de accionistas, de participación
equity-type loan; sponsored loan

crédito de avío
working capital loan

crédito de compradores
buyer credit; buyers' credit

crédito de contrapartida
matching credit

crédito de emergencia
bailout loan

crédito de exportación, a la exportación
export credit

crédito de proveedores
supplier credit; supplier's credit

crédito dirigido
directed credit

crédito documental
documentary credit

crédito en especie
credit-in-kind

crédito en tramitación
pipeline credit

crédito estacional
seasonal credit

crédito financiero
financial credit

crédito garantizado por el Estado
sovereign credit, loan

crédito impositivo, tributario
tax credit

crédito impositivo por inversiones
investment tax credit

crédito institucional
formal credit

crédito no institucional
informal credit

crédito oficial a la exportación
official export credit

crédito para importaciones con fines de reconstrucción
reconstruction import credit - RIC

crédito para importaciones con fines de rehabilitación
rehabilitation import credit

crédito por pago de impuestos en el extranjero
foreign tax credit

crédito presupuestario
allotment; appropriation [budget]

crédito recíproco [FMI]
swap

crédito renovable, rotatorio, refinanciable
revolving credit

créditos hipotecarios
mortgage financing

créditos que se traspasan
carryovers

créditos traspasados
carryovers

cresta arancelaria
tariff peak

cría de ganado, de animales
animal husbandry

criador
breeder [agriculture]

crisis de liquidez
liquidity squeeze

crisis petrolera, producida por los precios del petróleo
oil shock

criterio de contaminación total permisible
bubble concept

cronología
time pattern

croquis
sketch plan [architecture]

crudo de referencia
benchmark crude; marker crude [oil]

crudo liviano, ligero de Arabia Saudita
light Arabian crude; Saudi Arabian light crude

cruzamiento absorbente
line breeding

cruzamiento continuo
line breeding

cuadrar (una cuenta)
balance, to (an account)

cuadro
schedule

cuasicapital
quasi-equity

cuasidinero
near money; quasi-money

cubierta forestal
forest canopy

cubierta vegetal
plant cover

cuenca de captación
catch basin; catchment area

cuenca de captación
catchment area; catch basin

cuenca de rebalse
overflow basin

cuenta básica
basic account [balance of payments]

cuenta de anticipos
advance account; imprest account, fund

cuenta de anticipos para la preparación de un proyecto
project advance account

cuenta de capital
capital account

cuenta de cierre
summary account

cuenta de explotación
working account

cuenta de explotación, operación
operating account

cuenta de igualación de tipos de cambio
exchange equalization account

cuenta de ingresos
revenue account [national accounts]

cuenta de ingresos y gastos, de pérdidas y ganancias
income (and expenditure) account

cuenta de orden
memorandum account

cuenta de primas de emisión
share premium account [IFC]

cuenta de reconciliación
reconciliation account

cuenta de resumen
summary account

cuenta de tráfico
traffic count

cuenta de valores (en custodia)
securities (custody) account

cuenta del crédito
credit account [IDA]

cuenta del préstamo
loan account

cuenta especial secundaria
second generation special account - SGSA

cuenta reservada, especial
earmarked account

cuenta subsidiaria, auxiliar
subsidiary account

cuenta transitoria
suspense account

cuentas de ingresos y gastos
income and outlay accounts [national accounts]

cuentas diversas de caja
sundry cash accounts

cuentas económicas ajustadas conforme a consideraciones ambientales
environmentally adjusted economic accounts - EEA

cuentas por cobrar
accounts receivable; receivables

cuentas por pagar
accounts payable

cuentas sociales
social accounts

cuentas subsidiarias del medio ambiente
environment satellite accounts

cuerpo de funcionarios públicos
civil service

cuestión previa
preliminary question [ICSID]

cuestiones a las diferencias de roles del hombre y la mujer
gender issues

cuestiones que afectan a la mujer
gender issues

cuestiones relativas a las desigualdades entre los sexos
gender issues

cultivo
field crop

cultivo alimentario
food crop

cultivo alimentario básico
staple (food crop)

cultivo arbóreo
tree crop

cultivo comercial
cash crop

cultivo constante, continuo
continuous cropping

cultivo de decrecida
flood recession crop

cultivo de decrecida
recession crop

cultivo de secano
dry farming; dryland farming

cultivo de tejidos
tissue culture

cultivo de temporada corta
short season (crop)

cultivo en curvas de nivel
contour farming

cultivo en franjas
alley cropping; strip cropping

cultivo en pendiente
hillside farming

cultivo en recesión
recession, recessive cultivation

cultivo en tierras de aluvión
floodplain agriculture, cultivation

cultivo extensivo
field crop

cultivo intercalado
intercropping

cultivo intercalado, intermedio
catch crop

cultivo migratorio
shifting cultivation

cultivo protector, de cobertura
cover crop; nurse crop

cultivo único, de un solo tipo o especie
pure stand

cultivo(s) asociado(s)
associated crops, cropping

cultivos
crops

cultivos de fuera de estación, de temporada
out-of-season crop; off-season crop

cultivos de montaña, de tierras altas
upland crops

cultivos de raíces alimentarias
root crops

cultivos de rizomas
rhizomes; rootstock crops

cultivos dobles
double cropping; sequential cropping

cultivos en hileras
row crops

cultivos mixtos silvoagropecuarios
multistory farming; multilevel farming

cultivos múltiples
multicropping; multiple cropping

cultivos múltiples
multiple cropping; multicropping

cultivos para fines energéticos
energy cropping

cultivos simbióticos
companion crops

cultivos sucesivos
double cropping; sequential cropping

cumplimiento de contrato
contract performance

cuota arancelaria
tariff quota

cuota de importación
import quota

cupo arancelario
tariff quota

cupo de importación
import quota

cupones para la privatización
privatization vouchers

currículo
curriculum

currículo de estudios común
core curriculum

cursillo
workshop [training]

curso de actualización (para refrescar los conocimientos)
refresher course

curso de elementos intercambiables
course interchange [education]

curso de repaso
refresher course

curva de aprendizaje
learning curve

curva de indiferencia
indifference curve

curva de la oferta
supply curve

curva de posibilidades de producción
production possibility curve; transformation curve

curva de rendimiento
yield curve

curva de transformación
transformation curve; production possibility curve

curva salarial
payline

daños indirectos
consequential damages

daños y perjuicios previstos en un contrato
liquidated damages

dar de baja
scrap, to

dar en contrato
contract out, to

dar participación
empower

dar poder de decisión
empower

dar por terminado
terminate

dato aproximado
ballpark figure

datos antes del análisis de regresión
unsmoothed data

datos básicos
baseline data; fact sheet

datos básicos de un proyecto
project brief

datos brutos, sin elaborar
raw data

datos clave, básicos
key data

datos detallados
microdata

datos transversales
cross-sectional data [econometry]

de abajo arriba
bottom up (approach) [projects]

de alto coeficiente de mano de obra
labor-intensive

de base
grass root(s) level, at the

de conformidad con las leyes del mercado
market-friendly

de maduración tardía
late maturing [crop]

de maduración temprana, precoz
early (maturing) [crops]

de propiedad extranjera
foreign-owned

de rulo [Chile]
rainfed

de secano
rainfed

de temporal [México]
rainfed

de uso fácil
user friendly

de uso intensivo de energía
energy-intensive

de uso intensivo de mano de obra
labor-intensive

de visión hacia el futuro
forward-looking

debenture [EE.UU]
debenture (bond)

decano
dean (of the Board of Directors)

decisión tácita por vencimiento de un plazo
lapse-of-time decision

declaración
statement

declaración de gastos
statement of expenditure - SOE

declaración de impuestos
tax return

declaración de ingresos
tax return

declaración de intención, de intenciones
letter of intent - LOI

declaración de objetivos
mission statement [EDI]

declaración del impuesto sobre la renta
income tax return

declaraciones
representations

declinación de responsabilidad
disclaimer

deducción
tax allowance

deducción estándar
standard deduction [taxation]

deducción tributaria (por pérdida, etc.)
tax write off

deducción tributaria, de impuestos
tax deduction

deducidos los impuestos
net of taxes

deficiencia
shortfall

deficiencia de recaudación
undercollection [taxation]

déficit
gap; shortfall

déficit comercial
trade deficit

déficit de caja
cash deficit

déficit de explotación, operación
operating deficit

déficit de financiamento
financing gap; funding gap

déficit de inversiones
investment gap

déficit de la balanza en cuenta corriente
external current account deficit

déficit de recursos
resource(s) gap

déficit en cuenta corriente
current account deficit

déficit en cuenta corriente (excluidos los ingresos por concepto de intereses)
noninterest current account deficit

déficit excluido el pago de intereses
primary deficit; noninterest deficit

déficit fiscal
fiscal gap

déficit presupuestario
budget deficit; budgetary gap

déficit primario
primary deficit; noninterest deficit

deflación
deflation

deflactar
deflate, to

deflactor
deflator

deflactor de los compromisos
commitment deflator

deflactor de los desembolsos
disbursement deflator

deflactor de precios del PNB
GNP price deflator

deflactor implícito
implicit deflator

deflactor implícito del producto interno bruto
implicit gross domestic product deflator

deforestación
deforestation

degradación ambiental
environmental degradation

dejar de reunir las condiciones para recibir financiamiento del Banco
graduate, to [Bank, IDA]

delegación de atribuciones, facultades
delegation of authority

deliberaciones de sesión(es)
proceedings

demanda
claim

demanda agregada, global
aggregate demand

demanda bioquímica de oxígeno - DBO
biochemical oxygen demand - BOD

demanda bioquímica de oxígeno en cinco días - DBO5
biochemical oxygen demand over five days - BOD5; five day biochemical oxygen demand

demanda de los consumidores
consumer demand

demanda intensa
buoyant demand

demanda reprimida
pent-up demand

demora
lag; slippage

demora respecto del plazo previsto
time overrun

denominación común
nonproprietary name

denominado
denominated in (dollars, etc.)

densidad de carga
stocking rate [livestock]

densidad de siembra
plant population

denuncio
claim [mining]

departamentalización de la enseñanza
departmentalization [education]

departamento de (servicios de) apoyo
support department [IBRD]

departamento de operaciones
operating department; operational department [IBRD]

departamento de operaciones, sectorial, de ejecución
line ministry, department

departamento de servicio, de asesoramiento
staff department

departamento ejecutivo, de ejecución, de operaciones
line department

dependencia de la ayuda exterior
aid dependency

Depositario
Trustee [GEF]

depósito a la vista
demand deposit; sight deposit

depósito a plazo
term deposit

depósito a plazo, a término
time deposit

depósito de aduanas
bonded warehouse

depósito de decantación de residuos
tailing pond

depósito de pagarés
note deposit [IDA]

depósito en almacén de aduanas
bonding [customs]

depósito en custodia
escrow account

depósito en garantía, en custodia
escrow

depósito previo, anticipado
advance deposit

depósitos ácidos
acid deposition

depreciación acelerada, decreciente
accelerated depreciation

depreciación acumulada
accrued depreciation; accumulated depreciation

depreciación de equilibrio
breakeven (dollar) depreciation

depreciación diferida
deferred depreciation

derecho
claim

derecho (aduanero) ad valórem
ad valorem (customs) duty

derecho (aduanero) específico
specific (customs) duty

derecho antidumping
antidumping duty

derecho aplicable
governing law

derecho arancelario
tariff

derecho compensatorio
countervailing duty

derecho de aduana, de importación
tariff

derecho de expropiación
eminent domain

derecho de tenencia de la tierra
land tenure rights

derecho de usufructo
beneficial interest

derecho de vía
right of way

derecho de voto
voting right

derecho por pie
stumpage fee

derecho prioritario, preferencial, de preferencia, de prelación
first refusal right; preemptive right

derecho procesal, adjetivo, de forma
adjective law; procedural law

derecho procesal, adjetivo, de forma
procedural law; adjective law

derecho sustantivo, de fondo
substantive law

derechos arancelarios
tariff rates

derechos de matrícula
tuition fees

derechos de propiedad
proprietary rights

derechos de suscripción
stock rights [IFC]

derechos de voto
voting power

derechos portuarios
harbor dues, fees; port dues

desagregación
unbundling

desagregación de riesgos financieros
unbundling of financial risks

desahorro
dissaving

desajuste entre tipos de cambio
misalignment (of rates of exchange)

desarrollo
development

desarrollo institucional
institution building

desarrollo integral de la explotación agrícola
whole farm development

desarrollo participatorio, con participación
participatory development

desarrollo sostenible
sustainable development

desarrollo subregional
area development

desarrollo técnico
engineering development

desastre provocado por el hombre
man-made disaster

desatesoramiento
dishoarding

desbroce
clearing

descapitalizar
decapitalize

descarga de efluentes
effluent charges

descarga de gases ácidos, ricos en productos azufrados
sour gas discharge

descascarar
dehusking; husking

descascarar
husk, to; dehusk, to

descomposición
unbundling

descontar
discount, to [finance]

descripción de cargo, puesto
job description

descuento
discount

descuento cambiario
exchange discount

descuento de instrumentos de deuda
debt sales

descuento del impuesto potencial
tax sparing

descuento impositivo, tributario
tax credit

desechar
scrap, to

deseconomías
diseconomies

desembolsos concentrados al comienzo de un período
front loading

desempeño
performance

desempeño de la economía
economic performance

desempeño de las instituciones
institutional performance

desempleo encubierto, oculto, disfrazado
concealed unemployment; covert, disguised, hidden unemployment

desempleo estructural
structural unemployment

desempleo evidente, manifiesto
open unemployment

desempleo friccional
frictional unemployment

desempleo oculto, encubierto, disfrazado
disguised unemployment; concealed, covert, hidden unemployment

deserción
drop out [education]

desertar
drop out [education]

desertor escolar
drop out [education]

desestacionalizado
seasonally adjusted

desfase
lag; slippage

desfase (cronológico)
time lag

desfavorecido
underprivileged

desgaste (normal o natural)
wear and tear (fair)

desglose
breakdown; unbundling

desgravación
tax allowance

desgravación fiscal
tax relief

desgravación tributaria
tax rebate

desguazar
scrap, to

deshidratación por congelación
freeze drying

deshojar
husk, to; dehusk, to

desincentivo
disincentive

desinflación
disinflation

desinflacionario
disinflationary

desintermediación
disintermediation

desinversión
disinvestment

desistimiento (únicamente en el sentido del Art. 45 del Convenio)
discontinuance [ICSID]

deslizamiento (de un tipo de cambio dentro de una banda)
crawl [noun]

deslizamiento de troncos
skidding

desmantelamiento
rollback

desmonetización
calling in of a currency

desmonte
clearing

desmotado
ginning [cotton]

desnutrición
undernutrition

desnutrido
undernourished

despacho aduanero
clearance

desparasitar
deworm

despegue
take-off

despeje
clearance

desperdicio
waste; loss in weight [commerce]

despido
termination

desplazamiento
crowding out

desplazamiento de la demanda
demand shift

desreglamentar
deregulate

desregular
deregulate

destinado por su propia índole a determinados grupos de la población
self-targeting (commodity)

destinar (fondos) para un fin determinado
earmark, to (funds)

desutilidad
disutility

desutilidad marginal
marginal disutility

desviación de los salarios
wage drift

desviación estándar
standard deviation

desvinculación (de divisas)
delinking [foreign exchange]

desvinculación de la ayuda
untying of aid

desvincular
delink, to [foreign exchange]

desvincular (el tipo)
unpeg (a rate), to

deterioro ambiental
environmental degradation

determinación de costos
costing

determinación de costos directos
direct costing

determinación de precios sociales
social pricing

determinación de un proyecto, de proyectos
project identification

determinación del costo de un préstamo
loan pricing, costing

determinación del precio de costo
cost pricing

deuda amortizada
retired debt

deuda anulada
cancelled debt

deuda con garantía pública
publicly guaranteed debt

deuda con los bancos comerciales, privados
commercial debt

deuda consolidada
funded debt

deuda de pago dudoso
bad debt

deuda desembolsada y pendiente
debt outstanding and disbursed - DOD

deuda dudosa, de cobro dudoso
doubtful debt

deuda externa pendiente
external debt outstanding

deuda externa pendiente
outstanding external debt

deuda externa total
total external debt - EDT

deuda incobrable
bad debt

deuda notificada
reported debt

deuda pendiente
debt overhang

deuda prioritaria
senior debt, loan

deuda pública
official debt

deuda pública
public debt

deuda pública del Estado, en poder de particulares
publicly held government debt

deuda recíproca
reciprocal debt

deuda subordinada
junior debt; subordinated debt

deuda vencida
debt due

deuda(s) recíproca(s)
interlocking debt

deudas anteriores con condiciones menos favorables
lower quality old debt

devolución de impuestos
tax refund

día-hombre
man-day

diafanidad
transparency

diagrama de barras
bar chart

diagrama de dispersión
scatter chart, diagram; scattergram

diagrama de movimiento, de flujo, de producción, de secuencia, de procedimiento
flow chart; process chart

diagrama de red(es)
network diagram

diagrama de situación
working table; performance chart; management chart

días de atraso en el pago de las cuentas por cobrar
days receivable

dictamen con reservas
qualified opinion [auditing]

dictamen jurídico
legal opinion

dictamen legal
memorandum of law

diesel
diesel fuel; diesel oil

dieta
subsistence allowance

diferencia
gap

diferencia entre los márgenes
spread of spreads

diferencia entre los precios
price differential, spread

diferencia entre tipos, tasas de interés
interest-rate differential

diferencia negativa
carrying loss

**diferencia por la cual las cantidades devengadas
son inferiores a las previstas**
underaccruals

diferencia positiva
carrying gain

diferencia(s) de tipos de cambio
exchange rate differential

diferencias arancelarias
tariff wedges

diferimiento impositivo
tax deferral

dificultades económicas
economic hardship

dificultades financieras graves
financial distress

dilema del prisionero
prisoner's dilemma

dilución del capital (accionario)
stock dilution, watering; dilution

dinamismo
buoyancy [economics]

dinero a la vista
call money; day to day money; demand money;
money at call

dinero bancario
bank money

dinero barato, abundante
easy money

dinero de alta potencia [teoría monetarista]
high-power(ed) money

**dinero de la Reserva Federal de los EE.UU.
para uso de los bancos**
high-power(ed) money

dinero elástico
elastic money

dinero en el sentido estricto
narrow money

dinero en sentido amplio
broad money

dinero escaso, caro
tight money

dinero exigible
call money; day to day money; demand money;
money at call

dinero inactivo
idle cash

dinero negro
black money

dinero primario
reserve money; base money; high-power(ed)
money

dique
bund

dique en curva de nivel
contour bund

dirección
front office; governance; line management

dirección de impuestos
tax office

dirección de la institución, empresa
corporate management

dirección portuaria
port authority

directivo principal
senior manager

directivos
managers

director del proyecto
project manager

Director Ejecutivo
Executive Director

director ejecutivo con doble función (en el BIRF y el FMI)
dual executive director

Directorio Ejecutivo
Board of (Executive) Directors; Executive Board [IBRD, IDA]

Directorios del Banco y del Fondo
Boards of the Bank and the Fund

directrices
guidelines

discordancia entre los vencimientos
maturity mismatch

discrepancia impositiva
tax wedge

discriminación sexual
gender issues

discurso principal
keynote address, speech

diseñador
designer

diseño
design; layout

diseño con ayuda de computadoras
computer aided design - CAD

diseño conceptual
conceptual design

diseño de un proyecto, de proyectos
project design

diseño demasiado ambicioso
overdesign

diseño detallado
detailed design, engineering

diseño excesivo para las necesidades
overdesign

diseño técnico
engineering design

diseño técnico preliminar
engineering, preliminary

disminución
drawdown; shortfall

dispensa (de una obligación)
waiver

dispensar (de una obligación)
waive, to

dispensario
health post

disponibilidades
liquid assets; quick assets

disponibilidades (de equipo)
availability [transportation]

disponibilidades de viviendas
housing stock

disposición para pagar
willingness to pay - WTP

disposiciones de comercialización ordenada
orderly marketing arrangements - OMA

disposiciones de control de cambios
exchange control regulations

disposiciones procesales
procedural orders [ICSID]

disposiciones transitorias
bridging arrangement, credit

distribución
breakdown; layout

distribución de aguas
waterspreading

distribución de la carga [donantes]
burden sharing

distribución de las utilidades
allocation of profits; appropriation of profits

distribución de los costos
cost sharing

distribución de los recursos
allocation of resources

distribución del financiamiento (entre los países)
direction of lending

distribución del importe, de los fondos del préstamo
allocation of loan proceeds

distribución óptima de los vencimientos
market timing

distribución reservada
restricted distribution

disyuntiva
trade-off

divergencia entre tipos de cambio
misalignment (of rates of exchange)

diversidad biológica
biodiversity

diversificación de los riesgos
exposure diversification

dividendo en acciones
bonus issue; stock dividend

dividendo extraordinario
surplus dividend

divisa de reserva
reserve currency

divisa(s) de libre convertibilidad
free (foreign) exchange

divisas
foreign currency, exchange

división de la enseñanza
departmentalization [education]

divulgación
extension [agriculture]

doble clasificación
cross-classification

doble tributación, imposición
double taxation

documentación de apoyo
justification

documento de antecedentes, de información básica
background paper

documento de especificación de servicios laborales
performance work statement - PWS

documento de exposición de problemas
issues paper

documento de información sobre el proyecto
Project Information Brief - PIB

documento de política (sectorial, financiera, etc.)
policy paper

documento de referencia cruzada, comparación
crosswalk document

documento de trabajo
discussion paper

documento del Manual de Adquisiciones
Procurement Manual Statement - PMS

documento del Manual de Operaciones
Operational Manual Statement - OMS

documento del Manual del Personal
Personnel Manual Statement

documento expositivo sobre...
approach paper

documento para un seminario
seminar paper

documentos contractuales
contract documents

documentos de licitación
bidding documents; tender documents

documentos de precalificación
prequalification documents

documentos justificativos
justification

dolarización
dollarization

dominio eminente
eminent domain

donación
grant-in-aid

donación de contrapartida
matching grant

donación en capital
equity grant

donación en efectivo
cash grant

donación en, para equipos
equipment grant

donación para fines específicos, para un fin
específico
categorical grant; targeted grant

donante principal
lead donor

dos ritmos, trayectorias de desarrollo
two-track development

dosel forestal
forest canopy

dotación de capital
capital endowment

dotación de personal
staffing

dotación mínima de personal
core staffing

dotar de los medios
empower

dotar de personal
staff, to

drenaje de aguas lluvias, pluviales
storm water drainage system

dumping
dumping

duración
life (of a project)

duración de un proyecto
project life

duración útil
economic life

ecología, sí en mi barrio, no
NIMBY (not-in-my-backyard)

ecologistas
environmentalist

economía abierta
open economy

economía de consumo
consumption economy

economía de la oferta, basada en la oferta
supply side economics

economía de libre empresa
free market economy; free-enterprise economy

economía de monocultivo
single-crop economy

economía de planificación centralizada
centrally planned economy (country)

economía de subsistencia
subsistence economy

economía del bienestar
welfare economy

economía del retroceso
economics of regress

economía del sector público
public economics

economía dependiente de la exportación de un solo producto
export-enclave economy

economía dirigida
command economy; controlled economy; directed economy; managed economy

economía interna, nacional
domestic economy

economía monetaria
cash economy

economía no de mercado
nonmarket economy

economía subterránea, paralela
parallel economy; black economy; underground economy; submerged economy

economía(s)
avoided cost

economías de concentración
agglomeration economies

economías de diversificación
economies of scope

economías de escala
economies of scale

economías de ubicación
localization economies

economías de urbanización
urbanization economies

economista principal
principal economist

economista principal (de un departamento geográfico)
lead economist

economista principal (Oficina Regional)
chief economist

economista superior
senior economist

ecuación de regresión
regression equation

edición mediante microcomputadora
desktop publishing

editar
edit (texts for publication)

editor (de un texto)
editor

educación a distancia
distance learning, teaching

educación básica
basic education

educación extraescolar
out-of-school education

educación formal, académica
formal education

educación informal
informal education

educación no formal
nonformal education

educación permanente
continuing education; lifelong education; recurrent education

educación secundaria de ciclo superior
upper secondary education

educación secundaria de primer ciclo, de ciclo básico
lower secondary education

efectivos laborales
return of labor

efecto de anuncio
announcement effect

efecto de capilaridad, ascendente
bubble-up effect

efecto de captación incidental de beneficiarios
snatching effect

efecto de concentración
focusing effect

efecto de demostración
demonstration effect

efecto de (la) filtración
trickle-down effect

efecto de ingreso, de renta
income effect

efecto de invernadero
greenhouse effect

efecto de primera clase
prime bill

efecto de sustitución
substitution effect

efecto de trinquete
ratchet effect

efecto en, sobre los precios
price effect

efecto generalizado
blanket effect

efecto (o beneficio, etc.) mediato
downstream effect, benefit

efecto secundario
pass-through effect

efecto secundario, derivado
spinoff effect; spillover effect, impact

efecto secundario de urbanización
induced development effect; boomtown effect

efectos
paper [financial]

efectos comerciales
commercial bills; commercial paper

efectos de comercio por cobrar
trade receivables

efectos en cobro, cobranza
float [banking]

efectos externos
externalities [projects]

efectos financieros
financial paper

efectos negociables
eligible paper

efectos públicos
government paper

efectos públicos, del Estado
government securities

efectuar una operación de *swap*, de intercambio de monedas, de crédito recíproco
swap, to [finance]

eficacia
performance

eficacia en función de los costos
cost-effectiveness

eficaz en el uso de la energía
energy-efficient

eficaz en función de los costos
cost-effective

eficiencia del uso final de la energía
end use (energy) efficiency

eficiencia en la utilización del combustible
fuel efficiency

eficiencia estática
static efficiency

eficiencia marginal del capital
marginal efficiency of capital

eficiencia x
x-efficiency

eficiente y de costo más bajo
cost-effective

eficiente y de costo mínimo
cost-effective

egresados
output

ejecución (de una hipoteca)
foreclosure

ejecución de un contrato según sus términos
specific performance

ejemplar autenticado
conformed copy

ejercer efecto multiplicador [finanzas]
leverage, to

ejercer influencia
leverage, to

ejercicio (económico)
financial year; fiscal year

ejercicio (económico)
fiscal year; financial year

ejercicio contable
accounting period

elaboración
development; processing

elaboración de carne
meat processing

elaboración de material fabricado en otro país
offshore assembly, processing

elaboración de productos agropecuarios
agroprocessing

elaboración de un proyecto, de proyectos
project preparation

elaboración por vía húmeda
wet process [cement manufacture]

elaboración por vía seca
dry process [cement manufacture]

elasticidad-ingreso
income elasticity

elasticidad-ingreso de la demanda
income elasticity of demand

elasticidad-precio
own price elasticity; price elasticity

elasticidad-precio cruzada
cross price elasticity

elasticidad con respecto al ingreso
income elasticity

elasticidad con respecto al precio
price elasticity; own price elasticity

elasticidad constante de sustitución
constant elasticity of substitution - CES

elasticidad cruzada
cross elasticity

elasticidad de la demanda
elasticity of demand

elasticidad de la demanda en función del ingreso
income elasticity of demand

elasticidad de sustitución
elasticity of substitution

elasticidad del impuesto
tax elasticity

elasticidad igual a la unidad
unit(ary) elasticity

elasticidad tributaria global
tax buoyancy

elegibilidad para participar en una licitación
eligibility to bid

elegible
eligible [procurement]

elemento
component (of a project)

elemento concesionario, de donación
concessional, concessionary element

elemento concesionario, de donación
grant element

elemento de disuasión, disuasivo
deterrent

elemento en divisas
foreign exchange component

elementos estabilizadores, automáticos, internos, intrínsecos
built-in stabilizers

elementos no físicos
software

elementos nutritivos(as)
nutrients

eliminación de aguas negras, servidas
sewage disposal

eliminación de desechos
waste disposal

eliminación de tugurios, de zonas de tugurios
slum clearance

eliminar en libros
write off, to

eliminar por etapas, progresivamente
phase out, to

elusión del pago de aranceles (mediante el establecimiento de una empresa en el país)
tariff jumping

elusión legal de impuestos
tax avoidance

embargo preventivo
attachment [legal]; charge; lien [legal]

embarque
shipping

embarque, desembarque por propulsión propia
ro/ro [= roll-on/roll-off]

embarque, desembarque por propulsión propia
roll-on/roll-off - ro/ro

emisión
flotation [bonds]

emisión continua
issues on tap; tap issue

emisión de acciones (con derecho preferencial de suscripción)
rights issue, offering

emisión en divisas
foreign currency issue

emisión exploratoria
red herring issue

emisión fiduciaria
note issue

emisión ofrecida al público
public offering, borrowing

emisiones (de obligaciones) en Europa
European flotations

emisiones de organismos federales
agency securities, obligations [U.S.]

emitidos mediante oferta pública
publicly issued (bonds, etc.)

empalme
splicing

emplazamiento (de un proyecto)
site

empleado "fantasma"
ghost worker

empleado contratado localmente
local employee [IBRD]

empleo de (los) fondos
application of funds

empleos de referencia
benchmark jobs

empresa comisionista
commissioned company

empresa con pocos accionistas
closely-held corporation

empresa conjunta
joint venture

empresa de obras y servicios de infraestructura
infrastructure developer

empresa de servicios públicos
public utility corporation

empresa del proyecto
project enterprise [MIGA]

empresa en plena actividad y crecimiento
going concern; growing concern

empresa estatal
state-owned enterprise - SOE

empresa matriz
parent company

empresa mixta
mixed enterprise

empresa mixta, semipública, paraestatal
semipublic company

empresa productiva, que produce ingresos
revenue-earning enterprise

empresa pública
public corporation

empresa receptora del proyecto
project enterprise [MIGA]

empresario
entrepreneur

empresas asociadas, pertenecientes al mismo grupo
sister companies

empresas de servicios públicos
utilities

empresas maquiladoras
in-bond industries

empréstito
loan capital

empréstito de suma global
lump sum borrowing [IFC]

empréstito reembolsable de una sola vez a su vencimiento
bullet issue

empréstito reembolsable de una sola vez a su vencimiento
bullet issue

empréstitos calificados
qualified borrowing(s) [currency pool]

empréstitos compensatorios, contra depósitos
offset borrowings

empréstitos en el exterior
foreign borrowing

empréstitos gigantescos
jumbo borrowing(s)

empréstitos pendientes de utilización
undrawn borrowings

en armonía con, que armonice con el mercado
market-friendly

en condiciones concesionarias, muy favorables
concessional; concessionary

en el margen
at the margin

en el muelle (derechos por cuenta del comprador)
ex quay (duties on buyers' account)

en existencia
off-the-shelf

en pleno funcionamiento
full development, at [project]

en términos, cifras corrientes
current terms, in

en términos, cifras reales
real terms, in

enajenar a título oneroso
dispose (of) for value, to

enanismo nutricional
stunting; nutritional dwarfing

encaje circulante, flotante
floating cash reserve

encaje legal
legal reserve; minimum cash ratio; minimum cash requirement; reserve requirement

encaje legal adicional
marginal reserve requirement

encargado de una edición
editor

encargar
commission, to

encomendar
commission, to

encuesta
survey

encuesta (de sección) transversal
cross section(al) survey

encuesta básica
baseline survey

encuesta de actitudes
Attitude Survey [IBRD]

encuesta de gastos familiares
household expenditure survey - HES

encuesta longitudinal
longitudinal survey

encuesta muestral, por muestreo
sample survey [statistics]

encuesta por, de hogares
household survey

encuesta puntual
one-shot survey

endeudado en exceso
overgeared

endeudamiento forzoso
distress borrowing

energéticos de fuentes renovables
renewable energy

energéticos renovable(s)
renewable energy

energía a partir de biomasa
biomass energy

energía comercial
commercial energy

energía de biomasa
biomass energy

energía de fuentes convencionales
conventional energy

energía de fuentes renovables
renewable energy

energía entregada
delivered energy

energía final, secundaria
final energy; secondary energy

energía hidroeléctrica
hydroelectric power; hydropower

energía recibida
received energy

energía renovable(s)
renewable energy

energía secundaria, final
secondary energy; final energy

energía sustitutiva
alternative energy

enfermedad con base en el agua
water-based disease

enfermedad de transmisión vectorial
vectorborne disease

enfermedad transmitida por el agua
waterborne disease

enfermedad vinculada con la falta de higiene
water-washed disease

enfermero(a) auxiliar, no diplomado(a)
practical nurse

enfermero(a) diplomado(a)
registered nurse

engorde en establo
stall feeding

enlace
splicing

enlace UHF, en frecuencia ultraalta
UHF link [telecommunications]

enlace VHF, en frecuencia muy alta
VHF link [telecommunications]

enmienda presupuestaria presidencial
budget amendment [U.S.]

enmiendas al Convenio Constitutivo
amendments to the Articles of Agreement

ensayo de variedad(es)
variety trial

enseñanza a distancia
distance learning, teaching

enseñanza en doble jornada, de doble turno
double shift teaching system

enseñanza en múltiples turnos, jornadas
multishift teaching

enseñanza privada con método(s) patentado(s)
proprietary training

enseñanza simultánea de varios grados
multigrade teaching

enseres domésticos
household goods

entidad de préstamos en condiciones ordinarias,
no concesionarias
hard loan window

entidad paraestatal
parastatal [noun]

entorno propicio, favorable
enabling environment

entrada
intake

entrada de capital
capital inflow

entrada en vigor de un convenio
effectiveness of an agreement

entradas
returns; revenues

entradas de fondos
cash inflows

entrar en producción
stream, to go on

entrega futura, a plazo
forward cover

entregado con derechos pagados
delivered duty paid - DDP

entregado en frontera
delivered at frontier - DAF

entregar
release, to [capital]

envío
referral; shipping

envío en comisión de servicio
secondment

epizootia
epidemic disease [livestock]

equidad
equity

equidad horizontal
horizontal equity

equidad vertical
vertical equity

equilibrio fiscal, del presupuesto
fiscal balance

equipo de computación
hardware

equipo de conmutación
switching equipment [telephone]

equipo de evaluación
appraisal team [IFC]

equipo de perforación petrolera
oil (drilling) rig, platform

equipo(s)
equipment

equivalente de subsidio al consumo
consumer subsidy equivalent - CSE

equivalente de subvención de precios al productor
producer price equivalent - PPE

equivalente en años-personal
staffyear equivalent - SYE

equivalente en donación
grant equivalent

escala de precios
price range

escala decreciente
degressive scale

escalada de tarifas
tariff escalation

escapatoria tributaria
tax loophole

escasez de dólares
dollar gap

escorrentía
runoff [water]

escritura de constitución
articles of incorporation; charter (of a company)

escritura de constitución de deuda
deed of trust

escritura de fideicomiso
deed of trust

escritura social
charter (of a company)

escuela de aplicación
demonstration school; laboratory school; model
school; practice school

escuela diversificada, polivalente
comprehensive school

escuela experimental
demonstration school; laboratory school; model
school; practice school

escuela organizada por secciones
streamed school

escuela preparatoria
contributory school; feeder school; preparatory
school

escuela secundaria de primer ciclo
junior high school

escurrimiento
runoff [water]

esferas empresariales, comerciales
business community

esfuerzo propio
self-help

esfuerzo tributario
tax effort

eslabonamiento descendente de una industria
forward linkage of an industry

**eslabonamientos interindustriales, entre
industrias**
interindustry linkages

espaciamiento de los nacimientos
birth spacing

espacio libre
clearance

especialidad (farmacéutica)
brand name drug

especialización
advanced training

especies esenciales
key species

especificación de servicios laborales
performance work statement - PWS

especificaciones de funcionamiento
performance specifications

específico
brand name drug

espécimen de firma autenticado
authenticated specimen of signature

**especulación (en la Bolsa) aprovechando
información interna**
insider dealing, trading

**especulador (en la Bolsa) que aprovecha
información interna**
insider dealer, trader

esperanza de vida
life expectancy

esperanza matemática
mathematical expectation [mathematics]

espiral salarios-precios
wage-price spiral

espíritu empresarial
entrepreneurship

esquela
tombstone

esquisto bituminoso
oil shale

estabilización
leveling off

estación (de bombeo) de refuerzo, de rebombeo
booster (pumping) station

estación elevadora
step-up power station

estación reductora
step-down power station

estadía
laydays; laytime

estadísticas del estado civil, vitales
vital statistics

Estado
government

estado
status

Estado acreedor
sovereign creditor

Estado benefactor, providente
welfare State

estado consolidado de ingresos y gastos
consolidated income statement

Estado Contratante
Contracting State [ICSID, MIGA]

estado de cuenta
statement of account

estado de cuentas por cobrar según fecha de vencimiento
aging schedule [accounts receivable]

estado de cuentas verificado, auditado
audited statement of accounts

estado de flujo de fondos
statement of changes in financial position; sources and application of funds statement; funds statement; working capital statement; source and use of funds statement; funds flow statement; changes in working capital statement; statement of sources and applications of funds; statement of cash flows [World Bank]

estado de fuentes y utilización de fondos
statement of changes in financial position; sources and application of funds statement; funds statement; working capital statement; source and use of funds statement; funds flow statement; changes in working capital statement; statement of sources and applications of funds; statement of cash flows [World Bank]

estado de gastos
statement of expenditure - SOE

estado de ingresos y gastos, de pérdidas y ganancias
income statement [US]; profit and loss account [UK]

estado de pagos (certificado)
progress certificate [IBRD]

estado de situación financiera
statement of condition [IDA]

estado financiero
financial statement

estado financiero intermedio
interim financial statement

Estado que puede adherirse
State eligible to sign (the Convention) [ICSID]

estado resumido
summary statement

estado ribereño, costero
coastal state

estancamiento
stagnation (of the economy)

estanflación
stagflation

estanques de sedimentación
sedimentation ponds

estercoladura de base
basal dressing; bottom dressing

estercoladura de superficie
top dressing [agriculture]

estimación cuantitativa
bill of quantities

estimación cuantitativa con precios
priced bill of quantities

estimación de costos
cost estimate

estimación de la base impositiva
tax assessment; assessment for tax

estimaciones cuantitativas preliminares
preliminary estimates of quantities

estimaciones presupuestarias
budget estimates

estimador de materiales
quantity surveyor

estímulo
incentive

estipulaciones
covenants [loan agreements]

estrangulamiento
bottleneck

estrategia ante (de) la deuda
debt strategy

estrés ambiental
environmental stress

estrés por falta de humedad
moisture stress

estructura
structural work

estructura de cabecera
head gate structure [irrigation]

estructura de capital
capital structure

estructura de la producción
product mix

estructura del capital social
ownership structure (of a company)

estructura del comercio
trade pattern

estructura institucional
institutional framework

estructura orgánica
organizational structure

estructura social
corporate structure

estructura tarifaria escalonada
stepped tariff structure

estructuras metálicas
metal works

estudiante (que no ha recibido el primer título universitario)
undergraduate

estudio
survey

estudio (ambiental) preliminar
environmental screening

estudio (de evaluación) del sector privado
private sector assessment - PSA

estudio aeromagnético
aeromagnetic survey; airmag survey

estudio aeromagnético
airmag survey; aeromagnetic survey

estudio básico
baseline survey

estudio de factibilidad, de viabilidad
feasibility study

estudio de los efectos ambientales
environmental review

estudio de preinversión
preinvestment study, survey

estudio de recursos energéticos [de un país]
audit [energy]

estudio de recursos energéticos [de un país]
energy audit

estudio de seguimiento de egresados
tracer study [education]

estudio de suelos, edafológico
soil study, survey

estudio de un caso práctico, de casos prácticos
case study

estudio documental, de referencia
desk study

estudio preliminar
reconnaissance survey

estudio sísmico
seismic survey

estudio sobre un país, países
country study

estudios avanzados
higher training

estudios avanzados, superiores, de perfeccionamiento
advanced studies

estudios comparados entre países
cross-country studies

estudios de posgrado
postgraduate studies

estudios económicos y sectoriales
economic and sector work - ESW

estudios económicos y sectoriales de países
country economic and sector work - CESW

estudios operacionales
operational review

estudios posteriores al primer título universitario
postgraduate studies

estudios sobre finanzas nacionales
domestic finance studies

estudios técnicos detallados
detailed design, engineering

estudios técnicos preliminares
preliminary design, engineering

estudios técnicos, de ingeniería
engineering studies

estudios universitarios para obtener el primer título
undergraduate studies

etapa inicial
development period (of a project, of a company)

etiquetas verdes
green labeling

eurobonos
Eurobonds

euroemisiones
Euroissues

euroesterlina
Eurosterling

evaluación
performance evaluation [personnel]

evaluación (inicial) de un proyecto, de proyectos
project appraisal

evaluación administrativa
audit; management audit [management]

evaluación ambiental
environmental assessment - EA

evaluación con la participación de los beneficiarios
beneficiary assessment

evaluación con la participación de los habitantes de las zonas rurales
participatory rural appraisal, analysis - PRA

evaluación de funciones directivas
staff audit

evaluación de la pobreza con la participación de los afectados
participatory poverty assessment - PPA

evaluación de los costos durante la vida útil (de equipos)
life cycle cost evaluation

evaluación de los efectos ambientales
environmental impact assessment - EIA

evaluación de los efectos sociales
social impact assessment - SIA

evaluación de los resultados
audit [projects]

evaluación de recursos energéticos
energy assessment

evaluación de resultados
performance audit

evaluación del impacto ambiental
environmental impact assessment - EIA

evaluación ex ante
appraisal (technical and economic)

evaluación *ex post*
evaluation [projects]

evaluación *ex post* abreviada de un proyecto
pass-through audit [IBRD]

evaluación *ex post* combinada
cluster audit

evaluación *ex post* de un proyecto, de proyectos
project evaluation, audit

evaluación *ex post*, a posteriori
ex post evaluation

evaluación general, integral, a fondo
comprehensive auditing

evaluación incorporada en los proyectos
built-in evaluation [projects]

evaluación inicial (técnica y económica)
appraisal (technical and economic)

evaluación médica periódica
periodic health assessment - PHA

evaluación preliminar
preappraisal

evaluación previa
appraisal (technical and economic)

evaluación previa, ex ante
ex ante evaluation

evasión (ilegal) tributaria, fiscal, de impuestos
tax evasion

evasión legal de impuestos
tax avoidance

evolución
development

ex officio
ex-officio [ICSID]

ex participante
fellow [EDI]

examen
examination (of witnesses or experts) [ICSID]

examen (ambiental) sobre el terreno
environmental reconnaissance

examen de la ejecución de proyectos sectoriales
sector implementation review - SIR

examen de la ejecución del (de un) proyecto
project implementation review - PIR

examen de mediados del período (de una reposición)
Midterm Review - MTR [IDA]

examen de mitad del ejercicio, de mitad de año
midyear review

examen del uso de la energía
energy audit

examen médico
health screening

exámenes
achievement tests [education]

excedente
overhang

excedente de capacidad
excess capacity

excedente del consumidor
consumer surplus

exceder el objetivo
overshoot

excepción de incompetencia
objection to jurisdiction [ICSID]

exceso de empleo
overemployment

exceso de inversiones
overinvestment

exceso de oferta
overhang

exceso de personal
redundancy [staffing]

exclusión del régimen de contabilidad en valores devengados
nonaccrual status

excretas
night soil

exención (de una obligación)
waiver

exención de impuestos
tax exemption

exención parcial
waiver

exención tributaria
tax allowance

exento de derechos
duty-free

exigencia
claim

exigible
callable (capital, subscription)

exigir el agotamiento previo de las vías administrativas o judiciales (de un Estado)
exhaustion of local administrative or juridical remedies [ICSID]

exigir el reembolso anticipado de un préstamo
accelerate a loan

exigir el reembolso de un préstamo
call in a loan, to

exigir el reembolso de un préstamo antes de su vencimiento
accelerate a loan

eximir (de una obligación)
waive, to

existencias
inventory; inventories

existencias reguladoras
buffer stocks

exoneración temporal (parcial o total) de impuestos
tax holiday

expansión de la masa monetaria
monetary expansion

expansión monetaria
monetary expansion

expatriado
expatriate

expectativas inflacionarias
inflationary expectations

expectativas racionales
rational expectations

experiencia
skills

expertos
expertise

expertos en medio ambiente
environmentalist

explotación
development

explotación a cielo abierto, a tajo abierto [Chile]
strip mining; open pit, open cast, open cut mining

explotación agrícola
farm

explotación forestal
logging [forestry]

explotación inicial
initial operation

exportable o importable
tradable [adj.]

exportaciones de bienes y servicios
exports of goods and services - XGS

exportaciones de excedentes del mercado interno
spillover exports

exportaciones en régimen de trueque
bartered exports

exportador de petróleo con déficit de capital
capital-deficit oil exporter

exposición
statement

expresado
denominated in (dollars, etc.)

expresar en cifras netas
net out

extensión
extension [agriculture]

extensión agrícola
agricultural extension

extensionista
agricultural extension officer - AEO; extension agent, worker

externalidades [proyectos]
externalities [projects]

extracción
offtake [livestock]

extracción de madera
logging [forestry]

extracción excesiva de árboles
tree mining; forest mining

extracto
abstract (of a publication)

extracto de cuenta
statement of account

extraordinaria
below the line (item)

fabricación "justo a tiempo"
just in time (JIT) manufacturing

fabricación con ayuda de computadoras
computer aided manufacture - CAM

fabricación de acero en hogar abierto, en horno Martin-Siemens
open-hearth steelmaking

fabricación por vía húmeda
wet process [cement manufacture]

fabricación por vía seca
dry process [cement manufacture]

facsímil de firma autenticado
authenticated specimen of signature

factor concesionario, de donación
concessional, concessionary element; grant element

factor de carga
load factor [electricity]

factor de conversión basado en el consumo
consumption conversion factor - CCF

factor de conversión estándar
standard conversion factor - SCF

factor de descuento, actualización
discount factor

factor de disuasión, disuasivo
deterrent

factor de fondo de amortización
sinking fund factor

factor de interés compuesto
compounding factor

factor de recuperación del capital
capital recovery factor - CRF

factor de revaluación
revaluation factor [currency pool]

factoraje
factoring

factores de atracción (del lugar de destino) relacionados con la demanda
demand-pull factors

factores de rechazo (del lugar de origen) relacionados con la oferta
supply-push factors

facultad
authority [legal]

facultad de adquisición de contratos con interés tope
Global Cap Authority [IFC]

facultad de otorgar garantías
guarantee authority

facultad decisoria, de decisión
decision-making power

facultad legal
legal authority

facultad para conceder préstamos
lending authority

facultad para contraer compromisos
commitment authority; authority [IDA]

facultad para efectuar *swaps*
Global Swap Authority [IFC]

facultad presupuestaria
budget authority

falacia de composición
fallacy of composition

familia extensa
extended family

familia monoparental
one parent family; single parent family, household

fascículo
release [ICSID]

fase ascendente, de expansión
upswing

fase descendente, de contracción
downswing

fase inicial
development period (of a project, of a company)

favoritismo
cronyism

fecha de activación
trigger date [IBRD]

fecha de cierre
closing date

fecha de cierre, de liquidación
settlement date

fecha de desembolso
payout date

fecha de entrada en vigor
effective date

fecha de valor
value date

fecha límite
cutoff date [debt]

fenómeno de la doble tarea (de la mujer)
double-day phenomenon

fertilidad
fecundity

fertilizante compuesto
compound fertilizer; mixed fertilizer

fertilizante de superficie
top dressing [agriculture]

fertilizante nitrogenado
nitrogen, nitrogenous fertilizer

fertilizante simple
single fertilizer

fianza de cumplimiento
performance bond

fianza de la oferta
bid bond, garantee, security

fianza de pago
payment bond [US]

fianza de reembolso
repayment bond

fianza por pago anticipado
advance payment bond

fideicomiso
trust fund

fideicomiso "ciego"
blind trust

fideicomiso cuya composición es desconocida
por el beneficiario
blind trust

fijación anticipada del interés
anticipatory rate setting - ARS

fijación cálculo de precios sociales
social pricing

fijación de carbono
carbon fixation, sequestration

fijación de cargos por el uso de las carreteras
road pricing

fijación de precios
price fixing

fijación de precios al costo marginal
marginal cost pricing

fijación de precios de transferencia entre
empresas
intercompany pricing

fijación de precios en función del costo
cost pricing

fijación de precios equivalentes en operaciones de cofinanciamiento
loan equivalency pricing

fijación del costo de un préstamo
loan pricing, costing

fijación diferida de la tasa de interés y la moneda
deferred rate and currency setting

fijación diferida del interés
deferred rate setting - DRS

fijación ilícita de precios (entre productores)
price fixing

fijar
peg, to (prices, interest rates)

filtro de tela
bag filter; baghouse filter

financiación con, mediante déficit presupuestario
deficit financing

financiación mediante endeudamiento
debt financing

financialización
financialization

financiamiento a mediano o largo plazo
term financing

financiamiento combinado (del BIRF y la AIF)
blend financing; mixed financing

financiamiento complementario
complementary financing; follow-up financing; repeat financing

financiamiento con garantía
collateral financing

financiamiento con recurso limitado
limited recourse finance

financiamiento con tipo de interés fijo
fixed-rate financing

financiamiento concatenado
piggyback financing

financiamiento conjunto especial
Special Joint Financing

financiamiento contra factura
normal financing

financiamiento de contrapartida
matched funding [IFC]; matching funds

financiamiento de la deuda
debt funding

financiamiento de los últimos vencimientos
funding latter maturities

financiamiento en apoyo de reformas de políticas
policy-based lending; policy loans [IBRD]

financiamiento en condiciones comerciales
commercial lending

financiamiento en condiciones de mercado
market-related lending

financiamiento en valores
security lending

financiamiento estructurado
structured financing

financiamiento innovador, imaginativo
creative financing

financiamiento "mezzanine"
mezzanine financing

financiamiento para energía
energy lending

financiamiento para programas
program loan, lending

financiamiento para un proyecto, para proyectos
project loan, lending

financiamiento paralelo
parallel financing

financiamiento previo
prefinancing

financiamiento retroactivo
retroactive financing; retrofinancing

financiamiento sin posibilidad de recurso
nonrecourse finance

financiamiento transitorio
bridging arrangement, credit

financiamiento; plan de financiamiento
financing package

finca
farm

finca (de producción) de semillas
seed farm

firma consultora, de consultores
consulting firm

firmar un convenio, un acuerdo
execute an agreement, to

fiscalización del desempeño, de los resultados
performance monitoring

fiscalización por los pares
peer monitoring

fitogenética
plant breeding

flexibilidad monetaria
monetary ease

flota
fleet [transportation]

fluctuación de los tipos de interés debida a la fuga de capitales
interest leakage

fluctuación de precios
price swing

flujo de capital
capital flow; capital movement

flujo de estudiantes, alumnos
student flow

flujo de fondos
cash flow; funds flow; flow of funds

flujos de caja
cash flow

flujos de capital en condiciones no concesionarias
nonconcessional, nonconcessionary flows

flujos de costos y beneficios
streams of costs and benefits

flujo (de fondos) en condiciones concesionarias
concessional flow

flujos financieros
financial flows

flujos oficiales
official flows [development]

focalización
targeting

fomento
development

fomento del comercio
trade promotion

fondo común de inversiones
money market (mutual) fund - MMF; mutual fund

fondo común de monedas
currency pool

fondo de amortización
sinking fund

fondo de anticipos
imprest account, fund

fondo de capitalización de la deuda
debt-equity conversion fund [IFC]

fondo de cobertura del riesgo cambiario
foreign exchange coverage fund

fondo de comercio; "derecho de llave"
goodwill

fondo de conversión de la deuda en capital
debt-equity conversion fund [IFC]

fondo de estabilización
stabilization fund

fondo de estabilización cambiaria
exchange stabilization fund

fondo de igualación, de equiparación
equalization fund

fondo de inversión en acciones
equity fund

fondo de inversión que no cobra comisión
no load fund

fondo de inversiones
investment company, fund

fondo de inversiones de cartera
equity portfolio fund

fondo de regulación, de estabilización
buffer fund

fondo de seguridad social
social security fund

Fondo de Subvención de Intereses [= Tercera Ventanilla]
Interest Subsidy Fund [= Third Window]

fondo fiduciario
trust fund

fondo indicativo [fondo común de monedas]
reflecting pool

fondo internacional de garantías de crédito
international credit guarantee fund

fondo mutuo
money market (mutual) fund - MMF; mutual fund

fondo mutuo que cobra comisión
load fund

fondo para el fomento de las exportaciones
export development fund - EDF

Fondo para la Maternidad sin Riesgos
Safe Motherhood Fund [IBRD/WHO]

fondo rotatorio
revolving fund

fondos de contrapartida
counterpart funds

fondos de contrapartida
matched funding [IFC]; matching funds

fondos de explotación
working funds

fondos de libre utilización
free funds [IDA]

fondos de libre utilización de la AIF
IDA's "free-funds"

fondos de un día para otro
overnight funds

fondos de un préstamo o crédito
proceeds

fondos en efectivo
balances [cash]

fondos fiduciarios
funds-in-trust

fondos intercambiables, transferibles
fungible funds

fondos no disponibles para préstamos
unreleased funds

forestación
afforestation

forfetización
forfaiting

formación
educational background; skills development

formación avanzada, especializada
advanced training

formación bruta de capital fijo
gross fixed capital formation - GFCF

formación de capital
capital formation

formación de instructores
wholesale training

formación de recursos humanos, de la mano de obra
manpower development

formación en el empleo, trabajo
on-the-job training

formación en el propio país
retail training

formación en el servicio
in-service training

formación en la empresa
in-house training

formación interna de capital
domestic asset formation; domestic capital formation

formación para el puesto, cargo
job-related training

formación profesional
vocational training

formación técnica
technical background

formalización
delivery (of a contract)

formas novedosas de financiamiento
creative financing

fórmula de Filipinas
Philippines formula [MOV]

formulación
design

formulación de un proyecto, de proyectos
project design

forraje arbóreo
tree fodder

fortalecimiento institucional
institution building

forzamiento radiativo
radiative forcing

foscilación de precios
price swing

fosforita
phosphate rock; rock phosphate

foso séptico
septic tank

fraccionamiento de adquisiciones
slice and package [procurement]

franco a bordo - f.o.b.
free on board - FOB

franco al costado del buque - f.a.s.
free alongside ship - FAS

franco de avería particular
free of particular average - FPA

franco de carga y descarga - f.i.o.
free in and out - fio

franco en muelle
free on quay - FOQ; free on wharf - FOW

franco transportista
free carrier (named point) - FRC

franco vagón
free on rail - FOR

franquicia
deductible [insurance]

franquicia
franchise

franquicia correspondiente a la primera pérdida
first-loss deductible [insurance]

freno fiscal
fiscal drag

fuel oil
fuel oil

fuente (de contaminación) no identificable
nonpoint source

fuente puntual
point source [environment]

fuerza de ley
legal force

fuerza de trabajo, laboral
labor force

fuga de capitales
capital flight; flight of capital

fuga de cerebros, éxodo de intelectuales
brain drain

fumigación con tanque llevado a la espalda
knapsack spraying

función bienestar
welfare function; utility function

función catalizadora
catalytic role

función de bienestar social
social welfare function

función objetivo
objective function [economic analysis]

función utilidad
welfare function; utility function

funcionamiento y mantenimiento
Operations & Maintenance - O & M

funcionario autorizado
authorized officer

funcionario contratado localmente
local employee [IBRD]

funcionario de asistencia técnica
technical assistant

funcionario de extensión, de divulgación
outreach worker

funcionario destacado en el terreno
field worker

funcionario encargado de un país
desk officer

funcionario superior
senior manager

funcionarios
staff

funcionarios de contrapartida
counterpart staff

funcionarios de nivel profesional
higher level staff

funcionarios superiores
senior level staff

fusión
merger

fusión (mediante fundación de una nueva empresa)
consolidation (of companies)

futuros
futures

futuros financieros
financial futures

gama de precios
price range

ganadería
animal husbandry

ganado de doble finalidad
dual-purpose cattle

ganado en pie
cattle on the hoof

ganancia cambiaria
exchange premium

ganancia de capital
capital gain

ganancia neta
back value; netback value [energy]

ganancia neta no realizada
net unrealized gain

ganancia(s)
earnings

ganancias de capital realizadas
locked in capital gains

ganancias no realizadas
unrealized gains

ganancias ocasionales, eventuales
occasional earnings

garante
underwriter [securities]

garantía
collateral; security

garantía condicional
qualified guarantee

garantía de cumplimiento
performance guarantee [consultants]

garantía de cumplimiento, contra el riesgo de incumplimiento
performance security [contracts]

garantía de funcionamiento de acuerdo con las especificaciones garantizadas
"put right" guarantee

garantía de la oferta
bid bond, garantee, security

garantía de pago
payment guarantee

garantía de primer grado
first ranking security

garantía de reembolso
repayment guarantee

garantía irrevocable de reembolso
irrevocable agreement to reimburse

garantía pagadera a la vista
on demand guarantee

garantía por pago anticipado
advance payment bond; advance payment security

garantías relativas a la transformación de riesgos
risk transformation guarantees

garantizar un préstamo
secure a loan, to

gas asociado
associated gas

gas de horno de coque
coke oven gas

gas de petróleo licuado - GPL
liquefied petroleum gas - LPG

gas húmedo
wet gas

gas natural licuado - GNL
liquefied natural gas - LNG

gas no asociado
nonassociated gas

gas pobre
producer gas

gas que produce el efecto de invernadero
greenhouse gas - GHG

gas que produce retención térmica
heat trapping gas

gasificación del carbón
coal gasification

gasóleo
diesel fuel; diesel oil

gasto bruto de capital fijo
gross fixed capital expenditure; gross fixed
investment

gasto concentrado al comienzo de un período
front-loaded spending

gasto(s) de capital
capital expenditure; capital outlay

gasto de consumo final privado
private final consumption expenditure - PFCE

gasto discrecional
discretionary spending

gasto no asignable
unallocatable expenditure

gasto(s) público(s)
government expenditure

gastos admisibles, aceptables, financiables
eligible expenses

gastos capitalizados
capitalized expenses

gastos centralizados
centrally-managed costs

gastos concentrados al comienzo de un período
front loading

gastos (iniciales) de constitución
formation expenses; organization expenses

gastos de emisión
flotation costs [bonds]

gastos de explotación
running costs

gastos de explotación, de operación
business expenses

**gastos de explotación, operación,
funcionamiento**
operating expenses, costs

gastos de mantenimiento, conservación
upkeep costs

gastos descentralizados
unit-managed costs

gastos diferidos
deferred charges, expenses

gastos en efectivo
cash expenditures

gastos en petróleo
oil bill [national]

gastos extraordinarios
nonrecurring expenses

gastos fijos
fixed costs

gastos fiscales
tax expenditures

gastos generales
overhead costs; overheads

gastos generales directos
managed costs

gastos iniciales, de instalación
initial expenses

**gastos médicos del personal retirado no
cubiertos por el sistema de pensión**
non-pension retiree medical costs

gastos no monetarios
noncash expenses

gastos ordinarios (en presupuestos)
recurrent costs, expenditures

gastos periódicos
recurrent costs, expenditures

gastos preventivos
defensive expenditures

gastos públicos de capital
public (capital) expenditure

gastos superiores a los previstos
overexpenditures

generalización
stylized fact

genetista [especies vegetales]
breeder [agriculture]

gerentes
managers

germoplasma
germplasm

gestión de (los) riesgos
risk management

gestión de caja
cash management

gestión de la demanda
demand management

gestión de la institución, empresa
corporate management

gestión de la liquidez
liquidity management; liquidity portfolio
management

gestión de pasivos
liability management

gestión económica, de la economía
economic management

gestión financiera de las sociedades
corporate finance

gestión participatoria
participative management

gestión por objetivos
management by objectives - MBO

girar fondos
draw, to (funds)

giro
drawdown

giros pendientes de reembolso
outstanding drawings [IMF]

globalización
globalization

gobernable
manageable

gobierno
governance; government

grado de inclinación
steepness (of a curve)

**graduación (paso de las condiciones de la AIF a
las del Banco**
graduation [IBRD]

graduarse
graduate, to [Bank, IDA]

gráfico de barras
bar chart

gráfico de circulación
flow chart; process chart

gráfico de dispersión
scattered plotting

gráfico de ejecución
progress chart

gráfico de ejecución de las obras
construction progress chart

gráfico de situación
working table; performance chart; management chart

gran computadora
mainframe computer

gran ordenador [España]
mainframe computer

granja
farm

granja (de producción) de semillas
seed farm

granos alimentarios
food grains

gravamen
lien; charge [legal]

gravamen (tributario)
levy

gravamen a las importaciones
import levy

grupo
caucus (of countries at Annual Meetings)

grupo abierto
open-ended group

grupo beneficiario
target group

grupo de colocación
selling consortium, group, syndicate

grupo de dirección, directivo
management group; managing group

grupo de estudio
task force

grupo de evaluación ambiental
environmental (advisory) panel

grupo de expertos
panel of experts; thematic team; think tank

grupo de ingreso(s)
income bracket

Grupo de los Cinco
Group of Five

Grupo de los Diez
Group of Ten

Grupo de los Quince
Group of Fifteen

Grupo de los 77
Group of Seventy-Seven

Grupo de los Siete
Group of Seven

Grupo de los Veinticuatro
Group of Twenty-Four

grupo de participación abierta
open-ended group

grupo de trabajo
task force

Grupo de Trabajo Internacional de Compiladores de Estadísticas sobre la Deuda Externa
International Compilers Working Group on External Debt Statistics

Grupo del Banco Mundial
World Bank Group

grupo desfavorecido
disadvantaged group

grupo escogido (como meta)
target group

grupo impositivo
tax bracket

grupo muestra elegido
focus group

grupo objeto de ...
target group

grupo previsto
target group

grupo vendedor
selling consortium, group, syndicate

grupos de ingresos más elevados
higher income brackets

grupos homogéneos de diagnóstico
diagnostically related groups - DRG

grupos que viven en la pobreza absoluta
absolute poor

guerra y disturbios civiles
war and civil disturbance [MIGA]

guía del maestro
teacher's guide

habilitación
eligibility; eligibility conditions; empowerment

habilitación de tierras
land development

hacer inversiones en acciones comunes
take a straight equity position, to

hacerse cargo
take over, to

hambre oculta, encubierta
hidden hunger

hecho estilizado, de ocurrencia frecuente
stylized fact

hidrocarburos aromáticos policíclicos - HAP
polycyclic aromatic hydrocarbons - PAH

hidroclorofluorocarbono - HCFC
hydrochlorofluorocarbon - HCFC

hidrocraqueo
hydrocracking

hidrofluoroalcano - HFA
hydrofluoroalkane - HFA

hidrofluorocarbono - HFC
hydrofluorocarbon - HFC

higiene ambiental
environmental health, sanitation

hiperempleo
overemployment

hipótesis
counterfactual

hipótesis del progreso técnico incorporado
embodiment hypothesis

historia clínica
personal history [medicine]

hoja de asistencia
time sheet

hoja de plazos y condiciones
term sheet

hoja electrónica de cálculo
spreadsheet

homo economicus
economic man

honorario
consideration [legal, economic]

honorario anticipado
retainer

horario (de trabajo) básico
core hours; core (working) hours

horario flexible
flexitime; flextime

hortaliza de fruta
fruit vegetable

huerta (de producción) de semillas
seed garden

idea
design

identificación
borrower ownership; ownership (of programs)

identificación de un proyecto, de proyectos
project identification

importe de un préstamo o crédito
proceeds

imposición de precios por el fabricante
resale price maintenance - RPM

impresión (de computadora)
printout

impreso (de computadora)
printout

imprevistos
contingencies

imprevistos financieros
financial contingency

impuesto a las emisiones de carbono
carbon tax

impuesto a las empresas
corporate tax

impuesto a las sociedades
corporate tax

impuesto al consumo
excise tax

impuesto al, sobre el valor agregado, añadido - IVA
value-added tax - VAT; tax on value added

impuesto cedular
schedular tax; scheduled tax

impuesto de capitación
poll tax; head tax; capitation tax

impuesto de igualación, de equiparación de intereses
interest equalization tax

impuesto de la inflación
inflation tax

impuesto de origen
origin tax

impuesto de valorización
betterment levy, tax

impuesto de valorización, sobre la plusvalía
land betterment tax

impuesto en cascada
cascade tax

impuesto para fines específicos
earmarked tax

impuesto por etapas, en cascada
multiple stage tax

impuesto progresivo
graduated tax

impuesto que significa la inflación
inflation tax

impuesto retenido en la fuente
withholding tax

impuesto según uso final
end use tax

impuesto sobre el volumen, la cifra de negocios
turnover tax

impuesto sobre ganancias de capital
capital gains tax

impuesto sobre la plusvalía
betterment levy, tax

impuesto sobre la plusvalía
capital gains tax

impuesto sobre las utilidades
corporate income tax [US]; business (profit) tax; corporation tax [UK]

impuesto sobre las utilidades, los beneficios
profits tax

impuesto sobre nóminas
payroll tax

impuesto sobre, a la renta
income tax

impuesto sobre, a la(s) venta(s)
sales tax

impuesto sobre, a las utilidades, los beneficios
income tax [corporations]

impuesto territorial
land tax

impuestos en mora
delinquent taxes

impuestos fronterizos
border taxes

impuestos por beneficios
benefit taxes [IBRD]

impuestos según mercado final
destination taxes

impuestos sobre la renta presuntiva, presunta
presumptive taxation

impulso
take-off

inadmisible
ineligible

inamovilidad
security of tenure

incentivo
incentive

incentivo en dinero
incentive payment

incentivo tributario
tax incentive

incentivos de precios
price incentives

incentivos para la inversión
investment incentives

incidencia
incidence [medicine]

inclinación
bias [economy; statistics]

incorporar a las actividades habituales (del Banco)
mainstream, to

incremento anual medio
mean annual increment - MAI [forestry]

incumplimiento de contrato
breach of contract

incumplimiento de obligaciones
default on obligations

indemnización
compensation

indemnización compensatoria
compensatory damages

indemnización por accidentes de trabajo
workmen's compensation

indemnización por despido
severance pay

indemnización por terminación, rescisión, cese de funciones, despido
termination grant

independiente
free-standing; self-contained

indicador anticipado
leading indicator

indicador coincidente
convergent indicator

indicador contemporáneo
concurrent indicator

indicador económico
economic indicator

indicador primario de las tendencias económicas
bellwether (of economic trends)

indicador retrospectivo
lagging indicator

indicadores de las perspectivas económicas a corto plazo
Short Term Economic Monitor [IBRD]

Indicadores del desarrollo mundial
World Development Indicators - WDIs

indicadores del desempeño, de la actuación
performance indicators

índice combinado de desempeño de la cartera
current blend [IFC]

índice de aprovechamiento del forraje
feed conversion ratio

índice de cobertura de las importaciones
import coverage index

índice de eficiencia técnica
technical-efficiency index - TEI

índice de fletes marítimos
ocean freight rate index

índice de invernadero
greenhouse index

índice de la calidad material de la vida
Physical Quality of Life Index - PQLI

índice de octano
motor octane number - MON

índice de precios al consumidor
consumer price index - CPI

Indice de precios de los alimentos
Food Price Index [IBRD]

índice de precios de los metales y minerales
Metals and Minerals Price Index [IBRD]

índice de precios de los productos agrícolas no alimentarios
Non-Food Agricultural Price Index [IBRD]

índice de recuento de la pobreza
headcount index (measure) of poverty; headcount ratio - HCR

índice de recuperación de la renta económica
rent recovery index [projects]

índice de rendimiento total
Total Return Index [IFC]

índice de rentabilidad total
Total Return Index [IFC]

índice de variación
instability index

índice de vida dinámica
dynamic life index [commodities]

índice de volumen
quantum index

índice del valor unitario de las exportaciones
unit value export index

índice del valor unitario de las manufacturas - VUM
(World Bank) Manufacturing Unit Value (MUV) Index

índice del valor unitario de las manufacturas - VUM
Manufacturing Unit Value Index [World Bank]

índice en cadena
chain index

índice estático de las reservas (años)
Static Life Index [commodities]

índice global de precios de 33 productos básicos
33-Commodity Aggregate Price Index [IBRD]

Indices de Cobertura Amplia de la CFI (Indices IFCG)
IFC Global Indexes (IFCG Indexes)

Indices de la CFI de Valores para Inversión (Indices IFCI)
IFC Investable Indexes (IFCI Indexes)

industria auxiliar, abastecedora
supplier industry

industria basada en recursos naturales
resource based industries

industria con gran intensidad de mano de obra
labor-intensive industry

industria de apoyo a la agricultura
agrosupport industry

industria de elaboración de alimentos
food processing industry

industria de la construcción
construction sector

industria de servicios
service industry

industria del transporte por carretera
trucking industry

industria en decadencia, en crisis
depressed industry

industria familiar, casera, artesanal
cottage industry

industria fronteriza
border industry

industria ligera, liviana
light industry

industria metalmecánica
heavy engineering industry

industria naciente, incipiente
infant industry

industria no localizada, sin vinculación permanente
footloose industry

industria pesada
heavy industry

industria pionera, de vanguardia
pioneer industry

industria técnica, mecánica, metalmecánica
engineering industry

industrias de elaboración de productos agrícolas
agroprocessing industries

industrias de zona franca
in-bond industries

industrias maquiladoras
in-bond industries

inelasticidad con respecto al precio
price inelasticity

inestabilidad
volatility

inflación básica
core inflation

inflación de dos dígitos, de 10% ó más
double digit inflation; two digit inflation

inflación de los precios de los activos
asset price inflation

inflación desenfrenada, galopante
runaway inflation

inflación desfasada
lagged inflation

inflación galopante
galloping inflation

inflación inercial
inertial inflation

inflación latente, oculta
hidden inflation

inflación producida por la (presión de la) demanda
demand-pull inflation

inflación producida por los salarios
wage pull inflation

inflación progresiva
creeping inflation

inflación provocada por el alza de los costos
cost-push inflation

inflación subyacente
underlying inflation

influencia en el mercado
market power

información desactualizada
dated information

información obtenida
feedback (of information)

informatizado
computerized

informe corto de auditoría
short form audit report

informe de cuentas por cobrar según fecha de vencimiento
aging schedule [accounts receivable]

informe de evaluación de los efectos
impact (evaluation) report

informe de evaluación *ex post* de un proyecto
project performance audit report - PPAR

informe de evaluación inicial preparado por el personal
staff appraisal report - SAR

informe de fin de misión
end-of-mission document

informe de terminación del proyecto, de proyectos - ITP
project completion report - PCR

informe final de ejecución - IFE
Implementation Completion Report - ICR

informe inicial
inception report

informe largo de auditoría
long form audit report

informe presupuestario trimestral
apex report

informe sobre la marcha (de un proyecto), sobre la labor realizada, sobre las actividades
progress report; status report

informe sobre las repercusiones (de un proyecto)
impact (evaluation) report

informe sobre misión realizada
back-to-office report - BTO

infracostos
cost underrun; underrun cost

infraestructura (económica)
capital infrastructure

infraestructura física
physical infrastructure

infraestructura primaria
trunk infrastructure

infraestructura social
community facilities; social infrastructure; social overhead capital

infraseguro
underinsurance

ingeniería ambiental, del medio ambiente
environmental engineering

ingeniería de diseño
design engineering

ingeniería de procesos
process engineering

ingeniería del valor
value engineering

ingeniería ecológica
environmental engineering

ingeniería financiera [México]
financial engineering

ingeniero consultor
engineering consultant

ingeniero hidrólogo, hidráulico
water engineer

ingesta
intake

ingesta de alimentos
food intake

ingestión
intake

ingestión de alimentos
food intake

ingestión de calorías
calorie intake

ingreso ajustado conforme a consideraciones ambientales
environmentally adjusted income - EAI

ingreso discrecional
discretionary income

ingreso disponible
disposable income

ingreso imponible
assessed income

ingreso interno bruto - YIB
gross domestic income - GDY

ingreso marginal
marginal revenue product - MRP

ingreso monetario
money income

ingreso nacional ajustado conforme a consideraciones ambientales - INA
environmentally adjusted national income - ENI

ingreso nacional bruto - YNB
gross national income - GNY

ingreso neto por servicios de los factores
net factor service income

ingreso per cápita, por habitante
per capita income

ingreso(s)
earnings; income

ingreso(s) proveniente(s) de propiedades públicas
property income [government]

ingreso(s) agrícola(s)
farm income

ingreso(s) de equilibrio
equilibrium income

ingreso(s) de la propiedad, del patrimonio
property income [individuals, corporations]

ingreso(s) de los valores en cartera
portfolio income

ingreso(s) no proveniente(s) del trabajo; ingreso(s) no salarial(es)
unearned income

ingreso(s) proveniente(s) del trabajo
earned income

ingreso(s) salarial(es)
earned income

ingresos
returns; revenues

ingresos
revenues; returns

ingresos corrientes
current revenues

ingresos de explotación, de operación
operating income, profit

ingresos de exportación
export earnings, proceeds

ingresos de los factores
factor income

ingresos devengados, acumulados
accrued income

ingresos fiscales corrientes
current revenues

ingresos fiscales, tributarios
fiscal revenue

ingresos monetarios, en efectivo
cash income

ingresos netos [BIRF]
net income

ingresos no provenientes de las operaciones
nonoperating income

ingresos por (concepto de) inversiones, derivados de inversiones
investment income

ingresos por intereses
interest earnings, income

ingresos por intereses
interest income, earnings

ingresos públicos
government receipts, revenues

iniciación de la fase ascendente
upturn (economic)

iniciación de la fase descendente
downturn (economic)

iniciar (sus) actividades
stream, to go on

iniciativa (política)
political entrepreneurship

inmovilización de activos
warehousing (of financial assets)

inmunidad tributaria
immunity from taxation

innovaciones inducidas por el agricultor
farmer-pull innovations

innovaciones inducidas por el usuario
downstream innovations

innovaciones inducidas por la investigación
upstream innovations; research-push innovations

inscripción
perfection (of security); registration [Stock Exchange]

inscrito
registered

inspección previa al embarque
pre-shipment inspection

inspector administrativo
management auditor

inspector de bancos
bank examiner

instalación
facility

instalación de servicios en los lotes
plot servicing

instalación sanitaria mínima
wetcore

instalaciones
physical facilities

instalaciones comunitarias
social infrastructure; community facilities

instalaciones de elaboración, transporte y distribución
downstream plant, facilities

instalaciones físicas
capital works

instalaciones y bienes de equipo
plant and equipment

institución afiliada
affiliate

**institución afiliada que otorga el financiamiento
en condiciones concesionarias**
soft loan affiliate

institución de crédito, crediticia
lending agency, institution

institución de transferencia de hipotecas
secondary market mortgage institution

institución financiera de desarrollo
development finance company - DFC;
development finance institution - DFI

institución paraestatal
parastatal [noun]

institución principal
apex bank, institution

instituciones de ahorro contractual
contractual savings institutions

instituciones financieras internacionales
international financial institutions - IFIs

instituciones inversionistas
institutional investors

instrucciones
software

instrucciones permanentes
standing instructions, orders

instructor
trainer

instrumento (oficial)
instrument [ICSID]

instrumento de aceptación
instrument of acceptance

instrumento de compromiso condicionado
qualified instrument of commitment

**instrumento financiero con características
patrimoniales**
equity-like instrument

instrumentos cuasimonetarios
near cash instruments

instrumentos derivados
derivative instruments

instrumentos jurídicos, legales
legal instruments [agreements, etc.]

insuficiencia
shortfall

insuficiencia de ingresos
income shortfall

insuficiencia de las exportaciones
export shortfall

insuficiencia de liquidez
liquidity shortage

insuficiencia de los ingresos de exportación
export shortfall

insuficiencia de recursos
resource(s) gap

insuficiencia de(l) capital
capital inadequacy

insumo
input

insumo de fondos en efectivo
cash input [agricultural projects]

insumo no monetario
noncash input

integración horizontal
horizontal integration

integración progresiva
forward integration

integración regresiva
backward integration

integración vertical
backward-forward integration

integrador de irregularidades
bump integrator [highways]

integrante de la Lista (de Conciliadores o de Arbitros)
Panel member [ICSID]

intensidad constante de utilización de energía
constant energy intensity

intensidad de capital
capital intensity

intensidad de cultivo
cropping intensity

intensificación financiera
financial deepening

intensificación industrial
industrial deepening

intercambio de derechos de emisión, contaminación
emissions trading

intercambio de monedas
currency swap

intercambio de tipos de interés
interest (rate) swap

interés compuesto
compound interest

interés condicional, contingente
contingent interest

interés económico directo
working interest [oils, minerals]

interés mayoritario
proprietary interest

interés no financiado
unfunded interest

interés nominal
coupon rate (of a bond)

interesados
stakeholders

intereses (cobrados, pagados)
interest charges

intereses cobrados anticipadamente
unearned interest

intereses devengados, acumulados
accrued interest - AI

intereses durante la construcción
interest during construction - IDC

interfaz gráfica para el usuario
graphical user interface - GUI

intermediación
intermediation

intermediación del mercado
market intermediation

intermediario de crédito agrícola
agricultural credit intermediary

internacional
cross-border; transterritorial

internado
internship

interrogatorio
examination (of witnesses or experts) [ICSID]

interrupción del servicio
outage [electricity]

intervalo
time lag

intervención
statement

intervenciones dirigidas
targeted interventions

introducción [agricultura]
accession

intrusión de agua salada
salt water intrusion

invasión
crowding in

invención
development

inventario de recursos
survey of resources

inventario(s)
inventory; inventories

inversión (de capital)
capital investment

inversión admisible
eligible investment [MIGA]

inversión bruta en capital fijo
gross fixed capital expenditure; gross fixed
investment

inversión de tipo totalmente nuevo
greenfield investment

**inversión directa distinta de las contribuciones
al capital social**
nonequity direct investment

inversión en (el) capital social
equity financing, investment

inversión en activos fijos
physical investment

inversión en capital fijo
capital expenditure; capital outlay; fixed
investment

inversión en capital social corriente
net book value; current equity investment; net
investment

inversión en existencias
inventory investment

inversión en forma de préstamo
loan investment

inversión en infraestructura social
social overhead investment

inversión excesiva
overinvestment

inversión forzosa
forced investment

inversión insuficiente
underinvestment

inversión interna bruta - IIB
gross domestic investment - GDI

inversión nacional bruta - INB
gross national investment - GNI

inversión neta
net book value; current equity investment; net
investment

**inversión orientada a aumentar la eficiencia de
la producción y reducir los costos**
capital deepening investment

**inversión que no ha alcanzado su pleno
rendimiento**
unseasoned investment

inversiones de cartera
portfolio equity

**inversiones de cartera en capital social,
accionario**
portfolio equity investments

inversiones en acciones comunes, hacer
take a straight equity position, to

inversiones que han alcanzado su madurez, su fase productiva
mature investments [IFC]

inversionistas estratégicos
strategic investors

inversionistas que se estimen adecuados, apropiados
strategic investors

investigación académica
academic research

investigación aplicada
applied research

investigación básica
basic research

investigación con fines de adaptación
adaptive research

investigación inicial, de avanzada
pioneering research

investigación operativa, de operaciones
operational, operations research

investigación sobre sistemas de producción agrícola
farming systems research - FSR

investigación y desarrollo
research and development - R & D

investigación(es) en las explotaciones agrícolas
on-farm research - OFR

invitación a la precalificación
invitation to prequalify [contracts]

jarabe de maíz de alto contenido en fructosa
high fructose corn syrup - HFCS

jubilación
retirement benefits; superannuation

juego de gestión
management game

juego de suma cero, nula
zero sum game

juego de suma negativa
negative sum game

juego de suma positiva
plus sum game; positive sum game

juicio hipotecario
foreclosure

junta de comercialización
marketing board

Junta de Directores
Board of Directors [IFC, MIGA]

Junta de Gobernadores [Banco, AIF, CFI]
Board of Governors

jurisdicción
chair, constituency of an Executive Director [World Bank]

jurisdicción
constituent(s) of an Executive Director

kilómetro lineal
line kilometer [surveying]

laboreo con abrigo vegetal
trashy farming

labranza mínima
minimum tillage

laguna tributaria
tax loophole

lanzar una emisión de bonos
float a loan, to

lastre fiscal
fiscal drag

laudo
award [ICSID]

leasing
finance lease; financial, full pay out lease

lecho de un río
river channel

lenguaje de programación de computadoras
computer language

leña
woodfuel

letra aduanera garantizada
customs duty bill

letra de cambio
bill of exchange

letrina de cisterna y sifón
cistern flush latrine

letrina de cubo
bucket latrine

letrina de pozo
pit latrine; pit privy

letrina de pozo anegado
aqua privy

letrina de pozo mejorada con ventilación
ventilated improved pit (VIP) latrine; VIP latrine

letrina de pozo negro
vault toilet

letrina de sifón
pour flush latrine

levantamiento aeromagnético
aeromagnetic survey; airmag survey

levantamiento del mapa escolar, de mapas escolares
school mapping

levantamiento topográfico
survey

ley (de un metal precioso)
fineness (of a precious metal)

ley aplicable
governing law

ley de rendimientos decrecientes
law of diminishing returns

ley de utilidad marginal decreciente
law of diminishing marginal utility

ley del presupuesto
appropriation law [US]

ley(es) que autoriza(n)
enabling legislation

liberación con autorización de convertibilidad
convertible release (of 18% currency) [IBRD]

liberación incondicional, irrestricta
blanket release

liberación restringida (de los montos del 18%)
restricted release (of 18% currency)

liberalizar
deregulate

liberar
release, to [capital]

LIBOR [tipo, tasa de oferta interbancaria de Londres]
LIBOR [London interbank offered rate]

libre acceso a la información
disclosure of information

libre comercio
free trade

libre de derechos
duty-free

libre determinación
self-determination

libre intercambio
free trade

libro del maestro
teacher's guide

licencia
franchise

licencia de tiempo completo
day release; block release

licencia general de importación
open general licence - OGL

licitación anticipada
advance procurement action

licitación colusoria
collusive tendering

licitación internacional limitada
limited international bidding - LIB

licitación pública
competitive bidding; public tender; open tender

licitación pública internacional
international competitive bidding - ICB

licitación pública nacional
competitive bidding in accordance with local
procedures; local competitive bidding - LCB

**licitación pública según procedimientos
nacionales, anunciada localmente**
competitive bidding in accordance with local
procedures; local competitive bidding - LCB

**licitante (que somete la oferta más alta, más
baja)**
bidder (highest/lowest)

licitante calificado
qualified bidder

licitante cuya oferta ha sido aceptada
successful bidder

licitante favorecido
successful bidder

**licitante que presenta la oferta clasificada en
segundo lugar**
second lowest bidder

licitante que presenta la oferta de menor precio
lowest priced bidder

licitante que presenta la oferta más alta
highest bidder

licitante que presenta la oferta más baja
lowest bidder

licuefacción del carbón
coal liquefaction

ligero de Arabia Saudita
Saudi Arabian light (crude oil); light Arabian
crude

lignito
brown coal

limitación voluntaria (del comercio)
voluntary restraints (on trade)

limitación voluntaria de las exportaciones
voluntary export restraints - VER

limitaciones por razones de prudencia
prudential constraints

**límite (para la concesión de financiamiento de
la AIF o del Banco)**
cutoff point (for Bank or IDA financing)

límite de aprobación autónoma
free limit [IBRD]

límite de crédito
credit ceiling; credit limit

límite de crédito, de préstamos
lending limit

límite de redescuento
rediscount ceiling

límite estatutario de los préstamos
statutory lending limit - SLL

límite estatutario, legal, reglamentario
statutory ceiling

**límite máximo de los préstamos de aprobación
autónoma**
free limit of loan [DFCs]

límite oficial para recibir financiamiento de la AIF
formal eligibility threshold; eligibility threshold; eligibility ceiling

límite práctico para recibir financiamiento de la AIF
operational cut-off; effective cut-off; operational threshold

límites a la facultad para contraer compromisos impuestos por el principio de proporcionalidad
pro rata commitment authority limitations

limpieza (del medio ambiente)
clean-up (environmental)

línea de capital accionario
equity line [IFC]

línea de crédito
credit line [IFC]

línea de crédito a través de un agente
agency line; credit line on a agency basis [IFC]

línea de crédito a través de un agente
credit line on an agency basis; agency line [IFC]

línea de crédito para productos múltiples a través de agentes
multiproduct agency credit line [IFC]

línea de pobreza
poverty income threshold; poverty line

línea de subtransmisión, de transmisión secundaria
subtransmission line; secondary transmission line

línea de transmisión secundaria, subtransmisión
secondary transmission line; subtransmission line

liofilización
freeze drying

liquidación de activos
asset stripping

liquidación de impuestos
tax bill, demand

liquidación por concepto de mantenimiento del valor
maintenance of value settlement; settlement of maintenance of value

liquidez
cash flow; moneyness

liquidez discrecional
discretionary liquidity

liquidez internacional
international liquidity

líquidos de gas natural
natural gas liquids - NGL

Lista de Conciliadores, de Arbitros
Panel of Conciliators, Arbitrators [ICSID]

lista de efectivos laborales
return of labor

lista de precios
price schedule [procurement]

Lista de Sustancias Tóxicas Prohibidas
Restricted Toxic Materials List - RTML

lista final de selección
short list

lista positiva
positive list

llamada a licitación
invitation to bid, to tender

llamada de cobro revertido
collect call; transfer charge call; reverse charge call

llamada de cobro revertido
transfer charge call; collect call; reverse charge call

llanura inundada, de inundación
floodplain

lluvia ácida
acid rain

lote con servicios
serviced area, lot, site

lote de prueba
test plot

lote sin servicios, no urbanizado
undeveloped plot

lotes y servicios
sites and services

lucha contra [enfermedades, desastres, etc.]
control

lucha contra plagas y enfermedades
pest and disease control

lucha integrada contra las plagas
integrated pest management - IPM

lugar (de un proyecto)
site

lugar de destino
duty station

lutita bituminosa
oil shale

luz [entre cuerpos]
clearance

macrogestión
macromanagement

madera
timber

madera en pie
timber

madera redonda
roundwood

maduración
maturation (of borrowers from IDA to IBRD loans)

malnutrición
malnutrition

malnutrido
malnourished

mancomunado y solidario
joint and several

mandato
terms of reference [e.g. consultants]

manejable
manageable

manejo de rebaños
flock management; herd management

manipulación de la contabilidad (para aparentar una mejor situación)
window dressing

mano de obra calificada
skilled manpower

mano de obra no calificada
unskilled labor

mano de obra ocasional
casual labor

mano de obra semicalificada
semiskilled manpower

mano de obra; población activa
labor force

mantenimiento
sustainability

mantenimiento de rutina, rutinario
routine maintenance

mantenimiento del valor
maintenance of value - MOV (of IBRD capital)

manual del instructor
teacher's guide

máquina de tratamiento de textos
word processor

marcar
peg out, to [surveying]

marco de políticas
policy framework

marco institucional
institutional framework

marco normativo
policy framework

marco temporal, cronológico
time frame

margen
risk spread

margen (bancario) bruto
gross margin; banker's spread; banker's markup;
gross earnings margin [banks]

margen (de precio) en concepto de riesgos
risk allowance [projects]

**margen (entre las cotizaciones al contado y a
término)**
spread (between spot and forward quotations)

**margen (p.ej., entre el costo de los empréstitos y
el interés sobre los préstamos)**
spread (e.g. between borrowing cost and lending
rates)

margen de competitividad internacional
international competitiveness margin - ICM

margen de maniobra
headroom [World Bank]

margen de preferencia
margin of preference; preference, preferential
margin

margen de preferencia a empresas nacionales
domestic preference; preference margin;
preferential margin; margin of preference
[procurement]

margen de utilidad
mark-up

margen de utilidad, de beneficios
profit margin

margen entre los precios
price spread, differential

margen entre tipos, tasas de interés
interest-rate differential

margen estándar
benchmark spread

margen financiero
financial spread

**margen neto de interés sobre el promedio de
activos productivos**
net interest margin on average earning assets

marginado
underprivileged

masa salarial
wage bill

materia
subject matter [education]

material (de transporte)
equipment

material complementario
balancing equipment

material de propagación
planting material

material didáctico
educational material

material didáctico, pedagógico
instructional aid

material fungible
expendable equipment

**material genético, de mejora [especies
vegetales]**
breeding material

material no fungible
nonexpendable equipment

material pedagógico básico
teacher's kit

material vegetativo
planting material

materiales básicos
feedstock

materiales didácticos
learning materials; teaching aids

materias básicas
core subjects; basic subjects [education]; feedstock

matrícula
enrollments

matriculado
registered [vehicle]

matriz de contabilidad social
social accounting matrix - SAM

matriz de referencia cruzada, comparación
crosswalk document

máxima estacional
seasonal peak

mayor pago inicial de la porción pagada de las suscripciones de capital
front loading of the subscription [IBRD]

mayoría calificada
qualified majority

mayoría especial
special majority

mecanismo
facility

mecanismo administrativo
administrative machinery

mecanismo complementario
additional facility [ICSID]

mecanismo de emergencia
contingency mechanism [IMF/World Bank]

mecanismo de financiamiento transitorio
bridging facility

mecanismo de opciones
exit mechanism

mecanismo de participación
voice mechanism

mecanismo de precios de intervención
Trigger Price Mechanism - TPM [US]

mecanismo de préstamos a intermediarios
wholesale mechanism; wholesaling

mecanismo de reajuste automático (del tipo, de la tasa de interés)
automatic resetting mechanism [IFC]

mecanismo de salida de cesta
basket extractor, exit mechanism [GATT]

mecanismo de suscripción de reserva
backup (underwriting) facility

mecanismos de apoyo
backstopping

mecanismos de crédito, crediticios
credit facilities

mecanismos oficiales de control
command-and-control instrument, regulation

media armónica
harmonic mean [statistics]

media móvil
running average; moving average

media ponderada
weighted average

medicamento genérico
generic drug

médico "descalzo"
barefoot doctor

medida en que la asistencia es concesionaria, muy favorable
degree of concessionality

medida global de la ayuda - MGA
aggregate measure of support - AMS

medida provisional
provisional measure [ICSID]

medida temporal, de transición
stopgap measure

medidas de política
policy-based assistance

medidas de protección social
safety net; social safety net

medidas en materia de inversiones relacionadas con el comercio
trade-related investment measures - TRIMS

medidor de materiales
quantity surveyor

mediería
sharecropping

medio circulante
money stock, supply

medio de prueba
evidence [ICSID]

medio receptor
sink (e.g. of greenhouse gases)

medios
facility

medios de información, difusión, comunicación
mass media

medios empresariales, comerciales
business community

medios y arbitrios
ways and means

mejora de las condiciones de la deuda
debt enhancements

mejoramiento
development

mejoramiento ambiental
environmental enhancement

mejoramiento de tierras
land improvement

mejoramiento de zonas, barrios de tugurios
slum upgrading

mejorar las condiciones de la nueva deuda
enhance new debt, to

mejoras en las explotaciones agrícolas; adecuación predial
on-farm developments, improvements

memorando de acuerdo
memorandum of understanding

memorando de evaluación *ex post* de un proyecto
project performance audit memorandum - PPAM

memorando de transmisión
covering memorandum

memorando jurídico
memorandum of law

Memorando sobre Arreglos Administrativos
Memorandum of Administrative Arrangements [ICSID]

memorial
memorial [ICSID]

menú desplegable
pull-down menu

mercado abierto
open market

mercado activo
buoyant market

mercado al contado
spot market; cash market [foreign exchange]

mercado alcista
bull market

mercado bajista
bear market

mercado de capital(es)
capital market

mercado de competencia, competitivo
competitive market

mercado de compradores
buyer's market

mercado de divisas a término, a plazo
forward exchange market

mercado de divisas, de cambios
foreign exchange market

mercado de dos niveles
two-tier market

mercado de eurodivisas
Eurocurrency market

mercado de futuros
futures market

mercado de productos disponibles, de entrega inmediata
spot market [commodities]

mercado de *swaps*
swap market

mercado de trabajo, laboral
labor market

mercado de valores
securities market

mercado de vendedores
seller's market

mercado especializado, para productos específicos
niche market

mercado extrabursátil, fuera de bolsa
over-the-counter market; curb market

mercado extraterritorial
offshore market

mercado favorable a los compradores
buyer's market

mercado favorable al vendedor
seller's market

mercado financiero
open market

mercado gris
grey market; gray market

mercado monetario, de dinero
money market

mercado muy activo
deep market

mercado negro, clandestino
black market

mercado secundario
secondary market

mercado sustitutivo
surrogate market

mercados bien establecidos
mature markets [securities]

mercados emergentes, incipientes
emerging markets [securities]

mercancías de detalle
less than carload freight - LCL

mercancías en depósito, en almacén de aduanas
bonded goods

mercancías en existencia
off-the-shelf goods

mes-funcionario
staff-month

método contable, de contabilidad
accounting procedure

método de actualización de los flujos de fondos
discounted cash flow (DCF) method

método de "con y sin"
"with-and-without" test [projects]

método de la lista de opciones
menu approach

método de los cuadrados de rendimiento
crop-cut method

método de los efectos
effects method [project appraisal]

método de máxima verosimilitud
maximum likelihood method

método de mínimos cuadrados
least squares method

método de roza y quema
slash-and-burn cultivation

método del camino crítico
critical path method - CPM

MIBOR (tipo, tasa de oferta interbancaria de Madrid)
MIBOR [= Madrid Interbank Offered Rate]

microdatos
microdata

microenseñanza
microteaching

microgestión
micromanagement

miembro de pleno derecho
full member

miembro fundador
original member [MIGA]

miembro no fundador
nonoriginal member [MIGA]

miembros
membership [IFC]

millones de barriles diarios de equivalente en petróleo - mbdep
millions of barrels per day oil equivalent - mbdoe

minerales no combustibles
nonfuel minerals

mínimo
hard core [projects]

ministerio de ejecución
spending ministry

ministerio de operaciones, sectorial, de ejecución
line ministry, department

ministerio que efectúa gastos
spending ministry

ministerio responsable de una sola industria
branch ministry

ministerios de hacienda y de planificación
core ministries, departments

misión de estudio
survey mission

misión de estudio de oportunidades de inversión
investment review mission [IBRD]

misión de evaluación complementaria
post appraisal mission

misión de evaluación *ex post*
audit mission; evaluation mission

misión de evaluación *ex post*
evaluation mission; audit mission

misión de evaluación inicial, previa, ex ante
appraisal mission

misión de evaluación preliminar
preappraisal mission

misión de examen
review mission

misión de examen externo
external review mission

misión de finalización (previa a la terminación de un proyecto)
graduation mission [IBRD]

misión de supervisión
supervision mission

misión de supervisión general del proyecto a mediados del período de ejecución
midterm project review mission [World Bank]

misión en el terreno, de observación en el terreno
field mission, assignment

misión general
full mission

misión multidisciplinaria
composite mission

misión residente
resident mission

modalidad del comercio
trade pattern

modelo
design

modelo agregado, global
aggregate model

modelo computadorizado de equilibrio general
computable general equilibrium (CGE) model

modelo de (presentación de) ofertas
form of bid, tender

modelo de contrato
form of contract

modelo de insumo-producto
input-output model

modelo de las dos brechas
two-gap model

modelo de normas de diseño y mantenimiento de carreteras
Highways Design and Maintenance Model - HDM [IBRD]

modelo de oferta
bid form

modelo de paridad de los tipos de interés sin cobertura
uncovered interest rate parity model

modelo estándar mínimo modificado
revised minimum standard model - RMSM

modelo exhaustivo
ultimate model

modelo multisectorial de equilibrio general
multisectoral general equilibrium model

modelos de documentos de licitación
model bid documents

moderación
self-restraint

moderación financiera
financial restraint, stringency

modernización
rehabilitation

modernización de la estructura industrial
deepening of the industrial structure

modificación de los vencimientos
maturity transformation

modificación de productos fabricados en serie
custom retrofitting

módulos audiovisuales de capacitación
multimedia training modules [EDI]

moneda admisible
eligible currency

moneda de curso legal
legal tender

moneda de intercambio
trading currency

moneda de intervención
intervention currency

moneda de la garantía
guarantee currency

moneda de libre convertibilidad
freely convertible currency

moneda de libre uso
freely usable currency; unrestricted currency

moneda de reserva
reserve currency

moneda de uso restringido
restricted currency

moneda débil
soft currency

moneda distinta del monto del 18%
non-18% currency

moneda extranjera
foreign currency, exchange

moneda fronteriza
border currency (unit)

moneda fuerte
hard currency; strong currency

moneda importante
major currency

moneda nacional
domestic currency; local currency

moneda "vehículo"
vehicle currency

moneda vinculada
tied currency

moneda vinculada al oro
gold-pegged currency

monedas que integran la cesta del DEG
SDR currencies

monetización
monetization

monocultivo
monoculture; sole cropping

montaje de material fabricado en otro país
offshore assembly, processing

monto de la garantía contingente
standby amount of guarantee

monto de los préstamos bancarios vigentes
bank exposure

monto de los préstamos desembolsados y pendientes
bank exposure

monto del 2%
2% currency [IBRD]

monto del contrato
contract price

monto global
aggregate; lump sum price

monto global actuarial
actuarial lump sum

monto máximo de garantía
maximum amount of guarantee

monto neto de los giros
outstanding drawings [IMF]

monto pagado de las suscripciones de capital [BIRF]
paid-in capital subscriptions [IBRD]

monto(s) del 18% (pagado(s) por un miembro en su moneda)
18% currency [IBRD maintenance of value]

montos del 18% en préstamo
18% currency out on loan [IBRD maintenance of value]

montos retenidos en garantía
retention money

moratoria
tax deferral

mortalidad de niños menores de un año
infant mortality

mortalidad en la niñez [uno a cuatro años de edad]
child mortality

mortalidad infantil
infant mortality

motín
riot [MIGA]

motivación (política)
political entrepreneurship

movilización
harnessing

movilizar (fondos, etc.)
raise, to (funds, etc.)

movimiento
turnover

movimiento ascendente
upswing

movimiento de capital
capital flow; capital movement

movimiento de estudiantes, alumnos
student flow

movimiento del inventario, de las existencias
inventory turnover

movimiento descendente
downswing

movimientos de capital en condiciones no concesionarias
nonconcessional, nonconcessionary flows

muellaje
dockage; wharfage; wharfage charges

muestra aleatoria, al azar
random sample

muestra autoponderada
self-weighting sample

muestra representativa
cross section sample

muestreo por conglomerados, grupos
cluster sampling

multa
liquidated damages

multicopiado
processed

multiplicador del crédito
credit multiplier

multipropiedad
time sharing [computers]

necesidades de financiamiento del sector público
public sector borrowing requirement - PSBR

necesidades netas de efectivo
net cash requirements - NCR

necesidades sociales
social wants

negociación de bloques de acciones
block trading

negociación en pie de igualdad, entre iguales
arm's length negotiation

negociaciones arancelarias, sobre aranceles
tariff negotiations, round

negociaciones comerciales multilaterales
multilateral trade negotiations - MTN

negociaciones por vía expedita
fast-track procedures

nivel crítico de consumo - NCC
critical consumption level - CCL

nivel de alfabetización
literacy level

nivel de endeudamiento relativo al capital
leverage (ratio) [US]; gearing (ratio) [UK]

nivel de ingreso
entry level

nivel de ingreso(s)
income bracket

nivel de reemplazo, de renovación
replacement level [population]

nivel de vida
standard of living

nivel estable de préstamos
steady state lending

nivel freático
groundwater table

nivel impositivo
tax bracket

nivel sostenible de préstamos
sustainable level of lending - SLL

nivelación
flattening out; leveling off

niveles de supervisión
supervisory grades

niveles medios
supervisory grades

no contabilizado
unaccounted [e.g. water, electricity]

no disponible - n.d.
not available - n.a.

no especificado en otra parte - n.e.p.
not elsewhere specified - n.e.s.

no exportable o importable
nontradable [noun]

no garantizado
unsecured (note, loan, etc.)

no habilitado
ineligible

no indicado separadamente - n.i.s.
not included elsewhere - n.i.e.

no redimible antes del vencimiento
noncallable [bond]

no rescatable antes del vencimiento
noncallable [bond]

no se aplica - n.a.
not applicable - n.a.

nombramiento de plazo fijo
fixed term appointment

nombramiento ordinario, permanente
regular appointment [IBRD]

nombre genérico
nonproprietary name

nómina
payroll

norma (del Manual de Personal)
staff rule

norma de oferta firme
firm bid rule

normas de disciplina y control
prudential supervision and regulation

normas de diseño
design standards

normas de prudente discreción
prudent man rule

normas generales
guidelines

normativa
policy framework

nota sobre política económica
economic policy note [EDI]

nota técnica
technical note

notificación de desembolso
disbursement letter

notificación de impuestos
tax bill, demand

notificación de registro
notice of registration

nuclearización
nuclearization [education]

núcleo
hard core [projects]

núcleo habitacional
dwelling core

nueva circunstancia
development

nueva situación
development

numerario
numeraire

numerario del fondo común de monedas
pool unit

número de alumnos matriculados
enrollments

número de animales al final del período contable
closing stock [livestock]

número de estudiantes que pasan por el sistema escolar [educación]
throughput

nutrientes
nutrients

obligación contingente
contingent obligation

obligación tributaria
tax liability

obligaciones
liabilities

obligaciones a la vista
sight liabilities

obligaciones en, por concepto de depósitos
deposit liabilities

obligaciones relacionadas con el servicio de la deuda
debt service requirements

obligaciones sin financiamiento previsto
unfunded liabilities

obra gruesa
shell (of a building); structural work

obras civiles
civil works; public works

observación
monitoring

observación del desempeño, de los resultados
performance monitoring

obstáculo a la salida del mercado
exit barrier

obtención de cotizaciones
prudent shopping

obtención de empréstitos gigantescos
jumbo borrowing(s)

obtener (fondos, etc.)
raise, to (funds, etc.)

obtener cifras netas
net out

obtener un empréstito
float a loan, to

obtener un préstamo
secure a loan, to

octanaje
motor octane number - MON

ocupante sin título, ilegal, precario
squatter

ocupar terrenos ilegalmente, sin tener derecho
squat, to

oferta
tender

oferta alternativa
alternative bid [procurement]

oferta de acciones (con derecho preferencial de suscripción)
rights issue, offering

oferta de capital
capital supply

oferta evaluada como la más baja
lowest evaluated bid

oferta excesiva
oversupply

oferta fuera de plazo, tardía
late bid

oferta monetaria
money stock, supply

oferta no favorecida (con la adjudicación)
unsuccessful bid

oferta parcial
component bidding

oferta pública
borrowing from the public

oferta pública
public borrowing, offering

oferta pública de compra - OPT
takeover bid

oficial de desembolsos
disbursement officer

oficial de extensión de zona - OEZ
zone extension officer - ZEO [agricultural extension]

oficial de extensión, de divulgación agrícola
extension officer

oficial del préstamo, de préstamos
loan officer

oficial del proyecto, de proyectos
project officer

oficialización de la deuda
officialization (of debt)

oficina de centralización de trámites
one-stop agency, shop

oficina de impuestos
tax office

oficina del representante residente
resident office

oficina exterior, fuera de la sede
field office

oficinas en alquiler temporal
churn factor

oficinas provisionales
swing space

ofimática
office automation

oligopolio colusorio
collusive oligopoly

oligopolio colusorio explícito
(explicitly) collusive oligopoly

oncocercosis
onchocerciasis; river blindness

oncocercosis
river blindness; onchocerciasis

ONG autóctona
indigenous NGO

opción
trade-off

opción [proyectos]
alternative [projects]

opción a participar en el capital social
equity feature [IFC]

opción de compra
call option

opción de compra de acciones
stock option

opción de venta
put option

operación
venture [IFC]

operación bursátil
stock exchange transaction

operación concertada por, con un club bancario, consorcio
club deal

operación conjunta
joint venture

operación de compromiso de compra
standby commitment [IFC]

operación de demostración
demonstration activity

operación de garantía de emisión
underwriting commitment [IFC]

operación deficitaria
money-losing operation

operaciones "en reserva"
reserve operations [lending program]

operaciones de cobertura, de protección cambiaria
hedging

operaciones de pase [Argentina]
swap

operaciones invisibles
invisible transactions

operador(a) de tratamiento de textos
word processor

opinión jurídica
legal opinion

optimización de los recursos
value for money

óptimo de Pareto
Pareto optimum

orador principal
keynote speaker; keynoter

orden de compra
trading ticket [capital market]

orden de compra general
blanket purchase order - BPO

orden de proceder
notice to proceed [contracts]

orden de venta
trading ticket [capital market]

ordenación
control

ordenación de cuencas hidrográficas, de vertientes
watershed management

ordenación de las aguas
water management

ordenación de tierras áridas
dryland(s) management

ordenación de tierras de pastoreo
range management

ordenación forestal sostenible
sustainable forestry

ordenación monocíclica
monocyclic management

ordenación policíclica
polycyclic management

ordenación salarial
wage control

ordinaria, (partida)
above the line (item)

organismo afiliado de energía
energy affiliate

organismo agente de cobranza
billing agent

Organismo Anfitrión
Host Organization [ICSID]

organismo de centralización de trámites
one-stop agency, shop

organismo de clasificación de valores
rating agency

organismo de contrapartida
counterpart agency

organismo de crédito, crediticio
lending agency, institution

organismo de derecho público
statutory body

organismo de ejecución
executing agency [UNDP]; implementing agency

organismo de energía afiliado al Banco
energy affiliate

organismo del proyecto
project agency

organismo director, principal
lead agency

organismo especializado
specialized agency [UN]

organismo paraestatal
parastatal [noun]

organismo principal
parent body

organismo regulador
regulatory agency

organismo responsable del proyecto
project agency

organismo solicitante
Requesting Organization [ICSID]

organismos internacionales de productos básicos
international commodity bodies - ICBs

organización de base, comunitaria
grass roots organization

organización de medicina preventiva
health maintenance organization - HMO

organización gremial, patronal
trade organization

organización no gubernamental - ONG
nongovernmental organization - NGO

organización privada de voluntarios
private voluntary organization - PVO

organización sin fines de lucro
nonprofit organization; not-for-profit organization

organizaciones internacionales de productos básicos
international commodity organizations - ICOs

órgano decisorio, de decisión
decision-making body

órgano principal
parent body

orientación
student placement

orientación profesional
vocational guidance

orientado hacia el interior
inward-looking; inward-oriented [country; policy]

orientado hacia la exportación
export-oriented

orientar a grupos específicos
target, to

otras corrientes oficiales
other official flows - OOF

otros flujos oficiales
other official flows - OOF

óxido nitroso
nitrous oxide

óxidos de nitrógeno
nitrogen oxides (NO_x)

ozono estratosférico
stratospheric ozone

pagadero a la vista, contra presentación
payable on demand

pagaré
note [capital markets]; promissory note

pagaré a la vista
demand note

pagaré con interés variable, flotante
floating rate note

pagaré del Tesoro
Treasury note

pagaré del Tesoro a corto plazo
Treasury bill

pagaré descontado
discount note

pagaré no negociable
nonnegotiable note

pagaré participatorio
income note

pagaré que devenga intereses
interest bearing note

pagaré sin intereses
noninterest bearing note

pagarés con pago del principal vinculado a los tipos de cambio de diversas monedas
principal exchange rate linked securities notes

pago
consideration [legal, economic]

pago a cuenta
progress payment

pago al contado
cash payment

pago anticipado
advance payment

pago de cesantía
severance pay

pago de contrapartida
matching payment

pago en efectivo
cash payment

pago en el día
intra-day settlement

pago en especie
payment-in-kind - PIK

pago final, global
balloon payment

pago parcial
progress payment

pagos anticipados de exportaciones, por concepto de exportaciones
advanced export payments

pagos de transferencia
transfer payments

pagos en concepto de ingresos de los factores
factor income payments

pagos en mora
payment arrears

pagos internacionales corrientes
current international payments

pagos parciales por concepto de reintegro
recall installments [MOV]

país agobiado por la deuda
debt distressed country

país beneficiario, anfitrión
host country [MIGA]

país con economía de planificación centralizada
centrally planned economy (country)

país con superávit de capital
capital-surplus country

país de baja capacidad de absorción
low absorber [country]

país de desarrollo agroindustrial reciente
newly agro-industrialized economy - NAE

país de elevada absorción, de gran capacidad de absorción
high absorber [oil exporter]

país de franja litoral estrecha
coastal strip country

país de gran crecimiento económico
high performing economy

país de ingreso bajo
low income country

país de ingreso mediano
middle income country

país de ingreso mediano bajo
lower middle income country - LMIC

país de mediana capacidad de absorción
medium absorber [oil exporter]

país de nivel intermedio
second tier country

país de origen
home country [MIGA]

país de origen calificado
eligible source country

país de producción primaria
primary producing country

país de reciente industrialización, en vías de industrialización
newly industrializing country - NIC

país declarante, informante
reporting country

país deficitario
deficit country

país donante
donor country

país en desarrollo
less developed country - LDC

país en desarrollo no petrolero
nonoil developing country

país exportador de productos primarios
primary exporting country

país habilitado para recibir créditos de la AIF
IDA-eligible country

país industrial con economía de mercado
industrial market economy

país insular en desarrollo
developing island country; island developing country

país medianamente industrializado
halfway country

país menos desarrollado - PMD
less developed country - LDC

país muy endeudado, sumamente endeudado, fuertemente endeudado
highly indebted country

país no miembro y no declarante
nonreporting nonmember country

país orientado hacia el exterior
outward-looking, outward-oriented country

país parcialmente industrializado
halfway country

país prestatario de la AIF
IDA recipient

país que no influye en los precios internacionales
price taker

país que permite la contaminación sin restricciones
pollution haven

país que puede obtener financiamiento combinado (del BIRF y la AIF)
blend country

país que puede recibir créditos, financiamiento de la AIF
IDA-eligible country

país que recibió financiamiento para fines de ajuste antes de 1986
early intensive adjustment lending (EIAL) country

país que recurre a los servicios del Banco
client country

país receptor [inversiones]
host country [MIGA]

país receptor, beneficiario
recipient country

país receptor elegible
eligible host country [MIGA]

país recientemente industrializado
newly industrialized country - NIC

país(es) representado(s) por un Director Ejecutivo
chair, constituency of an Executive Director [World Bank]

país(es) representado(s) por un Director Ejecutivo
constituent(s) of an Executive Director

país sin litoral, mediterráneo
landlocked country

país solicitante
client country

país superavitario
capital-surplus country

país superavitario
surplus country

países ACP (Africa, el Caribe y el Pacífico)
ACP countries [Lomé Convention]

países asociados, que mantienen relaciones comerciales
partner countries

países de comercio estatal
state-trading countries

países de ingreso alto
high income countries

países de la Categoría I
Category I countries [IBRD]

países de la Categoría II
Category II countries [IBRD]

países de la Parte I
Part I countries [IBRD]

países de la Parte II
Part II countries [IBRD]

países de producción primaria
commodity producing countries

países del arco del Pacífico
Pacific Rim countries

países excluidos del régimen de contabilidad en valores devengados
countries in nonaccrual status

países inmediatamente afectados
most immediately impacted (MII) countries

países más gravemente afectados
most seriously affected countries - MSA

países (en desarrollo) menos adelantados - PMA
least developed countries - LLDCs

países que mantienen relaciones comerciales
trading partners

países que reciben financiamiento en condiciones predominantemente gravosas
hard-blend countries

países que se encuentran "en el umbral"
threshold countries

países que sólo reciben financiamiento de la AIF
pure IDA countries

países que tienen acceso al mercado financiero
market-eligible countries

países representado(s) por un Director Ejecutivo; jurisdicción
constituency, chair of an Executive Director

papel comercial
commercial bills; commercial paper

papeles de comercio
commercial bills; commercial paper

paquete financiero
financial package

paraíso tributario
tax haven

parámetro de cambio
shift parameter

parámetros de planificación presupuestaria
Budget Planning Framework [IBRD]

parcela de demostración
demonstration plot

parcela de prueba
test plot

parcela testigo, de control
controlled plot; control plot

parcialmente montado
partly knocked down - PKD

paridad
par value

paridad del poder adquisitivo
purchasing power parity - PPP

paridad móvil
crawling peg [rate of exchange]

parque
fleet [transportation]

parque industrial
industrial estate [UK], park [USA]

parte (en el procedimiento o en la diferencia)
party (to proceeding or to the dispute) [ICSID]

partes interesadas
stakeholders

participación de fundador
founder's share

participación de la mujer en el proceso de desarrollo
women in development - WID

participación del concesionario
working interest [oils, minerals]

participación en (el) capital social
equity financing, investment

participación en cada uno de los vencimientos (de un préstamo)
strip participation

participación en el capital social
equity ownership

participación en el financiamiento de los costos, gastos [beneficiarios]
burden sharing

participación en inversiones inmobiliarias
real estate equity

participación en la carga
burden sharing

participación en las ganancias, utilidades netas
net profits interest [oil]

participación en las utilidades
profit sharing

participación en los costos
cost sharing

participación en los impuestos
tax sharing

participación en los ingresos (fiscales)
revenue sharing

participación en una inversión
exposure

participación mayoritaria
controlling interest

participación pasiva
carried interest [petroleum industry]

participación proporcional
funding pro rata

participación sin posibilidad de recurso
nonrecourse participation

participante en un curso o programa de capacitación
trainee

participar en el capital social
share capital, to supply

partículas
particulate matter - PM

partículas en suspensión
suspended particulate matter - SPM

partida
item [budget]

partida (presupuestaria)
line item [budget]

partida arancelaria
tariff item; tariff position

partida compensatoria
balancing item, entry

partida de memorando
memorandum entry, item; memo item

partida de reconciliación
reconciliation item [accounting]

partida de transacción no monetaria
noncash item

partida extraordinaria
below the line (item)

partida informativa
memorandum entry, item; memo item

partida ordinaria
above the line (item)

partida pro memoria
memorandum entry, item; memo item

partidas que se compensan mutuamente
mutually offsetting entries

pasantía
internship

pasar de las condiciones de asistencia de la AIF a las del Banco
graduate, to [Bank, IDA]

pasar el punto más bajo
bottom out (of a recession)

pasivo
liabilities

pasivo acumulado
accrued liabilities

pasivo contingente
contingent liability

pasivo corriente
current liabilities

pasivo exigible a corto plazo
current liabilities

pasivos a largo plazo
long-term liabilities

pasivos monetarios
currency liabilities

pasivos transitorios
temporary liabilities

pasivos varios
sundry liabilities

paso gradual a tasas impositivas más altas
bracket creep, progression [taxation]

pastor nómada
pastoralist

pastoreo excesivo
overgrazing

patio de maniobra, de clasificación
marshalling yard

patrimonio
stockholders' equity; shareholders' equity; owners' equity; equity; net worth

patrimonio (neto)
equity

patrimonio natural de la humanidad
global commons

patrimonio neto
stockholders' equity; shareholders' equity; owners' equity; equity; net worth

patrocinador
sponsor

pauta cronológica
time pattern

pautas generales
guidelines

penalidades
liquidated damages

pendiente (de una curva)
steepness (of a curve)

pensión
retirement benefits

peón caminero
lengthman [highway maintenance]

pequeña empresa
small-scale enterprise - SSE

pequeña explotación agrícola
smallholding

pequeña industria
small-scale industry - SSI

pequeña y mediana empresa - PYME
small and medium enterprises - SME; small- and medium-scale enterprises - SMSE

pequeña y mediana industria
small and medium industries - SMI; small- and medium-scale industries - SMSI

pequeña zona, pequeño proyecto de riego
small-scale irrigation

pequeño agricultor
smallholder

pérdida
loss in weight; waste [commerce]

pérdida
waste; loss in weight [commerce]

pérdida cambiaria
exchange discount

pérdida de capital
capital loss

pérdidas de explotación, de operación
operating losses

pérdidas de peso muerto
deadweight (losses)

perdido
unaccounted [e.g. water, electricity]

perfeccionamiento
delivery (of a contract); upgrading of skills

perfeccionamiento de la función de gestión
management development

perfeccionamiento de los recursos humanos
human resource development

perfeccionamiento de recursos humanos, de la mano de obra
manpower development

perfeccionamiento del personal
staff development

perfeccionamiento del personal directivo
management development

perfiles ocupacionales normalizados
standardized occupational streams

perforación
drilling

perforación de explotación
development drilling

perforación exploratoria
wildcat (drilling)

perforación submarina, mar adentro
offshore drilling

pericia
expertise

período contable
accounting period

período de cumplimiento de obligaciones
performance period

período de eliminación gradual de los préstamos del Banco
phase out period [IBRD]

período de gestación de un proyecto
lead time of a project

período de gracia
grace period

período de sesiones
session [ICSID]

período exceptuado
excepted period

período previo a la exclusión del régimen de contabilidad en valores devengados
nonaccrual trigger point, date

período vegetativo, de crecimiento
growing period

peritaje
expert appraisal

permanencia (en el cargo)
tenure [education]

permiso negociable de contaminación
tradable emissions permit

persona a cargo
dependent

persona jurídica
corporate body, institution; body corporate; legal
entity, person

persona que recibe adiestramiento
trainee

persona responsable de adoptar decisiones
decision-maker

personal
staff

personal contratado a plazo fijo
fixed term staff

personal de contrapartida
counterpart staff

**personal de las oficinas exteriores, fuera de la
sede**
field staff

personal de nivel profesional
higher level staff

personal de supervisión
supervisory staff

personal ejecutivo, de operaciones
line staff

personal en el terreno
field staff

personal no permanente
nonregular staff - NRS

personal permanente
regular staff

personalidad jurídica
legal existence; juridical personality

personas que viven en la pobreza absoluta
absolute poor

perturbaciones del medio ambiente
environmental stress

pesca
capture fishery; harvest fishery

pesca con luz (artificial), al encandilado
lamplight fishing; fishing by lamplight

pesca con luz artificial, al encandilado
fishing by lamplight; lamplight fishing

pesca con trasmallos
trammel fishing

pesca de altura
deep sea fishing

pesca de arrastre
trawl fishing

pesca de deriva
drift fishing

pesca (con redes) de tiro
seine fishing

pesca en aguas interiores
inland fisheries, fishing

pesca fantasma
ghost fishing

pesca por enmalle
gill fishing

peso muerto
deadweight (losses)

petróleo combustible pesado
heavy fuel oil

petróleo crudo liviano
Saudi Arabian light (crude oil); light Arabian
crude

petróleo crudo liviano, ligero de Arabia Saudita
light Arabian crude; Saudi Arabian light crude

petróleo para calefacción
heating oil

petróleo pesado
heavy oil

petróleo residual, combustible
fuel oil

PIB comercial
commercial, commercialized GDP

PIB monetizado
monetized GDP

PIB sectorial
sector GDP

pila de combustible
fuel cell

piquetear
peg out, to [surveying]

piscicultura
culture fishery

plan contractual
program contract

plan de acceso anticipado a las aportaciones
advance contribution scheme (for IDA-10)

plan de acción nacional relacionado con la función de la mujer en el proceso de desarrollo
country WID action plan

plan de actividades (empresariales)
business plan

plan de amortización
amortization schedule; repayment schedule

plan de cuentas
chart of accounts

plan de distribución
layout plan

plan de estudios
curriculum

plan de estudios común
core curriculum

plan de existencias reguladoras
buffer stock scheme

plan de financiamiento
financing plan

plan de jubilación anticipada
early retirement scheme

plan de jubilación mínima
top-up scheme; minimum pension guarantee

plan de ordenación ambiental
mitigation plan; environmental management plan; action plan

plan de pagos
payment schedule

plan de pensiones según, conforme a las necesidades, con comprobación previa de medios de vida
means-tested pension plan

plan de protección ambiental
environmental action plan - EAP

plan de seguridad social
social security scheme

plan de seguro global
"wrap-up" insurance arrangement

plan de sucesión para cargos de dirección
management succession planning

plan de utilización de tierras
land use plan

plan de vivienda por el sistema de esfuerzo propio y ayuda mutua
self-help housing scheme

plan financiero
finance plan; financial plan

plan maestro
master plan

plan modelo de presupuesto de finca
pattern farm plan

plan nacional de protección ambiental - PNPA
national environmental action plan - NEAP

plan para situaciones imprevistas
contingency plan

plan presupuestario
agreed budget plan; contract plan

plan preventivo
mitigation plan; environmental management plan;
action plan

plan renovable
rolling plan

**planificación de recursos humanos, de la mano
de obra**
manpower planning

planificación de tierras
land use planning

planificación del avance profesional
career development

planificación del desarrollo
development planning

planificación del espacio físico
physical planning

planificación detallada
blueprint planning

planificación familiar, de la familia
family planning

planificación global, agregativa
aggregative planning

planificación global, integral
comprehensive planning

planificación obligatoria, preceptiva
mandatory planning

**planificación presupuestaria en valores de caja,
en efectivo**
cash-based budget planning

planificación presupuestaria nominal
(full cost) nominal budget planning, budgeting

**planificación y evaluación del desempeño (del
funcionario)**
Performance Planning and Review - PPR [IBRD]

planificador de obras, de instalaciones
physical planner

planificador del desarrollo
development planner

planilla de cálculo electrónica
spreadsheet

plano
design

plano del emplazamiento, del lugar
site plan

planos definitivos
final design

planos generales (de un proyecto)
layout

planos preliminares
preliminary design, engineering

planos técnicos detallados
detailed design, engineering

planta alimentaria
food plant

planta de elaboración secundaria [petróleo]
downstream plant, facilities

planta de semillero, vivero
seedling

planta de simiente
seed plant

planta de tratamiento de aguas negras, servidas
sewage (treatment) plant

planta eléctrica diesel
diesel (fired) power plant

planta para semilla
seed plant

planta textil
fiber crop

planta totalmente nueva
greenfield plant; grass root plant

plantación cortavientos
windbreak

plantación de árboles
afforestation

plantación de bosques comunitarios
social forestry

plantación en franjas
strip planting

plantación núcleo
nucleus estate

plantón (de árboles)
seedling

plántula
seedling

plataforma de perforación petrolera [mar.]
oil (drilling) rig, platform

plazo
time limit [ICSID]

plazo de amortización, de reembolso
payback period

plazo de recuperación (de inversiones)
payback period

plazo de vencimiento
maturity (of a loan, bond, etc.)

pliego de condiciones de la licitación
bidding conditions

plusvalía
capital gain

población activa
working population

población en edad de trabajar
working age population

poblaciones indígenas
tribal peoples

poder (jurídico)
proxy

poder calorífico
heat value

poder calorífico bruto - PCB
gross heating value - GHV; gross calorific value - GCV; higher heating value

poder calorífico neto - PCN
net heating value - NHV; net calorific value - NCV; lower heating value

polígono industrial
industrial estate [UK], park [USA]

política
policy-based assistance

política cambiaria
exchange rate policy

política comercial restrictiva
restrictive trade policy

política coyuntural
business cycle policy

política crediticia restrictiva
tight credit policy

política de austeridad
restraint policy

política de avance intermitente
stop-go, stop and go policy

política de contracción
contractionary policy

política de empobrecer al vecino
beggar-my-neighbor policy

política de precios
pricing policy

política de reactivación
pump priming policy [economics]

política de restricción crediticia
tight credit policy

política de servicios gratuitos
zero fee policy

política expansionista
expansionary policy

política favorable a la economía de la oferta
supply side politics

política fiscal
fiscal policy

política subóptima
second-best policy

política tarifaria
pricing policy

políticas
policy-based assistance

políticas de reasignación de recursos
switching policies

póliza de seguro global
wrap-up insurance policy

ponderación distributiva
distributional weight

poner en servicio
commission, to

por administración
force account, by/on [US]; direct labour [UK];
direct work; departmental forces

por encima de la cuota
above quota

porcentaje de préstamos excluidos del régimen de contabilidad en valores devengados
nonaccrual rate [World Bank]

porcentaje de reserva mínima obligatoria
minimum cash requirement

porcentaje estándar para el establecimiento de reservas para pérdidas
benchmark provisioning rate

porcentaje garantizado
guaranteed percentage

porción
slice [contracts]

porción de cada uno de los vencimientos de un préstamo
strip of maturities

poscalificación de licitantes
postqualification of bidders

posibilidad de capacitación
trainability [EDI-World Bank]

posibilidad de colocación
saleability [securities]

posibilidad de comercialización, de colocación
marketability

posibilidad de extracción
subtractability

posibilidad de repetición financiera
financial replicability

posibilidad de repetición, de duplicación
replicability

posición de balanza de pagos
balance of payments position

posición de capital
capital position

posición de reserva(s)
reserve position

posición de riesgo
risk posture

potenciación
empowerment

potencial de agotamiento de la capa de ozono - PAO
ozone-depleting potential - ODP

potencial de recalentamiento atmosférico, de la Tierra
global warming potential - GWP

pozo de ozono
ozone sink

pozo entubado
tubewell

pozo exploratorio
wildcat well

práctica óptima
best practice

práctica(s)
internship

prácticas contables
accounting practices

prácticas de avalúo aduanero, de aduana
customs valuation (practices)

preámbulo de un convenio
preamble to an agreement; recital of an agreement

preámbulo de un convenio
recital of an agreement; preamble to an agreement

precalificación de licitantes
prequalification of bidders

precedente establecido por Brasil y Yugoslavia
Brazil-Yugoslavia Precedents

precio a nivel de la explotación agrícola
farm gate price

precio administrado, controlado, impuesto
administered price

precio al consumidor
consumer price

precio al contado, para entrega inmediata
spot price

precio al desembarque
landed price

precio al productor
producer price

precio c.i.f./puerto de entrada
cost, insurance and freight (CIF) port of entry/border point price

precio contractual
contract price

precio corriente, vigente
going price

precio de compra, de adquisición
historical cost

precio de compuerta [avicultura]
lock gate price; sluice price; sluice gate price

precio de costo
cost price

precio de cuenta
accounting price; shadow price

precio de eficiencia
economic price; efficiency price

precio de incentivo
incentive price

precio de intervención
intervention price

precio de lista, cotizado, de cotización
posted price [oil]

precio de los factores
factor price

precio de mercado, de plena competencia
arm's length price

precio de necesidad
distress price

precio de oferta
bid price [contract]

precio de paridad
parity price

precio de referencia
benchmark price; marker price [oil]

**precio de referencia para fines tributarios
[petróleo]**
tax reference price [oil]

precio de reserva
reservation price (of labor)

precio de sostén, de apoyo, de sustentación
support price

precio de transferencia
transfer price

precio de venta
selling rate

precio desleal
predatory price

precio económico
economic price; efficiency price

precio efectivo, de realización
realized price [oil]

precio en (la) frontera
border price

precio en almacén
off-the-shelf price

precio en el exterior
foreign price

precio en fábrica
ex factory price; price ex factory; factory gate price

precio en la boca, en la cabeza del pozo
wellhead price

precio f.o.b. puerto de embarque
free on board (FOB) port of shipment price

precio global
lump sum price

precio indicativo
guiding price; target price

precio mínimo
floor price

precio neto
payout price

precio nominal, simbólico
nominal price

precio paritario de exportación
export parity price

precio paritario de importación
import parity price

precio por pie
stumpage price

precio puesto en fábrica
price to factory

precio recibido por el productor
producer price

precio social
social price

precio sombra
shadow price

precio tope, máximo
ceiling price

precio umbral
threshold price

precio unitario
unit cost

precio vendedor
selling rate

precios constantes
constant prices

precios corrientes
current prices

precios de equilibrio del mercado
market-clearing prices

precios en plaza (lista de)
posted values

precipitador
precipitator; dust collector; dust separator

predisposición
bias [economy; statistics]

preferencia
margin of preference; preference, preferential
margin

preferencia por los amigos
cronyism

preferencia por los productos nacionales
domestic preference; preference margin;
preferential margin; margin of preference
[procurement]

prefinanciamiento
prefinancing

prelectura
pre-reading

preparación
development

preparación de un proyecto, de proyectos
project design; project preparation

preparación del terreno
site development

preparación técnica
technical background

presa de almacenamiento
storage dam

presa de derivación
diversion dam

presa de terraplén
earthfill dam

prescindencia
redundancy [staffing]

presentación de ofertas
bid submission; delivery of bids

presentación de reclamaciones
filing of claims [MIGA]

presentaciones [demandas, alegatos, etc.]
pleadings [ICSID]

presentar y ofrecer pruebas
marshal evidence, to [ICSID]

presidente en funciones
serving chairman

presión de los salarios
wage pressure

presión fiscal
tax burden

prestación de cesantía
severance pay

prestaciones
benefits [social security]

prestaciones de (la) seguridad social
social security benefits

prestaciones sociales
social benefits

prestaciones suplementarias
fringe benefits

prestamista en última instancia
lender of last resort

prestamista subordinado
subordinate lender

préstamo "A"
"A" loan

préstamo a corto plazo para salvar una dificultad temporal
carryover loan

préstamo a la vista
call loan

préstamo a mediano o largo plazo
term loan

préstamo a un intermediario financiero
financial intermediary loan - FIL

préstamo activo
active loan

préstamo (para fines de) ajuste de la política de comercio exterior
trade adjustment loan

préstamo amortizable en su mayor parte al vencimiento
balloon loan

préstamo anterior al sistema del fondo común de monedas
prepool loan

préstamo "B"
"B" loan

préstamo "balloon"
balloon loan

préstamo bancario de primera categoría
top-rated bank loan

préstamo cofinanciado
coloan

préstamo complementario
repeater loan

préstamo con interés tope
cap

préstamo con riesgo de posibles pérdidas
jeopardy loan

préstamo con vencimiento elegido a la suerte
serial loan

préstamo concedido por un club bancario, por un consorcio
club loan

préstamo contingente
standby loan

préstamo convertible en acciones de capital [CFI]
equity feature [IFC]

préstamo cuyo vencimiento se ha anticipado
prematured loan

préstamo de amortización negativa
negative amortization loan

préstamo de aprobación autónoma
free-limit loan [DFCs]

préstamo de calidad
quality loan [IBRD]

préstamo de contrapartida con tasa fija
fixed rate matched funding loan

préstamo de emergencia
bailout loan

préstamo de emergencia para recuperación
emergency recovery loan - ERL

préstamo de rápido desembolso
quick disbursing (loan); fast disbursing (loan)

préstamo de suma global
lump sum loan

préstamo de un consorcio, concedido por un consorcio
syndicated loan

préstamo de vencimiento escalonado
serial loan

préstamo en condiciones concesionarias, blando, liberal
soft loan

préstamo en condiciones ordinarias, de mercado
hard loan

préstamo (que se halla) en dificultades
distressed loan

préstamo en especie
commodity loan

préstamo en forma de participación en el capital
equity loan

préstamo en pirámide, en cascada
apex loan

préstamo en tramitación
pipeline loan

préstamo en una sola moneda
single currency loans, [IBRD]

préstamo en valores
security lending

préstamo garantizado
secured loan

préstamo inactivo
inactive loan

préstamo incluido en el sistema de fondo común de monedas
pooled loan

préstamo independiente, autónomo
free-standing loan

préstamo indizado, reajustado según un índice
indexed, index-linked, index-tied loan

préstamo no redituable, improductivo
nonperforming loan; nonaccruing loan

préstamo para ajuste de la(s) política(s) industrial y comercial
industrial and trade policy adjustment loan - ITPAL [World Bank]

préstamo para ajuste del sector agrícola
agricultural sector adjustment loan - ASAL [World Bank]

préstamo para ajuste del sector exportador, de exportación
export adjustment loan - EAL

préstamo para (fines de) ajuste sectorial
sector adjustment loan - SECAL; SAD

préstamo para asistencia técnica
technical assistance loan - TAL

préstamo para capital de trabajo
working capital loan

préstamo para cubrir posibles excesos de costos
overage loan

préstamo para importaciones con fines de rehabilitación
rehabilitation import loan

préstamo para inversión y mantenimiento sectoriales
sector investment and maintenance loan - SIM

préstamo para programas
program loan, lending

préstamo para programas de un país, de países
country loan [IBRD]

préstamo para proyecto de inversión
investment loan

préstamo para racionalización de empresas públicas
public enterprise rationalization loan - PERL

préstamo para reconstrucción de emergencia
emergency reconstruction loan - ERL

préstamo para recuperación económica
economic recovery loan - ERL [World Bank]

préstamo para reforma de empresas públicas
public enterprise reform loan - PERL

préstamo para rehabilitación de empresas públicas
public enterprise rehabilitation loan - PERL

préstamo para un proyecto, para proyectos
project loan, lending

préstamo para una inversión específica
specific investment loan - SIL [IBRD]

préstamo participatorio con obligación contingente de pago de intereses
deferrable participating loan

préstamo poco rentable, de escaso rendimiento
badly performing loan

préstamo por etapas
time-slice loan

préstamo prioritario
senior debt, loan

préstamo problemático
problem loan [IFC]

préstamo que entraña un riesgo soberano
sovereign risk loan

préstamo representado por obligaciones convertibles [CFI]
convertible debenture loan investment [IFC]

préstamo sectorial, para un sector
sector loan

préstamo sin finalidad específica
nonpurpose loan

préstamo sólido, seguro
sound loan

préstamo subordinado
subordinated loan

préstamo subsidiario
subsidiary loan

préstamo transitorio, de transición, "puente"
bridge, bridging loan

préstamos (a un país) desembolsados y pendientes
country exposure [IBRD]

préstamos en apoyo de reformas de políticas
policy-based lending; policy loans [IBRD]

préstamos en condiciones comerciales
commercial lending

préstamos en moneda única
single currency loans, [IBRD]

préstamos hipotecarios
mortgage financing

préstamos no voluntarios
involuntary lending

préstamos obtenidos de intermediarios financieros
intermediative borrowing

préstamos para (fines de) ajuste estructural
structural adjustment lending - SAL

préstamos pendientes
exposure; outstanding loans

préstamos voluntarios
voluntary lending; spontaneous lending

prestar de nuevo (el importe de un préstamo)
onlend, to

prestar de nuevo (el importe de un préstamo)
relend, to

prestatario activo
active borrower

prestatario inactivo
inactive borrower, nonactive borrower

prestatario preferencial, preferente, de primera clase
prime borrower; premier borrower

presupuestación a partir de cero
zero base budgeting - ZBB

presupuestación completa
full budgeting

presupuestación en dólares constantes
constant dollar budgeting

presupuestación en dólares corrientes
current dollar budgeting

presupuestación incremental
incremental budgeting

presupuesto
cost estimate; resource envelope

presupuesto (de una unidad del Banco)
unit budget envelope

presupuesto basado en los costos efectivos
dollar budgeting

presupuesto bruto
gross budget

presupuesto de caja
cash budget

presupuesto de capital
capital budget

presupuesto de divisas
exchange budget

presupuesto de explotación, operación
operating budget

presupuesto de gastos discrecionales
discretionary expense budget

presupuesto de gastos generales directos
direct overhead budget

presupuesto de inversiones
investment budget

presupuesto de la explotación agrícola
farm budget

presupuesto extraordinario
extraordinary budget; special budget

presupuesto global de la explotación agrícola
whole farm budget

presupuesto igual, sin cambio, sin aumento
flat budget

presupuesto multianual
forward budgeting

presupuesto ordinario
regular budget

presupuesto ordinario, corriente
current budget

presupuesto para programas reembolsables
reimbursable budget

presupuesto parcial
partial budget

presupuesto por funciones
performance budget

presupuesto por programas
program budget

presupuesto por unidad de actividad
unit activity (crop) budget

prevalencia
prevalence [disease]

previsión social
social insurance

previsiones de caja
cash forecast

previsiones inflacionarias
inflationary expectations

previsiones para fines de planificación
planning forecasts

prima
bonus; incentive payment; premium [MIGA];
premium [securities]

prima cambiaria
exchange premium

prima contingente
standby premium [MIGA]

prima de, por calidad
quality premium

prima de emisión
premium [stocks]

prima de inflación
inflation premium

prima por descarga rápida
despatch money; dispatch money

prima por reembolso anticipado
premium on prepayment [IBRD]

prima por trabajo en el exterior
overseas allowance

primer memorando oficial
initiating memorandum - IM [World Bank]

primeros procesos
upstream process

principal
principal

principal sostén económico
principal (income) earner

principales productos básicos, primarios
core commodities [IBRD]

principiante
trainee

principio de proporcionalidad
pro rata rules [IDA]

principio de quién contamina paga
polluter-pays principle - PPP

**principio de utilización de los fondos del Banco
en primera instancia**
"Bank first" principle

**principio de utilización de los fondos del Banco
en última instancia**
"Bank last" principle

**principio del trato entre iguales, entre
compañías independientes**
arm's length principle

principios relativos al empleo del personal
Principles of Staff Employment [World Bank]

privatización
divestiture; divestment

privatización mediante cupones
voucher privatization

probabilidad de pérdida de carga
loss of load probability - LOLP

problema de las colas
queuing theory, problem

**problemas de cobertura efectiva, de
incorporación al plan, de participación en el
plan**
take-up problems (of means-tested pension plans)

problemas iniciales
teething problems

procedimiento contable, de contabilidad
accounting procedure

procedimiento de aprobación tácita
"no objection" (procedure)

procedimiento de dos sobres
two-envelope procedure [consultants]

procedimiento oral
oral procedure [ICSID]

procedimiento simplificado (para proyectos...)
streamlined project procedure

procedimientos de adquisición
procurement (procedures)

procedimientos separados
two-stage, two-step procedure [IBRD]

proceso de evaluación del desempeño (del funcionario)
Performance Management Process - PMP

proceso presupuestario
budget process

producción
output

producción a escala comercial
commercial production

producción a que se renuncia
forgone output; foregone output

producción agrícola, de cultivos
crop production

producción alimentaria, de alimentos
food production

producción antieconómica
uneconomic production

producción combinada de calor y electricidad
combined heat and power - CHP

producción de abonos a partir de desechos
composting

producción de alimentos para consumo propio
autoconsumption of food

producción en gran escala, en serie
mass production

producción medida, efectiva
measured production

producir efecto multiplicador [finanzas]
leverage, to

productividad del capital
capital efficiency

productividad marginal del capital
marginal efficiency of capital

productividad total de los factores
total factor productivity - TFP

producto
output; proceeds

producto agrícola bruto
gross value product - GVP

producto agrícola para elaboración de bebidas
beverage crop

producto básico agrícola no alimentario
non-food agricultural commodity

producto básico, primario
commodity

producto de marca registrada
brand name product

producto destinado por su propia índole a determinados grupos de la población
self-targeting (commodity)

producto estrella
flagship product

producto farmacéutico genérico
generic drug

producto físico marginal
marginal physical product - MPP

producto geográfico bruto - PGB [Chile]
gross domestic product - GDP

producto interno ajustado conforme a consideraciones ambientales - PIA
environmentally adjusted domestic product - EDP

producto interno bruto - PIB
gross domestic product - GDP

producto interno bruto a precios de mercado
gross domestic product at market prices

producto interno bruto al costo de los factores
gross domestic product at factor cost

producto material bruto - PMB
gross material product - GMP

producto material neto - PMN
net material product - NMP

producto nacional bruto - PNB
gross national product - GNP

producto nacional neto sostenible - PNNS
sustainable net national product - SNNP

producto primario, básico
primary product, commodity

producto sensible a la coyuntura
sensitive product

producto territorial bruto [Perú]
gross domestic product - GDP

producto útil neto
net beneficial product

productor compensador, de compensación
swing producer

productos agrícolas
crops

productos alimentarios
foodstuffs

productos industriales
industrial goods

productos pesados
heavy commodities

programa
schedule

programa (de financiamiento) básico
base (lending) program [IBRD]

programa (de financiamiento) de reserva
standby (lending) program [IBRD]

programa cuya magnitud depende del volumen de actividad
volume driven program

programa de alcance exterior, de extensión, de divulgación
outreach program

programa de alimentos por trabajo
food-for-work programme

programa de atención especial
program of special emphasis - PSE

programa de cooperación
cooperative program

programa de demanda de alimentos
food demand program

Programa de Desarrollo de la Capacidad de Evaluación Ex Post
Evaluation Capability Development Program - ECDP [IBRD]

programa de eliminación gradual de los préstamos del Banco
phase out program [IBRD]

programa de financiamiento
lending program

Programa de intervenciones dirigidas
Program of Targeted Interventions

programa de medidas, etc.
package

programa de medidas de rescate, de salvamento
rescue package

programa de operaciones
operating program [IBRD]

programa de operaciones crediticias
lending program

programa de "quinta dimensión"
Fifth Dimension Program

programa de reestructuración de la deuda
debt work-out program [World Bank]

programa de ventas subvencionadas
social marketing program [population]

programa integrado de capacitación y
perfeccionamiento de funcionarios que ocupan
cargos de dirección
integrated management training program

programa ordinario de financiamiento
regular lending program [IBRD]

Programa para la Maternidad sin Riesgos
Safe Motherhood Initiative [IBRD/WHO]

programación lineal
linear programming

programas
software

programas de fortalecimiento institucional
institutional programs [IBRD]

programas focalizados, dirigidos a grupos
específicos
targeted programs

programas preparados por el gobierno mismo
government-owned programs

progresividad arancelaria
tariff escalation

progreso
development

proliferación de algas
algae, algal bloom

proliferación de asentamientos urbanos
urban sprinkling

promediados
rolled (costs)

promedio móvil
running average; moving average

promedio ponderado
weighted average

promesa de contribuciones
pledging

promesa de participación en el capital
accionario
pledge (of shares) [IFC]

promoción de la autonomía
empowerment

promoción del comercio
trade promotion

promotor
motivator [family planning]; outreach worker;
sponsor

promotor inmobiliario
real estate developer

propensión marginal (al consumo, al ahorro,
etc.)
marginal propensity (to consume, to save, etc.)

propietario registrado
record owner

proporción de importaciones sujetas a barreras
no arancelarias
trade coverage ratio

propietarios de las acciones
ownership (of a corporation)

propuesta
tender

propuesta de candidatura
nomination

prospecto
prospectus [financial markets]

proyección del flujo de fondos
cash projections

proyectista
designer

proyecto
design

proyecto agropecuario; proyecto de cultivos múltiples
mixed farming project

proyecto aislado
outlier project

proyecto básico
core project

proyecto compensatorio
shadow project

proyecto complementario
follow-up project

proyecto complementario
repeater project

proyecto concatenado
piggyback project

proyecto de alcantarillado
sewerage project

proyecto de ámbito nacional
country-wide project

proyecto de carácter social
soft project

Proyecto de Comparación Internacional - PCI
International Comparison Project - ICP

proyecto de contenido mínimo
minimum package project

proyecto de desarrollo rural integrado
integrated rural development project

proyecto de exposición
showcase project

proyecto de fines múltiples
multipurpose project

proyecto de inversión
investment project

proyecto de muy corto plazo, relámpago
hit-and-run project

proyecto de "nuevo estilo"
"new style" project [IBRD]

proyecto de presupuesto
budget estimates

proyecto de rápido rendimiento
quick yielding project [IBRD]

proyecto de rehabilitación del sector exportador, de exportación
export rehabilitation project - ERP [IBRD]

proyecto emprendido a instancias gubernamentales
behest project

proyecto en avanzado estado de ejecución, próximo a terminarse
mature project

proyecto en que se hará todo lo posible para lograr la participación de la mujer
"best effort" project [IBRD]

proyecto en tramitación, en reserva
pipeline project

proyecto en un sector específico
area specific project

proyecto enclave
enclave project

proyecto financiable (por el Banco)
bankable project

proyecto global
umbrella project

proyecto independiente
stand-alone project

proyecto independiente, autónomo
free-standing project

proyecto integrado de conservación y desarrollo
integrated conservation-development project - ICDP

proyecto llave en mano
turnkey contract, project

proyecto modelo
good practice project

proyecto no básico
noncore project

proyecto no incluido en la cartera
nonportfolio project [IFC]

proyecto puntero, de punta
flagship project

proyecto que se autofinancia
self-liquidating project

proyecto que sirve de marco para otros
umbrella project

proyecto totalmente nuevo
greenfield project

proyectos azules
blue projects

proyectos en tramitación, en reserva
lending pipeline; pipeline of projects

proyectos en tramitación, en reserva
pipeline of projects; lending pipeline; project
pipeline

proyectos en tramitación, en reserva
project pipeline; pipeline of projects; lending
pipeline

proyectos marrones, pardos
brown projects

proyectos verdes
green projects

prueba
evidence [ICSID]

prueba de "antes y después"
"before-and-after" test

prueba de "con y sin"
"with-and-without" test [projects]

prueba de variedad(es)
variety trial

prueba del rendimiento de los proyectos
yield test of projects

**pruebas de aprovechamiento, de progreso
escolar, de rendimiento**
achievement tests [education]

pruebas documentales
documentary evidence

**publicación especializada para determinada
industria, negocio o profesión**
trade publication

publicación estrella
flagship product

publicación mediante microcomputadora
desktop publishing

pueblos tribales
tribal peoples

puente-báscula
weighbridge

puerto de aguas profundas
deep water port

puerto franco, libre
free port

puesto de atraque de fines múltiples
multipurpose berth

puesto de monta
service station [livestock]

puesto de monta, de cubrición, de reproducción
breeding station [commercial breeding]

puesto de salud
health post

puesto de venta de productos subvencionados
fair price shop

puesto ejecutivo, de operaciones
line position

punto (porcentual)
percentage point

punto máximo estacional
seasonal peak

punto muerto, de equilibrio
breakeven point

que genera deudas
debt-creating

que impone los precios
price leader, setter, maker

que impone los precios
price maker, setter, leader

que impone los precios
price setter, maker, leader

que no afecta al presupuesto
budget neutral

que no cumple los requisitos
ineligible

que no se ajusta (a las estipulaciones, normas, etc.)
nonresponsive

que se ajusta (a las estipulaciones), normas, etc.
responsive

que se beneficia sin asumir carga alguna
free rider [economics]

que tiene en cuenta...
responsive

quema de gas
gas flaring

racimo de frutas frescas
fresh fruit bunch - FFB

racionalización
streamlining

raíces alimentarias
root crops

ramo
business line

rápido desembolso
quick disbursing (loan); fast disbursing (loan)

rápido desembolso, préstamo de
fast disbursing (loan); quick disbursing (loan)

raza
breed [livestock]

reactivación
recovery; upturn (economic)

readiestramiento
retraining

reajuste
adjustment

reajuste financiero
financial adjustment

reaseguro contractual
treaty reinsurance

reaseguro facultativo
facultative reinsurance

reaseguros
reinsurance

reasentamiento involuntario
involuntary resettlement

reasignación (de fondos)
redeployment (of funds)

reasignación de fondos presupuestarios
input switching

rebaja de intereses
interest rebate

rebajar de categoría
downgrade, to (a loan)

rebajar el valor en libros
write down, to; expense, to

rebeldía (únicamente en el sentido del Art. 45[2] del Convenio)
default [ICSID]

rebrote
regrowth

recalentamiento atmosférico, de la Tierra
global warming

recargo a la(s) importación(es)
import surcharge

recargo o multa para reducir las emisiones de carbono
carbon tax

recargo tributario
tax surcharge

recaudación de impuestos
collection of taxes

recaudación tributaria
tax yield

receptor de créditos de la AIF
IDA recipient

recesión
recession; slump

recesión con inflación
slumpflation

recibo
certificate of payment

reciclaje
recycling (of capital)

recinto (ocupado por una familia extensa)
compound [West Africa]

recirculación (de capital)
recycling (of capital)

reclamación
claim

reclamación salarial
wage claim

reclasificación
regrading [personnel]

recolocación
outplacement

recompras en efectivo
cash buybacks

reconciliar
reconcile

reconocimiento médico
health screening

reconocimiento sísmico
seismic survey

reconocimiento y ejecución (de un laudo)
recognition and enforcement (of award) [ICSID]

reconstitución de los recursos
replenishment of resources

reconstituir
replenish (an account), to

reconversión industrial
retrofitting

recopilación de datos
collection of data

recopilación de datos
data collection

recorte de la demanda de punta
peak (load) shaving [electricity]

recubrimiento
overlay [highways]

recubrimiento de grava
graveling; regraveling

recuento de tráfico
traffic count

recuperación
recovery

recuperación
retrieval; upturn (economic)

recuperación acelerada
accelerated recovery

recuperación de costos
cost recovery

recuperación de la inversión
return of investment

recuperación de tierras
land reclamation

recuperación de un préstamo, de préstamos
loan recovery

recuperación del capital
return of capital

recuperación diferida
deferred recovery

recuperación estándar
standard recovery

Recuperación Garantizada del Principal de las Inversiones - GRIP
Guaranteed Recovery of Investment Principal - GRIP [IFC]

recuperación mejorada
enhanced recovery [oil]

recuperación secundaria
secondary recovery

recuperación terciaria
tertiary (oil) recovery

recuperar
reclaim

recurso (legal)
legal remedy

recurso provisional
stopgap measure

recursos básicos
core fund [GEF]

recursos en divisas
foreign exchange resources

recursos inexplotados
untapped resources

recursos propios
internally generated funds; cash generation; internal cash generation

recursos provenientes de las operaciones
internally generated funds; cash generation; internal cash generation

recursos reservados (para un determinado proyecto)
tied resources

recusación
disqualification [ICSID]

red de área local - LAN
local area network - LAN

red de distribución, de reparto
delivery system; supply system

red de energía eléctrica
power system

red de seguridad social
social safety net

red interurbana
trunk network

red principal
main power grid [electricity]

redactor jefe
editor

redención
redemption

redescontar
rediscount

redescuento
discount window [central bank]; rediscount

redimible
redeemable

redistribución (de fondos)
redeployment (of funds)

reducción
drawdown; rolling back

reducción de costos
avoided cost

reducción de impuestos
tax rebate

reducción de las tasas máximas de cada tramo arancelario, del arancel
concertina reduction

reducción de los impuestos
tax mitigation

reducción de los márgenes de utilidad
profit squeeze

reducción de personal
redundancy [staffing]

reducción del capital
capital impairment

reducción del valor en libros
writing down

reducción inicial
down payment (on the budget deficit)

reducciones arancelarias radiales
radial reductions

reducciones presupuestarias
budget cuts

reducir de tamaño
downsize, to

reembolso
refunding

reembolso anticipado
advance repayment; prepayment [IBRD]

reembolso de impuestos
tax refund

reembolso (anticipado) de la deuda
retirement of outstanding debt

reembolso en cuotas iguales
level repayment

reembolsos concentrados al comienzo de un período
front loading

reembolsos de los créditos de la AIF
IDA reflows

reemplazo de personal extranjero por personal nacional
indigenization

reestructuración empresarial, de empresas
corporate restructuring

reestructuración financiera
workout [financial]

refinanciación
refinancing

refinanciación
refunding

refinanciamiento
refinancing

refinanciamiento continuo
rollover

refinar
upgrade, to [oil]

reflación
reflation

reflujos de los créditos de la AIF
IDA reflows

reforestación
reforestation; reafforestation

reforma de la tenencia de la tierra
land reform

refugio tributario
tax shelter

régimen cambiario
exchange system

régimen de licencias de importación
import licensing

régimen de pagos con cargo a los ingresos corrientes
pay-as-you-go system [social security]

régimen de tenencia de la tierra
land tenure system

registrado
registered (e.g. tradesmen)

registrador
registrar [ICSID]

Registro
Register [ICSID]

registro (de valores)
perfection (of security)

registro catastral
land register

registro de ingresos
revenue recognition

regla de los dos años
two-year trigger rule

regla del primer año
first year rule - FYR [project analysis]

Reglamento del Mecanismo Complementario
Additional Facility Rules [ICSID]

Reglamento del Personal
Staff Rules [IBRD]

Reglamento Interno para las Reuniones del Directorio
Rules of Procedure for Meetings of the Executive Directors

Reglamento y Reglas (del Centro)
Regulations and Rules (of the Centre) [ICSID]

reglamento; estatutos
bylaws

Reglas de Arbitraje
Arbitration Rules [ICSID]

Reglas de Conciliación
Conciliation Rules [ICSID]

Reglas de Iniciación
Institution Rules [ICSID]

Reglas Procesales Aplicables a la Iniciación de los Procedimientos de Conciliación y Arbitraje (Reglas de Iniciación)
Rules of Procedure for the Institution of Conciliation and Arbitration Proceedings (Institution Rules) [ICSID]

Reglas Procesales Aplicables a los Procedimientos de Arbitraje (Reglas de Arbitraje)
Rules of Procedure for Arbitration Proceedings (Arbitration Rules) [ICSID]

Reglas Procesales Aplicables a los Procedimientos de Conciliación (Reglas de Conciliación)
Rules of Procedure for Conciliation Proceedings (Conciliation Rules) [ICSID]

regulación de (las) aguas
water control

regulación de la demanda
demand management

regulación de la oferta
supply management

regulación salarial
wage control

rehabilitación
rehabilitation

reintegro
drawback [customs]; recall [MOV]

reintegro a pro rata, proporcional
pro rata recall

reintegro acelerado
accelerated recall [MOV]

reintegro de impuestos
tax refund

reintegro de los montos en préstamo
recall under loans [MOV]

reivindicación salarial
wage claim

relación activo disponible-pasivo corriente
acid-test ratio; liquid ratio; quick ratio

relación activos de riesgo-patrimonio
IFC risk assets-equity ratio

relación alumnos-profesor, alumnos por profesor
pupil-teacher ratio - PTR; student-teacher ratio - STR; teacher-pupil ratio

relación beneficio neto-inversión
net benefit investment ratio

relación capital-activo
equity ratio

relación capital-producto
capital-output ratio

relación capital-servicio
capital-service ratio

relación capital-trabajo
capital-labor ratio

relación contractual (bipartita)
privity [legal]

relación corriente [América Latina]
current ratio; working capital ratio

relación costos-beneficios
benefit-cost ratio [US]; cost-benefit ratio [UK]

relación costos-beneficios empresariales, de las empresas
entrepreneurial benefit-cost ratio - EBC

relación costos-beneficios privados
private benefit-cost ratio - PBC

relación costos-beneficios sociales
social benefit-cost ratio - SBC

relación de Bruno
Bruno ratio

relación de cobertura de intereses
interest coverage ratio - ICR; times interest earned ratio

relación de cobertura de las importaciones
import coverage ratio

relación de cuenta
accounting ratio

relación de dependencia (por edades)
dependency ratio

relación de desmonte
stripping ratio [mining]

relación de endeudamiento
debt ratio

relación de endeudamiento a largo plazo
long-term debt ratio

relación de energía neta - REN
net energy ratio - NER

relación de gastos
statement of expenditure - SOE

relación de inestabilidad
volatility ratio [stocks]

relación de intercambio
terms of trade

relación de intercambio de dos factores
double factorial terms of trade

relación de intercambio de ingresos
income terms of trade

relación de intercambio de trueque
barter terms of trade

relación de intercambio de un solo factor
single factorial terms of trade

relación de recaudación de impuestos
tax performance ratio

relación deuda-capital
debt-equity ratio; debt-to-equity ratio;
debt-to-capital ratio

relación dosis-efecto
dose-response relationships

relación endeudamiento-capital propio
gearing [UK]; leverage

relación endeudamiento-capital propio
leverage (ratio) [US]; gearing (ratio) [UK]

relación gastos de vivienda-ingresos
housing expenses/income ratio; affordability ratio

relación impuestos-ingresos
tax ratio

relación impuestos-PIB
tax/GDP ratio

relación incremental capital-producto
incremental capital-output ratio - ICOR

relación insumo-producto
input-output ratio

relación intereses de la deuda - exportaciones
debt burden ratio

relación pasivo-capital
gearing ratio; free resource ratio; capital gearing
ratio; leverage (ratio) [US]; gearing (ratio) [UK];
gearing ratio [IFC]

relación personal-población
staffing ratio

relación precio-utilidades
price-earning ratio; P/E ratio - PER

**relación préstamos desembolsados y
pendientes-capital y reservas [Banco Mundial]**
gearing ratio; free resource ratio; capital gearing
ratio

relación profesor-alumnos
student-teacher ratio - STR; pupil-teacher ratio -
PTR; teacher-pupil ratio

relación riesgo-activos
risk-asset ratio

relaciones entre empleados y empleadores
industrial relations; labor-management relations;
labor relations

relaciones financieras
financial ratios

relaciones obrero-patronales
labor-management relations; labor relations;
industrial relations

relajación monetaria
monetary ease

relajación monetaria
monetary ease

**remediar los daños sufridos por el medio
ambiente**
clean-up (environmental)

remesas
remittances

remesas de los trabajadores (emigrados, expatriados)
workers' remittances

remisión
referral

rémora fiscal
fiscal drag

remuneración
compensation; earnings

remuneración neta
take-home pay

rendición de cuentas
accountability

rendimiento
performance

rendimiento a escala
returns to scale

rendimiento al vencimiento
yield to maturity - YTM

rendimiento corriente
current yield

rendimiento de la inversión
investment return, yield; return on, to investment

rendimiento del capital
return on, to capital

rendimiento en función de la escala
returns to scale

rendimiento en la fabricación, la molienda, el maquinado
milling yield

rendimiento equivalente a un interés nominal
coupon equivalent yield

rendimiento escolar
educational achievements

rendimiento medio neto de los activos productivos
average earning assets - AEA

rendimiento mínimo
floor return

rendimiento térmico
heat rate

rendimientos decrecientes
diminishing returns

renglón arancelario
tariff line

renivelación
regrading [highways]

renovación
retrofitting; rollover

renovación de la superficie
resurfacing [highways]

renta
income

renta de monopolio
monopoly rent

renta económica
economic rent

renta per cápita, por habitante
per capita income

renta presunta
assessed income

renta(s) proveniente(s) de propiedades públicas
property income [government]

rentabilidad
earning power

rentabilidad de equilibrio del mercado
market-clearing returns

rentabilidad de la inversión
investment return, yield; return on, to investment

rentabilidad del capital
capital efficiency; return on, to capital

rentabilidad media neta de los activos productivos
average earning assets - AEA

rentas
revenues; returns

rentas públicas
government receipts, revenues

renuncia
droppage [IFC]; waiver (of a right) [ICSID]; waiver (of immunity) [ICSID]

renuncia (a un derecho)
waiver

renunciar (a un derecho)
waive, to

reorganización
rehabilitation

reorientación del gasto
expenditure-switching

reparación de baches
patching; spot improvement, patching; road, surface patching [highways]

reparación de los daños ambientales
clean-up (environmental)

reparación general de equipo
overhaul [equipment]

repartición en porciones, tramos
tranching [loans]

repercusiones de las alzas de precios
ripple price effects

repetición de un proyecto, programa
rollover project, program

repoblación forestal
afforestation; reafforestation; reforestation

repoblación forestal
reforestation; reafforestation

reponer
replenish (an account), to

reposición de existencias
restocking

reposición de los recursos [AIF]
replenishment of resources

represa de almacenamiento
storage dam

represa de derivación
diversion dam

represa de terraplén
earthfill dam

representación
representative office [bank]

representante de ...
chair representing ... [World Bank Executive Directors]

representativo
proxy

represión financiera
financial repression

représtamo
onlending; onward lending

represtar
onlend, to; relend, to

reproductor [ganadería]
breeder [agriculture]

reproductores
breeding stock

reprogramación (del servicio) de la deuda
debt rephasing; rescheduling of debt; rephasing of a debt; debt rescheduling

reputación en materia de crédito
credit standing

requerimiento de capital
call for capital; call of capital

requisito de depósito previo, anticipado (a la importación)
advance deposit requirements (on imports)

requisito(s) en materia de informes
reporting requirement(s)

requisitos de desempeño, cumplimiento, funcionamiento
performance requirements [contracts]

requisitos que deben cumplirse
eligibility; eligibility conditions

resarcimiento
recoupment [insurance]

rescatable
redeemable

rescate
redemption

rescate (anticipado) de la deuda
retirement of outstanding debt

rescate de la deuda
debt retirement

rescindir [nombramiento]
terminate

rescisión
termination

resellado
resealing [highways]

reserva
provision [accounting]

reserva de biosfera
biosphere reserve

reserva de valor
store-of-value

reserva del Presidente
President's Contingency

reserva especial
Special Reserve [World Bank]

reserva flotante en efectivo
floating cash reserve

Reserva General
General Reserve(s) [IBRD]

Reserva general para pérdidas
General Loss Reserve [IFC]

reserva genética, génica
gene pool

reserva mínima obligatoria
minimum cash requirement

reserva obligatoria
legal reserve; reserve requirement

reserva obligatoria marginal
marginal reserve requirement

reserva para depreciación
capital consumption allowance; reserve for depreciation; allowance for depreciation; depreciation allowance

reserva para imprevistos
contingent reserve

reserva para imprevistos, para contingencias
allowance for contingencies; reserve for contingencies; contingency allowance

reserva para pérdidas
loss provision; provision for losses; reserve for losses; reserve against losses

reserva por agotamiento
depletion allowance, reserve

Reserva Suplementaria para pérdidas en préstamos y por devaluaciones de monedas (Reserva Suplementaria)
Supplemental Reserve against Losses on Loans and from Currency Devaluations (Supplemental Reserve)

reservas de divisas
foreign exchange reserves

reservas de oro
gold holdings

reservas disponibles
free reserves

reservas internacionales
international reserves

reservas ocultas
hidden reserves

reservas primarias
primary reserves

reservas recuperables definitivas - RRD
ultimate recoverable reserves - URR

resometimiento (en el sentido del Art. 52[6] del Convenio)
resubmission [ICSID]

responsabilidad
accountability

responsabilidad ante más de una autoridad, entidad, jefe
matrix reporting

responsabilidad global máxima
maximum aggregate liability [MIGA]

responsabilidad macroeconómica
macro-level accountability

responsabilidad microeconómica
micro-level accountability

responsabilizar
empower

resquicio
window (in a market)

resquicio tributario
tax loophole

restricción a la admisibilidad de licitantes
bracketing

restricción del crédito
credit squeeze; credit tightening

restricción del crédito
credit tightening; credit squeeze

restricción oficiosa del crédito
window guidance [central bank]

restricción pronunciada del crédito
credit crunch

restricción salarial
wage restraint

restricciones crediticias
tightening of credit

resultado final
bottom line

resultado(s) financiero(s)
financial performance, results

resultados
performance

resultados económicos
economic performance

resultados escolares
educational achievements

resumen
executive summary

resumen de actividades previstas
activity brief [EDI]

retención (de impuestos) en la fuente
pay-as-you-earn - PAYE; pay-as-you-go [taxation]

retención del impuesto
tax withholding

retención en, como garantía
retention money

retención térmica
heat trapping

retirar fondos
draw, to (funds)

retiro de una moneda de la circulación
calling in of a currency

retraso
lag; slippage; time lag

retroacción
feedback (of information)

retroarriendo
leaseback

retrocesión en arrendamiento
leaseback

retroinformación
feedback (of information)

reubicación
outplacement

Reunión Anual
Annual Meeting [ICSID]

reunión de conclusiones
wrap-up meeting

reunión en dos niveles
two-tier meeting

Reunión Inaugural
Inaugural Meeting [ICSID]

reunión informal (del Directorio)
Board seminar

reunión oficiosa
informal meeting

Reuniones Anuales del Banco Mundial y del Fondo Monetario Internacional
Annual Meetings (of the Boards of Governors) of the World Bank and the International Monetary Fund

reuniones de grupos de representantes de los interesados
focus group

reutilización de las ganancias
rollover of gains

revalorización
revaluation

revaluación
revaluation

revestimiento
overlay [highways]; surfacing [highways]

riego por anegación controlada
flood control irrigation

riego por aspersión
spray irrigation; sprinkle irrigation

riego por aspersión con pivote central
center pivot sprinkle irrigation

riego por compartimientos
basin irrigation; level border irrigation

riego por corrugación
corrugation irrigation

riego por desbordamiento natural
wild flooding

riego por escorrentía, por escurrimiento
runoff irrigation

riego por goteo
drip irrigation; dribble irrigation; trickle irrigation

riego por gravedad
gravity irrigation

riego por gravedad con retenes
border check irrigation; border ditch irrigation;
border irrigation; border strip irrigation; gravity
check irrigation; ribbon check irrigation; strip
check irrigation; strip irrigation

riego por inundación
flood irrigation; spate irrigation

riego por microaspersión
micro-sprayer irrigation

riego por surcos
furrow irrigation

riego por surcos pequeños y próximos
corrugation irrigation

riego por tablares, por eras
border check irrigation; border ditch irrigation;
border irrigation; border strip irrigation; gravity
check irrigation; ribbon check irrigation; strip
check irrigation; strip irrigation

riego subterráneo
subirrigation; subsoil irrigation

riego superficial, de superficie
surface irrigation

riesgo
exposure

riesgo admisible
eligible risk

riesgo cambiario
exchange risk; foreign exchange risk

riesgo conjunto
co-exposure [insurance]

riesgo de expropiación
risk of expropriation [MIGA]

riesgo de incumplimiento de contrato
breach of contract risk [MIGA]

riesgo de los bancos
bank exposure

riesgo de pérdida en, por concepto de intereses
interest rate risk

riesgo de transferencia de moneda
currency transfer risk [MIGA]

riesgo moral
moral hazard

riesgo que plantea el Estado prestatario
sovereign risk

riesgo soberano
sovereign risk

riesgos no cubiertos
excepted risks

rizomas
rhizomes; rootstock crops

roca fosfatada, fosforita
rock phosphate; phosphate rock

roce
ash farming; burn-beating; burning

rociado con tanque llevado a la espalda
knapsack spraying

rociado de muy bajo volumen
ultra low volume (ULV) spraying

rodal
stand [forest]

Ronda Uruguay
Uruguay Round [GATT]

rotación
turnover

rotación del inventario, de las existencias
inventory turnover

rotafolio
flip chart

roza
ash farming; burn-beating; burning

ruido de fondo
background noise

sacar de apuros
bail out, to

sacudimiento
shakeout (of the market)

salario
wage rate

salario-producto
product wage

salario de cuenta
shadow wages

salario de cuenta social
social shadow wage rate - SSWR

salario de eficiencia
efficiency wage

salario de reserva
reservation salary, wage

salario monetario, nominal
money wage

salario neto
take-home pay

salario sombra
shadow wages

saldo acreedor no utilizado
unspent credit balance

saldo de, en caja
cash balance; cash holdings; cash in hand; cash on hand

saldo no utilizado
undrawn balance

saldo traspasado
balance carried forward

saldos en efectivo
balances [cash]

saldos pendientes
overhang

saldos que se traspasan
carryovers

saldos retenidos para cubrir operaciones a término, a plazo
balances held on a covered basis

saldos traspasados
carryovers

salegar
salt lick; mineral lick

salida en el orden de adquisición, fabricación, etc.
first in, first out - FIFO

salida en orden inverso al de adquisición, fabricación, etc.
last in, first out - LIFO

salida impresa
hard copy

saneamiento
sanitation

saneamiento ambiental
environmental health, sanitation

saneamiento de la cartera
portfolio cleanup

saneamiento de tierras
land reclamation

sanear
reclaim

satélite de exploración de los recursos terrestres
earth resources satellite

satélite para el estudio de los recursos terrestres
earth resources satellite

sección de evisceración
dressing section, hall [slaughtering]

sección estándar (del presupuesto)
standard charge section

Secretario General Adjunto
Deputy Secretary General [ICSID]

sector de la construcción
construction sector

sector empresarial
corporate sector

sector estructurado
formal sector

sector informal
informal sector

sector no estructurado
informal sector

sectores de producción primaria
commodity producing sectors

sectores productivos
real sectors

secuestro
seizure [legal]

seguimiento
follow-up; monitoring

seguimiento del desempeño, de los resultados
performance monitoring

seguimiento y evaluación
monitoring and evaluation - M & E

según registro de caja
cash basis, on a

segunda alternativa
second-best optimum

segunda línea de reservas
secondary reserves

seguridad
security

seguridad alimentaria
food security

seguridad de tenencia
security of tenure

seguridad en el cargo
security of tenure

seguridad social
social insurance

seguridades aceptables para los bancos
bankable assurances

seguro contra todo riesgo
all risk insurance; comprehensive insurance

seguro de desempleo
unemployment compensation, benefit

seguro de inversión
investment insurance

seguro multilateral de inversiones
multilateral investment insurance

seguro social
social insurance

selección
triage

selección automática interurbana
subscriber trunk dialing - STD

selección de lo mejor
cherry picking

sellado superficial, de superficie
surface dressing [highways]

selva (pluvial) tropical
tropical rain forest

selva pluvial
rain forest

sementales
breeding stock

semilla básica
foundation seed

semilla certificada
certified seed

semilla de primera reproducción, del mejorador
breeder seed

semilla registrada
registered seed

semillas de campo
field seeds

semimontado
semiknocked down - SKD

Seminario de políticas de...
Senior Policy Seminar on... [EDI]

Seminario de políticas generales
Senior Policy Seminar [EDI]

sensibilidad a las tasas de interés
interest (rate) sensitivity

señal de alerta, de prevención
warning signal

separación de riesgos financieros
unbundling of financial risks

separación del servicio
separation [employment]

serie cronológica
time series

serie de beneficios
benefit stream

serie de disposiciones, equipos, proyectos, actividades, financiamiento
package

serie de medidas financieras
financial package

servicio
facility

servicio a cambio del pago de honorarios
fee-based service [IFC]

servicio bancario internacional
international banking facility - IBF

servicio de emisión de pagarés - SEP
revolving underwriting facility - RUF; note issuance facility - NIF; prime underwriting facility - PUF

Servicio de financiamiento a largo plazo para la compra de bienes de capital por los países en desarrollo
Long-term Facility for Financing Purchases of Capital Goods by Developing Countries [IBRD]

servicio de financiamiento transitorio
bridging facility

servicio de préstamos en condiciones ordinarias, no concesionarias
hard loan window

servicio de reestructuración de la deuda
Debt Restructuring Facility - DRF

servicio de sobregiro
overdraft facilities

servicio de transmisión
wheeling

Servicio especial de financiamiento para productos mineros de los países ACP y PTUM
Sysmin (= Special financing facility for ACP and OCT mining products) [European Communities]

servicio financiero de ajuste estructural (SAE) dentro del marco de la Cuenta Especial de Desembolso
Structural Adjustment Facility (SAF) within the Special Disbursement Account [IMF]

servicio mínimo
nominal service

servicio para la transformación sistémica
Systemic Transformation Facility [IMF]

servicio para préstamos concesionarios
soft loan window

servicio paraestatal
parastatal [noun]

servicios bancarios para consumidores
retail banking

servicios comunitarios de salud
community health services

servicios conexos
incidental services

servicios de apoyo
backstopping

servicios de crédito, crediticios
credit facilities

servicios no atribuibles a factores
nonfactor services - n.f.s.

servicios no comerciales
nonmarket services [national accounts]

servicios públicos
public utilities; utilities

servidumbre de paso
right of way

sesgo
bias [economy; statistics]

sesgo (por defecto) de margen, de borde
border bias

sesgo (por exceso) de margen, de borde
edge bias

sesión
sitting [ICSID]

setos vivos
live fencing

sí, muy bien, pero no en mi barrio
NIMBY (not-in-my-backyard)

SIBOR (tasa de oferta interbancaria de Singapur)
SIBOR [= Singapore Interbank Offered Rate]

siembra a voleo
broadcasting (seed, fertilizer)

silvicultura sostenible
sustainable forestry

simientes de campo
field seeds

simplificación
streamlining

sin efecto sobre los recursos
resource-neutral

sin garantía
unsecured (note, loan, etc.)

síndrome de inmunodeficiencia adquirida - SIDA
acquired immune-deficiency syndrome - AIDS

sinopsis de actividades (no relacionadas con proyectos específicos)
activity brief [EDI]

síntesis informativa sobre un (el) proyecto
summary of project information

síntesis sectorial
approach paper

sirope de maíz de alto contenido en fructosa
high fructose corn syrup - HFCS

sistema (de amortización, de depreciación) de saldo decreciente
declining balance method; reducing charge method

sistema (o planes) de reparto
pay-as-you-go system [social security]

sistema administrativo
administrative machinery

sistema cambiario
exchange system

sistema de alcantarillado "en condominio"
condominial sewerage system

sistema de alcantarillado (alcantarillado) para efluentes líquidos
effluent sewerage; solids-free sewerage; small-bore sewerage

sistema de alerta anticipada
early warning system

sistema de arbitraje administrado por una institución
administered arbitration system [ICSID]

sistema de capacitación y visitas
training and visit [T & V] system

sistema de capitación
capitation approach [health financing]

sistema de captación de rentas
rent-seeking

sistema de cultivo
cropping pattern

sistema de cultivo sin laboreo, de cero labranza
zero tillage system

sistema de determinación de precios en función del costo más honorarios
cost-plus pricing system

sistema de distribución, de reparto
delivery system; supply system

sistema de explotación agrícola
farming system

sistema de fijación de tipos, tasas de interés
pricing system [financial markets]

sistema de honorarios por servicios
fee-for-services basis

sistema de información para la administración
management information system - MIS

sistema de licencias de importación
import licensing

sistema de modelos algebraicos generales
General Algebraic Modeling System - GAMS [IBRD]

sistema de múltiples procedimientos para las transacciones
multiple trading approaches

Sistema de notificación de la deuda al Banco Mundial
Debtor Reporting System [World Bank]

sistema de notificación de la deuda externa
external debt reporting system

sistema de pagos iguales de principal e intereses
annuity system [debt service]

sistema de pagos totales iguales (de principal e intereses)
level annuity system

sistema de participación en la gestión, administración
comanagement; codetermination; management participation system

sistema de planificación y evaluación del desempeño (del funcionario)
Performance Planning and Review - PPR [IBRD]

sistema de planificación, programación y presupuestación - SPPP
planning, programming, budgeting system - PPBS

sistema de presentación de informes
reporting system [projects]

sistema de prestación de servicios de salud
health delivery system

sistema de prestación, de suministro (de un servicio)
delivery system; supply system

sistema de prestador preferido - SPP
preferred provider organization (PPO) system

sistema de programación orientado a objetos
object-oriented programming system - OOPS

sistema de puntos
merit point system

sistema de seguridad social
social security scheme

sistema de tipos de interés basados en una cesta de empréstitos pendientes
Pool-Based Lending Rate System [IBRD]

sistema de votación ponderada
weighted voting system

sistema financiado con aportaciones
unfunded system [insurance; social security]

sistema financiado con fondos propios
fully funded system

Sistema Generalizado de Preferencias - SGP
Generalized System of Preferences - GSP

sistema impositivo con deducción de gastos efectuados en el mismo año
cash flow system of taxation

sistema internacional de garantías de crédito
international credit guarantee system

sistema múltiple de mensajes financieros
message front-end system

sistema nacional de investigaciones agronómicas
national agricultural research system - NARS

sistema radial
hub and spoke system

sistemas de crédito, crediticios
credit facilities

sistemas simplificados de alcantarillado
simplified sewerage

situación
status

situación de autosostenimiento
self-sustaining state

situación de balanza de pagos
balance of payments position

situación de efectivo, de liquidez
cash position

situación de emergencia latente
slow onset emergency; quiet emergency

situación de las reservas
reserve position

situación de liquidez
liquidity position

situación de pagos (de un país)
payments position (of a country)

situación de pagos externos
external payment position

situación de pagos internacionales
international payments position

situación en materia de reservas de divisas
foreign exchange position

situación financiera
financial intrinsics

situación socioeconómica
socioeconomic status - SES

sobrante
overhang

sobre una base semestral
semiannual coupon equivalent basis, on a [bonds]

sobrecostos
cost overrun

sobreempleo
overemployment

sobreprecio
price premium

sobrestadía
demurrage

sobretasa
tax surcharge

sobrevaloración de las monedas
exchange rate overvaluation

sociedad anónima
stock corporation

sociedad cuyas acciones se cotizan en bolsa
publicly traded company

sociedad de ahorro y crédito
savings and loan association

sociedad de ahorro y préstamo
savings and loan association

sociedad de cartera, de inversiones
holding company

sociedad de inversión con número de acciones fijo
closed-end investment company, fund [US]; investment trust [UK]

sociedad de inversiones
investment company, fund

sociedad de inversiones con número de acciones variable
open-end (investment) fund; unit trust [UK]

sociedad de responsabilidad limitada
limited liability company

sociedad de valores
securities dealer; securities firm

sociedad en comandita por acciones
joint stock company

sociedad en participación
joint venture

sociedad ficticia
shell company

sociedad matriz
parent company

sociedad no accionaria
nonstock corporation

sociedad pública
public corporation

sociedad simple, colectiva
partnership

socorro
relief

solicitud de ingreso
application for membership

solicitud de ingreso
membership application

solicitud de préstamo
loan application

solicitud de propuestas
request for proposal - RFP

solicitud de retiro de fondos (de la cuenta del préstamo o crédito)
application for withdrawal (from loan account or credit account)

solicitud definitiva de garantía
definitive application for guarantee

solicitud preliminar de garantía
preliminary application for guarantee [MIGA]

sólidos en suspensión
suspended matter

solución de compromiso
trade-off

solvencia
creditworthiness; financial standing

solvencia económica
economic soundness [MIGA]

sostén de la familia
breadwinner

sostén de precios
price support

sostenibilidad
sustainability

sostenibilidad ambiental
environmental sustainability

STABEX (Sistema de estabilización de los ingresos de exportación de los Estados ACP y PTUM)
Stabex (System for the stabilization of ACP and OCT mining products) [European Communities]

statu quo
standstill

subasta de divisas
foreign exchange auction

subcapitalizado
undercapitalized

subcontratista
subcontractor

subcontratista propuesto
nominated subcontractor

subcontrato
subcontract

subdivisión política u organismo público (de un Estado Contratante)
constituent subdivision or agency (of a Contracting State) [ICSID]

subempleo
underemployment

subfacturación de exportaciones
underinvoicing of exports

subgarante [CFI]
subunderwriter [IFC]

subida por efecto de trinquete
ratcheting up

subinversión
underinvestment

subocupación
underemployment

subóptimo
second-best optimum

subpréstamo
subloan

subpréstamo de aprobación autónoma
free-limit subloan

subprestatario
subborrower

subproyecto
subproject

subproyectos gestionados a través de agentes
agency (line) subprojects

subrasante
subgrade [highways]

subsidiaria en propiedad absoluta
wholly owned subsidiary

subsidiariedad
subsidiarity

subsidio a las exportaciones
export subsidy

subsidio a las importaciones
import subsidy

subsidio a los consumidores
consumer subsidy

subsidio cruzada(o) interna(o)
internal cross subsidy

subsidio cruzado
cross subsidization

subsidio de explotación, de operación, de funcionamiento
operating subsidy

subsidio para instalación
settling-in grant [IBRD]

subsidio por lugar de destino difícil
hardship allowance

subsidio por reasentamiento, por reinstalación
resettlement grant

subsidio por traslado
relocation grant

subsidios de asistencia social
welfare payments

subvaloración de las facturas de exportación
underinvoicing of exports

subvención
grant-in-aid

subvención a las exportaciones
export subsidy

subvención a las importaciones
import subsidy

subvención a los consumidores
consumer subsidy

subvención cruzada
cross subsidization

subvención cruzada(o) interna(o)
internal cross subsidy

subvención de explotación, de operación, de funcionamiento
operating subsidy

subvención de intereses
interest subsidy, subsidization

subvención equilibradora
balancing subsidy

subvención para insumos
input subsidy

subvención para inversión
investment grant

sueldos y salarios
salaries and wages

suelo(s) de fertilidad marginal, de baja fertilidad
marginal soil(s)

suficiencia de(l) capital
capital adequacy

sujeto al cobro, al pago de derechos
dutiable

sujetos (potenciales) del impuesto
tax handles

sujetos, bienes y actividades imponibles
tax net

suma alzada
lump sum price

suma por la cual las cantidades devengadas son inferiores a las previstas
underaccruals

suma total
aggregate

sumidero
sink (e.g. of greenhouse gases)

suministro de agua
water supply

suministro de energía alimentaria - SEA
dietary energy supply - DES

superar el punto más bajo
bottom out (of a recession)

superávit de explotación, operación
operating surplus

superávit de las transacciones invisibles
surplus on invisibles

superávit presupuestario
budget surplus

superficie agrícola útil
useful farm space - UFS

superficie habitable
living area

superfosfato triple
triple superphosphate - TSP [fertilizer]

superintendencia bancaria, de bancos
superintendency (of banks)

superintendente de bancos
bank examiner

supervisión
line management; monitoring

supervisión de un proyecto, de proyectos
project supervision

supervisión y reglamentación
prudential supervision and regulation

supervisor directo, inmediato
line manager

supervisor inmediato
next-in-line manager

suplente
Deputy [Dev. Comm.; IDA]

supresión de puestos
redundancy [staffing]

suprimir
disestablish, to

susceptibilidad de capacitación
trainability [EDI-World Bank]

suscripción al capital, de acciones del capital
capital subscription [IBRD]

suscripción de capital social, de capital accionario
equity subscription [IFC]

suscripción en exceso de la emisión
oversubscription [capital markets]

suscripción inicial
initial subscription [IDA]

suscripción no sujeta a restricciones
unrestricted subscription [IDA]

suscriptor
underwriter [securities]

suspender por etapas, progresivamente
phase out, to

suspensión de la ejecución (del laudo)
stay of enforcement [ICSID]

suspensión no oficial de los desembolsos
informal suspension of disbursements [IBRD]

suspensión oficial de los desembolsos
formal suspension of disbursements [IBRD]

sustancia que agota la capa de ozono
ozone-depleting substance - ODS

sustancias nutritivos(as)
nutrients

sustitución de combustibles
interfuel substitution

sustitución de importaciones
import substitution

sustitución de recursos para reducir costos
input shifting

sustitutivo
proxy

sustituto
proxy

swap de monedas
currency swap

swap **de tipos de interés**
interest (rate) swap

swap; **intercambio de monedas**
swap

Sysmin (Servicio especial de financiamiento para productos mineros de los países ACP y PTUM)
Sysmin (= Special financing facility for ACP and OCT mining products) [European Communities]

tabla de conexiones de datos
panel data set

tabla de insumo-producto
input-output table

tala selectiva
selection felling, cutting

tanque de inmersión
dipping tank

tanque séptico
septic tank

tanto alzado
lump sum price

tarea de reparación de los daños ambientales
clean-up (environmental)

tarifa
tariff

tarifa [precios]
tariff schedule

tarifa de recolección de basura(s)
household waste collection charge

tarifa mínima, vital
lifeline tariff

tarifa por bloques
block tariff

tarifa uniforme, a tanto alzado
flat rate

tarifas
charges [utilities]

tarifas de agua
water charges

tarifas portuarias
port charges, tariffs

tarifas progresivas
inverted rates [electricity tariffs]

tarifas según hora de consumo
time-of-use (TOU) rates [electricity tariffs]

tasa activo(a)
lending rate

tasa arancelaria media ponderada
weighted average tariff rate - WATR

tasa bruta de matrícula (primaria)
gross (primary) enrollment ratio - GER

tasa bruta de mortalidad
crude death rate

tasa bruta de natalidad
crude birth rate - CBR

tasa central
key money rate; central rate

tasa compuesta de crecimiento
compound rate of growth

tasa crítica de rentabilidad
hurdle rate

tasa cruzada
cross rate

tasa de aceptación
acceptance rate (by beneficiaries of a project)

tasa de actividad
labor force penetration; labor force participation rate

tasa de actualización
discount rate [project appraisal; securities]

tasa de actualización de equilibrio
crossover discount rate; equalizing discount rate

tasa de actualización social
social discount rate; social rate of discount

tasa de acumulación
accrual rate

tasa de analfabetismo
illiteracy rate

tasa de asimilación de conocimientos
learning rate

tasa de aumento, crecimiento de las importaciones
import growth rate

tasa de carga
stocking rate [livestock]

tasa de continuidad de utilización
continuation rate [contraception]

tasa de depreciación de equilibrio
breakeven (dollar) depreciation

tasa de descuento sombra, de cuenta
shadow discount rate

tasa de desempleo que no modifica el nivel salarial
nonaccelerating-wages rate of unemployment - NAWRU

tasa de deserción
dropout rate [education]; wastage; waste [education]

tasa de desgaste, de eliminación, de atrición
attrition rate

tasa de emisión
coupon rate (of a bond)

tasa de extracción
offtake rate [livestock]

tasa de fecundidad
fertility rate

tasa de fecundidad total
total fertility rate - TFR

tasa de importaciones afectadas
trade coverage ratio

tasa de inflación de dos dígitos, de 10% ó más
double digit inflation; two digit inflation

tasa de inflación de dos dígitos, de 10% o más
two digit inflation; double digit inflation

tasa de interés de cuenta
shadow rate of interest

tasa de interés efectivo(a)
effective interest rate

tasa de interés inmodificable
locked in interest rate

tasa de interés negativa
negative rate of interest

tasa de interés sobre los depósitos
depositor rate of interest; borrowing rate [banks]

tasa de interés sobre los préstamos
lending rate

tasa de interés sombra
shadow rate of interest

tasa de intermediación
intermediation rate

tasa de los fondos comunes de inversiones
money market rate

tasa de matrícula
enrollment ratio

tasa de mortalidad normalizada según la edad
age-standardized death rate

tasa de parición
calving rate

tasa de preferencia pura en el tiempo
rate of pure time preference

tasa de preferencia social en el tiempo
social time preference rate

tasa de promoción
pass rate; promotion rate [education]

tasa de redescuento
discount rate [central bank]

tasa de rendimiento
yield rate

tasa de rendimiento económico, de rentabilidad económica
economic rate of return - ERR; economic internal rate of return - EIRR

tasa de rendimiento financiero, de rentabilidad financiera
financial rate of return; internal rate of financial return; financial internal rate of return - FIRR

tasa de rentabilidad aceptable, de desistimiento
cutoff rate (of return) [projects]

tasa de rentabilidad de equilibrio
equalizing rate of return

tasa de rentabilidad económica a la terminación
completion economic rate of return

tasa de rentabilidad interna
internal rate of return - IRR

tasa de rentabilidad requerida, exigida
required rate of return - RRR

tasa de rentabilidad social
social rate of return - SRR

tasa de rentabilidad, de rendimiento
rate of return

tasa de repetición
repeater rate [education]

tasa de reproducción neta - TRN
net reproduction rate - NRR

tasa de retención
retention rate; grade ratio [education]

tasa de supervivencia escolar
survival rate [education]

tasa de uso de anticonceptivos
contraceptive prevalence rate - CPR

tasa del mercado monetario
money market rate

tasa diferencial de rentabilidad
incremental rate of return

tasa impositiva efectiva marginal
marginal effective tax rate - METR

tasa impositiva efectiva media
average effective tax rate - AETR

tasa límite de rentabilidad aceptable
cutoff rate (of return) [projects]

tasa marginal de ahorro nacional
marginal national savings rate

tasa oficial de descuento
bank rate [UK]

tasa pasivo(a)
depositor rate of interest; borrowing rate [banks]

tasa preferencial
prime rate

tasa preferencial a largo plazo
long-term prime rate - LTPR

tasa tendencial
trend rate

tasa uniforme, a tanto alzado
flat rate

tasa (de interés) vigente
standard rate (of interest)

tasa vigente en el mercado
prevailing market rate

tasación para fines impositivos
tax assessment; assessment for tax

tasación pericial
expert appraisal

tasas arancelarios
tariff rates

tasas de interés clave
key interest rates

tasas de interés crecientes
step-down, step-up interest rates

técnica de análisis de decisiones tomando en cuenta múltiples atributos
multiattribute decision analysis

técnica de evaluación y revisión de programas - PERT
program evaluation and review technique - PERT

técnica de variables múltiples
multivariate technique

técnicas de administración tributaria
tax technology

técnicas de reducción de la contaminación
abatement technologies

técnicas disponibles
off-the-shelf technology

técnicas financieras
financial engineering

técnico agrícola
agriculturist

técnico especializado
subject matter specialist - SMS [agricultural extension]

tecnología apropiada
appropriate technology - AT

tecnología avanzada, de vanguardia
frontier technology

tecnología de estado sólido, de semiconductores, de transistores
solid state technology

tecnología óptima disponible
best available technology - BAT; best practicable means - BPM

teledetección
remote sensing

teleobservación
remote sensing

temario anotado, comentado
annotated agenda

Temas del Banco Mundial [IBRD]
issues paper

temporada corta
short season (crop)

tendencia
bias [economy; statistics]

tendencia a condiciones de préstamo más gravosas
hardening of loan terms

tendencia a muy largo plazo
secular trend

tendencia alcista, ascendente
upward trend

tendencia descendente
downward trend

tendencia hacia categorías más altas de clasificación del personal
grade creep

tendencia intrínseca
built-in tendency

tenedor de bonos
bondholder

tenedor de la garantía
guarantee holder [MIGA]

tenencia comunitaria de bosques
tree tenure

tenencias [en, de divisas, oro]
holdings [foreign exchange, gold]

tenencias en oro
gold holdings

tenencias oficiales
official holdings

tensión ambiental
environmental stress

tensión debida a la sequía
drought stress

teoría cuantitativa del dinero
quantity theory of money

teoría de la elección social
theory of public choice

teoría de las colas
queuing theory, problem

teoría de los precios en operaciones de arbitraje
arbitrage pricing theory - APT

teoría de recuperación de los bosques
gap theory

teoría del control del dinero implícito
implied money control theory

terapia de rehidratación oral
oral rehydration therapy - ORT

Tercera Ventanilla
Third Window

terminación
termination

terminación de las instalaciones
mechanical completion [projects]

terminación del derecho a financiamiento del Banco)
graduation [IBRD]

terminar
terminate

términos de intercambio
terms of trade

términos de referencia
terms of reference [e.g. consultants]

términos de referencia, parámetros (de un estudio)
terms of reference [study]

terraplén
bund

terraplén en curva de nivel
contour bund

terreno aluvial, de aluvión
floodplain

terreno comprendido, cubierto
site coverage

terreno no parcelado
unsubdivided plot

testigo
drill core

tiempo compartido
time sharing [computers]

tiempo de inactividad
down time

tiempo de rotación, del viaje de ida y vuelta
turnaround (time)

tiempo necesario para un servicio
turnaround (time)

tierra de pastoreo
rangeland

tierras húmedas
wetlands

timbre fiscal
revenue stamp

tipo activo(a)
lending rate

tipo central
key money rate; central rate

tipo cruzado
cross rate

tipo de alojamiento
accommodation type

tipo de cambio a término, a plazo
forward exchange rate

tipo de cambio al contado
spot exchange rate

tipo de cambio central
central rate [exchange rates]

tipo de cambio comprador
buying rate of exchange

tipo de cambio de cuenta
shadow exchange rate - SER; shadow pricing of
the exchange rate

tipo de cambio de equilibrio
equilibrium exchange rate

tipo de cambio de referencia
reference rate of exchange [MIGA]

tipo de cambio efectivo
effective exchange rate

tipo de cambio efectivo nominal
nominal effective exchange rate

tipo de cambio efectivo real
real effective exchange rate

tipo de cambio flotante
floating rate

tipo de cambio interno
modified Bruno ratio; internal exchange rate

tipo de cambio mínimo
floor rate of exchange

tipo de cambio real de equilibrio
equilibrium real exchange rate

tipo de cambio sombra
shadow exchange rate - SER; shadow pricing of
the exchange rate

tipo de descuento sombra, de cuenta
shadow discount rate

tipo de interés contable - TIC
accounting rate of interest - ARI

tipo de interés de cuenta
shadow rate of interest

tipo de interés efectivo(a)
effective interest rate

tipo de interés inmodificable
locked in interest rate

tipo de interés negativo
negative rate of interest

tipo de interés real *ex post*
ex post real interest rate

tipo de interés sobre los depósitos
depositor rate of interest; borrowing rate [banks]

tipo de interés sobre los préstamos
lending rate

tipo de interés sombra
shadow rate of interest

**tipo de interés variable basado en una cesta de
empréstitos pendientes**
pool-based variable lending rate [IBRD]

tipo de redescuento
discount rate [central bank]

tipo oficial de descuento
bank rate [UK]

tipo pasivo(a)
depositor rate of interest; borrowing rate [banks]

tipo preferencial
prime rate

tipo preferencial a largo plazo
long-term prime rate - LTPR

tipo (de interés) vigente
standard rate (of interest)

tipo vigente en el mercado
prevailing market rate

tipos cruzados dispares
broken cross rates

tipos de cambio concordantes
unified cross rates

tipos de interés clave
key interest rates

título
security

título de crédito
financial claim

título de crédito [finanzas]
claim

título híbrido, estructurado
structured security

título nominativo
registered security

título otorgado por dos universidades
split degree

títulos de organismos federales
agency securities, obligations [U.S.]

títulos del mercado monetario
money market paper

toma (de agua)
intake

toma de agua
standpipe; standpost; hydrant

toma de fuerza
power takeoff - PTO

tonelada de equivalente en carbón - tec
ton of coal equivalent - tce

tonelada de equivalente en petróleo - tep
ton of oil equivalent - toe

tonelada en seco, secada al aire
air dried ton

toneladas de peso muerto
deadweight tonnage - DWT

tonelaje (de registro) bruto
gross (register) tonnage - GRT [shipping]

tonelaje de registro neto
net register tonnage - NRT

tope
cap

tope de crédito
credit ceiling; credit limit

tope de los tipos de interés
interest rate cap [IBRD]

torre de perforación petrolera
oil (drilling) rig, platform

torta (de semillas) oleaginosa(s)
oilcake

torta de estiércol
dung cake

total de partículas en suspensión
total suspended particulates - TSP

total de sólidos disueltos - tsd
total dissolved solids - TDS

total de sólidos en suspensión
total suspended solids - TSS

total neto de los giros
outstanding drawings [IMF]

trabajador a nivel de poblado
village level worker - VLW

trabajador ambulante
unlocated worker

trabajador calificado
skilled worker

trabajador de extensión, de divulgación
outreach worker

trabajador de salud de la comunidad
community health worker - CHW

trabajador desplazado
dislocated worker

trabajador no sindicado
unorganized worker

trabajador por cuenta propia, independiente, autónomo
self-employed person

trabajador semicalificado
semiskilled worker

trabajadores ocasionales
casual labor

trabajo a destajo
jobbing

trabajo en el terreno
field work

trabajos de urbanización
site development

traducción de monedas
currency translation

tráfico de detalle
less than carload freight - LCL

tráfico de regreso
backhaul traffic

tráfico directo
through traffic

tráfico en tránsito
through traffic

tráfico generado
generated traffic

tramitación
processing

tramitación del (de un) préstamo
loan processing

tramo impositivo
tax bracket

transacción
trade-off

transacción cubierta contra riesgos cambiarios
currency-hedged transaction

transacción fuera de mercado
off-market transaction

transacciones conforme a márgenes de riesgo y rendimiento
credit spread trades

transacciones entre grandes bancos y entre éstos y otras instituciones financieras
wholesale banking

transacciones interbancarias
wholesale banking

transacciones invisibles
invisible transactions

transferencia con, de contrapartida
requited transfer

transferencia de activos (de una sociedad) a cambio de acciones (de otra sociedad nueva)
spinoff [financial market]

transferencia de capital
capital transfer

transferencia desde el sistema principal
downloading

transferencia electrónica de fondos
electronic funds transfer - EFT

transferencia hacia el sistema principal
uploading [computers]

transferencia inversa de tecnología
reverse transfer of technology

transferencia sin contrapartida [cuentas nacionales]
unrequited transfer

transferencia unilateral [balanza de pagos]
unrequited transfer

transferencias [empresas]
remittances

transferencias de capital (no reembolsables)
capital grants

transformación
processing

transformaciónde empresas (públicas) en sociedades comerciales, entidades previstas en la ley de sociedades
corporatization

transfronterizo
cross-border; transterritorial

transitable
serviceable [highways]

transnacional
cross-border; transterritorial

transnacional
transterritorial; cross-border

transparencia
transparency

transparencia fiscal
fiscal transparency

transporte de productos empacados
nonbulk traffic

transporte entre terminales
line-haul [transportation]

transporte marítimo
shipping

transporte multimodal
multimodal transport

transterritorial
cross-border; transterritorial

transterritorial fronterizo; internacional
transterritorial; cross-border

traslación del impuesto
shifting of tax

traspaso de intereses
divestiture; divestment

tratamiento
processing

tratamiento ambulatorio
outpatient treatment

tratamiento por separado
two-stage, two-step procedure [IBRD]

tratamiento superficial
surface dressing [highways]

trazar
peg out, to [surveying]

tregua tributaria
tax holiday

tren bloque
block train

trenes unidades
unit trains

triaje
triage

Tribunal de Arbitraje
Arbitral Tribunal [ICSID; MIGA]

tribunales competentes o cualquier otra autoridad (para ejecutar laudos)
competent court or other authority (to enforce awards) [ICSID]

trimestre del año civil
calendar quarter

tubérculo feculento, raíz feculenta
starchy root crop

tubérculos alimentarios
root crops

tubería de presión, de carga
penstock [hydroelectricity]

umbral de pobreza
poverty income threshold; poverty line

umbral de veto de una minoría
minority threshold [IBRD]

unidad agrícola, de explotación agrícola
farming unit

unidad contable
accounting unit

unidad de administración del proyecto
project management unit - PMU [IBRD]

unidad de capacitación práctica
training production unit

unidad de cuenta
numeraire

unidad de cuenta
unit of account - UA

unidad de cuenta basada en una cesta de monedas
basket unit of account

unidad de eficiencia
efficiency unit

unidad de extensión (agrícola)
field unit [agricultural extension]

unidad de ganado
animal unit - AU

unidad de ganado tropical
tropical cattle unit - TCU; tropical animal unit - TAU; tropical livestock unit - TLU

unidad de la cesta de monedas
basket unit

unidad de moneda fronteriza
border currency (unit)

unidad de producción
unit of output

unidad del proyecto
project unit

unidad directiva
managing unit

unidad familiar con intereses en común
glued-together household

unidad forrajera
feed unit; forage unit

unidad ganadera
cattle unit

unidad mínima de vivienda
core housing; nuclear housing

unidad monetaria
currency unit

unidad monetaria compuesta
basket unit; composite currency unit

unidad monetaria europea - ECU
European Currency Unit - ECU

unidad móvil de formación, de capacitación
mobile training unit

unidades de 20 pies (de contenedores) - TEU
twenty equivalent units - TEU [containers]

unión
pooling

urbanización
development

urbanización
land development

urbanización de lotes
plot servicing

urbanizador
real estate developer

usar un enfoque selectivo
target, to

uso de (los) fondos
application of funds

uso de contenedores
containerization

uso de recursos por el gobierno
financial claims of government

uso final
end use (of a commodity)

uso, utilización de (los) fondos
application of funds

usuario
consumer [telecommunications]

usufructo
beneficial interest

usufructuario
beneficial owner

utilidad bruta de operación, de explotación
gross operating profit

utilidad imprevista, extraordinaria
windfall profit

utilidad marginal
marginal utility

utilidad sobre la venta de inversiones
profit on sales of investments

utilidad(es)
earnings

utilidades acumuladas
accumulated profit [accounting]

utilidades en libros
paper profit

utilidades encubiertas
leakage

utilidades netas [sociedades]
net income

utilidades netas derivadas de un proyecto
project rent

utilidades no distribuidas
earned surplus; retained earnings

utilidades no distribuidas y no asignadas
unappropriated (earned) surplus

utilidades reinvertidas
plowed-back profits

utilización
drawdown

utilización de recursos
claim (on resources)

utilización del capital
drawdown of equity

utilización escalonada de energía
energy cascading

utilizar fondos
draw, to (funds)

vaca de desecho
culled cow

vado pavimentado
submerged bridge

valor
security

valor a la par (monedas)
par value

valor a precio de comprador
purchasers' values [national accounts]

valor a precio de productor
producers' values [national accounts]

valor actual de una anualidad constante
present worth of an annuity factor

valor actual neto a precios económicos
net present value in efficiency prices - ENVP

valor actual, actualizado
present value, worth

valor actualizado (principal)
current value

valor agregado, añadido en el país
domestic value added

valor atípico
outlier

valor calculado
constructed value

valor comercial, de mercado
market value

valor contable neto
net book value; current equity investment; net investment

valor contable, en libros
book value

valor crítico
switching value [sensitivity analysis]

valor de contribución
contribution value [MIGA]

valor de existencia
existence value

valor de liquidación, de realización
selling value

valor de opción
option value

valor de primera clase
blue chip; blue chip security

valor de primera clase
prime bill

valor de protección
hedge [securities market]

valor de realización
current exit value; exit value; net realizable value [UK] [accounting]

valor de recuperación, de rescate
salvage value

valor de reposición
current (entry) value; replacement value; current cost [accounting]

valor de venta forzosa
liquidation value; forced sale value

valor del producto marginal
marginal value product

valor en boca de mina
minehead price

valor en razón de la escasez
scarcity value

valor esperado
expected value

valor estimado de la cartera
evaluated portfolio [IFC]

valor híbrido, estructurado
structured security

valor imputado
imputed value

valor inicial
historical cost

valor intrínseco
existence value

valor justo, equitativo de mercado
fair market value

valor neto actual, actualizado
net present worth, value - NPW, NPV

valor neto actualizado
net discounted value

valor nominal
face value

valor nominal (valores)
par value

valor nominativo
registered security

valor oro
gold value

valor residual neto
netback value [energy]

valor residual, de desecho
scrap value

valor social neto actual, actualizado
social net present value - SNPV

valor temporal del dinero
time value of money

valor unitario
unit value

valoración a costo total
full cost pricing

valoración aduanera
valuations for customs purposes

valores
paper [financial]

valores a más largo plazo de oferta continua - COLTS
Continuously Offered Longer-Term Securities - COLTS

valores acreditados
seasoned securities

valores de primer orden
gilt-edged securities

valores de segundo orden
secondary securities

valores del mercado monetario
money market paper

valores en cartera
portfolio securities

valores en circulación
outstanding securities

valores extrabursátiles, fuera de bolsa
over-the-counter securities

valores financieros
financial paper

valores negociables
eligible paper; marketable securities

valores normales, corrientes, estándar
standard values [trade]

valores públicos, del Estado
government securities

valorización
appreciation (in value)

variable ficticia, artificial, simulada
dummy variable

variable independiente, predictiva
explanatory variable; predictor; predicated, independent variable; fixed variate; regressor [statistics]

variable independiente, predictiva
fixed variate; predictor; independent variable;
predictor; predicated variable; predictor

variaciones climáticas inducidas por la radiación solar
radiative forcing

variaciones estacionales
seasonal movements

variante
alternative [projects]

variedad pura
pure variety; true to type variety [agriculture]

variedad pura
true to type variety; pure variety [agriculture]

velocidad de diseño, nominal
design speed

vencimiento (de un préstamo, obligación, etc.)
maturity (of a loan, bond, etc.)

vencimiento de un día para otro
overnight maturity

vencimientos a menos de un año
current maturities

venta (de una empresa)
divestiture; divestment

venta a cualquier precio, de urgencia
distress sale, selling

venta a plazos
extended payment plan

venta con prima
premium sale

venta de bienes embargados, secuestrados
distress sale, selling

venta de un crédito fuera del consorcio
sell down

venta de valores en cartera
portfolio sale

venta de vencimientos de préstamos
sale of loan maturities

venta simple, al contado
outright sale

venta sin compromiso de garantía de emisión
"best efforts" sale

venta sin recurso de rescisión, irrevocable
no recourse sale

ventaja comparativa
comparative advantage

ventaja comparativa manifiesta, explícita, evidente, etc.
revealed comparative advantage - RCA

ventaja relativa
trade-off

ventajas sociales, colectivas
social advantages

ventana
window [computers]

ventanilla para préstamos concesionarios
soft loan window

ventas
merchandising

verificación
monitoring

verificación de cuentas
audit [finance]

verificación de precios previo al embarque
pre-shipment price inspection

verificación de prueba
test check [accounting]

verificar cuentas
audit, to

vertedero
landfill

vertical
top-down (approach) [projects]

vetiver
vetiver

vía de comercialización
channel [trade]

vía de servicio
service road

vía navegable
waterway

viabilidad de la balanza de pagos
external viability

viaje de observación, estudio, etc.
field trip

viaje en grupo
group travel [World Bank]

viajero frecuente o cotidiano (por razones de trabajo, de negocios)
commuter

viajes oficiales relacionados con operaciones
operational travel

viático
subsistence allowance

vicepresidencias centrales
central vicepresidencies [IBRD]

vida útil
economic life

vida útil
life (of a project); useful life

vida útil de un proyecto
project life

vigencia de un préstamo
life of a loan

vigencia media de los préstamos
average loan life - ALL

vigilancia
monitoring

vinculación de los salarios con los precios
wage-price indexing

vinculación regresiva
backward linkage

vinculación vertical
backward-forward linkage

vincular
peg, to (prices, interest rates)

vínculo a una combinación de monedas
composite peg [foreign exchange]

vínculo ajustable
adjustable peg [foreign exchange]

vínculo compuesto
composite peg [foreign exchange]

vínculo móvil
crawling peg [rate of exchange]

violación de contrato
breach of contract

virus de la inmunodeficiencia humana - VIH
human immunodeficiency virus - HIV

virus informático
computer virus

vivienda ilegal
illegal housing

vivienda mínima
core housing; nuclear housing; dwelling core

vivienda semipermanente
semipermanent housing

viviendas multifamiliares
multidwelling houses

viviendas no sujeta(s) a reglamentaciones
unregulated housing

volumen de deserción
wastage; waste [education]

volumen de material elaborado [manufacturas]
throughput

volumen de negocios
turnover

voluntad de pagar
willingness to pay - WTP

votación formal
formal vote [ICSID]

votación sin convocar a reunión
vote without meeting

votos básicos más votos de adhesión
uniform votes [IBRD]

votos de adhesión
membership votes

xenodivisas
xenocurrencies

xenomonedas
xenocurrencies

yacimiento de carbón
coal field

yacimiento geotérmico
geothermal deposit

yacimiento rentable
commercial deposit [mining]

yacimiento submarino, mar adentro
offshore field

zona atmosférica
airshed

zona bajo riego controlado
command area [irrigation]

zona de absorción de carbono
carbon sink

zona de absorción, de disipación
sink (e.g. of greenhouse gases)

zona de captación [riego]
catchment area; catch basin

zona de captación, de influencia [educación, etc.]
catchment area; catch basin

zona de contratación de mano de obra
labor shed

zona de libre comercio
free trade area

zona de ocupantes ilegales, sin título
squatter area, settlement

zona de referencia
reference zone; target zone [foreign exchange]

zona de singular riqueza ecológica
environmental hotspot

zona de soberanía económica
exclusive economic zone - EEZ

zona del proyecto
project area

zona en desarrollo
development area

zona expropiada
right of way

zona franca
free trade zone - FTZ; bonded area

zona franca industrial
export processing zone - EPZ

zona industrial
industrial estate [UK], park [USA]

zona industrial en régimen de franquicia aduanera
bonded industrial estate

zona infestada, de infestación
infected area

zona silvestre protegida
wildland management unit - WMU

zona urbanizada
serviced area, lot, site

zonas silvestres
wildlands

zonas silvestres administradas
wildland management area - WMA

zootecnia
animal husbandry

Distributors of World Bank Publications

Prices and credit terms vary from country to country. Consult your local distributor before placing an order.

ALBANIA
Adrion Ltd.
Perlat Rexhepi Str.
Pall. 9. Shk. 1, Ap. 4
Tirana
Tel: (42) 274 19; 221 72
Fax: (42) 274 19

ARGENTINA
Oficina del Libro Internacional
Av. Cordoba 1877
1120 Buenos Aires
Tel: (1) 815-8156
Fax: (1) 815-8354

AUSTRALIA, FIJI, PAPUA NEW GUINEA, SOLOMON ISLANDS, VANUATU, AND WESTERN SAMOA
D.A. Information Services
648 Whitehorse Road
Mitcham 3132
Victoria
Tel: (61) 3 9210 7777
Fax: (61) 3 9210 7788
URL: http:www.dadirect.com.au

AUSTRIA
Gerold and Co.
Graben 31
A-1011 Wien
Tel: (1) 533-50-14-0
Fax: (1) 512-47-31-29

BANGLADESH
Micro Industries Development Assistance Society (MIDAS)
House 5, Road 16
Dhanmondi R/Area
Dhaka 1209
Tel: (2) 326427
Fax: (2) 811188

BELGIUM
Jean De Lannoy
Av. du Roi 202
1060 Brussels
Tel: (2) 538-5169
Fax: (2) 538-0841

BRAZIL
Publicacões Tecnicas Internacionais Ltda.
Rua Peixoto Gomide, 209
01409 Sao Paulo, SP.
Tel: (11) 259-6644
Fax: (11) 258-6990

CANADA
Renouf Publishing Co. Ltd.
1294 Algoma Road
Ottawa, Ontario K1B 3W8
Tel: 613-741-4333
Fax: 613-741-5439

CHINA
China Financial & Economic Publishing House
8, Da Fo Si Dong Jie
Beijing
Tel: (1) 333-8257
Fax: (1) 401-7365

COLOMBIA
Infoenlace Ltda.
Apartado Aereo 34270
Bogotá D.E.
Tel: (1) 285-2798
Fax: (1) 285-2798

COTE D'IVOIRE
Centre d'Edition et de Diffusion Africaines (CEDA)
04 B.P. 541
Abidjan 04 Plateau
Tel: 225-24-6510
Fax: 225-25-0567

CYPRUS
Center of Applied Research
Cyprus College
6, Diogenes Street, Engomi
P.O. Box 2006
Nicosia
Tel: 244-1730
Fax: 246-2051

CZECH REPUBLIC
National Information Center
prodejna, Konviktska 5
CS – 113 57 Prague 1
Tel: (2) 2422-9433
Fax: (2) 2422-1484
URL: http://www.nis.cz/

DENMARK
SamfundsLitteratur
Rosenoerns Allé 11
DK-1970 Frederiksberg C
Tel: (31)-351942
Fax: (31)-357822

ECUADOR
Facultad Latinoamericana de Ciencias Sociales
FLASCO-SEDE Ecuador
Calle Ulpiano Paez 118
y Av. Patria
Quito, Ecuador
Tel/Fax: (2) 542 714; 542 716; 528 200
Fax: (2) 566 139

EGYPT, ARAB REPUBLIC OF
Al Ahram
Al Galaa Street
Cairo
Tel: (2) 578-6083
Fax: (2) 578-6833

The Middle East Observer
41, Sherif Street
Cairo
Tel: (2) 393-9732
Fax: (2) 393-9732

FINLAND
Akateeminen Kirjakauppa
P.O. Box 23
FIN-00371 Helsinki
Tel: (0) 12141
Fax: (0) 121-4441
URL: http://booknet.cultnet.fi/aka/

FRANCE
World Bank Publications
66, avenue d'Iéna
75116 Paris
Tel: (1) 40-69-30-55
Fax: (1) 40-69-30-68

GERMANY
UNO-Verlag
Poppelsdorfer Allee 55
53115 Bonn
Tel: (228) 212940
Fax: (228) 217492

GREECE
Papasotiriou S.A.
35, Stournara Str.
106 82 Athens
Tel: (1) 364-1826
Fax: (1) 364-8254

HONG KONG, MACAO
Asia 2000 Ltd.
Sales & Circulation Department
Seabird House, unit 1101-02
22-28 Wyndham Street, Central
Hong Kong
Tel: 852 2530-1409
Fax: 852 2526-1107
URL: http://www.sales@asia2000.com.hk

HUNGARY
Foundation for Market Economy
Dombovari Ut 17-19
H-1117 Budapest
Tel: 36 1 204 2951 or 36 1 204 2948
Fax: 36 1 204 2953

INDIA
Allied Publishers Ltd.
751 Mount Road
Madras – 600 002
Tel: (44) 852-3938
Fax: (44) 852-0649

INDONESIA
Pt. Indira Limited
Jalan Borobudur 20
P.O. Box 181
Jakarta 10320
Tel: (21) 390-4290
Fax: (21) 421-4289

IRAN
Kowkab Publishers
P.O. Box 19575-511
Tehran
Tel: (21) 258-3723
Fax: 98 (21) 258-3723

Ketab Sara Co. Publishers
Khaled Eslamboli Ave.,
6th Street
Kusheh Delafrooz No. 8
Tehran
Tel: 8717819 or 8716104
Fax: 8862479

IRELAND
Government Supplies Agency
Oifig an tSoláthair
4-5 Harcourt Road
Dublin 2
Tel: (1) 461-3111
Fax: (1) 475-2670

ISRAEL
Yozmot Literature Ltd.
P.O. Box 56055
Tel Aviv 61560
Tel: (3) 5285-397
Fax: (3) 5285-397

R.O.Y International
PO Box 13056
Tel Aviv 61130
Tel: (3) 5461423
Fax: (3) 5461442

Palestinian Authority/Middle East
Index Information Services
P.O.B. 19502 Jerusalem
Tel: (2) 271219

ITALY
Licosa Commissionaria Sansoni SPA
Via Duca Di Calabria, 1/1
Casella Postale 552
50125 Firenze
Tel: (55) 645-415
Fax: (55) 641-257

JAMAICA
Ian Randle Publishers Ltd.
206 Old Hope Road
Kingston 6
Tel: 809-927-2085
Fax: 809-977-0243

JAPAN
Eastern Book Service
Hongo 3-Chome,
Bunkyo-ku 113
Tokyo
Tel: (03) 3818-0861
Fax: (03) 3818-0864
URL: http://www.bekkoame.or.jp/~svt-ebs

KENYA
Africa Book Service (E.A.) Ltd.
Quaran House, Mfangano Street
P.O. Box 45245
Nairobi
Tel: (2) 23641
Fax: (2) 330272

KOREA, REPUBLIC OF
Daejon Trading Co. Ltd.
P.O. Box 34
Yeoeida
Seoul
Tel: (2) 785-1631/4
Fax: (2) 784-0315

MALAYSIA
University of Malaya Cooperative Bookshop, Limited
P.O. Box 1127
Jalan Pantai Baru
59700 Kuala Lumpur
Tel: (3) 756-5000
Fax: (3) 755-4424

MEXICO
INFOTEC
Apartado Postal 22-860
14060 Tlalpan,
Mexico D.F.
Tel: (5) 606-0011
Fax: (5) 606-0386

NETHERLANDS
De Lindeboom/InOr-Publikaties
P.O. Box 202
7480 AE Haaksbergen

NEW ZEALAND
EBSCO NZ Ltd.
Private Mail Bag 99914
New Market
Auckland
Tel: (9) 524-8119
Fax: (9) 524-8067

NIGERIA
University Press Limited
Three Crowns Building Jericho
Private Mail Bag 5095
Ibadan
Tel: (22) 41-1356
Fax: (22) 41-2056

NORWAY
Narvesen Information Center
Book Department
P.O. Box 6125 Etterstad
N-0602 Oslo 6
Tel: (22) 57-3300
Fax: (22) 68-1901

PAKISTAN
Mirza Book Agency
65, Shahrah-e-Quaid-e-Azam
Lahore 54000
Tel: (42) 7353601
Fax: (42) 7585283

PERU
Editorial Desarrollo SA
Apartado 3824
Lima 1
Tel: (14) 285380
Fax: (14) 286628

PHILIPPINES
International Booksource Center Inc.
Suite 720, Cityland 10
Condominium Tower 2
H.V dela Costa, corner
Valero St.
Makati, Metro Manila
Tel: (2) 817-9676
Fax: (2) 817-1741

POLAND
International Publishing Service
Ul. Piekna 31/37
00-577 Warzawa
Tel: (2) 628-6089
Fax: (2) 621-7255

PORTUGAL
Livraria Portugal
Rua Do Carmo 70-74
1200 Lisbon
Tel: (1) 347-4982
Fax: (1) 347-0264

ROMANIA
Compani De Librarii Bucuresti S.A.
Str. Lipscani no. 26, sector 3
Bucharest
Tel: (1) 613 9645
Fax: (1) 312 4000

RUSSIAN FEDERATION
Isdatelstvo <Ves Mir>
9a, Lolpachnii pereulok
Moscow 101831
Tel: (95) 917 87 49
Fax: (95) 917 92 59

SAUDI ARABIA, QATAR
Jarir Book Store
P.O. Box 3196
Riyadh 11471
Tel: (1) 477-3140
Fax: (1) 477-2940

SINGAPORE, TAIWAN, MYANMAR, BRUNEI
Asahgate Publishing Asia Pacific Pte. Ltd.
41 Kallang Pudding Road #04-03
Golden Wheel Building
Singapore 349316
Tel: (65) 741-5166
Fax: (65) 742-9356

SLOVAK REPUBLIC
Slovart G.T.G. Ltd.
Krupinska 4
PO Box 152
852 99 Bratislava 5
Tel: (7) 839472
Fax: (7) 839485

SOUTH AFRICA, BOTSWANA
For single titles:
Oxford University Press
Southern Africa
P.O. Box 1141
Cape Town 8000
Tel: (21) 45-7266
Fax: (21) 45-7265

For subscription orders:
International Subscription Service
P.O. Box 41095
Craighall
Johannesburg 2024
Tel: (11) 880-1448
Fax: (11) 880-6248

SPAIN
Mundi-Prensa Libros, S.A.
Castello 37
28001 Madrid
Tel: (1) 431-3399
Fax: (1) 575-3998
http://www.tsal.es/mprensa

Libreia Internacional AEDOS
Conseil de Cent. 391
08009 Barcelona
Tel: (3) 488-3009
Fax: (3) 487-7659

SRI LANKA, THE MALDIVES
Lake House Bookshop
P.O. Box 244
100, Sir Chittampalam A. Gardiner Mawatha
Colombo 2
Tel: (1) 32105
Fax: (1) 432104

SWEDEN
Fritzes Customer Service
Regeringsgaton 12
S-106 47 Stockholm
Tel: (8) 690 90 90
Fax: (8) 21 47 77

Wennergren-Williams AB
P.O. Box 1305
S-171 25 Solna
Tel: (8) 705-97-50
Fax: (8) 27-00-71

SWITZERLAND
Librairie Payot
Service Institutionnel
Côtes-de-Montbenon 30
1002 Lausanne
Tel: (021)-320-2511
Fax: (021)-320-2514

Van Diermen Editions Technique
Ch. de Lacuez 41
CH1807 Blonay
Tel: (021) 943 2673
Fax: (021) 943 3605

TANZANIA
Oxford University Press
Makiaba Street
PO Box 5299
Dar es Salaam
Tel: (51) 29209
Fax: (51) 46822

THAILAND
Central Books Distribution
306 Silom Road
Bangkok
Tel: (2) 235-5400
Fax: (2) 237-8321

TRINIDAD & TOBAGO, JAMAICA
Systematics Studies Unit
#9 Watts Street
Curepe
Trinidad, West Indies
Tel: 809-662-5654
Fax: 809-662-5654

UGANDA
Gustro Ltd.
Madhvani Building
PO Box 9997
Plot 16/4 Jinja Rd.
Kampala
Tel/Fax: (41) 254763

UNITED KINGDOM
Microinfo Ltd.
P.O. Box 3
Alton, Hampshire GU34 2PG
England
Tel: (1420) 86848
Fax: (1420) 89889

ZAMBIA
University Bookshop
Great East Road Campus
P.O. Box 32379
Lusaka

ZIMBABWE
Longman Zimbabwe (Pte.)Ltd.
Tourle Road, Ardbennie
P.O. Box ST125
Southerton
Harare
Tel: (4) 662711
Fax: (4) 662716